European Economic History

European Economic History

VOLUME
I

THE ANCIENT WORLD

WILLIAM I. DAVISSON   JAMES E. HARPER
University of Notre Dame

APPLETON-CENTURY-CROFTS
Educational Division
New York   MEREDITH CORPORATION

55461

72   73   74   75   76/10   9   8   7   6   5   4   3   2

Library of Congress Card Number: 75-172518
PRINTED IN THE UNITED STATES OF AMERICA
390-25735-4

THE PLAN OF THE WHOLE WORK

The early societies of the ancient Near East ordered their economies on principles which at first seem to us utterly foreign and strange but which are not unknown today among primitive peoples. They lacked markets altogether, as far as can be discovered. Even barter, which is the free exchange of goods for other goods thought to be of equal value, was not their central integrating principle. Rather production and distribution were determined by status relationships and controlled by political authority. This system was capable of brilliant results, as the early histories of Sumeria and Egypt show, but the unit of economic integration must be relatively small if it is to be controlled and directed by political authority. The progressively greater empires of the ancient Orient never attempted to impose anything like a general economic integration upon their territories. Having accepted the imposition of political authority, taxation, and forced services, conquered tribes and cities were allowed to retain their ancient economic systems based upon nonmarket institutions. There are limits to the complexity and flexibility as well as to the size which these economies could achieve. In ages possessing limited means of transport, weak administrative cadres, and limited techniques of control, systems of political control over production and distribution can quickly become oppressive, wasteful, and destructive of economic innovation. The organization of the economy about an institution which is not politically controlled, that is, about the market, was an innovation first made by the Greeks in the sixth and fifth centuries B.C. The inability of the ancient Near East to invent institutions suitable to a larger political order and more complex technology gave the Greeks the lead and in the course of their colonization and the later Macedonian conquests they either imposed their economic system on the Near East and the Mediterranean or their methods were imitated by more backward peoples, of whom the Romans were far the most important.

Thus for a long part of human history, from the invention of the market among the Greeks to the recent past, economic progress, increased production, more efficient administration, and the liberation of individual capacities have been closely connected with the advance of the market's role in the economy, while a decline in the part that the market has played in the distributive system has generally been connected with a decline in prosperity and economic development. Certainly this correlation is evident in the late Roman Empire, the age of state control and economic regression with which this volume ends. The survival and restoration of market techniques in the eastern Mediterranean are closely related to the superiority of the eastern Mediterranean vis-à-vis the western Mediterranean in the early Middle Ages and with the survival there of a higher economy. The collapse of the international market system and the decline of the more local exchanges during the course of the early Middle Ages accounts for the backwardness of Western Europe at least as much as do the barbarian invasions from the third to the tenth centuries A.D. The renewed growth from the tenth century onwards was largely a function of the reappearance of the market economy and of the professional merchants. The impersonal market undertook the task of economic integration that no state in the period could attempt. To be sure, the high Middle Ages did not have an economy controlled simply and solely by the market. The market for land, for example, was largely circumscribed by social and political controls and the serf was able to dispose of his labor on market principles only to a limited extent. But the social history of the high and late Middle Ages and of modern times to the end of the nineteenth century can be viewed as a progressive increase in the scope and depth of market activity. In spite of the collapse of the 1340s and 1350s, land and labor in Europe were increasingly drawn into the market.

In the period from the eleventh to the fifteenth century A.D. an economy developed in Western Europe ordered about an interrelated double market system—very local in scope on the one hand and international on the other. With the emergence of national monarchies and princely states in northern Europe from the late fifteenth century A.D., something like national economies emerged. These were larger units which only gradually moved toward internal free trade, but which were subject to a degree of control by policies of a central government. These proto-mercantilist and mercantilist policies, however, made little effort to replace or to stifle the play and expansion of the market in the economy which can hardly be said to have contracted under governmental supervision.

After the voyages of the Portuguese and Spaniards, lands overseas were increasingly drawn into the European market system. While non-European states and societies might and did imitate European productive techniques, Europe itself repeatedly revolutionized its technology so that the gap between the productive power of Europe and that of the rest of the world was progressively increased. So dependent did the plantation economies of colonial regions become that it might be truer to say that they were subject to the European market system rather than integrated with it. The American plantation South producing cotton, tobacco, rice, indigo, and naval stores; the precious metals of Latin America; the coffee, chocolate, and spices of the East Indies were all subject to the European market dictates.

The astounding explosion of productive forces in England at the end of the eighteenth century goes by the name of the Industrial Revolution and it is with this phenomenon that we open our fourth volume. This world domination by the European market continued until the long generation before the first world war. European economic hegemony never appeared more complete than after the Berlin Conference of 1884 at which European diplomats divided an Africa still largely unseen by European eyes. Yet forces were at work which would bring down the system. One was the adoption of European industrial techniques and market methods by non-European peoples. Here the Japanese achievement was the most striking. It was clearly in evidence by 1900. The growth of the United States and Russia was perhaps even more ominous. Since both were outside of the European continent and of European civilization, their possession of European techniques did not disturb the system as long as they did not separately exceed the size of the European states nor collectively overshadow Europe as a whole. Russia's immense expansion to the east, her occupation of the Urals and Siberia, and her presence on the Pacific Ocean created a state comparable in size to Europe as a whole and at the same time drew her away from the European community. From the time of the building of the American transcontinental railroads, American growth began to accelerate at such a rate that it was clear that it would not long be contained within the European system.

Taken alone, the developments of Japan, Russia, and the United States might simply have meant the replacement of European market hegemony with a system based on an entire northern temperate zone. However, the end of the nineteenth century saw the renewal of old demands that the market not control the economy so completely as it had in the past. In order of their effectiveness and priority the demands appear to us to have been: that business not be left to suffer periodically the consequences of the business cycle, that governments make some attempt to stabilize economic and other instability; that the landlord and peasant be protected from the competition of cheap grain brought from the midwest of America and from the Russian Ukraine by the new transatlantic steamer and railroad; and that the now vast wage-earning population not be left to the mercy of the market. Social insurance became a political cry.[1]

The first world war destroyed what had seemed so stable as to be a law of nature—the autonomous workings of a market independent of political decisions and a European domination of the world economy. Outside of the United States, the death of the old system was evident by 1919, although few contemporaries understood how momentous was the demise. The system survived intact or apparently so in the United States until the Great Depression and the New Deal.

Efforts to deal with the Great Depression by political action and by international cooperation among the independent states of Europe were a failure during the 1930s not only because of the animosities generated by the first

---

[1] The reader should note that the demands were not by any means all "socialistic" nor did they come exclusively from the "left," or from those who suffered most from the system.

world war, but because men's minds were hardly prepared for the scale of change required for the old economic faiths to be abandoned. It might be noted that the "socialistic" Left was not so very much more realistic in this respect than was the industrial and commercial Right. Only after the catastrophe of the second world war was Europe able to grasp the kind of international planning that may hopefully produce a new economic system and a new economic stability and prosperity.

PREFACE TO VOLUME I

It was William James who said that any subject, even science, when studied from the historical point of view, becomes a humane study. Communism and National Socialism, for example, become something quite different when they are viewed as the culmination of a long line of millenary dreams of the dispossessed from the time of Maccabeean Jews down to Thomas Muenzer and the Peasant Revolt during the German Reformation.[1] Lenin—if not Stalin—might have had second thoughts about the use of the secret police, if he had not been completely captive of the Marxian view of history as a theory. Either might have acted differently if he had seen that the structure he was rearing was the continuation of the Czarist police, itself the descendent of the Byzantine, which in turn derived from the *agentes in rebus* of the Emperor Hadrian in the second century A.D.

So, too, the study of economic history should tell us something of the direction in which we are moving and should liberate us from the dogmas of the recent past by making clear that, whatever the validity of particular theories of economics, none possesses an absolute value and any number of past experiences may be of value in today's choices. Economics, when looked at from the historical point of view, has a real existential value, for it helps us make decisions by revealing something about what choices are open to us today.

From the time of Adam Smith economics has largely been treated as a science and, therefore, as a dogma; that is to say, it has sought to extract general rules from contemporary experience, to rectify those general rules in the light of reason, and then to propound them as statements about the proper ordering of the economy. Now whatever may be the analytical and normative value of the theories propounded in the nineteenth century and still propounded today, they are in fact models which correspond only imperfectly to the economic conduct of any society and which differ immensely from any economic conduct possible in most of the societies of history. The study of models, then, without the study of the real economic organization of human societies in the past leads to dogmatism and sometimes even to the strange assertion that the models are right and a society that does not conform to them is wrong or even immoral. Whatever may be the weaknesses of historical thought—and they are many—history can lead men away from such follies as these.

W.I.D.
J.E.H.

[1] Norman Cohn, *The Pursuit of the Millennium* (New York: Essential Books, 1957).

CONTENTS

MAPS   *between* 278–279

FIGURES   *between* 278–279

ABBREVIATIONS

The following abbreviations are used in the footnotes.

Ann. ESC.	Annales: économies, sociéties, civilisations
CAH	Cambridge Ancient History
CEH	Cambridge Economic History, ed. H. H. Postan
EcHR	Economic History Review
ESAR	Economic Survey of Ancient Rome, ed. Tenney Frank
F.A.	Finanz-Archiv
History of Technology	History of Technology, ed. Charles Singer et al.
JNES	Journal of Near Eastern Studies
NH	Pliny, Natural History
SHA	Scriptures Historiae Augustae (trans. David Magie; Loeb Classical Library)

EUROPEAN ECONOMIC HISTORY

AN INTRODUCTION TO ECONOMIC HISTORY

THE NATURE OF ECONOMIC HISTORY

Certain fundamental relationships characterize the study of economic history. The primary focus of the present study is the relationship between the market and society in Western cultures. This has often involved the relationship between the market and the government—as we shall see in Roman times, during much of the Middle Ages, and early in the modern period.

Economic history ought to attempt to determine why particular relations exist between the productive-distributive system and other institutions in a particular society and should also attempt to examine the general influence of these relationships on the society and its people. These basic relationships involve:

A. The market and the society (government)
B. Relations of production
C. Investments in capital goods and in consumer goods
D. Merchants and producers

The history of civilization and economic history can then be written from a number of viewpoints. One of the commonest illustrates how man was able to progress from a food-gathering and unsettled mode of life to a stable, civilized community because of his growing ability to develop tools and weapons to manipulate his natural environment. Such a view commands the study of prehistory for almost the whole surviving record consists of artifacts. Only more advanced societies, which have left clues about their social organization, can be studied from different points of view.

Societies are groups of persons held together by common necessities, beliefs, and institutions. They are usually called civilizations when a significant number of their members are not directly engaged in producing food goods and other basic necessities. Many societies have developed from the primitive to the civilized, but most have received a stimulus from more advanced civilizations. The Mesopotamian civilization, however, was the first to rise above the level of neolithic village agriculture and therefore could not have achieved civilization by imitation of a higher culture. We must concern ourselves with the technical and economic achievements of primitive

1

peoples that made possible this first birth of civilization. The study of the economic history of the earliest people is limited to the technology as revealed by their artifacts. Because they were illiterate, we can never recover their institutions.

With the appearance of written records and of monumental architecture, we can produce not simply technological but social interpretations of history. Economic history can be seen as an institutional development. With this change it ceases to look simply like a slow progress of productive techniques. For example, the characteristic Egyptian conception of the role of the pharaoh and his relation to society found its first pictorial expression in the Narmer Palette and its first literary embodiment in the Memphite Theology.[1] They give a monarchical perspective to society and to history. The significance of the Memphite Theology is that it demonstrates the overwhelming importance of kingship in Egyptian society and thus in Egyptian history, including economic history. It is one of our earliest glimpses of the way production might be integrated in society by social institutions and systems of distribution through the pharaoh rather than the market.

Economic history concerns the relation between the distributive system and the social order, often characterized as the relation between the market and the government. The economic history of a literate society, then, can discover the relation of the market to the society and attempt to determine why that relationship existed and what its significance was for that society, its people, and its historical development.

An economic system is one of several foundations on which a society organizes itself. The economic system of a society is concerned with the activity of production, with distribution of goods and services, and with allocation of all (including human) resources between present and future use—i.e., using labor to plant corn or to build an irrigation dike. It involves the organization of labor and the maintenance of artisans and others who do not live directly on their own production. But in addition to an economic system, a civilized society has a political superstructure composed of persons not immediately concerned with production: scribes, priests, kings. If a political superstructure is imposed on the economic organization and consists of persons not directly engaged in producing goods and services, the economist (economic historian) must inquire into the composition of the political superstructure and its relation to the economic base.

The first question may be answered provisionally by saying that in these early societies the political superstructure seems to include all persons who are not engaging directly in producing the necessities of life. Priests, scribes, artisans producing metal tools and weapons or ritual and cult objects, rulers and governors, servants, professional soldiers, and police are all part of the

---

[1] Henri Frankfort, *The Birth of Civilization in the Near East* (Bloomington: Indiana University Press, 1951).

political system. There appears to be nothing like private wealth capable of supporting independent leisure in the early civilizations of Mesopotamia and Egypt.

Most people today naturally think of a market in modern terms as the primary characteristic of an economic system and of private property as a second essential of that system. The market and private property involve the assumption that the individual naturally spends his time and energy in an effort most effectively to promote the accumulation of private wealth and in its expenditure. A further assumption is that wants are unlimited so that there is no natural limit to the desire to produce, accumulate, and consume. We say, then, that the institutions and basic beliefs of our society compel individuals to allocate their resources (money, time, labor) most efficiently, that is, to economize.[2] The accumulation of wealth is regarded as a positive and distinct good. Any activity that tends to promote the accumulation of wealth by individuals is regarded as good. (Other things are recognized as good, but the economist largely ignores them, and we all ignore them when thinking about economics.) The market and private property are the institutional framework to compel economizing—that is, efficient or rational economic activity, which then makes the economy susceptible to analysis. The economy, in such circumstances, can be analyzed independently of the rest of society's institutions and aims, of its religion, of the family, and even of government.

In the market-oriented society, the market is the center of economic activity and gives direction to the production, distribution, and resource allocation of the society. Governmental interference in the freely operating market structure is justified only if it is necessary to save the system, as it ostensibly is in war, and really is in those cyclical market crises we call depressions and in those prolonged doldrums called stagnation. Even so, the government will not directly do anything that can be done by private persons. It will not, for example, build a military camp, if it can contract to have the work done by private concerns on the basis of competitive bids. If it must act itself, the government will at least attempt cost analyses that imitate (perhaps) conditions of the competitive market. But what happens when a society has no market, no money, no institution of private property, and no "economizing" behavior? What happens when the economic historian cannot apply modern economic analysis to the society he is examining?

The aim of the economic historian, then, in dealing with ancient nonmarket societies must be to determine the central force which gave the society its economic direction. He is concerned specifically with examining the relationship between the economic system and the political superstructure. But he faces a major difficulty when dealing with societies in which no market existed or societies in which the market did not control the economy or fix prices or allocate resources.

[2] The reader should keep in mind this peculiar definition of "economize" since we shall have to come back to it.

The point should be made perfectly clear. Modern readers normally think of such societies as the American, which have a basic acquisitive aim and where the economic workings are dictated by a free market. It is common to use the terms "American society," "American economy," "American nation," "American civilization," or "American capitalism" when referring to the same thing. The thing referred to is a particular set of natural resources in a given geographical location, a particular way of organizing production, and certain features in the political superstructure.

Most earlier ages did not have the presuppositions of the market, nor did they have a market, although they did have economic systems and political superstructures. Max Weber was the first to clearly point out that ancient societies were based on different sorts of principles than are modern, Western societies and that, therefore, it made little sense to attempt to analyze ancient societies as though they resembled modern ones. To be sure there was no lack of interest in acquiring wealth in the ancient world. Greed is universal. But ancient oriental societies were organized differently, and economic advantage was not to be gained through market activity.[3]

THE SOURCES

An economic history of the Ancient
Near East is yet to be written.

—A. T. Olmstead

If such relationships as those discussed above are the main objects of economic history, Professor Olmstead's dictum, written in 1930, is still broadly true, in spite of very considerable progress in the last thirty years. We know a great deal about some aspects of the economic history of the ancient Near East from the origins of civilized life somewhere c. 3000 B.C. to the conquests of Alexander the Great at the close of the fourth century B.C. However, our knowledge is fragmentary, which presents great difficulties. New discoveries can do a great deal to upset old views, and the interpretation of the evidence is so difficult that a better understanding of well-known texts can upset long established doctrines.

Let us begin, then, by looking at the state of our knowledge and its sources. Everything we know, of course, comes ultimately from diggings.[4] In Mesopotamia and Syria and much of Asia Minor the best sites are the tells,

[3] Max Weber, *General Economic History*, trans. Frank H. Knight. Glencoe, Ill.: The Free Press, 1927, pp. 244–5.
[4] An exception, of course, is the Old Testament, which from about 1000 B.C. becomes an independently useful source.

the great mounds above the plains which mark the sites of ancient cities. Most building in these regions, all of it in some parts, was done in brick and most of the brick was not fired as modern brick is, but simply dried in the sun. So the cores of the great temple mounds, the ziggurats, were of sun-dried brick and only the crusts were of fired brick. All private houses were certainly of sun-dried brick. The length of their life, then, was not great. When a rainstorm or old age weakened the walls, it was customary to remove all valuables from a house and to pull down the walls. Animals would be brought in to trample down the loose brick of the old walls into a new floor of something like adobe. The new house was then built on a higher level than the old. Much junk, like broken pottery and tools, of course was lost in the old foundation. Even better, from the archaeologist's point of view, was the destruction of the whole city and its temporary desertion. If rehabilitation were delayed some years, the new settlement would be on a higher level than the old one and would leave most of the old walls and foundations now underneath the surface intact. In Mesopotamia, such buried buildings might typically include not only rubbish, but the remains of palaces and temples, great art objects like the Assyrian and Persian winged bulls, statues of the gods, mosaic pavements, and the tile walls, and—best of all—archives and libraries of cuneiform records on clay tablets. When excavations of such a site are undertaken, they can produce a lively and full picture of the life of the city through successive stages.

The situation is rather different in Egypt. There the inundations of the Nile have destroyed or deeply buried almost everything in the valley and delta. Our chief materials are found in the adjacent desert in the tombs and in the temples attached to them. It is the dead that we know best in Egypt. Fortunately from our point of view, the Egyptians spent immense efforts on housing their dead, particularly their pharaohs. The desert sometimes does yield other resources. Papyrus, not clay tablets, was the writing material of the ancient Egyptians and will last almost indefinitely in the dry climate of the Egyptian desert. Such papyri as the *Book of the Dead* are found in tombs, where they were placed to aid the dead man in his progress through the terrors and trials of the afterlife. Rubbish heaps have yielded private records of various sorts; papyri used to make *papier mâché* for coffins have yielded bits and pieces of the most varied sorts, including even scraps of the archaic Greek poets copied in the Ptolemaic period. Then, too, people sometimes hid books in the desert, as the Jewish monks in the Dead Sea area hid their scrolls from the Roman soldiers.

The evidence, then, is generous, if enough effort is made to find it, and certainly a great deal has been accumulated. But it is not wholly coherent. First, it is one-sided. From Egypt it chiefly concerns the dead. In Babylonia we have little direct evidence about the countryside and, even in the cities, excavators are irresistibly tempted to excavate the ceremonial and administrative centers rather than the ordinary houses. The considerable bodies of literary, administrative, religious, or commercial documents are of the first importance, but they come from relatively few sites and from particular ages. They do not make a smooth series from the origins of civilization down to the Macedonian conquest, and they do not reveal generalities for large areas. The administrative documents discovered at Lagash may not apply to Ur at that same period. We cannot tell whether the system described was peculiar to Lagash or generalized, or whether it was a recent development or a tradition of long standing. Moreover, our documents come overwhelmingly from government sources and, when they deal with the economy, primarily discuss the government's role in it.

Finally another *caveat*. When we hear that a language has been deciphered, we are tempted to assume that linguists can read and understand anything in it. But even when a foreign language is fairly well known,[5] difficulties can arise, and this is perhaps particularly true in business and administrative texts. Literary and religious texts are generally written to speak to a broad audience and to be understood by people at a distant time. Thus the intellectual and moral meaning of the Hebrew Bible and of Greek and Latin literatures are not generally obscure. But contracts are written in technical and legal language; most of us cannot understand a contract written yesterday in English. Administrative documents are written by clerks for clerks. They can use all kinds of technical jargon and abbreviations, since they know what the document is for and do not have to reveal its purpose to outsiders.[6] Documents relating to tenures in even so well known a language as Latin can, as we shall see, raise great problems in interpretation.

Under such circumstances, almost everything that is said about the economy of the ancient Near East before the Macedonian conquest—and not a little after it—must be taken as hypothesis. It is particularly hard to draw a sound generalized picture. The student can be quite certain that the general picture of classic and medieval history will not be upset. Errors no doubt will be corrected and new information may be revealed; new interpretations will be developed, but the texts and the excavations are full enough to make their interpretation in general certain, and the general picture is not subject to the danger of wholesale revision as the result of some chance find. This is certain because all the various pieces of evidence fit coherently together. Because of

[5] The reader is asked to consider the immense linguistic difficulties. The Mycenaean Greek of Linear B is an Indo-European language; Hittite is partly an Indo-European language; Egyptian appears to be in part distantly related to the Semitic languages but is almost *sui generis*; Hebrew, Aramaic, and Akkadian are all Semitic but are distinct languages; Sumerian is completely unrelated to any other known language family. And these are only a few of the languages with which orientalists must deal.

[6] The reader can see the sort of problems we have in mind either by a quick look at Michael Ventris and John Chadwick, *Documents in Mycenaean Greek. Three Hundred Selected Tablets from Knossos, Pylos, and Mycenae with Commentary and Vocabulary* (Cambridge: Cambridge University Press, 1959), or by looking over the memoranda passed about by the administration of his school.

the nature of our sources and the difficulties of interpretation, that is not yet true of the history of much of the ancient Near East and, most especially, is not true of its economic history.[7]

[7] A number of partial syntheses that have been put to great service in the following chapters may be conveniently cited here: A. Leo Oppenheim, *Ancient Mesopotamia* (Chicago: University of Chicago Press, 1964); Georges Roux, *Ancient Iraq* (London: Allen and Unwin, 1964); Fritz Heichelheim, *An Ancient Economic History from the Palaeolithic Age to the Migrations of the Germanic, Slavic, and Arabic Nations*, Vol. I, trans. Joyce Stevens, 2d ed. (Leiden: A. W. Sijthoff's Uitgeversmaatschappij, 1958).

1 THE NEOLITHIC PERIOD

THE NEOLITHIC ECONOMY

Man was always a hunter and a food gatherer and perhaps a fisherman, and he has always been distinguished from animals which hunted and grazed by his use of tools. To be sure, man is not the only animal capable of using tools or learning more than instinctual behavior. Monkeys will pile boxes on top of each other in order to reach bananas hung from the roofs of their cages and certain Japanese monkeys have been observed to wash their food by carrying it to the water on the trays on which men had placed it, walking upright in order to carry the trays.[1] But no other animal, it appears, is able to make tools for anything more than immediate use. When primates began regularly to make tools and weapons of wood and stone to serve permanent and distant needs, they had clearly formed images of the ends toward which they labored. But the primates who did this were human, or were to become human, and there is considerable thought that the development of tools and weapons accelerated the pace of primate evolution among the species that preceded *Homo sapiens*.[2]

When we are first concerned with him, man was already leading a life characterized by traditions learned from the past; he was a cultural rather than a natural animal. The creation of this culture had been, of course, the result of a long process of innovation. A clan's economic conduct, then, was socially conditioned, that is to say, conditioned by the past behavior of the group and by the innovations that had taken place in its collective past; each clan, therefore, could be expected to respond differently to environmental challenges. They had gradually made considerable, although slow, progress in learning to exploit their environment, progress which it is easy to lose

[1] See K. P. Oakley, "Skill as a Human Possession," *History of Technology,* I (Oxford: Oxford University Press, 1956), pp. 13ff.; Bronislaw Malinowski, "Culture," *Encyclopedia of the Social Sciences,* IV (New York: Macmillan, 1932), pp. 621ff. On the Japanese monkeys, see *The New York Times,* September 31, 1963, p. 20.

[2] J. Hawkes, *Prehistory and the Beginning of Civilization,* Vol. I of *The History of Mankind* (New York: Harper and Row, 1963), p. 41; Sherwood L. Washburn, "Tools and Human Evolution," *Scientific American* (September 1960), 3–15. There are a number of general surveys of technology to which reference will be made frequently: Charles Singer et al., eds., *History of Technology* (Oxford: Oxford University Press, 1954) ; Maurice Daumas, ed., *Histoire générale des techniques,* Vol. I: *Les origines de la civilisation technique* (Paris: Presses universitaires de France, 1962). Even more recent is Henry Hodges's beautifully clear and simple exposition, *Technology in the Ancient World* (New York: Alfred A. Knopf, 1970).

sight of. Neolithic men lived in communities whose compositions and order-
ings we can never hope to know with much certainty, though the groups were
certainly larger than the nuclear or elementary family of a father and mother
and their minor offspring. They had language and traditional ways of making
a living, but even before the emergence of agriculture, there was considerable
variety of ways of life. Some bands or tribes hunted, other fished, others
gathered such food as berries and nuts, and still others did some several of
these things. They made stone tools by chipping siliceous materials and
domesticated the dog.[3] They had learned the use of digging sticks to grub out
roots and tubers and could make baskets and rafts. Slightly more advanced
men had mastered the canoe and the boomerang. The great hunters who
dominated the continental plains were masters of a complicated arsenal of
weapons including the bow and arrow and polished stones. Some tribes had
developed nets or hooks for fishing; many—probably most—were largely
dependent upon fleshy plants, but the technique of grinding enabled some, at
any rate, to make use of hard seeds. In short, there is a long prehistory of the
economy and of man's slow technological mastery of his environment.[4] All
these bands, however, fed themselves without much changing their environ-
ments or increasing the food supply.[5] They preyed on other animals and
plants but did little or nothing to cultivate them. The early evolution of man's
ways of making a living, however, belongs to other disciplines than economic
history. Our effort at some kind of a continuous history must start from the
revolution that made man a cultivator of food and a herder of animals. That
tremendous revolution still dominates our lives. No other event before the
industrial revolution of the nineteenth century is even remotely comparable.[6]

[3] On which see the imaginative reconstruction by a great student of animal behavior, Konrad
Lorenz, in the first chapter of *Man Meets Dog* (London: Methuen, 1954).

[4] See for example Carl Sauer, "Early Relations of Man to Plants," in *Land and Life, A
Selection from the Writings of Carl Ortwin Sauer*, ed. John Leighly (Berkeley: University
of California Press, 1963), pp. 155–81.

[5] The use of fire by hunters may be an exception. If frequent, it could turn forest into grassland. Elsewhere it might open the forest and increase the number of animals that it would
support. See Sauer, "A Geographic Sketch of Early Man in America" and "Fire and Early
Man," *ibid.*, pp. 221–4, 288–99.

[6] On the neolithic period and the development of agriculture (which Professor Childe has
dubbed the neolithic revolution), see Jacquetta Hawkes, *Prehistory and the Beginnings of
Civilization*, pp. 219–351; Robert Braidwood, *Prehistoric Man*, 7th ed. (Glenview, Ill.: Scott,
Foresman and Co., 1967); and V. Gordon Childe, *The Prehistory of European Society*
(Pelican Books; Harmondsworth, Middlesex: Penguin Books, 1958); *The Dawn of European Civilization*, 6th ed. (London: Routledge and Kegan Paul, 1957); *What Happened
in History*, 2d ed. (Pelican Books; Harmondsworth, Middlesex: Penguin Books, 1954);
New Light on the Most Ancient Near East, 4th ed. (London: Routledge and Kegan Paul,
1952); *Social Evolution* (London: Watts and Co., 1951); *Man Makes Himself*, 2d ed.
(The Thinker's Library; London: Watts and Co., 1941). The reader should keep in mind
that our information about these distant times is very sketchy and that, therefore, our views
may be profoundly altered at any time by new discoveries. Hence it is especially important
to consult recent works and not hold to views formulated a generation ago.

By c. 5000 B.C. a large and growing number of bands in the Near East had transformed themselves from food gatherers into villagers who farmed and cared for animals. The techniques they invented then spread slowly both east and west to transform the lives of many other tribes of the Old World. Many had made the transformation by 2000 B.C.; some had not, and indeed some few groups still have not.[7] We must look at the origins of the technique of neolithic dry farming and then review its diffusion throughout the Old World. The central feature of this revolution is agriculture—in particular the cultivation of spelt, six-rowed barley, and a primitive, coarse kind of wheat called emmer.[8] This innovation must have occurred first in the Near East, where these grains survive even today in a wild state.

Archaeologists have unearthed a number of sites in the Near East which, taken together, provide a fairly continuous succession of stages from the level of the hunter and food gatherer to that of the farmer (see Map I). The caves of Mount Carmel in Israel have revealed the remains of a culture that the archaeologists call Natufian. These Natufians were the earliest people known to have used the sickle, a grooved haft of bone in which short flint teeth were mounted. These sickles are not certain proof that the Natufians, whom we can date somewhere about 6000 B.C., actually cultivated grain; they may simply have harvested wild grasses. But it is clear that cultivation soon followed the invention of the sickle and that the spread of agriculture can be traced in part by the diffusion of the sickle.[9]

The sites in Iraq above the Tigris valley uncovered in 1950–1951 by an American expedition headed by Professor Braidwood are of even greater importance for the origins of agriculture. The cave of Bâlîkawrah and a slightly later site at Karîm Shahir, dated about 6000 B.C., revealed bones of the first domesticated animals, polished stone axes, and sickles of stone which certainly indicate the beginnings of agriculture. At Jarmo the same team discovered the oldest known village. Instead of a natural cavern, the population of Jarmo lived along a road in some fifty huts of pressed clay. Jarmo can be dated by radio-carbon tests at about 4800 B.C.[10]

[7] The Eskimo's habitat does not permit farming, but a number of peoples like the Australoids never learned cultivation, although their environment permitted it.

[8] The curious reader may learn something about the botany of these and of the cultivated plants mentioned later from Clarence J. Hylander, *The World of Plant Life*, 2d ed. (New York: Macmillan, 1956).

[9] It is possible that another similar revolution took place somewhere in the south or southeast of Asia, where agriculture was based upon rice and certain root crops. At a later date certainly these regions had an agricultural regime profoundly different from that of the grain-growing peoples of the Near East and one which contributed much to the development of both the Chinese and Indian economies. See William H. McNeill, *The Rise of the West* (Chicago: University of Chicago Press, 1963), pp. 10–2, 23–4. No direct evidence of a separate origin of agriculture in southeastern Asia can be hoped for in the absence of far more extensive digging.

[10] At various sites in Asia Minor still earlier evidence of agriculture and the domestication of animals has been found. It is still too early to tell just how the excavations at Çatal

The earliest sites with evidence of harvesting like Mount Carmel may not reveal true agricultural communities. It seems reasonable to suppose that hunting continued to be a major occupation and that the invention of the sickle preceded the art of sowing. Even when men—or more likely women—learned to sow grain, the clan may very well have continued to be itinerant, returning to its fields only seasonally for the harvest. But such hunters who supplemented their food supply by occasional sowing might eventually build villages and settle down. In these Palestinian sites, then, we are near the origins of agricultural life. Some later archaeological discovery might depose the Natufians and the people of Jarmo from their proud position as the first farmers, but their techniques are so crude, their instruments so simple, and their continuity with cave dwellers so close that we feel certain that they are close to the earliest agriculture.

Of more interest to a history of man's civilized economy than these earliest discoveries is the new complex of tools and institutions that the neolithic revolution brought into service. As long as man moved about in pursuit of herds, even the discovery that grains could be sown and harvested cannot have brought a major transformation of his life. He was rather in the position of those Arabian nomads who in the rare years when rain falls within their herding areas, sow a little grain along a wadi and get a catch crop to supplement their diet of meat and milk. But Jarmo is clearly a different thing: it is a permanent village, and with permanent settlement a series of radical innovations was ushered in. At Jarmo itself, ovens have been discovered in which clay as well as bread was baked. The houses, to be sure, are of pressed earth, not of baked brick, but the people of Jarmo did make pottery and figurines. Though pots are important to archaeologists who develop relative chronologies from their styles, to the people of Jarmo they were useful for boiling food and absolutely essential for its preservation. The hunting community is always subject to periodic dearth and famine; agricultural societies are, of course, subject to the weather, to the failure of rain, and to crop shortages. (Western Europe was not freed of the danger of years of want and famine until the nineteenth century.) Even in normal years an agricultural people faces a crisis after the plenty of the harvest. Without means of preservation—of which ceramics are an essential part (except in the tropics where root crops provide continuous rather than seasonal harvests)—a predominately agricultural way of life would be impossible; even with them the month before the harvest is a period of want. It is not accident that July is the month of revolutions in Western Europe; the earliest new supply of food

Hüyük and Hacilar and elsewhere will effect our general picture of the origins of agriculture, but they certainly give earlier dates and suggest that the development covered a wider area. See James Mellaart, *The Chalcolithic and Early Bronze Ages in the Near East and Anatolia* (Beirut: Khayats, 1966) and *Çatal Hüyük, a Neolithic Town in Anatolia* (London: Thames and Hudson, 1967).

comes there in August and only in good years was a large part of the population not hungry by that time.

But with the knowledge that grains could be sown, with the sickle to harvest them, and pottery in which to cook and preserve them, a new way of life came into being: the peasant society, reflected in verse from Hesiod to Virgil and from Virgil to Frédéric Mistral in the nineteenth century. But Mistral was perhaps the last poet of the peasant, for he lived in the last generation of European life dominated by the peasantry and its political and social forms. The twentieth century may well see its complete disappearance.

WHAT IS A PEASANT?

The peasant's way of life has dominated all advanced society from the neolithic revolution at Jarmo in the fifth millennium B.C. down to the nineteenth century. All higher civilizations have been raised upon the peasant's shoulders. Today an American farm worker produces enough food to support some forty persons, but until the nineteenth century it took many peasant families to feed a single family in town, as it still does in many parts of the world. And yet so radical has been the revolution of the nineteenth century in Western societies that few Americans have ever seen a peasant or really understand what he is. America is full of farmers, not peasants. Perhaps, however, statements by people who have seen both are the best means by which an American reader can be brought to an imaginative leap, to view the matter from the side of the vastly greater part of human experience.

When I say that America outside the old South is industrial, I am thinking even of those parts that are devoted almost wholly to agriculture, for the mentality of the American [farmer] is industrial. He uses much modern machinery; he is intimately dependent upon the railway and the telephone; he is very conscious of the distant markets to which his products are sent; he is in fact a capitalist who might just as well be in some other business. A peasant, as he exists in Europe and Asia, is practically unknown. This is an immense boon to America, and perhaps its most important superiority as compared to the Old World, for the peasant everywhere is cruel, avaricious, conservative, and inefficient. I have seen orange groves in Sicily and orange groves in California; the contrast represents a period of about 2000 years. Orange groves in Sicily are remote from trains and ships; the trees are old and gnarled and beautiful; the methods are those of classical antiquity.[11] The men are ignorant and semisavage, mongrel descendants of Roman slaves and Arab invaders; what they lack in intelligence towards trees they make up for by cruelty to animals. With moral degradation and economic incompetence goes an instinctive sense of beauty which is perpetually reminding one of

[11] In fact those of medieval Islam, for the Muslims seem to have introduced citrus fruits to the Mediterranean.

Theocritus and the myth about the Garden of the Hesperides. In a California orange grove the Garden of the Hesperides seems very remote. The trees are all exactly alike, carefully tended and at the right distance apart. The oranges, it is true, are not all exactly of the same size, but careful machinery sorts them so that automatically all those in one box are exactly similar. They travel along with suitable things being done to them by suitable machines at suitable points until they enter a suitable refrigerator car in which they travel to a suitable market. The machine stamps the words "Sunkist" upon them, but otherwise there is nothing to suggest that nature has any part in their production. . . . The men engaged in agriculture of this kind do not feel themselves, like the agriculturists of former times, the patient servants of natural forces; on the contrary, they feel themselves the masters, and able to bend natural forces to their will. There is therefore not the same difference in America as in the Old World between the outlook of industrials and that of agriculturists.[12]

Sybille Bedford makes the same contrast:

The Tarrascan Indians . . . live in an economic pattern now obsolete in the West and diluted in the East that was, *mutatis mutandis*, the pattern of agrarian civilization since before Babylon. This pattern is called primitive, but the people who live in it are no more savages than the rural inhabitants of Yorkshire or Normandy. The differences are ones of outlook and domestic objects. The Tarrascan Indians live from hand to mouth, but once more, after a lapse of four hundred years, own the means of production: the land and raw materials. They are not farmers *or* fishermen, shipwrights *or* masons. They grow what they eat and wear, and sometimes a little more; where there is water, they fish; they are competent to build their own or their neighbor's house and boat and even turn a neat, small dome called a half-orange; weave cloth, plait straw, knit hammocks, cure hides, make nets and harnesses and cook-pots. Bricks are made of adobe, the clay dug from their land; the thatch comes off the palms, matting off their coconuts, wicker from reeds. There is sugar-cane in the fields, tobacco grows in the kitchen garden and coffee in the shrubbery. In lucky regions there is also a vile kind of cactus that can be tapped for a mildly alcoholic liquid which looks like cloudy beer and tastes like buttermilk. They have no capital outlay on seeds, stocking and chemical fertilizers. What they cannot raise or make, they do without. Livestock are hardy and prolific beasts—donkeys, pigs, goats and a species of tough hens. What one man lacks or is not so good at, another one in the community can supply or do in exchange for services or goods. The larger acquisitions: knives, firearms, formal riding clothes, musical instruments, silver ornaments or a cow, can also be made by way of barter. It is all a big round not of taking in each other's washing but of producing each other's food and toys. Schools, when there are schools, are free, and the witch doctor will always accept a chicken. Money is indispensable only for salt, matches, and such per-

---

[12] Bertrand Russell, "Modern Homogeneity," *In Praise of Idleness and Other Essays* (London: George Allen and Unwin, 1960), pp. 117-8.

sonal expenses as drink (for those who cannot grow their own), lottery tickets, baptism, the marriage service, funerals and taxes. As occasions for these arise, a man will sit down and spend a day or two weaving a blanket or turning out a batch of soup-pots, then seize a piglet and a cluster of bananas, bundle everything up and pile it on his or his wife's back and set off to market.[13]

Simone de Beauvoir can still see into both worlds, the peasant's and the modern:

> It is the first Indian village that we have visited, and it charms us without surprising. On the contrary, the small houses of beaten earth, the barns, the stacks of straw and hay, the enclosures where the cattle stand behind wooden fences, all that is very much closer to a French hamlet than Lone Pine or Ojai. What we find here is that ancient rural civilization, several thousand years old, which is perpetuated in the fields of Europe as it is here in these privileged territories where the Americans have not assassinated the past—while to our eyes the American villages have the ungrateful exoticism of things that are too new. . . .[14]

While the type is recognizable across a vast era of time and experience, nothing is more erroneous than to view the peasant's technological or social experience as changeless. It is an error induced by urban myopia. (Might the peasant view the city man's experience as timeless and unchanging?) The agricultural technique of the neolithic peasant was far more limited than that of later times and suitable only to a limited geography. All the earliest communities are found on the uplands, on small alluvial plains in the mountains, or on spurs of the hills above the river valleys. Primitive peasants using fire and tools of stone and wood had not the means to deal either with the tangle of marsh and jungle or with the great forests and steppes of northern Europe. Trees could be girdled and burned, but the primeval forests could not be cleared. Clearing grassland was difficult enough, for the hoe was the earliest means of attacking the sod. While the mattock to break the clods may have followed, the plow remained unknown for centuries. Under such conditions, the early peasant carried out a slash-and-burn kind of clearing— a field was opened by burning off the wood. It was then hoed, and the grain scattered. After a few years, when its fertility was greatly reduced, another field would be cleared. It was possible to slow the decline in fertility by leaving a field fallow every other year, but the system demanded great areas for the support of a single village of fifty families such as Jarmo. Soil exhaustion was unavoidable in the absence of fertilizers, crop-rotation, and legumes which could be plowed under for green manure.

[13] Sybille Bedford, *The Sudden View, A Traveller's Tale from Mexico* (New York: Atheneum, 1963), pp. 93–4.
[14] Simone de Beauvoir, *L'Amérique au jour le jour* (Paris: Gallimard, 1954), p. 188.

The adoption of an extensive system of agriculture became imperative when the early peasant learned to attract herbivorous animals. The dog had long been domesticated by the hunter, but the hunter's prey had not been attracted to his camp. With the cultivation of grain, men domesticated a great number of animals—the sheep, the ox and the cow, the goat, the donkey, and the pig. Extensive areas were needed for pasturage but the products (milk, cheese, wool, and, more rarely, meat) were necessary supplements to bread and to the hunter's game which still played an important part in the diet. We can picture a village like Jarmo, then, surrounded by fields, some of them in grain, some fallow, and some deserted. Farther out were more extensive and perhaps rougher areas given over to pasture. Even in the most thickly populated areas, fields of one village did not lie alongside the next but were separated by great wastes and pastures.

Such villages were scattered widely about the Near East in the fifth and early fourth millennia B.C. (see Map I). Improved technology certainly produced a greatly increased population. The archaeological evidence is clear that the social and economic configuration of the neolithic village spread widely. While it is possible, even probable, that the techniques were borrowed by more distant peoples, the spread of agriculture certainly involved migrations as well. The neolithic village had a limited and precarious economy, especially subject to soil exhaustion and to the dangers of overpopulation. On the other hand, though we speak of the neolithic village as a permanent habitation, there was little to prevent the village from moving, since its crops were annual. When the population became too great, the village presumably would produce a colony. We find the process still going on in the European Middle Ages, when a New Sarum was the colony of Old Sarum. Certainly there would be a change when the soil near the old home had given out. On occasion, these migrations undoubtedly involved not a single village or clan, but large groups of villages which for the enterprise of the migration came to form a tribe or nation.

By these methods—borrowing by more primitive peoples, colonizing, and migrations—the culture originated in the Near East spread throughout much of the Old World. Before c. 5000 B.C. agriculture was confined to the Fertile Crescent, northern Iran, and southern Anatolia, and it was not extended to the alluvial valleys of the Nile and the Tigris and Euphrates until about 3000 B.C. By then the rest of Asia Minor, the Balkans, Central Europe and most of the Mediterranean littoral on the west, the Indus Valley, and the arable lands of Turkestan on the east were under cultivation. By about 2000 B.C. agriculture had reached all of Western Europe and the shores of the Baltic and Northern seas, the Ukranian steppe, and northern China on the east (see Map II). Near Eastern agricultural techniques may have come in contact with a gardenlike wet cultivation of rice and tubers originating independently in southern Asia. South of the Sahara in Africa, agriculture began perhaps as early as the third millennium but probably gathered momentum only during the second and first millennia, when millets were cultivated in the Sudan (that belt of savanna between the desert and the rain forest).[15] The introduction of agriculture into the river valleys of the Tigris, Euphrates, and Nile brought more significant changes than simple extension; we shall speak about that process in the next chapter when discussing the rise of civilization.

It is much harder to define, even so tentatively and inexactly, the spread of nomadism. The nomad must not be confused with the hunter; his way of life is entirely different, for he tends and herds animals which he must follow regularly from one pasture to another. The two ways of life have the absence of a settled habitation in common, but little more. It is to be supposed that the herder appeared later than the farmer and that his way of life derived from the peasant's, for animals must first have been tempted into domestication by men who grew grain. Gradually a different way of life made its appearance, but one often in close association with the peasantry.

Great areas of the Near East are not suitable to cultivation but can afford light grazing for animals. In the mountains, goats and, to a lesser degree, sheep can be fed, though the process many require transhumance, that is, the moving of the herds from the highlands in the summer, where there are more rains, down to the lowlands in the winter. Sheep and, at a later date, camels were pastured in the northern Syrian desert and in much of Arabia, northern Libya, and the steppe land north of the Caucasus Mountains and the Black and Caspian seas. Mountain tribes did not ordinarily move great distances and might build up a way of life in close symbiosis with the village. They had goods like raw wool, hides, cheese, and meat to offer the villagers in return for grain and for manufactured articles like pottery and cloth. Such a symbiosis might also develop along the border of the desert, where sometimes the survival of the herds through the withering heat of summer might depend upon grain stored by sedentary populations. Something of this way of life at a later date is reflected in the stories of the patriarchs in the book of Genesis, some of which reflect the precamel nomadism of the later second millennium.[16]

At a greater distance from important sedentary populations, however, a more independent and probably more warlike way of life developed, although

[15] On the spread of neolithic agriculture to Europe, see V. Gordon Childe, *The Prehistory of European Society*, pp. 44–55, and *The Dawn of European Civilization*, passim. On China, see McNeill, *Rise of the West*, pp. 10–2, 23–4. On Africa south of Egypt and the Sahara, see Roland Oliver and J. D. Fage, *A Short History of Africa* (Penguin African Library; Baltimore: Penguin Books, 1962), pp. 23–33. The rain forests of the Congo Basin and Guinea Coast did not see agriculture until a much later date. Almost none of the important crops that can be raised in these regions are native to Africa. Cultivation had to wait until the introduction of the banana and yam from southeastern Asia probably in the early Christian era, and of the sweet potato, maize, and cassava from South and Central America during the sixteenth and seventeenth centuries.

[16] W. F. Albright, *The Biblical Period from Abraham to Ezra* (Harper Torchbooks; New York: Harper and Row, 1963), pp. 21, 41.

the nomads of this era before the domestication of the camel were far less mobile and dangerous. The economy depended not only upon raising sheep, goats, and, eventually, camels, but also upon regular raiding, if we may judge by what we know of later times. The nomad's life is always a hard one and he is constantly tempted by the sown. (The Arabs call Mesopotamia "Iraq," "the green.") When a bit of rain falls in the Syrian desert, bedouin will sow a handful of grain in the wadis where water collects and return in several months to harvest their crop. When an opening not occupied by peasants appears in the border region, the nomad may gradually settle down and take up village life. Such appears to have happened in Palestine among the various tribes of herders of sheep and goats who eventually came to compose the Hebrews. They settled in the more barren upland first, in the southern mountain land (the Negeb), and to the west of the Jordan River in the highlands. In Palestine the newcomers, coming into conflict with the settled inhabitants, formed a confederation of tribes and eventually wrested most of the country from the resident Canaanites and the Philistines. The conflict between the nomad and the peasant, however, could take more spectacular forms and produce such momentous events as the Arab conquests of the seventh century A.D. or the Mongol conquests of the thirteenth.

2 THE ORIGINS OF CIVILIZATION IN THE GREAT RIVER VALLEYS

INNOVATIONS OF EARLY CIVILIZATION

The double culture of the isolated neolithic village and the nomadic herders of sheep and goats lays at the root of the new social configuration which developed in the great river valleys of the Tigris and Euphrates, the Nile, and the Indus, all of which show a social order recognizable to us as civilization.[1] It is difficult to define civilization, even if we manage to avoid imposing our own ideas of civilized conduct and morality. Yet we do sense easily enough that at several places in human history there have appeared recognizably similar societies that might be called primitive civilizations: Sumeria in southern Mesopotamia; then Egypt, Minoan Crete, and the Indus valley cities of Mohenjo-Daro and Harappa; the Yellow River valley of north China; and much later, the central valley of Mexico, the Yucatan, and Peru. Although it is as yet hard to make out the archaeological record, the medieval civilizations of the African Sudan, too, seem to bear a generic resemblance to these cultures.

All these early civilizations made use of a technology more advanced than the neolithic and developed a new sort of social organization. Because they were all without writing during the periods of their origin and early growth, we are again forced to view social change largely from the point of view of the technological innovations revealed by the archaeologist's spade, although certainly such innovations depended as much on individual genius and the state of the social order as either of these things depended upon technology.[2]

By the fourth millennium the neolithic farming economy appears to have reached a crisis in some regions. That system of livelihood suffered from serious limitations. The appearance and spread of extensive dry agriculture

---

[1] The standard work in English on the history of the ancient Near East is the first two volumes of *The Cambridge Ancient History*. A second edition is being published in fascicles; upon completion it will be published as two bound volumes and a volume of plates will be added.

[2] Robert Redfield, *The Primitive World and Its Transformations* (Ithaca, N.Y.: Cornell University Press, 1953).

18

had greatly increased the population;[3] its methods however were not infinitely expandable. A great deal of space was needed to support a neolithic village, the return per acre was feeble, and it was necessary to maintain great areas out of cultivation for grazing animals and for such raw materials as wood and reeds and perhaps as a hunting ground. Many of the richest soils were waterlogged or, in such places as Western Europe, covered with great forests. The great plain of Eurasia was covered with heavy grass sod which resisted the tools of the neolithic farmer. When all the land about his village had declined in productivity as a result of what agronomists call mining the soil, the early peasant could only move. Manuring and crop rotation were possible escapes from this Malthusian dilemma, but in fact they were developed only slowly and after two other innovations.

One such innovation appears to have been war.[4] When the population had risen to a point that there was no longer enough free land available for such extensive methods of cultivation, men for the first time—or at least peasants for the first time—appear to have taken to conquest. The earliest Danubian farming settlements in Europe show no signs of defensive walls, only fences against browsing and grazing animals. But in later stages, after contact with a mysterious Western European culture more largely devoted to herding, the peasantry of Europe began to raise fortifications. Weapons that seem to be designed for use against other men made their appearance; war became a human institution.

[3] The increase of population is certain, but there were complications which cannot now really be traced. Disesases, for example, that prey on human populations almost certainly increased as well. From Marston Bates, *The Forest and the Sea. A Look at the Economy of Nature and the Ecology of Man* (Signet Science Library; New York: The New American Library, 1961), p. 135:

> This meant that men could increase greatly in numbers and could aggregate into villages where they could continue to live in the same place for long periods of time. Among other things, this altered man's relation to his parasites. I suspect that the human contagions, the diseases that are "catching," that can pass directly from host to host without vectors or intermediate states, started to appear during this period. It is hard to imagine diseases like measles, smallpox, gonorrhea, syphilis, tuberculosis, being maintained in the Old Stone Age. There were not enough hosts, and the hosts would not come in contact often enough, to keep the pathogens going. Man got an increased load of disease along with his increased food supply. Even the non-contagious diseases, like malaria and yellow fever, could take on a new importance.
>
> The contagious diseases today cannot maintain themselves in scattered hunting of food-gathering populations. They are diseases of civilization, often introduced into hunting populations by outside contact, where they may cause fearful epidemics before they disappear again, but they do disappear unless outside contact is frequent enough. These diseases have a long history in the Mediterranean and in the thickly settled parts of Asia—they started in the very regions where the Neolithic revolution started—and they have spread to the rest of the world only in modern times. . . .

See also M. Bates, *The Prevalence of People* (New York: Charles Scribner's Sons, 1955), pp. 154–72.

[4] V. Gordon Childe, "War in Prehistoric Societies," *Sociological Review*, XXXIII (1941), 126–38.

The other possible solution open to the postneolithic peasant was to innovate in agricultural methods. Instead of making improvements in techniques of dry farming (crop rotation and fertilizers), the neolithic peasant entered the wet river valleys of southern Mesopotamia and Egypt where he created a radically different kind of agriculture. Consequently a radically different social order arose—the agriculture of drainage and irrigation, the social order called civilization. This change depended upon several technological innovations developed in the late neolithic period. One set involved the working of copper and some other less important metals like lead, gold, and silver. Meteoric iron had long been used by savages and barbarians. It is pure enough to be beaten into a form, but, while useful for very small cutting edges, it is too rare to affect society profoundly. The scarcity of gold and silver, as well as their softness, made their contribution negligible also. Copper, too, had been beaten cold without startling social consequences, but the neolithic period learned to smelt copper and to cast it into any desired shape. Copper is a fairly soft metal and its usefulness for tools and weapons is limited, but within several hundred years of the discovery of smelting, men learned to add a quantity of tin (or some other metals) to produce bronze, a far harder metal, suitable for tools and weapons.[5] Gold, silver, and lead could be smelted and cast in the same fashion. The melting point of iron however is very much higher than that of these metals and therefore iron played no important role in the earliest civilizations. The later development of kilns that could smelt it would produce revolutionary results.

The late neolithic age also learned to build better than the earliest village at Jarmo. Sun-dried bricks, a better material than *terre pisée*, were used, while techniques of stonework, too, were improved. Monumental architecture is one of the most startling characteristics of the early civilizations. The progress of the Sumerian temple from a village shrine can be traced at the site of al'Ubaid near Ur in southern Mesopotamia. Such great constructions as the ziggurats of Mesopotamia, the pharaonic pyramids, and the immense temples of Peru, the Yucatan, and Mexico resulted. These called for a number of other innovations, one of which was terra cotta (cooked or baked brick). This development must have been closely linked with the development of pottery. An efficient potter's kiln appeared in the late neolithic period as well as the potter's wheel, which permits a single worker to mold a pot in a few minutes instead of hours.

Transportation underwent great improvement as moving became more complicated. The cart was invented, a heavy, cumbersome vehicle drawn by oxen. The invention of the ox yoke and harness called for considerable ingenuity. Men had long made dugout canoes and perhaps some other kinds of boats, but now the sail made its appearance, the first, and for long the only, use of inanimate power. Yet by c. 3000 B.C. men's sources of power had im-

---

[5] Childe, *What Happened in History*, pp. 73–7; *Man Makes Himself*, pp. 116–21.

proved considerably—as they had to if they were to produce the immense monuments of some early civilizations.

Cities, too, are a product of such early civilizations, although they did not appear in them all. They may have developed from military needs or around temple centers. Even if cities did not develop—as in early dynastic Egypt—the size of the political community increased to something greatly exceeding the isolated agricultural village. With this larger size came greater specialization of function. The neolithic village had, in a fashion, known division of labor. Work, like everything else, was divided according to sex and perhaps between shepherd and peasant. The women made the pottery just as they made the cloth and prepared skins; the men carved and made stone tools. Individuals might acquire a specialty: among some modern West African tribes, a man who carves spoons never carves anything else. Yet he is hardly a specialist, for though he does some one thing better than anyone else, everyone could do his special task and he does the same basic work that everyone else does; he is first of all a peasant, not a woodworker. With the increased labor pool and the complexity of new manufacturing techniques, specialization had gone much farther: the bronzesmith was necessarily a professional, and the potter working on a wheel and with a kiln probably also became a specialized artisan.

Increased specialization can probably be related to the development of class lines. Rulers and priests made their appearance, and later we shall see the city developing into the territorial state. With the development of a priestly and administrative class exercising control over a territory and receiving taxes or shares of the community's produce, a need to keep records might come to be felt, and such cultures often developed instruments for that purpose. Some early methods, like the Peruvian *quipu*, were capable of little development; the Sumerians however turned their pictures into writing.

At the base of all these early civilizations, and far more basic than the innovations we have been describing, was a more intensive system of agriculture that exploited a kind of environment profoundly different from the highlands of the neolithic village. It may not have been more economical in terms of labor, but it certainly was in acreage needed to support a man. New crops also appeared. The mobility of the neolithic village was largely lost and a denser and more permanent settlement on the land became the rule. In the Near East, the Mediterranean, and Europe, the plow and water control were essential elements.[6]

In summary the early civilizations present a configuration of intensive agriculture, the territorial state, government, a society of unequal classes including priests and persons holding political power, a leisured class exploiting others, record keeping (often writing), skilled artisans, monumental architecture, and often towns and cities.

[6] The techniques of tropical agriculture and of rice production are quite different.

THE ORIGINS OF SUMERIAN CIVILIZATION

Basic to the change from neolithic barbarism to early civilization was the development of a radically new system of cultivation, one far more intensive. Many of the innovations spoken of above—the potter's wheel and the smelting of copper and the various complicated processes involved in it—may have been invented in the neolithic uplands but did not coalesce into a distinctly new form of society. That happened in a place where a more intensive agriculture could produce a denser population and a greater surplus of food. The great step from the upper barbarism of the neolithic village to civilized societies has been taken at a number of times and places, but each appears in some degree dependent upon the impetus or catalytic action of a more advanced civilization. Egypt was influenced in important and apparently essential ways by Sumeria;[7] both the Indus Valley civilization of Harappa and Mohenjo-Daro and the Chinese civilization appear to have borrowed seminal ideas from the Near East.[8] Only the civilizations of the New World—in the central valley of Mexico, the Yucatan, and Peru—may have been entirely independent, and even that appears to be becoming increasingly doubtful. More and more evidence points to influences (even migrations) across the immense width of the Pacific Ocean, amazing as that appears.[9] Only once can we speak with any confidence of a completely original development, independent of any imitation of a higher culture. That development is the first appearance of Sumerian civilization in the swamps and alluvial plain of the lower valley of the Tigris and Euphrates rivers in southern Mesopotamia during the centuries before 3000 B.C.

In order to understand or describe this development, it is necessary to have fairly clearly in mind the geography and climate of Mesopotamia (see Map III).[10] Today the life and the urban order of Los Angeles and New York are strikingly similar; their divergences are largely the results of their

---

[7] Frankfort, *The Birth of Civilization*, pp. 123ff.

[8] McNeill, *Rise of the West*, pp. 84, 107–9.

[9] *Ibid.*, pp. 239–43; J. Alden Mason, *The Ancient Civilizations of Peru* (Baltimore: Penguin Books, 1964), pp. 20ff.; Edgar Anderson, *Plants, Man and Life* (Boston: Little, Brown and Co., 1952), pp. 66–72.

[10] It would be well to begin by reminding the reader of the chief features determining the climate. In the northern temperate zone, the water supply is carried chiefly by westerlies from the Atlantic. In summer these winds pass to the north across the great plain of Eurasia. In the winter the Mediterranean lands lie in their path. Now, when winds are intercepted by mountains, they are forced up and at the same time cooled. Because cool air will hold less moisture than warm air, the result of the rising of the winds, then, is rain on the windward side of mountains and a rain shadow on the lee. The prevailing westerlies of the winter are partly intercepted by the Atlas Mountains and the plateau of Spain and deposit much of their moisture on the western slopes before they enter the Mediterranean through

having been built at different stages of a rapidly transforming technology: New York before and Los Angeles after the widespread use of the automobile. This does more to determine Los Angeles's peculiarity than its celebrated climate. Ancient man—and, indeed, modern man until very recently—was far more dependent upon the climate and the immediate geography, as the farmer still is. For ancient man was overwhelmingly a peasant, with a technology far less capable of coping with his environment. He was the patient servant of nature, barely learning to coax and persuade her. But it should not be assumed that even in a primitive society the environment determines the nature of society, as Montesquieu thought.[11] Rather, the environment sets limitations and offers opportunities. Nor should it be supposed that the regions which have housed the greatest and most original social developments are necessarily those pleasantest or easiest for human habitation. For example, the Indians of southern California were among the most backward peoples on the continent.

Mesopotamia is the product of the rivers; it is the two valleys and the steppe between them. Both rivers rise in the mountains of Armenia, but while the Tigris flows more or less directly southeast to the Persian Gulf, the Euphrates makes a wide arc to the west before passing through the Middle Euphrates gorge at the ancient cities of Melitene and Samosata, then swings southeast toward the Gulf. Except in northern Mesopotamia where the border mountains of Iran (the Zagros) induced rain enough for some neolithic agriculture, the country is almost completely dependent upon the rivers for water, for in the lower part of the plain the total annual rainfall does not exceed six to eight inches which is insufficient to produce crops. Whatever land, then, is not reached by the rivers' waters and cannot be irrigated is barren steppe affording little more than rough herbage for sheep. The Euphrates above the ancient city of Babylon, at the point where it approaches nearest to the Tigris (about on the parallel of modern Baghdad), cuts deeply into the plateau and does not, therefore, either flood or offer much opportunity for irrigation. Consequently much of northern Mesopotamia is open steppe not suitable to agriculture. Even in the south, in the ancient land of Sumer, those regions above the flood plain remained dry and barren. But in the south, due to the deposits of silt it lays down in its bed, the Euphrates

---

the Straits of Gibraltar and the funnel between the Pyrenées and Cévennes Mountains of southern France. The Mediterranean lands themselves are generally mountainous and as a result the annual waterfall is very unevenly distributed. But broadly there is a little less rain in the eastern parts than the western. Beyond the sea itself desiccation becomes extreme. The Anatolian plateau, the mountains of modern Turkey and Armenia, where the Tigris and Euphrates rise, and the mountains parallel to the coasts of Syria and Palestine catch almost the last of the rain. To the east of them lies the plateau of the Syrian desert.

[11] *De l'esprit des lois*, pt. 3.

sometimes flows above the plain.[12] An extraordinarily high flood in the spring causes it to overflow, break its embankment, and flood the country about it. Pools of stagnant water are left behind, while the river perhaps takes a new course. In place after place the swampy former river beds can still be discovered. Silt accumulated, too, at the mouths of the rivers, as in the deltas of the Nile and the Mississippi, but whether the Persian Gulf extended much farther north in the late fourth millennium than it does today appears doubtful. The deposits laid down by the Karun River flowing from the coastal mountains of Iran and the wadis of Arabia had perhaps formed very much the modern northern coast of the Persian Gulf, but behind this seacoast lay a land of salt lagoons and low islands, a region gradually silting up with the deposits of the great rivers from the north.[13] The whole of Sumer then must have been a swamp interspersed with lagoons and areas of upland steppe. In crossing the north Syrian steppe, the Euphrates receives two important tributaries from the east: the Balikh and the Khabour, both of which also rise among the mountains of Asia Minor, but below this it receives none at all. In its long trip from the Khabour to the Persian Gulf, on the contrary, the Euphrates loses considerable volume by evaporation. The Tigris, on the other hand, receives numerous tributaries from the Zagros Mountains all along its length, and some of them like the Great and the Little Zab and the Diyala are considerable streams.

These differences have consequences to the people of the lower valley. The volume of the Euphrates does not vary rapidly in its middle and lower courses, because it depends upon rainfall that has percolated through porous rock strata or upon the melting snows of the mountains of Asia Minor, but the Tigris can be affected by local direct surface run-off from mountain torrents. Thus a local rainstorm in the Zagros can produce great changes within a few hours, and rises of some eight or twelve feet in twenty-four hours can occur.

Most of the fall of both rivers occurs above the Baghdad region, where even on the Euphrates the current is too swift for any but highly powered boats to move upstream. The fall of the Tigris is even sharper. The speed of the current means that both rivers erode considerable soil and carry much

[12] This seems odd and perhaps needs clarification. As a river leaves the mountains of its source and enters the flood plain towards its mouth, the momentum of its waters naturally slows. As it slows, it deposits silt and raises its bed. But since the water flows faster in the middle of the river than along its banks, its deposit is greater along the sides, which are thus built up and maintain the river in its bed until a great flood sweeps them away at some point and lets the waters run over the low lands. The same phenomenon is seen in the lower Mississippi and Sacramento rivers in the United States.

[13] On the coast line, see the opinions expressed by W. B. Fisher, *The Middle East, Physical, Social, and Regional Geography* (London: Methuen, 1950), pp. 34–5; and Georges Roux, *Ancient Iraq* (London: George Allen and Unwin, 1964), pp. 19–20. The eastern shore of Arabia along the Persian Gulf seems to be rising: Geoffrey Bibby, *Looking for Dilmun* (New York: Alfred A. Knopf, 1969), pp. 373–4.

sediment. Both appear all year as turbid and rapid streams, in contrast to the Nile, which is placid and clear for eight months. The volume of water carried by the Tigris is much greater than that of the Euphrates. Since its fall is also steeper and it receives direct run-off from the mountains, it is especially subject to floods. Below Baghdad, which may have been the primitive head of the Persian Gulf, the fall of the river is far less sharp, as would be expected in what was originally delta country. Here the flow of the river is slower, a fall of only one inch per mile over the last one hundred miles of the Euphrates, and of about two inches per mile along the Tigris. One result is that the rivers deposit immense amounts of silt in their beds so that they actually flow above the level of the plain about them and the flooding spoken of above occurs. Even without such a disaster, the lower reaches of the river are permanent marsh, whose inhabitants today follow a radically different way of life from the people farther north.

The annual regimes of the two rivers differ. Both are at their lowest in September and October. When the temperature falls in autumn, there is a slight, but noticeable, rise in the Euphrates, though not in the Tigris, as evaporation declines. The first winter rains, however, affect the Tigris immediately; the Euphrates rises more slowly on account of the porous soils at her mountain sources. The maximum flood of the Tigris comes during April; that of the Euphrates not until May. The volume of the Tigris is much greater than that of the Euphrates at all times, its increase is sharper, its volume in flood is a greater increase over its lowest level, and its height in flood above the level of low water—some eighteen feet—is greater than that of the Euphrates, even though its bed is narrower. It clearly is the more dangerous river. The levels of the two rivers are not the same. From Qurna as far as Baghdad, the Tigris lies at a slightly higher level than the Euphrates. In the vicinity of Baghdad their relation is reversed. For centuries this peculiarity has been used for irrigation.

The climate is generally difficult and unpleasant. The lowlands have two seasons: a dry and intensely hot summer from May to October and a comparatively cool, damp winter from December to March. Spring and fall are short. The summer monsoons of the Indian Ocean and the Persian Gulf set up a wind, known as the *Shamal*, which blows without interruption during the summer. The air is dry, there are no clouds, and the sun beats down without relief. On most days the temperature reaches 95 degrees and far too often 120. There is some relief at night, but most of the population which cannot move to the hills takes refuge in underground shelters. Daily dust storms add to the general discomfort. Near the rivers and swamps the humidity is high and heat exhaustion common.

It rains only in the winter, and rains are due almost entirely to the arrival of moist maritime air from the Mediterranean. Since this air has already passed over the mountains of Syria, there is only reduced rainfall. Late January and early February are the wettest periods, and there is ordinarily no rain between the end of May and the end of September. Over most of the country the annual precipitation does not exceed five inches, a level that produces desert, but in the foothills of the Zagros, the Assyrian region receives some 15 inches, which is sufficient to support a rather precarious cultivation without irrigation. Elsewhere cultivation is completely dependent upon irrigation.[14]

But the rivers made life possible and even enviable. The Euphrates carries only about half as much water as the Tigris, but because its banks are lower, it overflows more readily onto the plain and spreads its waters and silt more freely once it is south of Babylon. Since, too, its floods are less dangerous, the first inhabitants preferred its banks for the foundations of their earliest settlements. The annual flood in Mesopotamia comes in the early summer, too late for the farmer to take advantage of the gentler spring warmth. The waters recede in June, at the beginning of the hot season when the burning sun parches the earth. The very modest rains come in October and November, and the next month plowing begins.

The plow was one of the major innovations of the new agricultural system. The early plow was, indeed, little more than a hoe or a digging stick harnessed to a yoke of oxen, but its consequences were tremendous. It did much to change the role of the sexes in agriculture, making the tilling of the fields men's work. It also made possible the cultivation of a much larger area in a day by a single man, or rather by a single plow team. This may have increased the surplus product of the individual peasant, but not too much should be made of this in comparison with the uplands, for the new burden of diking, draining, and irrigating was extremely laborious. Without the plow, these burdens would perhaps have been excessive. Oxen, too, when they are working, must be fed something more than grass, and they must be fed over the parched Sumerian summer, so that a part of the produce of the land must go to animals rather than men. But the plow did enable men to plant much more quickly, and that is a very considerable advantage. Its transformations over the next five thousand years will mark great revolutions in agriculture.

The harvest in the southern and central parts of the country is made in the middle of May. Thereafter the heat becomes so fierce that no work can be done in the fields until the September–October rains again soften the soil.

The products of the more intensive agriculture of the lower valley of Mesopotamia were very largely those of its neolithic predecessor: barley throughout the third millennium B.C. was by far the most important grain, though emmer wheat and wheat were also grown.[15] Barley was eaten as

---

[14] Fisher, *The Middle East*, pp. 339–53; Max Cary, *Geographical Background of Greek and Roman History* (Oxford: Clarendon Press, 1949), pp. 178–82.

[15] The relative importance of different grains at different times is a matter only now being carefully studied and complete agreement has not been reached. Perhaps in the earliest times wheat was as common as barley, but barley became increasingly important in the river valleys. It withstands salinity better than wheat, and T. Jacobsen and R. M. Adams,

porridge and as leavened and unleavened bread. It was also made into beer, which we must not think of as a luxury or a self-indulgence. Beer certainly played an essential part in the diet of all the agricultural populations, having a food value somewhat different from the bread or porridge into which grain can also be turned. Oil came largely from sesame rather than from the olive as in the Mediterranean and many rough upland districts. Among vegetables, many of which were grown as field crops, onions were perhaps the most important. Garlic was put on the table of the gods, but beets, something like the turnip or carrot, radishes, chicory (which is a root something like the carrot or parsnip), and many varieties of cucumbers were grown as well as garden products of less food value like cress, dill, cardamon (perhaps), coriander, saffron, hyssop (a small perennial whose bitter aromatic leaves were brewed into a tea for certain illnesses), thyme, caraway, cassia, asafetida [16] and flowers, of which the poppy was especially popular. Most of these small annuals were probably an inheritance from the neolithic past.

There were innovations, however. The vine was known in Assyria but does not flourish in the lower valley. Certain fruit trees also were now cultivated, and their appearance was important both economically and socially, for the cultivation of fruit trees, which take years of attention, ties men to their habitations and necessarily marks the end of that seminomadism characteristic of the neolithic farmer. Trees played an important part in the Sumerian economy: the pistachio, the pear, the almond, the carob, and perhaps the lemon were all known at some period, though how early is not always clear. By far the most important, known from the earliest times, was the date palm. Indeed the swamps of southern Mesopotamia still produce most of the dates in international commerce. The date palm demands a hot head and wet feet; few places in the world offer this combination better than the river banks of the lower parts of the rivers and the Shatt el-Arab. The date produces not only fruit—and a fruit that can be dried and preserved— but also a juice that can serve in the place of honey, for the bee is less common and honey less cheap than in the uplands. Date stones were fed to cattle and burnt as fuel.

The animals were largely those long domesticated: oxen, donkeys, sheep, and goats. Some, however, surprise us today, for gazelles seem to have been

---

"Salt and Silt in Ancient Mesopotamian Agriculture," *Science*, CXXVIII (1958), 1251–8, argue that increasing salinity of the alluvium caused the change. Spelt was valued as equivalent to barley, while wheat was twice as valuable. Barley was also the common bread grain in Palestine, and early Greek sources show freemen eating barley bread, although later it became the food of slaves and the poor. At least by Hellenistic times and earlier in some places, wheat was the common food of Greeks living in cities: E. Ashtor, *Ann. ESC.*, XXIII (1968), 1019. One reason was the cost of transport, for barley is bulkier than wheat.

[16] A gum resin used for medicine as an antispasmodic or as a calming medicine for persons having spasms of fits. It is derived from a plant of the carrot family.

raised and to have played a real role in the economy. (They are permitted the Jews in the Deuteronomic law.) It seems surprising, too, that Sumeria was considered important grazing country; the flocks were certainly very large. Perhaps the explanation is that with the autumn rains cattle could be widely herded in the desert, but the nomads, if nomads rather than Sumerian peasants tended the herds, were dependent upon supplies of fodder from the peasants during the great summer drought. Oxen pulled the plow; cattle, sheep, and goats all supplied milk, butter, and probably cheese, but the goats, like sheep, were primarily raised for their wool. Donkeys and asses were the chief beasts of burden. Pigs were allowed to run more or less loose and were cheap, for their flesh was already surrounded by taboos. The dog was not valued by the peasant, though of course dogs were used by the hunters of the hills and probably by the shepherd. Whether the cat was known even by Assyrian times in the early first millennium is uncertain (his early history is curiously obscure). The horse did not become important until the later part of the second millennium and the camel not until the first. The goose was domesticated early, but the chicken took a long time to arrive from the east, and the duck was only beginning to be domesticated in Roman times. Both fresh and salt-water fish appear to have been caught in large quantities, for sanctuaries have been discovered strewn with their bones.[17]

It was in this not wholly enviable environment that the earliest civilization made its appearance. The radically new demands that the change in agricultural technique put upon the community forced the creation of new social forms and resulted in an increased population in the river valleys comparable to the increase produced by the first introduction of agriculture in the highlands. When the greatly increased labor involved in working heavy soil, in draining, and diking and irrigating is considered, it is not at all certain that the marginal productivity of labor in Sumeria was greater than that in the earlier or contemporary neolithic villages of Assyria to the north, but the fertility of the lower valley was vastly greater. When Strabo says that barley reproduced 300-fold, he was, of course, talking nonsense, as Romans usually did when they wrote about numbers, but the yield is now some 36-fold. The Romans at a much later date considered tenfold an extraordinarily good yield for dry agriculture, and the harvests of northern France in the ninth century A.D. may have sometimes given as little as threefold. As a result, large numbers of men began to dwell more closely together than ever before in history, and perhaps no condition of society does more to determine its nature than the density of settlement: consider the differences between the great plains of wheat in Manitoba and the crowded Nile Valley.

[17] B. Meissner, *Babylonien und Assyrien*, I (Heidelberg: C. Winter, 1920), pp. 202ff.; P. Anton Deimel, *Sumerische Tempelwirtschaft zur Zeit Urukaginas und seiner Vorgaenger. Abschluss der Einselstudien und Zusammenfassung der Hauptresultate*, Vol. II of *Analecta Orientalia* (Rome: Pontificio Instituto Biblico, 1931), p. 4. On domestic birds, Pierre P. Grassé, ed., *Traité de Zoologie*, Vol. XV: *Oiseaux* (Paris: Masson, 1950), pp. 1101–15.

The beginnings of things are always obscure, and the origins of cultivation in the valleys are no exception. We do not know with any certainty just how men first tackled the problem of farming among the swamps and lakes of lower Mesopotamia. Presumably some clans of neolithic villagers migrated to the banks of the great rivers—we may suppose reluctantly—and were forced to attempt some control of the waters. Irrigation techniques may not have been wholly unknown. It has been suggested that the earliest farmers may indeed have made some use of irrigation, for many of the earliest sites are in lands where the rainfall is barely adequate for an assured crop and were on the alluvial terraces formed by mountain streams. The flood of the autumn rains, then, may have early been directed into small channels and rivulets to irrigate. This could be done by a village community with considerable labor, but little ingenuity. In the great valley, however, the problems are considerably more complicated, for the force of the stream in flood time makes irrigation difficult and dangerous, and much of the fertile land is likely to be waterlogged much of the year. Since the rivers flow above the general level of the valley, much diking and ditching are needed to drain the land, while other ditches are needed to lead waters into the fields and to keep it there long enough to provide a crop. The flood itself was not regular or gentle enough and did not last long enough to irrigate without control. Such efforts at some point demanded resources and organization beyond the means of the neolithic village and appear to have been the prime cause of the emergence of a new power structure among the Sumerians settled in the southernmost parts of the Tigris and Euphrates valleys.[18] This new form is the city, and Professor Childe has popularized the term "the urban revolution" to describe the origins of civilized life here.

At a number of sites in Sumeria, the archaeologist's work has revealed the successive stages by which some of the neolithic villages of the alluvium turned into cities, including al'Ubaid, the nearby Ur, and a number of others (see Map III). The decay and renewal of successive villages on the same site produced a mound, the familiar "tell" standing above the flat plain which clearly indicates a site of early habitation. The lower levels of such a tell will consist of mud-brick houses and reed huts, the very first standing on the alluvium itself. In the successive levels increasing size, greater use of metals, the introduction of the potter's wheel, and other postneolithic developments can be traced.

But new elements not found in neolithic villages successively make their appearance. The temple at al'Ubaid developed from a simple shrine to a considerable temple raised upon an artificial mound, the first of those ziggurats,

[18] There are discussions of the techniques and problems of drainage and irrigation in R. J. Forbes, *Studies in Ancient Technology,* II (Leiden: E. J. Brill, 1955), pp. 1–77; by Robert M. Adams, *The Evolution of Urban Society; Early Mesopotamia and Prehispanic Mexico* (Chicago: Aldine Press, 1966); and by M. S. Drower, "Water-Supply, Irrigation, and Agriculture," *History of Technology,* I, ed. Singer et al., pp. 520–57.

which became a part, indeed the central part, of every Sumerian town. Such temples fell into disrepair and were rebuilt time and time again. The larger and wealthier communities also built fortifications. Clearly the wealth revealed by Sir Leonard Woolley's excavations of the "royal cemetery" at Ur indicates a social order very much larger than a village. The cemetery contained most elaborate goldwork, carved stone, and jewelry, all indicating a courtly society. The city had become a center of political power exercised over the surrounding countryside. Sumerian civilization crystallized about such city-states: Eridu, Larsa, Erech, Nippur, Lagash, and Ur, familiar as Abraham's home and the site of Sir Leonard Woolley's astounding discoveries.[19]

The cities of ancient Sumeria were profoundly different organisms from the modern industrial and commercial city. The greater part of their population certainly was peasants, direct tillers of the soil who left the city daily to plow and sow. These cities are far more comparable to the Greek *polis* and the Roman *civitas*, not places established for commercial or industrial reasons, but rather places where the countryside could assemble for political and religious purposes. (Ortega y Gassett has suggested that the first city was simply a circle with an empty space in which public business might be transacted.) It seems likely, though, that the purpose which induced the Sumerians to move from the countryside to town and to alter their traditional ways of life so radically was the need to make common decisions about water control (although war and rivalry with other tribes of peasants may have played a part).

It can be argued that the need to control waters, to dike and to ditch, called for an authoritarian govenment, and there is indeed much evidence to support this contention. Such societies require a bureaucratic organization and must be able to summon huge bodies of manpower at short notice for great undertakings. This is the thesis of Professor Wittfogel, and the entire later history of the Near East in a measure supports him,[20] for the Sumerian city-states, the Egyptians, the Akkadians, the Assyrians, and the Persians all had divine and absolute monarchs. Still, there is some evidence that the earliest Sumerians did not live under absolute kings or priesthoods but were in fact citizens of free republics.[21] We know too little of that social order to speak confidently of democracy, but there do appear to have been deliberative assemblies of a sort that had passed away by historical times. This is not very surprising after all: the coming together of the people into a city prob-

[19] Sir Leonard Woolley, *Digging Up the Past* (New York: C. Scribner's Sons, 1931); *Ur of the Chaldees: A Record of Seven Years of Excavation* (London: E. Benn, 1929); *Excavations at Ur: A Record of Twelve Years' Work* (London: E. Benn, 1955).

[20] Karl A. Wittfogel, *Oriental Despotism, A Comparative Study of Total Power* (New Haven, Conn.: Yale University Press, 1957).

[21] Thorkild Jacobsen, "Primitive Democracy in Ancient Mesopotamia," *JNES*, II (1943), 159–72. This point is discussed more fully in the next chapter.

ably occurred only under great pressure, for it involved a radical transformation of traditional life. How radical can be judged from the fact that the surviving records of Sumerian life show no remnants, not the least trace, of the clan and tribal organizations which must have preceded the city, while among the Greeks and Romans such vestiges are everywhere evident even in the first century B.C., 700 or 800 years after the creation of the polis. But even if it took place under pressure, the union was made for common ends about which men would naturally deliberate. It must also have been voluntary, for no village could produce the power necessary to coerce other villages into a union. It must have been deliberative, for the problems raised by water control in Mesopotamia demanded rational rather than traditional solutions. In short, that union of villages into the city created political society.

THE ORIGINS OF EGYPTIAN CIVILIZATION

Although the development of civilized life in Egypt was more or less contemporary with that in Mesopotamia, a number of considerations suggest that the Egyptians should be considered after the Sumerians. As we shall see, the neolithic Gerzean cultures of fourth-millennium Egypt seem to have been stimulated into the activities that produced civilization by innovations from Sumeria, and, therefore, in some sense to be dependent upon it.[22] Then, too, the influence of Egypt was never as central or important as that of the peoples and cultures of Mesopotamia, for Egypt is a remarkably isolated land. Once Egypt had achieved her distinctive social order, she continued her own course with remarkable indifference to the world outside the Nile valley, and her history can be discussed without constant reference to the peoples about her. Egypt does, however, resemble Mesopotamia and all other early peoples in the close dependence of her society upon her climate and geography, and her economy resembles Mesopotamia's in particular in its dependence upon the peculiarities of a river. The study of her history and economy, then, must begin with geography.

Egypt is, quite simply, the Nile valley [23] and its delta (see Map IV). Above Aswan the valley narrows to little more than a gorge which has been described as 200 miles long and five yards wide. The desert closes in on either side. From Aswan to the Mediterranean is a distance of some 750 miles, but for 600 miles of that distance the cultivable land is never more than thirteen miles wide and less in some places. The river provided the long and narrow land with transportation and the possibility of unity. Like the Tigris and

[22] Frankfort, *Birth of Civilization in the Near East*, Appendix.
[23] Hawkes, *Prehistory*, pp. 232–3. Until late in the nineteenth century, the modern world knew no more of the sources of the Nile than did Herodotus. Their discovery has been delightfully chronicled by Alan Moorehead in *The Blue Nile* (New York: Harper and Row, 1962) and *The White Nile* (New York: Harper and Row, 1960).

Euphrates, the Nile floods periodically, but its flood is far more regular and less dangerous. It rises and falls with extraordinary precision. The rise is first noticed at the beginning of July. By September the river is at its peak and the land covered by six feet or more of water. The water recedes and is back within its banks by the end of October. Planting begins almost immediately, and the crops mature through the mild winter. The harvest begins in the middle of May. By the end of May the river is at its lowest ebb, and between April and July the sun and heat crack the land and nothing grows without artificial irrigation.[24] The flood cycle begins again early in July.

Despite the regularity of the Nile, there was always the possibility that not enough or too much water might arrive each year. A Hellenistic statue of the Nile god, now in the Vatican, holds a horn of abundance and is surrounded by sixteen children, each one cubit (about twenty inches) high. The infants symbolize the sixteen cubits' flood (measured at Memphis) which guaranteed abundance. A flood of twelve or thirteen cubits brought hunger; eighteen cubits meant disaster, for an extraordinarily high flood could do great damage. But the Nile, unlike the Tigris and Euphrates, has such a slight fall after it enters Egypt and is so well contained within its banks that it never really rampages.

As it spreads over the country, its movement, of course, slows, and as a result silt is deposited on the land. Land is built in this way (or rather, it was until the building of the high dam at Aswan): the entire delta has been deposited in the Mediterranean by the river, and the level of the valley is calculated to have been raised some twenty feet since the First Dynasty.[25] But since the flood is regular and gradual, the deposits do not, as in many rivers, occur chiefly at the banks or raise the river about the surrounding land. They tend rather to be particularly heavy at the edge of the flood, where the current is slowest, so that the valley slopes down smoothly to the river. The Nile, then, is not diked and does not break its embankments in disastrous floods like those on the Tigris, Euphrates, Mississippi, and Yellow rivers, and some rivers of California. Usually it rises, covers the land, and recedes without serious damage.

The silt also replenishes the productivity of the soil with vegetable matter and phosphates so that manuring and fallow are both unnecessary if only one

---

[24] Much of the extraordinary progress by which modern Egyptian agriculture has kept pace with population growth is the result of artificial irrigation and the summer crops it produces, but such irrigation on a large scale is made possible only by barrages and high dams, like that under construction at Aswan, which store vast acres of water for the dry season. In the ancient and medieval periods, artificial irrigation was practiced only for garden crops and date trees.

Note that the flood does not correspond with the wet season of the Mediterranean and of the northern temperate zone generally, but with the rains of the East African highlands which are brought by the monsoons. This flooding during a period of drought was a cause of constant amazement to the ancients.

[25] Drower, *History of Technology*, I, p. 539.

crop is to be taken a year. Moreover the way the river floods and drains prevents the accumulation of salts of the sort that have ruined so many acres of Mesopotamia since late in the third millennium B.C. Salt has become a problem only in some regions of the delta as the result of summer irrigation in the present century. No other land is so fortunate in these respects.

Given such a water system, the irrigation of the Nile developed differently from that of Mesopotamia. Earthen embankments some four to eight feet high divided the fields into shallow basins. (Today such basins may contain from 2,500 to 50,000 acres, but they were small in antiquity.) Flood water from the river is allowed to fill the basins through gaps in the embankment. It deposits a layer of silt and as the river level declined late in the season, the water was retained in the fields for a few weeks by closing the dike until the soil was saturated. Such a system is suited to crops that can grow well in the relatively cool winter months. Today Egypt's chief export is cotton; maize is the most important cereal crop, and rice the second. But cotton and rice, along with the citrus fruits and sugar cane, were introduced into the Mediterranean by the Arabs under the caliphate. None of them are very suitable to basin agriculture, for they prefer the Egyptian summer when temperatures reach 100 degrees daily in most places. Millet, too, is an important summer crop today. Such crops depend upon irrigation waters held in barrages and dams.

The ancient crops were much the same as those of Mesopotamia. In the Old Kingdom barley seems to have been the chief crop; in the New Kingdom emmer and einkorn wheat were more important, but both were grown from the earliest times. An improved wheat was introduced in the Hellenistic period. Flax was also a winter crop, and Egypt was famous throughout the ancient world for her linen (the Egyptians had a taboo against wearing woolen cloth). Flax, safflower, and sesame (at least from the New Kingdom), and the castor oil plant all supplied oil. Lettuce, lentils, gourds, and melons were grown in gardens. Orchards in the valley contained sycamores, acacias, dates, and figs.

Along the river it was sometimes possible to irrigate crops in the summer. Otherwise in the earliest period they must have been watered by hand. The *shaduf* was invented at some uncertain period: it is simply a bucket attached to a pole that swings on a pivot that will thus raise enough water from the river for a garden. In Ptolemaic times, in the last few centuries B.C., the *saliye*, a wheel with pots attached for the same purpose, was invented. The olive grew on the coast, in Libya, and near the site of modern Alexandria, but perhaps not much inland. The vine was widely cultivated, generally on the border regions, in the oases, along the coast at Tanis and Pelusium, and in the great Fayyum. Beer however was the national drink.[26]

[26] Hermann Kees, *Ancient Egypt, A Cultural Topography*, ed. T. G. H. James and trans. Ian F. D. Morrow (Chicago: University of Chicago Press, 1961), pp. 47ff.; Fisher, *The Middle East*, pp. 461ff.

It is clear both from the surviving records of property and from Egyptian paintings that herds played an important role in ancient Egypt. In the earliest period (before c. 2000 B.C.) this may have been partly because the desert was not so completely dry as it is today, having some grass on it, and because the land watered by the Nile was not yet entirely cultivated. There was room for grazing and even for hunting and fowling. Much of the delta is still swamp today. The cattle of the Old Kingdom were longhorned and rinderpest-resistant,[27] somewhat like those of the Watusi of the Masai plains in East Africa today; there were also shorthorned and hornless breeds, which had vanished by the New Kingdom. Egypt, like Mesopotamia, however, is hard on cattle. Epidemics have rendered attempts at improving the breeds nugatory in modern times, and it would appear that the ancient Egyptians imported better strains to try to improve their breeds. Along with the donkey (an African animal) these cattle must have filled the place of the modern water buffalo at the plow as well as supplying milk and meat. The Old Kingdom sheep with horns twisted like those of a goat had already been replaced in the Middle Kingdom by the fat-tailed sheep. This breed is not much prized in Europe and America, for it tends to be skinny, the weight going to the enormous tail (as much as twenty pounds of fat), but this fat was—and still is—much prized in the Middle East. They were probably bred for their tails rather than their wool, which the Egyptians would not wear. Geese and goats were kept everywhere. Pigs like a moist soil and were kept in the delta, although there were already some taboos on the eating of pork, at least among the upper classes and priests. In ancient times great flocks of birds settled in Egypt in their migrations: ducks, storks, and geese were all trapped and eaten, while the nobles and pharaohs hunted gazelles and even lions. The horse, however, was not introduced to Egypt until the Hyksos period, c. 1600, and the camel not until Hellenistic times.[28]

But the Nile does even more than provide and impose a certain agricultural regime on Egypt. It almost imposes a view of the world and of society. In modern Egypt all land that can be reached by the waters is cultivated. It is possible to stand with one foot on the moist black soil of the river and the other on the red desert. No doubt the contrast was not quite so clear in the Old Kingdom, when there were still marshes inhabited by the crocodile and hippopotamus and visited by immense flocks of cranes, geese, and ducks and when there were still some areas of steppe and acacia woods, the haunts of such game as is now found in the Sudan.[29] But the desert and the sown must still have dominated the Egyptian's view of the world; he could always turn

---

[27] This disease is a problem even today in parts of Africa.

[28] Sir Alan Gardiner, *Egypt of the Pharaohs* (Oxford: Clarendon Press, 1961), pp. 27ff.; Kees, *Ancient Egypt*, pp. 86ff.

[29] *Ibid.*, pp. 71–2; John Wilson, *The Culture of Ancient Egypt* (Chicago: University of Chicago Press, 1956), Ch. 1; and Henri Frankfort et al., *The Intellectual Adventure of Ancient Man* (Chicago: University of Chicago Press, 1946), pp. 41ff.

his eyes from the mud of the Nile to the cliffs which lined the valley on either side, beyond which was an awful world of rocks and salt, inhabited only by a few bedouin and the monsters of his imagination. Yet most of his fears were imaginary. Only in Libya was there a nomadic population comparable to the Arabs who from time to time threatened Mesopotamia. Most of the desert was too sterile to maintain any population dangerous to the people of the valley. Only from the north or the south could Egypt be invaded, and on the south the country was provided with something very like natural fortresses in the cataracts of the Nile, where the desert comes down almost to the river and closes off the country from the herders of the distant Sudan.

Indeed, the desert supplied Egypt with just those materials that the valley lacked. The earliest great Egyptian monuments were, like those of Sumeria, built of brick. In the Third Dynasty the Egyptians learned to build in stone, which their country, unlike southern Mesopotamia, supplied in abundance. The quarries opposite Gizeh, near Cairo, supplied a magnificent limestone and a less pleasing sandstone. There was costly hard stone for gates and columns and sarcophagi: the showy red granite of the First Cataract; the hardly less appreciated grey black basalt from the eastern desert at the level of Coptos; brilliantly translucent alabaster for jars and vases; the reddish quartzite from near Cairo, the hardest and one of the most beautiful of Egyptian stones. With architecture in stone came sculpture: only recently has the source of the diorite used for statues been discovered some forty miles northwest of Abu Simbel. There were numerous semiprecious stones: amethyst, carnelian, garnet. Mines in Sinai were sources of turquoise, and gold was so plentiful that until Dynasty XX it was valued less than silver, which Egypt lacked and had to import. The sources of tin are unknown, and some copper had to be imported, but until the introduction of iron metallurgy into the Middle East late in the second millennium B.C., Egypt could supply all the really essential materials for an advanced civilization except timbers for buildings and ships which had to be sought abroad, chiefly from Lebanon.[30] No doubt this extraordinary self-sufficiency did as much as geographical isolation to make Egyptians conservative and self-satisfied and increased the rigidity of their social order.

In both Egypt and Mesopotamia the precivilized era ended sometime about 3200 B.C.—in Mesopotamia with the appearance of cities, in Egypt with the pharaonic dynasties.[31] The precivilized cultures of Mesopotamia are termed "proto-literate" and began about 3900 B.C. The comparable Egyptian period is called Gerzean and must have been nearly contemporary. Yet there is a distinct difference in the rhythm of progress in the two lands. We have seen that in Mesopotamia a slow and continuous development can be traced from neolithic communities to the temple cities of Sumeria. In Egypt the

[30] Kees, *Ancient Egypt*, pp. 116ff., 135ff.; Gardiner, *Egypt of the Pharaohs*, pp. 41ff.
[31] On the difficulties of Egyptian chronology and its uncertainties, see *ibid.*, pp. 46ff.

neolithic Gerzean villages, rather than being continuously progressive, appear to have received a sudden impetus which in a few generations produced changes profound enough to create a civilization. The catalyst here certainly was not conquest by peoples from outside the valley but appears to have been the introduction of certain ideas from the more progressive cultures of Sumeria. The most concrete evidence of this is the discovery of three Mesopotamian cylinder seals which were imitated in Egypt from the beginning of the First Dynasty (c. 3100 B.C.). This type of cylinder seal is an intaglio and appropriate to writing on clay, but not on the paper the Egyptians had learned to make from the papyrus plant. The Egyptians therefore would never have invented such a thing; clearly it was a foreign import which was imitated because of the prestige of a superior civilization. Hence it soon passed out of Egyptian life and art and never reappeared.[32]

The cylinder seal itself, of course, is not very important, but it provides concrete evidence that Sumeria influenced Egypt in the late fourth millennium. Art motifs and influences are harder to trace, but the late predynastic and early dynastic art of Egypt does have certain themes, like balanced heraldic animals in mirror images of each other, that seem to be Mesopotamian. Yet the creation of Egyptian civilization was the work of the Egyptians not of the Mesopotamians. In the rapid formation of a new society, ideas are most important, and here archaeology helps us less. It does appear, however, that the idea that words, and sounds as well, can be put into visual symbols that can be written down was learned from outside. The proof of borrowing here is more tenuous, for none of the techniques of Egyptian hieroglyphic writing in any way resemble the cuneiform of the Sumerians. The symbols are not borrowed, as the Greeks borrowed the Phoenician characters for their alphabet, but the initial concept of writing probably was, for there are no tentative first steps in Egyptian writing; it appears from the beginning as a coherent and satisfactory system. It is often felt that to say a culture has borrowed something is disparaging. Perhaps this is some reflection of the modern cult of originality. But borrowing itself can be a creative act. If the Egyptians learned from the Sumerians that syllables can be represented by signs, they nevertheless worked out their own symbols suitable to their very different language [33] and then developed techniques based on different writing materials.

A more profound originality lies in the uses to which the Egyptians put writing. The Sumerian priests who had first devised it used writing for keeping records and tallies of temple property. The Egyptians, in their early period, appear to have devoted writing to the purposes of religion, and their

---

[32] Frankfort, *The Birth of Civilization in the Near East*, Appendix.

[33] Sir Alan Gardiner, *Egyptian Grammar, Being an Introduction to the Study of Hieroglyphs*, 3d ed. (London: Oxford University Press, 1957), goes far beyond the probable interests of any but an egyptologist, but its opening pages are a clear statement of the character of the language and of the methods of writing.

beautiful hieroglyphics decorated the walls and columns of their temples. This suggests the extent of the originality involved in borrowing. A society can borrow only those things that its society can use, but at the same time it must modify the loan and also reform itself deeply in order to make use of it. At the beginning of the dynastic period around 3000 B.C., the Egyptians did this on a scale probably a good deal greater than we can prove directly. No doubt much of the late predynastic record of Egypt is buried deep under the Nile mud or has been destroyed by its waters, but the Gerzean culture shows evidence of conservative stagnation, and all of Egypt's early development bears the mark not of gradual progress and tentative tries, but of sudden and profound changes which quickly crystallized into the style and form of historic Egypt.

3 THE ANCIENT NEAR EASTERN PREMARKET ECONOMY

Neolithic villages seem to have been able to survive with the sole purpose of self-preservation; that is, the production of food was the main reason for their establishment, and no attempt need be made to explain further what holds people together in such a community (although its members were, of course, conscious of other ties, such as those of kinship and religion). It is, however, necessary to inquire what holds a civilized society together and to discover the fundamental beliefs and traditions that form a common bond among the people of a civilized community and that can transcend their differences. These beliefs and traditions, whatever they are, are often called the institutional foundations of society.

THE CITY IN PRIMITIVE SUMERIA

The first appearance of an economy more complicated and advanced than that of the neolithic village community comes to the archaeologist only with the appearance of cities. There are, indeed, few things more determinative of human society and experience than the simple density of population. Social integration is, no doubt, possible without the development of the city,[1] but in Sumeria it took place in an urban context. Now essentially the city differs from the village not just in size, but in function. The word "village" should be reserved for places inhabited by persons directly connected with agriculture: the peasant, the lord of the land perhaps, and any number of persons of immediate service to the peasant. The city by definition is the habitation of persons with a variety of occupations. We tend first to think of commerce and industry as the functions of the city, for they dominate most modern cities overwhelmingly. But administration and religion played a more important part in the creation and development of the ancient city. Lewis Mumford, indeed, brilliantly describes them as the storehouses of power and culture.[2]

[1] Witness the absence of cities from Egypt during the Old Kingdom.
[2] In a work which cannot be too strongly recommended, *The City in History* (New York: Harcourt, Brace, and World, 1961).

Since we shall have little to say about them, it may be appropriate here to point out that a number of other civilizations were founded on a similar technology and produced a

The ancient Sumerian cities and the Babylonian and Assyrian cities that
followed them were not dominated by economic concerns. The very plan of
the city was determined by ritual interests and by the temple precinct. The
gates of the city were oriented for ritual purposes. The palace later came to be
a central dominating feature, but never the market nor the needs and interests
of artisans. The city was not made up of artisan quarters, bazaars, and commercial streets. Aside from the separate and rigidly patterned temple precinct,
and the (probably) later palace precinct of the king (*lugal* or *ensi*), the
houses of the citizens were set in an unplanned maze of alleys. Built about
courts in a fashion suitable to a hot climate, their thick earthen walls turned
a blank back to the narrow streets. In the extensive area of habitation there
seems to have been no place of meeting, no open spot suitable for a market
or an assembly of the citizens, nor any wider street lined with the shops of a
particular trade.[3] Each precinct of the city was administered from a "gate"
by a mayor and the assembly of the quarter.

The city, strictly speaking, was not simply the area of concentrated
habitation enclosed within the walls, but the entire territory. The Sumerian

---

somewhat similar social order. Besides Egypt, of which we shall speak, the Indus River valley knew an urbanized agricultural civilization in the third millennium. In terms of simple
size, it surpassed Sumeria and its two chief cities, Mohenjo-Daro and Harappa, which have
been excavated, were huge by contemporary standards. In some ways its technology was
superior to that of Mesopotamia: cotton was the common cloth and burnt bricks appear to
have been commoner than in Sumeria; the humped bull, the buffalo, sheep, elephant, and
the camel were domesticated. But little writing has been discovered and it not deciphered,
so that the social order cannot be clearly understood. See R. C. Majumdar et al., *Advanced
History of India*, 2d ed. (London: Macmillan, 1958); and Stuart Piggott, *Prehistoric India*
(Harmondsworth: Penguin Books, 1950). The destruction of this civilization is usually
attributed to an invasion of Indo-European-speaking peoples c. 1500 B.C., but perhaps the
only reason is that we know of no other event in Indian history early enough to account
for the disappearance of the civilization of which these cities are evidence.

The first Chinese civilization which can be seen with any clarity later tradition assigned
to the Shang. It appeared with surprising swiftness about the middle of the second millennium B.C. Whether both or either of these civilizations was somehow dependent upon those
of the Near East is hotly disputed, but it does seem probable that certain seminal ideas
were borrowed.

The much later civilizations of Peru, the Yucatan, and central Mexico share the same
general characteristics. These may be defined as a dense peasant population, monumental
architecture devoted to sacred purposes, a small ruling class surrounded by religious sanctions, wonderful works of artisanship devoted to religious purposes, and a close integration
of economic, religious, and social activities. The case for technological borrowing by these
civilizations or their forerunners from across the Pacific Ocean—immense as are the distances—seems to be becoming stronger: Carl O. Sauer, *Agricultural Origins and Dispersals*
(Bowman Memorial Lectures; New York: The Amerian Geographical Society, 1952);
Edgar Anderson, *Plants, Man and Life* (Boston: Little, Brown and Co., 1952), pp. 66–72.
[3] The largest Mesopotamian city was undoubtedly Babylon, which reached a total area of
2,500 acres; Nineveh, 1,850; Uruk, 1,110. Others were much smaller, but 60,000 persons
seems a fair estimate for Lagash: Roebuck, *World of Ancient Times*, p. 29. Athens in the
fifth century B.C. had a walled area of 550 acres and was the largest city of Greece.

cities, in this respect, were like the Greek city-states. At one gate or at the river or waterway on which the city was located was a *kar*, a port of trade under a special legal status, administratively independent, at which the townsmen, or more probably the officials of the community, met the peoples of the desert and other foreigners who came to exchange goods for the grain and manufactures of the temple and palace. Here, outside the walls, foreign merchants camped with their stores. They were provided for by the tavern-keeper of the kar, who must have been some sort of a public official.[4] We shall return to this institution of the kar later; here it is only necessary to note that it was a circumscribed area outside the town proper and that it was not an open market for private exchanges nor a seasonal fair for the same purpose.

Beyond the walls of the city spread a district of clumps of houses, cattle folds, and gardens in which vegetables and fruits were raised, which the Sumerians called "the outer city." Beyond lay the less intensively cultivated grain fields. Even in its plan the ancient Mesopotamian city was something *sui generis*, quite as unique as the Greek polis and even more enduring.[5] Its general structure and plan would endure until Hellenization under the successors of Alexander the Great in the third century B.C.

Within this community it was first about the temples that the ancient Sumerians organized their states as they grew more complex and came to demand more economic and social integration than could be provided by the traditions of the neolithic village.

THE ECONOMY IN PRIMITIVE SUMERIA

It may seem strange to begin a discussion of the economy of the earliest urbanized civilization with religion, but religion was central to the life of the ancient Sumerians. While they lacked a vocabulary of economic analysis and, therefore, the ability to think in strictly economic terms, they had a highly developed mythology in which they expressed their central convictions about the way in which the universe and society were and should be ordered. From as early an age as we can trace their thoughts on the subject, the Sumerians conceived the gods as the owners of the land and of the people who dwelt on it. On one momentous occasion the gods had met together in assembly and divided the earth up among themselves. But the earth did not freely yield up its fruits to satisfy their needs. The gods, therefore, created

[4] Oppenheim, *Ancient Mesopotamia*, p. 116. One finds this "tavernkeeper" again performing the same function in medieval Bruges, particularly with respect to the Hanseatic merchants.
[5] A. Falkenstein, "La cité-temple sumérienne," *Journal of World History*, I (1954), 784–814; Anna Schneider, *Die Anfaenge der Kulturwirtschaft: Die sumerische Tempelstadt* (Essen, 1920) ; and R. von Uslar, "Stadt, Burg, Markt und Temenos in der Urgeschichte," *Festschrift Gustav Schwanzes* (Neumuenster, 1951), pp. 33–44.

men to labor upon the earth and to serve them. The Sumerians thought of themselves, quite simply, as the serfs of whatever god ruled and owned their city. The city was organized to serve the temple in which the god lived. To put the matter differently, the temple was the god's house and the city, his estate. Its inhabitants were his serfs, whose duty it was to feed and clothe him, to provide him with concubines perhaps, and to perform whatever arbitrary—and probably expensive—rituals he demanded.[6]

This view was, in fact, a theological explanation and a justification of the historical experience of the Sumerians and of the actual organization of their society. Throughout the al'Ubaid period before the crystallization of Sumerian society into city-states and the invention of writing, archaeology reveals increasingly larger agricultural villages with ever greater temples in their midst. The ancient neolithic village economy of the upland had produced nothing really like a temple, only small shrines. But in the river valley from the al'Ubaid period from perhaps about 4000 B.C. to the Jemdet-Nasr period in the two centuries before 3000 B.C., the temple grew and clearly became the organizing principle in the city that emerged from the neolithic village.

From later evidence about the household of the god, we can gain a clear general picture of what the service of the deities demanded. The god was conceived literally to dwell in the cella of the temple (although he could also be conceived of as acting elsewhere, for he was present at the assemblies of the gods and other places). His needs were much like those of human beings but were far more exacting. A text of the Seleucid period (third and second centuries B.C.) from Uruk stipulates two meals a day: the first and principal one was brought in the morning when the temple was opened, the other at night. Each meal consisted of two courses. A table was brought in and placed before the image; the water for washing was offered in a bowl. A number of liquid and semiliquid dishes were placed on the table in a prescribed order and style, and containers with beverages were set out. Specific cuts of meat were served as the main dish. Finally fruit was brought in. At the same time musicians performed and the cella was fumigated. Finally the table was cleared and was itself removed, and water in a bowl was offered to the image to clean its fingers.[7] The particular rules of this ceremony cannot be applied to a period almost three thousand years earlier, but generally the services must have been similar. We may assume that the tableware of the god was the best society could afford and produce. Each of various colleges or corporations of priests and attendants had specific and peculiar functions at such a ceremony. The temple personnel, in short, served the same functions in the god's house as did slaves and servants in the king's.[8]

---

[6] Thorkild Jacobsen in Frankfort, ed., *The Intellectual Adventure of Ancient Man*, pp. 174–5, 201ff.

[7] Oppenheim, *Ancient Mesopotamia*, pp. 183ff.

[8] Compare the personnel of Jehovah's temple at Jerusalem in Ezra 2:36–58; I Chron. 23–26.

On other occasions different services were required. The god demanded dressing and on occasion called for new clothes. On high festivals the image was taken from the cella and carted about the city or out of the city to some place in the vicinity and then back. These greater festivities called for the participation of all of the god's servants and slaves, that is, of all the people of the city. No doubt they called for greater expense than the daily ceremonies. Periodically, too, the temple had to be repaired or rebuilt, since it was built chiefly of sun-dried brick. This called for large-scale gang labor from the community as a whole.

When the community faced some threat or was experiencing some misfortune, when famine, drought, flood, or foreign enemies threatened or struck, the Sumerians, like the later Jews, usually found the explanation in the displeasure of their divinities and sought means of learning their will and of propitiating them. The care and feeding of the gods was thus central to the needs and concerns of the Sumerians, and consequently the economy was first organized about the temple.

Although such a society cannot be individualistic, it need not necessarily be autocratic. The survival of certain popular institutions at a later date and the mythical projection of a democratic assembly into the Sumerians' divine pantheon both suggest that originally the Sumerian cities were governed by a democratic assembly.[9] We must picture the primitive economy, then, as composed of peasants of nearly equal status, holding from the temple nearly equal allotments of land and practicing special crafts on the side, and of simple shepherds and fishermen, all of whom surrendered to the temple a large part of their produce and simple handicrafts.

The Sumerians' view of the city as the god's property was based upon an economic and social necessity. Individual property and exploitation were not practicable in southern Mesopotamian conditions where control of the rivers was the great concern of society. Perhaps those landholders next to the river did not need the cooperation of their neighbors for irrigation, but even they were concerned with the maintenance of dikes and the natural level along the river which flowed above the level of the surrounding plain. Everyone else was concerned with the digging of canals for irrigation and drainage. Under such physical conditions, when large crews of labor needed to cooperate for the public good, individual initiative was useless.

In a subsistence economy without markets and elaborate specialization of occupation, unemployment, or rather seasonal underemployment, seems to be endemic. It is impossible for the peasant to "economize" by producing simple goods for sale in his free time. There is no market or great demand for such goods, which can be produced anywhere by almost anyone. Thus when work does not have to be done in the fields, there is little useful individual occupation and it is possible to recruit the great gangs of unskilled

[9] Jacobsen, *JNES*, II (1943), 159–72.

labor for public projects. The pyramids were built without the wheel, and it was millennia before the simple wheelbarrow was introduced into the West from China. Yet the earliest civilizations have raised some of mankind's most stupendous monuments: the ziggurats of Sumeria, the pyramids and the other temples of Egypt, the immense mounds of the central plateau of Mexico and of Peru, the temples of the Yucatan.[10] The Sumerians used this labor for their temples, but also for the great operations of diking and ditching for irrigation and drainage. Some lands, too, were higher and called for water's being carried to them, a very laborious enterprise. We do not know of any mechanisms that may have been used. The result was a rigid and detailed water law about such things as the opening of sluices, the carrying away of water at high flood, the conservation of water in deep holes, dues for the care of the canals and dams, fines for damages and breaks, and the use of forced— or at least required—labor for the digging of new canals and the cleaning out of silt.[11]

Such enterprises were, of course, a common concern, but they called for organization, command, and probably coercion and were centered first, it would seem, in the temple. The temple was thus the regulatory agency, and even from an early age it did more than take the surplus produce not necessary to the survival of the peasant household. It possessed large granaries and storage bins for reeds, wood, onions, and dried and salted fish. It is likely that even the seed for the next year's crop was stored by the temple, not by the individual peasant household. The whole community, not the individual family, was the basic economic unit. The raw materials for manufacturing were also granted out by the temple and the finished products received back by it. Hence, specialized occupations came to be ordered about the temple. Like more primitive societies, the earliest Sumerian cities presumably had shepherds. The sheep in their flocks may have belonged individually to peasant households or to the temple as a whole, but they were pastured by specialists directed by the temple management and the temple took their wool. So, too, the fishermen's catch went to the temple and was distributed by it.

The earliest specialists, however, were probably—to judge by better-known primitive societies—the sacred personnel of the shrine. We may loosely call them the priestly class. Even in a period before the emergence of cities, from the al'Ubaid and Jemdet-Nasr periods in the fourth millennium

[10] For the stupendous works accomplished in the New World without either the wheel or any very satisfactory draft animal, see J. Alden Mason, *The Ancient Civilizations of Peru*, 2d ed. (Baltimore: Penguin Books, 1964), especially the plates; and Victor W. von Hagen, *World of the Maya* (Mentor Books; New York: New American Library, 1960), pp. 140ff. To build the chief pyramid at Tikal it was necessary to carry some 250,000 cubic feet of limestone rubble, a task estimated to have required 25,000 man-hours.

[11] Deimel, *Sumerische Tempelwirtschaft zur Zeit Urukaginas*, pp. 80ff.; and the earlier "Die Reformtexte Urukaginas," *Orientalia Commentarii de rebus Assyro-bablyonicis, arabicis, aegypticis*, etc., II (1920), 3–31, and "Die Bewirtschaftung des Tempellandes zur Zeit Urukaginas," *ibid.*, V (1922), 1–25.

B.C., they may have been released from all labor that we would call productive, though their fellow townsmen would have considered that they were
indeed engaged in productive activities. They ensured the benevolence of the
deities and, therefore, the fruitfulness of the land.

The picture drawn here is simplified, hypothetical, and schematic, but
it will serve the student well to grasp clearly this picture of primitive Sumeria
in order to be able to understand the complications which can develop from it.
A small number of shepherds and of fishermen, a great majority of the population devoted to raising grain and dates—each contributes his food products
and handicrafts to a central storage economy, to the granaries of the god.
They and the temple personnel draw from this common storehouse according
to their needs regulated by traditional rules.[12] The temple rather than the
patriarchal household was the center of production and distribution, and
even at a later date the private household in Sumeria did not develop handi-
craft production for home consumption as it would among the Greeks and
Romans.[13]

Such a central storehouse economy in which exchanges play no important part may be described as a status-distributive system or a redistributive
economy. It does not operate by voluntary exchanges of goods of equal value
on a market, rather what each family gives and what each receives depends
upon its status in the community (peasant, shepherd, fisherman, priest, man,
woman, slave, or free) and upon traditional and established relationships.
Economic activity is closely integrated with the general texture of society,
for there is no production for an anonymous market, only crafts produced
for a recognized and known purpose. In the simple, egalitarian, and traditional society we have described, such a status-distributive system is capable
of immense development and complication as we shall see. Indeed, such development and complication is precisely the story of the ancient Near Eastern
economy, where the market played no important part until the Hellenistic
age after Alexander the Great's conquests at the end of the fourth century B.C.

THE SUMERIAN CITY: ECONOMY AND POLITY

The advance of civilization destroyed this primitive egalitarian democracy and disrupted the monolithic economic integration of the earliest civilized age. As one might expect, the forces behind this change are not any
longer perfectly clear, but sheer physical growth and an improvement or
elaboration of productive techniques were both important driving forces. The
actual documents that survive from the third millennium B.C., from Lagash
in Urukagina's time (c. 2400 B.C.), from Drehem, and from the Third Dynasty of Ur, in fact show a much more complicated economy than the primi-

[12] I. J. Gelb, "The Ancient Sumerian Ration System," *JNES*, XXIV (1965), 230–43.
[13] Oppenheim, *Ancient Mesopotamia*, pp. 74ff.

tive one we have hypothesized. For one thing, the demands of the gods became greater for goods of unprecedented splendor which could not be simply the by-products of peasant craftsmen. Skilled specialists became a regular part of the temple community.

The achievements of the most skilled of Sumerian artisans are of breathtaking beauty and difficulty. The methods of the modern jeweller are, no doubt, more efficient and, with the aid of modern chemistry, he can command more numerous and purer materials, but his products are in no artistic way superior to the objects found in the "Royal Cemetery" of Ur—the harp with a bull's head of solid gold, the gold helmet, the gold tumbler, or the dazzling headdress of a lady-in-waiting.[14] Such things were not produced by peasants or shepherds during a slack time of year, nor were comparable cloths for the gods produced by their wives. Such products demanded the maintenance of specialized artisans. They called, too, for raw materials that could not be found in the alluvium of lower Mesopotamia. Therefore the economy had to be organized to produce for foreign exchange.

At the same time, the growth of civilization brought with it one of civilization's most characteristic institutions—organized warfare.[15] It seems unlikely that the cities of Sumeria during the period of their earliest development were much involved in struggles against each other. Each must have been engaged in draining and irrigating, and while unexploited resources at home need not deter men from trying to seize their neighbors', each settlement must have been separated from its neighbors by swamps or desert. Herdsmen or fishermen probably quarreled, but the struggles were not important enough to engage the energies of the community as a whole. Later, however, as the population grew, the fields of one community might run up against those of another. Boundary disputes became far more important, and much of Sumerian history in the third millennium concerns such disputes and the quarrels of gods and men, for the gods were conceived to fight on the side of their people.

It was probably the growing importance of warfare that created a new office among the Sumerians. In the archaic texts he is called *en*, which is

---

[14] The truly thrilling story of their discovery should be read in the discoverer's own words: Woolley, *Ur of the Chaldees; Digging up the Past;* and *Excavations at Ur.*

[15] It is easy to think of warfare as a natural human activity, so closely does it seem to the modern bourgeois to be related to the love of violence. The passions that war invokes are certainly present everywhere, but organized warfare is a social institution. The archaeological record, at any rate, suggests that at some times men have found it advisable to fortify their homes and possessions and at others found it unnecessary. Among historical societies, some organized themselves for waging war, and its demands deeply influenced their institutional structure and their training of the young (the Greeks of the peninsula in classic times, for example) while others have looked upon war as a peripheral and exceptional state, something that hardly affects the average man. The Chinese during the long course of imperial history have taken this attitude. Other peoples, like the Navaho, seem scarcely to be able to wage it. Oddly enough, they have not been particularly unsuccessful. See Childe, *Sociological Review,* XXXIII (1941), 126–38.

usually translated "lord," although the word implies, too, the most important sacerdotal functions. Perhaps in primitive times he had been the high priest. In early dynastic times, however, the ruler was known as ensi, "governor," or as lugal, "king." The difference between the two—if, indeed, there was a consistent difference—is hard to make out.[16] The ruler lived in a palace separate from the temple. Those at Eridu and Kish have been excavated and are very similar in plan. Each consists of two large buildings with numerous rooms opening onto courts. At Kish there was a majestic court with a row of four columns down the center. The care and feeding of kings, especially if their purpose is to wage war and to rebuild temples and palaces and to lead the population in pleasing the god, is quite as expensive as the maintenance of a temple. Thus alongside the redistributive system centered about the temple and its priesthood, there arose another about the palace. The two were never perfectly separate, for the king combined the functions of leader in war with the administration of the property of the god, the direction of the clergy, judge, and director of public works. Yet there were separate households and the general tendency throughout the course of Mesopotamian history was to separate the palace from the temple and then to subordinate the temple to the palace.

This subordination was accompanied by another development. The earliest Sumerian cities appear to have been wholly independent of one another, bound together only by a common sense of their culture and a sense that their way of life differed from and was superior to that of the outer barbarians of the desert and mountains. The earliest struggles were border disputes. This warfare brought the kings to power and enabled them to create a military system and a military class. The desire to conquer and subject other cities followed. The first surviving royal inscription (c. 2700) indicates that a dynasty at Kish enjoyed some kind of hegemony over all of the land. The leadership of Ur, which followed, was ended by an invasion of Elamites from the mountains to the east, who imposed two foreign dynasties, the Awan and the Hamazi, on at least a part of Sumer. The conflict between Elam and Sumer may, indeed, stretch back to prehistoric times. Foreign domination was ended by a new dynasty at the city of Lagash, c. 2550, and again a succession of local dynasties succeeded one another until a second foreign invasion, this time by Semites from the north.

Their leader, Sargon of Akkad (c. 2371–2316), not only conquered Sumer, but also a great empire stretching all the way to the Taurus Mountains and the Mediterranean (or so our sources seem to indicate; Sargon may have been boasting). Sargon's conquests begin the age of empires, of successively wider conquests, and of successively more enduring imperial states down to the Persian Empire of the sixth, fifth, and fourth centuries B.C. Each of these

[16] On the titles, see Roux, *Ancient Iraq*, p. 115.

empires was created by a military people who maintained themselves by exploiting their conquered. The repeated disruption of these empires led to periods of minor states lasting until some other conqueror could unite the greater part of the Near East.

Before turning to the different, but in many ways parallel development of Egypt, let us describe as well as our sources permit the economy of the third millennium B.C. in a Sumerian city, for this is the type of the local economies on which the great empires were built. That which is most clearly seen is Uruk at the time of Urukagina, shortly before c. 2350 B.C.[17] But for some purposes it will be necessary to draw on other sources, some of them much later. The composite picture thus formed is a possible one, adhering to historical reality in each particular—as far as we understand our texts. Even when all the texts shall have been discovered and understood, our picture will remain incomplete, for many things were never put down in texts. The activities of small landholders, mountain and desert tribes, and peoples on the edge of the town were never reduced to writing.[18] In some ways, then, contemporary literary accounts like the Bible can reveal more about how society looked and felt to the people who lived in it than do archival records.[19]

The most basic concern of the community was, of course, the exploitation of the land. Some was farmed directly by the temple with the labor of freeholders in return for wages in kind. Agricultural slavery would have been

---

[17] Deimel, *Sumerische Tempelwirtschaft zur Zeit Urukaginas*, pp. 80ff.

[18] The uses to which any people put writing are of considerable interest and vary greatly. The Egyptians, we shall see, made rather different uses of hieroglyphics than the Mesopotamians did of cuneiform. In all the long history of the Minoans of Crete and the Mycenaean Greeks, there is not a single inscription surviving; probably there never were any. The classic Greeks and Romans delighted to see their names and offices on stone, and this compensates us some little bit for the almost complete loss of their administrative and business records, written on fragile papyrus and parchment.

The matter of land ownership raises considerable problems. Much belonged to the temples, but it does not appear that—as Deimel thought—all the agricultural land of Uruk was in their possession. We have no particular information about small possessors; as far as we can see, they do not make their appearance in the temple accounts on which we depend. Our sources do not reveal what institutions of barter or cooperation their needs may have given rise to.

[19] For the classic world we probably have a more balanced view, for we have only the literary record. Administrative documents have not—except in Egypt to some degree—survived. Of the Carolingian era in Western Europe, c. A.D. 800, we have, of documentary evidence, only some registers of estates drawn up by great ecclesiastical corporations. They reveal the large manor in a systematic fashion and led earlier historians to speak of a typical manor and to suppose that all or almost all of Western Europe was so farmed. But later more varied documentation suggests how false this view is. Had we from the twelfth and thirteenth centuries only the registers of the great monasteries, we should have a very different picture, for by then other sources tell something of lay estates and of the life of peasants and of independent peasant holdings. Imagine the twentieth century described only from the records of DuPont, Ford, and General Motors.

wasteful, since farm labor in Babylonia lasts only five or six months of the year. Hence slavery did not play an important role in the Sumerian economy. A second category of land was that parcelled out in carefully measured, individual plots by an official of the temple. Most of the males of the community received such holdings. Reapportionment was frequent, if not annual, but the size of the parcels varied with the importance of the holder's civil or military office. A third sort of holding was rented land for which a part, usually one-third, of the crop had to be delivered to the temple. Though the rent might sometimes be figured in value of silver, it was probably always or almost always paid in grain.

At the beginning of the agricultural season, in late November or early December when the winter rains had softened the sun-baked soil, the workmen received supplies from the temple: seed corn, plow animals and fodder for them, and the plows themselves, for all were temple possessions. Since it distributed the seed, the temple clearly made decisions about what crops would be grown. Barley was by far the most important grain, but emmer and wheat were also grown, the last being more valuable per bushel than either barley or emmer. The chief source of oil was sesame, apparently a field crop.

The grinding of grain into flour for porridge or bread was done by the women in a mortar of wood or in hand mills. (The water mill was yet far in the future and even the circular quern which can be driven by a draft animal was unknown.) This is a long, time-consuming job, perhaps the chief occupation of the women. It must have been done in every household, but the temple, too, had troops of women for the purpose, because it had a numerous personnel to maintain. The field work must have called for overseers, and we must assume a considerable body of officials in charge of canals and water rights. In addition to the fields, considerable food was grown in gardens: onions were a field crop, but most vegetable and trees, especially the important date, were garden crops. The temple at Lagash in Urukagina's time possessed nine gardens, each with its gardener and crew.

Beasts were kept by the temple in great numbers. The account divided them into great (oxen and cattle) and small (sheep and goats); pigs were handled separately. Early in the year, feeding cattle was no problem, for the meadows were covered with grass, but later they had to be fed off the stubble of the harvested fields, and in high summer they were kept mostly in the reed beds and cattail stands of the river and canals. We do not possess complete records of the cattle of the temple of Lagash, but it possessed 150 asses or donkeys. Goats were raised chiefly for their wool, but some of the kids were slaughtered for their meat and as offerings to the gods. Cows, sheep, and goats all gave milk, and the herders had to render a certain amount of butter, and probably of cheese, for each animal in their care. The smaller animals—pigs, kids, and lambs—were eaten, but large cattle rarely were. In such a hot climate their flesh would either have to be salted or eaten the same day they were slaughtered.[20] Meat was an unusual item in a diet of bread or porridge, vegetables, fruit, vegetable oils, fish, and beer. The temple at Lagash appears to have had only one troop of pigs, or at least a single chief swineherd.

It employed some hundred fishermen, one-third of them fresh-water and two-thirds salt-water fishermen. If the other temples of the city are added, we can estimate some five hundred fishermen. They appear to have fished both the brackish waters of the lagoons and the high seas. They certainly owed fixed and definite dues in kind to the temple, although they were not slaves but freemen. It is a bit hard for us to understand on what legal basis the temple took its due, for the sea, unlike the lands of the city, could hardly be distributed by the temple. Probably the question did not arise in the Sumerian mind, so close was social integration about the temple. Fish were dried and salted to keep in storehouses; there is no evidence that the art of smoking was yet known. Records for the distribution of fish are scarce, but certainly it was an important part of the diet.[21]

The revenues in kind of the temple (we have referred chiefly to the temple of the goddess Bau at Lagash in the late third millennium B.C.) were thus immense. But the temple had great obligations. The first was, of course, the maintenance of the goddess. This particular temple, too, was presided over, perhaps we could say owned, by the ruler's wife, and the maintenance of her and her household was an obligation. It also had to pay for the upkeep and repair of the barns and magazines and the cleaning and redigging of canals. The repair of brickwork was a constant effort, for unbaked brick could hardly survive the winter rains. When the ensi Urukagina boasts that he rebuilt the temple of Bau, we may suppose that the temple estate itself paid the costs of maintaining and feeding the labor. The temple had to maintain its officials, the singers and dancers, and also its considerable administrative personnel. At a later date each official seems to have been entitled to definite fees and perquisites. Whether this was true in Urukagina's time is uncertain, but the chief swineherd of the temple had six female slaves to grind his grain, and he was not a very important official.

[20] There survive from Drehem, near Nippur, the records of the government's center for receiving and disbursing birds and animals (including, oddly, gazelles) for sacrifices, the palace, support of the priests, officials, soldiers, foreign emissaries, and workers. Thousands of animals were brought in and sent out each month. The lists of receipts and disbursements were made each day and totalled for each month or for a longer period: Tom B. Jones and John W. Snyder, *Sumerian Economic Texts from the Third Ur Dynasty. A Catalogue and Discussion of Documents from Various Collections* (Minneapolis: University of Minnesota Press, 1961), pp. 212–8.

[21] The status of the fishermen is not clear at Lagash but probably resembled that of those at Babylon in the time of Hammurabi (1792–1750) and his successors. Heichelheim thought that these documents indicated sales and the accumulation of capital, but Paul Koschaker has shown that the activity of the fishermen was rather a part of the distributive economy: "Zur staatlichen Wirtschaftsverwaltung in altbabylonischer Zeit, insbesondere nach Urkunden aus Larsa," *Zeitschrift fuer Assyriologie*, XLVII (1942), 135–80.

There was, indeed, a large number of women belonging to the temple. Their status is a bit baffling. The translations often call them slaves, and they are inferior in some legal ways to the landholding members of the community. However, since they are subject to the public authority, they are hardly chattel slaves, and marriage to freemen seems to have been possible. The six women who ground grain for the swineherd were the property of the temple, not of the swineherd. Because in a very real way all the Sumerians were the property of the god and held property and reecived tasks from him, it is a bit misleading to impose modern terminology on Sumerian social classes.

The development of class evident in such an organization so early is remarkable. Within the temple organization were great variety of classes and status: handworkers, tenure holders subject to military service, herdsmen, fishermen; slave and free. Some of the overseers as well as workers were slaves. Most of the females serving the temple seem to have been wool cleaners, spinsters, cooks, brewsters, and keepers of pigs. But free women also worked for the temple, for it was customary for the male servants of the temple to put not only their own slaves, but also their families into the service of the temple. Something of the military organization is clear from these Lagash texts. The temple had many men capable of bearing arms; they were ordered in hundreds under chiefs: the temple of Bau appears to have had some five to six hundred such men.[22] But the military was not yet an independent occupation. These men were peasant holders, drawn from the substantial class of responsible citizens. The professional soldier had yet to make his appearance. This class differentiation, however, was much different from that with which we are familiar as private property had hardly made its appearance. Class depended upon status in a graded hierarchy of function and reward corresponded to status.

A great deal of industrial and artisanal activity was done at the temple or by its dependents. Records survive of the wool turned over to the temple by the shepherds and goatherds. It was cleaned (picked, combed, washed, and defatted) by the women of the temple, while others spun and wove. Skins, some of them perhaps imported from Elam, which was richer in cattle, were tanned by the temple's people and made into harnesses for the oxen and asses and into armor for soldiers. (Metal armor was unknown as yet, and shoes were rare; most of the population went barefoot.)

The temple made carefully recorded payments. The most important form of payment was in barley, but there were others in wheat, wool, bread, milk, and fruit. Wages in barley were paid to persons holding temple land. They were generally made every two or three months and appear to have been for labor in digging and cleaning the canals. Payments were made to certain gardeners who were not paid by their overseers. They appear to have had the task

22 Deimel, *Anal. Orient.*, II, 113.

of watering the gardens, a most laborious task in the absence of any machinery. (There is some reason to believe these persons were blind.) The porters who carried sacks in the sacred magazines were given payments. Barley was rationed to the female slaves and their children who worked at wool, in the brewery, in the temple kitchen and bakery, and in the pigsty and to those who belonged to the children of the wife of the ensi. There are also lists of payments made on feast days.

All this activity clearly called for an elaborate organization. The temple found it necessary to keep exhaustive records of its income and of its expenditures, done in cuneiform characters on clay tablets which could be fired to make them permanent. It can hardly be doubted that writing was invented for this purpose rather than for literary reasons; it was the creation of bureaucrats, not of *literati*. The characters of the earliest writing were numerous and difficult. Progress came with successive simplifications until the alphabet was reached early in the first millennium. But the earliest writing, derived from signs for things, was syllabic and called for an elaborate set of auxiliary signs to indicate relations between words and was difficult to learn, so that rather than widespread literacy, the earliest literate societies gave rise to a clerical class. The great bulk of surviving documents indicates that this class was numerous and industrious.

The need to keep such records, ledgers indeed, gave rise not only to writing, but also to money—not to coinage, but to money of account. It was often possible, sometimes necessary, to record actual goods: so many sheep, so many oxen. But this could be extremely awkward when it was necessary to make equivalences. How many bushels of barley were equal to an ox or to a sheep? If such equivalences could be worked out, the economy could be made far more manageable and elastic. Goods could be received or issued equal to what was due. Often units of barley appear to have been used as standards; but silver weights were even more convenient, for silver was almost imperishable, always in demand, and infinitely divisible. Anything could be measured in—set as the equivalent of—silver.[23] (It was easy, of course, to establish relations between silver and other metals, but no other metal appears to have been used for the recording of values for many centuries.) Such equivalences were not really prices, for they did not vary according to a market or to the laws of supply and demand. This accounts for the fact, at first sight unbelievable, that all through the third millennium B.C. a certain measure of barley, the gur-sag-gal, was the equivalent of one silver shekel.

---

[23] Money of account continued to have a function long after the creation of coinage. The early Middle Ages knew only one coin, the silver penny, but kept accounts also in shillings and pounds. Even when the English issued notes of pounds sterling worth 20 shillings, they continued to use the guinea, worth 21 shillings, for keeping books.

FOREIGN TRADE

Southern Mesopotamia is a grain-raising and cattle-producing country; it produces almost nothing else. It possesses no metals at all, no stone, no good timber or other products of trees. (The date palm is the only exception and its timber is very inferior; some of the purposes to which other peoples put wood could be met with reeds or bundles of reeds.) All these things had to be imported. In exchange southern Mesopotamia could offer: barley, dates, and sesame; the products of cattle-raising, such as butter, cheese, leather, and wool cloth; and the work of its artisans. Barley, however, was raised in most parts of the Near East. Only the coasts of the Persian Gulf, southern Persia, and the Arabian Peninsula perhaps imported it. Livestock, too, was raised everywhere. Moreover, agricultural products were reasonably inexpensive and bulky and could have been moved economically only by water. They were not suitable for donkeyback or—most especially in the absence of roads—by donkey cart. Hence we must suppose that what Sumeria offered in return was chiefly the export of industrial articles such as garments and the works of fine craftsmanship, like cylinder seals. There may also have been a considerable reexport of expensive articles, for silver was used to pay for foreign goods although silver itself was imported.[24]

It is clear that the community's exportable surplus was in the hands of the king or the temple. They alone commanded the agricultural surplus and the skilled craftsmen capable of making goods for export. Foreign trade inevitably was in their hands.[25] Information about foreign trade is, naturally, imperfect but is better than might be hoped, because it was not in private hands, but in the hands of "merchants" who in their dependence on the temple or palace resembled the artisans and peasants in a status-distributive economy. They were merchants, but not capitalists seeking profits.

The best example we have of the organization of foreign trade comes from the Assyrian merchant *karum* at Kultepe in modern Turkey.[26] The exact

---

[24] W. F. Leemans, *Foreign Trade in the Old Babylonian Period as Revealed by Texts from Southern Mesopotamia*, Vol. VI of *Studia et Documenta ad Iura Orientis Antiqui Pertinentia*, ed. M. David et al. (Leiden: E. J. Brill, 1960); review by Elena Cassin, *Ann. ESC* (1964), 1005–9.

[25] An exception should perhaps be made. We have spoken only of the city-state, but a more or less nomadic and herding population certainly lived on the steppe along the edge of the desert or the mountains. Their relation with the sown is complicated and important, and it was often peaceable. Though the temple and king owned flocks, they might, too, barter grain and other goods for the wool and hides of the nomad and so might their subjects. This was possible because the nomad would come to the gate of the city. But such barter is of a very different order from the merchants' distant foreign trade.

[26] On the records of the Assyrian karum, merchant colony, in Cappadocia from the period c. 1975–1950 and following: Benno Landsberger, *Assyrische Handelskolonien in Kleinasien aus dem dritten Jahrtausend*, Vol. XXIV, Pt. 4 of *Der Alte Orient* (Leipzig: J. C.

meaning of the Semitic word *karum* is a bit difficult in a modern language. It is borrowed from Sumerian *kar*. "Colony" is not quite distinct enough, and while the word certainly means "settlement," it has also a legal meaning. The karum was a community of merchants established in a foreign country under conditions established by treaty. It resembles what the medieval Italians would have called a *fondaco* and our ancestors in the seventeenth century, who were doing business in the Far East, a "factory." The merchants lived in a community under a law laid down by their own state but under conditions determined by treaty. Their commerce was also conducted according to treaty arangements. Political conditions in Cappadocia in the nineteenth century B.C.[27] are little understood and those at Ashur are hardly known, except that it was then tributary to Ibbi-Sin, the last king of the Third Dynasty at Ur. The merchants at Kultepe were occupied with buying goods, chiefly cloth, lead, and copper. They paid in gold and silver, which were always weighed except among men who knew each other within the gild of Assyrian merchants doing business in Cappadocia. The prices paid appear to have been set by treaty, and the merchants, working on commission from their city, were interested in neither profit nor loss, but in giving a careful and acceptable account to the authorities at home in Ashur.[28]

At an earlier period in the late third millennium, at both Lagash and Ur, foreign trade was organized in a similar fashion. Here we have a far better idea of the extent of trade and its lines and products than for Ashur. Copper was imported from Dilmun (the island of Bahrein in the Persian Gulf) in exchange for barley, cedar, oil, flour, wool clothes, and silver (only some of which were native Sumerian products). The copper probably came to Dilmun from Oman.[29] Barley and oil were exported to Elam and silver brought back.

Hinrichs'sche Buchhandlung, 1925). On the documents of the Third Dynasty of Ur (2050–1950), see W. F. Leemans, *The Old Babylonian Merchant, His Business and His Social Position*, Vol. III of *Studia et Documenta ad Iura Orientis Antiqui Pertinentia*, ed. M. David et al. (Leiden: E. J. Brill, 1950) and *Foreign Trade in the Old Babylonian Period*. John B. Curtis and W. W. Hallo, "Money and Merchants in Ur III," *Hebrew Union College Annual*, III, 103–39; George Gottlob Hackman, *Temple Documents of the Third Dynasty of Ur from Umma. Babylonian Inscriptions in the Collection of James B. Nies* (New Haven, Conn.: Yale University Press, 1937); Jones and Snyder, *Sumerian Economic Texts;* James Hornel, "Sea-Trade in Early Times," *Antiquity*, XV (1941), 233–56; and A. L. Oppenheim, "The Seafaring Merchants of Ur," *Journal of the American Oriental Society*, LXXIV (1954), 6–17.

27 On the date H. Lewy, "Anatolia in the Old Assyrian Period," *CAH*, 2d ed., I, Ch. xxiv.
28 Karl Polanyi et al., *Trade and Market in the Early Empires: Economies in History and Theory* (Glencoe, Ill.: The Free Press, 1957), p. 19.
29 Bibby, *Looking for Dilmun*, pp. 187ff., 219–22. The work of Geoffrey Bibby and the expeditions of the Danish Prehistoric Museum of the University of Aarhus between 1953 and 1968 have revealed the unexpected extent and antiquity of civilized life on the Arabian coasts of the Persian Gulf and the interior of Arabia. They have definitely established Bahrein as the site of ancient Dilmun and provided further evidence of its close contact with the civilization of the Indus.

Timbers of various kinds, including those used for boats, were also imported from Elam. Ur imported gold from sources that cannot be identified, and copper, which Ashur at this time was importing from Asia Minor, came to Ur from Magan, whose site is uncertain, but which appears to have been reached by sailing down the Persian Gulf and may have been Oman, although there are other places along the Arabian coast that copper might have come from. Its value—rather surprisingly—was lower than in Assyria. The sources of tin are a bit doubtful: perhaps Elam and certainly Asia Minor from which Ashur received it. Precious and semiprecious stones were imported into Mesopotamia from all the peripheral zones; some could have come only from Afghanistan. Ivory must have come by sea, either from Africa or the west coast of India. The names of the woods are hard to identify. Cedar and cypress were floated down the Euphrates from Syria, but others were imported from Magan and Meluhha, which cannot be very confidently identified.[30] A kind of reed, perhaps bamboo, came from Magan. Oils and essences, which were very popular, were among the most important imports, including cypress oil, cedar oil, and gums from conifers came from Lebanon and the Amanus Mountains. Wine came down the Euphrates to Mari and would later be imported to Babylon. The scale of trade is, of course, impossible to estimate, but its total value must have been considerable, for the working capital and the amounts involved in some exchanges were considerable—thirty minas of gold and sums of half a talent of silver.

We know less than we might like about the organization of the trade of places like Lagash and Ur in the southern part of Mesopotamia, but some things are certain. Like the Assyrians at Kultepe, the merchants of Ur resided abroad. In the trade between Ur and Dilmun we see natives of Ur sailing to Dilmun and residents of Dilmun coming to Ur and residing in the kar outside the city. The city of Sippar had a permanent agency at Mari on the Middle Euphrates and one at Mishlan. Probably there was a colony of Larsan merchants in the country of Eshnunna on the Diyala River northeast of modern Baghdad and perhaps a similar colony at Susa in Elam. Whether the merchants of Ur had permanent agencies at Dilmun is not known, but probable.

It is clear that the state took great interest in this trade. The entire economy of Sumeria was dependent upon some of these imports: copper and tin were essential and the other things very important. Nor could the mer-

---

[30] The place the Sumerian texts call Meluhha cannot be Nubia or Ethiopia and was probably the west coast of India (Sind). From here could come the lapis lazuli of Afghanistan and ivory worked into combs and objets d'art, accomplishments of which Nubia and Ethiopia were hardly yet capable. Magan is more and more thought to be Oman, while Tilmun or Dilmun was the island of Bahrein, where a Danish excavation has brought to light a city: Elena Cassin, *Ann. ESC.*, XIX (1964), 1008. The excavator of an extremely interesting site at Tepe Yahya near Bandar Abbas in southern Iran, C. C. Lamberg-Karlovsky, has suggested that it may be Magan, which hence would lie on the north coast of the straits of Hormuz.

chants possibly act abroad without arrangements with foreign governments; they could have resided abroad only under treaty arrangements and probably needed treaty arrangements in order to carry on any trade at all. But while it seems that the goddess at Ur took a tithe of the copper imported, it is not clear that the merchants were acting solely as agents for the temple. They seem to have acted in some way as private entrepreneurs. There is, incidentally, no evidence that they were organized into gilds, as they certainly were at Kultepe.

At Lagash under Urukagina, state control of the economy was extensive and the merchant acted exclusively in the trade of goods, never as far as can be seen as a moneylender. Examples of his activities are the purchase of 234 minas of copper alloy in the island of Dilmun, whence it was brought to the palace and checked by the *patesi* (ruler, king). Another merchant brought 6½ minas of silver from Elam for the wife of the patesi, and a third purchased three asses in another town for an estate and delivered them to its plowmen. Thus it was mainly the commerce with other towns and countries that was in the hands of professional merchants of Lagash, but they figured also in the local economy in some way. A man with the title of "great merchant" appears to have been one of the highest of officials of the state. He somehow acted in the same sort of function for the catch of the local fishermen, which was distributed by the patesi and his wife.[31] Perhaps there was something comparable to sales of fish within the country, but it seems far more likely that what look like sales in the records were simply put into the form of sales in order to keep records. Thus just as money of account preceded real coinage, sales of account came before real sales. The role of the merchant at Shuruppak appears to have been similar to his role at Lagash in this age.

In the Third Dynasty at Ur, c. 2000 B.C., the whole of Sumeria and Akkad were, for the first time, united under a single political authority, but the method of integrating foreign commerce appears much the same. A merchant received "a field for feeding," just as did other servants of the temples or the state. In another document a merchant receives various quantities of barley; in another, merchants figure as suppliers of bitumen [32] to the temple. A third table records deliveries of precious metals and stones to the temple. Thus the system of govenment-controlled economy could and in fact did survive into an age of great sophistication in commercial transactions. But while the temple and the palace continued to play a large—perhaps a dominating—part in the economy of the Third Dynasty of Ur, merchants no longer acted solely on behalf of the temple or palace. They began to carry on business in their own interest as well. When, after the fall of the Third Dynasty

---

[31] E. Leemans, *Foreign Trade in the Old Babylonian Period;* cf. Paul Koschaker, *Zeitschrift fuer Assyriologie*, XLVII (1942), 135–80.

[32] Mineral pitch or asphalt used for waterproofing, storage, etc.

of Ur, legal and economic texts again come to light from the Babylonian period under the dynasty of Hammurabi, private property and trade had reached a very high development. Thereafter the history of the economy in the Near East, if sufficient documentation were available, might be told in terms of fluctuations between state control and private control of productive property and activity with a tendency for the latter to increase. In general the private sector of the economy appears to have grown, until in the fourth century, much of the economy of the Near East, of Syria, Palestine, and Mesopotamia was ready for the introduction of the market and private, market-controlled and market-determined enterprises by the Macedonian conquest.

4 OTHER BRONZE AGE CIVILIZATIONS
Egypt and the Aegean

Partly through diffusion from Sumeria a number of other societies in the third millennium reached a level which we would recognize as civilized. The process was partly one of diffusion from Sumeria, to which Elam was almost an appendage, and a very old one. More slowly, urbanization and larger states spread northward in Mesopotamia itself and into Assyria. The city-states of northern Syria exhibited a mixed culture under strong influence from Mesopotamia. The civilization of the Indus River valley has been briefly mentioned. In Anatolia the Konya plain had early been a center of intensive neolithic agricultural development, and the transition to the Bronze Age was made by the indigenous population itself. There urban communities and petty kingdoms arose, but our knowledge of them is recent and our understanding of the general part they played in the development of the ancient Near East will have to await further excavations.

Only two of these societies need detain us here: the Egyptian civilization of the Nile Valley and the Minoan civilization that dominated the Aegean from Crete. Both play an important part in the development of the Western economy and each has a peculiar interest in respect to economic history. Under circumstances very similar to those of the Sumerians, Egypt developed a status-determined redistributive system which was profoundly different from that of Mesopotamia, while Minoan Crete shows that a nonmarket, status-distributive society could operate on a large scale even outside a river valley. Her experience, too, in some ways points to the future economic development of the Greeks in the Iron Age.

EGYPT

We have seen that the development of civilized life in the Nile valley was stimulated by the influence of Mesopotamia at a very early date. Consequently Egypt's early development was remarkably fast: a stagnant folk culture scattered along the margin of the Nile was crystallized in a remarkably short time into the institutions and civilization of historic Egypt.[1] Archae-

---

[1] For the general accounts of Egyptian history, see Wilson, *The Culture of Egypt*; Gardiner, *Egypt of the Pharaohs*; S. R. K. Granville, ed., *The Legacy of Egypt* (Oxford: Oxford

ology reveals no gradual development of successively advanced societies in Egypt like those found in the al'Ubaid period in Sumeria.

While the material basis for Egyptian civilization was strikingly similar to that of the Sumerian, and while Egypt borrowed much from Sumeria and had basically the same technology, its social order developed in a profoundly different fashion. It was late in Egyptian history before anything recognizable as a city appeared, and the city never played the political or cultural role in Egypt that it did in Mesopotamia, Syria, and Greece. Egypt was and remained a society of villages. The provincial divisions of the country, which the Greeks later called "nomes," were essentially rural districts. Egyptian civilization at the opening of the third millennium was formed not about the city, nor about the temple—which may surprise one who has heard much about the intense religiosity or superstition of the Egyptians—but rather about the divine king, the pharaoh. The foundation act in Egyptian thought was and until Christian times remained the unification of the two lands, Upper and Lower Egypt, by King Menes. We do not know, and it is likely that we shall never know, whether Menes was a real man, but the rightness of the Egyptian view is clear, as it appears that the First Dynasty was founded by the conquest of Lower Egypt (the delta) by Upper Egypt (the valley) in late prehistoric times. This unification of the whole land—immense by ancient political standards—about the person of the divine king dates the nation of Egypt as an historical and cultural entity. Historical Egypt appears an overgrown village governed by a central court presided over in person by a god-king, the pharaoh.

By the time of the Third Dynasty, which raised the immense piles of the pyramids near modern Cairo, all the chief features which formed the peculiar Egyptian style had appeared. Life in Mesopotamia centered about the city and its temples, and they directed the economic integration of society. In Egypt true cities—anything more than villages and the temporary residences of the pharaohs and court near the site at which the royal tomb was being built— seem to have been unknown until the Middle Kingdom (c. 2100–1788). The economic system of the whole land, a vast unity by Bronze Age standards, revolved about the pharaoh and his court.[2] The whole of Egypt was, in a sense,

---

University Press, 1942); George Steindorff and K. C. Seele, *When Egypt Ruled the East* (Chicago: University of Chicago Press, 1957). Many of the sources can be found in English translation in James H. Breasted, *Ancient Records of Egypt*, 5 vols. (Chicago: University of Chicago Press, 1906–1907).

[2] The cultivated area of Egypt in antiquity was about 10,000 square miles. The primary area of Mesopotamia from the gulf to a point a bit above Babylon is about equal. But the total population of modern Iraq, a much larger area, is today only about 8,500,000 persons, while Egypt is bursting with a population of about 31,000,000. Even when ancient Sumer was united by some conquering power, it did not have a unified economy of the sort that was normal in Egypt, and much of the time it was not unified.

an immense village stretching along the Nile from the swamps at its mouth to the first cataract in the south (Map IV). Its only center of integration, its only capital, was the court surrounding the pharaoh's person.

The pharaoh was the chief priest of the Egyptian people, but he was also a god—perhaps, when the Egptians looked at the matter from one point of view, the greatest of the gods. The first beginning of things, as far as the Egyptians were concerned, was when the god Re had ruled Egypt in person as the first pharaoh. He structured the country and established its religion and polity; it was the duty of his descendents, the line of mortal pharaohs, to maintain that order. They were the possessors of the whole land; their sacrifices and spells caused the Nile to rise and inundate the valley and kept the seasons to their appointed rounds. The pharaoh assigned tasks and overseers to the people, and the whole produce of the country was his to distribute. Strictly there was not and could not be any class system, for no one but the pharaoh could possess the means of production. He had unlimited power to elevate and debase his servants, even the members of his own family. In the Old Kingdom (c. 2700–2200 B.C.), at least during its prosperity, there seems to have been no hereditary official class which could, in fact, limit his control, though, of course, the entire land of Egypt was far too large for the pharaoh's personal attention.[3]

It appears that in the Old Kingdom, and perhaps for long afterwards, the exploitation of mines and quarries of the desert was the monopoly of the pharaoh. Certainly his interest was far greater than any other. The desert supplied the many excellent building stones of Egypt; some semiprecious stones (turquoise, amethyst, carnelian, and garnet, which were prized not only for their beauty, but for their magical properties as well); and gold, though not silver.[4] Copper mines in the Sinai peninsula were exploited at an early period, though it is uncertain whether the first direct workings by the Egyptians date from the First or the Third Dynasty.

For both prehistoric and historical periods, we must depend very largely upon archaeology to trace Egypt's foreign trade from finds of foreign objects in Egypt or of Egyptian objects abroad. Millennia before the appearance of large states and cities, the lands of the eastern Mediterranean were bound together by trade of some sort, but Egypt appears to have been a latecomer. The same appears true of her trade to the Sudan in the south and on the Red Sea. Her lack of certain useful raw materials would naturally move the Egyptians to seek goods abroad, but her isolation, it will be remembered, is remarkable. To the south she is separated from the fertile lands of the Sudan by the cataracts at Wadi Halfa and by the approach of the desert to the river. The Red Sea can be approached only across the desert, it lacks good harbors,

---

[3] We follow Wilson's account in *The Culture of Egypt.*

[4] Kees, *Ancient Egypt,* discusses the resources of the desert in considerable detail.

and it is an extraordinarily difficult and dangerous body of water.[5] The
Mediterranean is certainly more approachable, but very little of Egypt is close
to it and very few Egyptians in any age can have had intimate or frequent
knowledge of the sea. Even the delta, which in ancient times was very largely
waste, was separated from the sea by great marshes often inhabited by barbarian peoples from Libya, only partially subject to the pharaoh. Much or
most of Egypt's foreign trade therefore has been conducted by foreigners (the
Hellenistic Greeks would call their chief city Alexandria-by-Egypt, and even
in the 1950s the city was largely Greek and English rather than Egyptian).

Egypt's isolation, however, was not simply the result of geographical
isolation. The closely knit Egyptian economic system had no place for freely
operating foreign merchants, nor for Egyptians freely importing goods from
abroad.[6] Yet certain goods were necessary and even in predynastic times
Egypt had traded abroad. Egypt had no silver; until the Twentieth Dynasty
(c. 1200–1090 B.C.) silver remained rarer and more valuable in Egypt than
gold. There is no satisfactory timber for sacred buildings or boats. Nor does
Egypt produce tin, for which reason she was slow to advance from copper to
bronze. (We do not know the place from which Egypt imported tin.) Other
rare and exotic products like ivory and valuable stones were desired. Hence,
though the most nearly self-sufficient of countries, Egypt needed imports, and
after the great consolidation under the pharaohs of the Third Dynasty, the
amount of trade increased considerably.

Providing imports was the pharaoh's business, and foreign trade seems
from earliest times to have been a state monopoly. Seaborne commerce was

[5] For a lively description of its difficulties and dangers, see Jacques Cousteau and James
Dugan, *The Living Sea* (New York: Harper and Row, 1964), Ch. iii. Even today many
reefs have not been charted, and ships follow the central channel by radar. The coasts are
desolate, as are the islands, and survivors of a wreck, once they get ashore, still face almost
uniformly hostile natives.

We have already noted that the Sumerians were capable of sailing the Persian Gulf
and that they had contact of some sort, probably by sea, with the Indus Valley and northwestern India as well as with the coasts of Arabia. The earliest boats were presumably
hollowed-out logs; sails were a neolithic invention, for long man's only use of inanimate
power. The early sails were set in such a fashion as to make tacking almost impossible. As
a result ships could sail with the wind, but not almost into it, as can a modern sailboat
by tacking. The draft of early ships was certainly inconsiderable and their loads very
small, but our knowledge of Bronze Age shipbuilding is meagre in spite of a number of
drawings, reliefs, and frescoes picturing ships. On the subject, see: James Hornell, "Sea-
Trade in Early Times," *Antiquity*, XV (1941), 233–56; T. Säve-Söderbergh, *The Navy of
the Eighteenth Egyptian Dynasty* (Uppsala: Lundequiska bokhandeln, 1946) (on Hatshepsut's expedition to Punt and Thutmose's use of the navy in his Syrian campaigns);
and Lionel Casson, *The Ancient Mariners, Seafarers and Sea Fighters of the Mediterranean
in Ancient Times* (New York: Macmillan, 1959).

[6] For the tendency of monarchies with an "early" technology to isolate themselves from
outside contact, protect themselves by control of trade with foreigners, and use control of
trade to build states, see Catherine Coquery-Vidrovitch, "La fête des coutumes au Dahomey:
Histoire et essai d'interprétation," *Ann. ESC.*, XLIX (1964), 696–716.

often conducted in the pharaoh's ships. Trade with Lebanon for the various coniferous woods we summarize under the name "cedar" was centered at Byblos even in predynastic times. We have some texts concerning this trade. In writing for home consumption, the pharaohs regularly picture objects received from abroad as tribute, and while it does seem true enough that foreign trade was easier when Egypt's political prestige was great, Egyptian papyrus, linen, and gold were still returned as "gifts." Already at the beginning of the Fourth Dynasty, Snofrue built many ships and received from Lebanon—presumably from Byblos—forty ships laden with cedar wood.[7] Indeed, the excavations at Byblos have yielded stone vessels bearing the names of many pharaohs of the Old Kingdom. It would be too much to describe Byblos as an Egyptian colony, but at least the Egyptian envoys were always welcome there in the days of Egypt's prosperity, and connections were so close that a temple of the goddess Hathor came to be identified with the native Semitic Astarte.

The "Story of the Shipwrecked Sailor" relates an expedition sent by the pharaoh from some harbor on the Red Sea to the mines of the Sinai peninsula in a very large ship (60 by 20 meters) with a crew of 120 Egyptian sailors. The ship was wrecked and only the narrator survived, cast up on an island the like of which is not really to be found in the Red Sea, fruitful in everything, and ruled by a supernatural serpent. Though the story is fabulous, the list of goods with which the narrator returned to Egypt is fairly close to those the Egyptians sought from the incense-producing countries at the south end of the sea: myrrh and other perfumes and incenses, eye cosmetics, giraffes' tails, elephant tusks, greyhounds, monkeys, and apes.[8] Such a shipment, of course, was worth a fortune, but on his return, the narrator went to the residence of the pharaoh and "presented unto him all this treasure which [he] had brought from this island." The tale of Wen Amon relates another official trade expedition, and Queen Hatshepsut, who ruled as pharaoh during the late sixteenth and early fifteenth centuries, recorded in hieroglyphics on the walls of her temple at Deir el-Bahri, as one of her proudest achievements, a great expedition to Punt, the land of myrrh. (Punt's location was probably vague to most Egyptians, but it probably meant not only modern Somaliland, but southwestern Arabia as well, for that was the source of frankincense.) Five ships set out with the manufactures of civilized Egypt—jewelry, tools, and weapons—and returned with small cattle, apes, incense trees (which were to be cultivated in Egypt), ivory, myrrh, and rare woods.[9]

Egyptians did not always go abroad to trade; foreigners came to her borders. They were not permitted to enter the country but did business at ports of trade, *emporia*, comparable to the Assyrian and Sumerian *tamkarum*

[7] Gardiner, *Egypt of the Pharaohs*, pp. 77ff.

[8] Adolf Erman, ed., *The Ancient Egyptians, A Sourcebook of Their Writings*, trans. Aylward M. Blackman (Harper Torchbooks; New York: Harper and Row, 1966), pp. 29–34.

[9] Säve-Söderbergh, *The Navy of the Eighteenth Egyptian Dynasty*.

or karum. It is possible that there was a Cretan emporion at the west side of the delta on the later site of Alexandria during the first half of the second millennium and that Cretans were commissioned to bring cedars from Lebanon by Thutmose III in 1467 B.C.[10] At the south end of Egypt, at the First Cataract, lay a town which the Greeks later called Syene and an island they called Elephantine. Syene is Greek for the Egyptian Sewen, the modern Aswan, and means "mart," while Elephantine, the Egyptian Yeb, referred not only to the island, but to the whole area to the south from which ivory was drawn. Aswan was a port of trade facing the desert of the south and its nomads.[11]

Foreign merchants were not allowed to do business in Egypt itself; the distribution of foreign goods within the country was in the pharaoh's sphere. If private enterprise and greed had been permitted to develop unchecked, the redistributive system would have been exploded, and the government would have lost one of its most effective means of keeping control and gaining support. From the earliest civilizations down to the age of mercantilism in seventeenth-century Europe, control of foreign commerce has played a great part in state building and the maintenance of order. In Egypt, foreign trade was a necessity for a Bronze Age technology, and the distribution of its goods was in the pharaoh's hands. Thus he controlled the production and distribution of bronze and of the tools and ornaments made from it, as well as the distribution of precious ointments, perfumes, and incense from abroad to royal officials and to the temples for the cult of the gods. The distribution of such marks of honor as ostrich feathers and giraffes' tails was a matter of court ceremonial. Foreign goods were distributed to favorites and courtiers as part of their perquisites and honors; they in turn made gifts to their subordinates and dependents. Stone for a courtier's tomb, similarly, would necessarily be a gift from the pharaoh's quarries; the courtier's wife, relatives, and dependents would profit from the gift by subordinate places in the tomb complex. Such a system kept economic control in the hands of those with political power, prevented an indiscriminate rush for wealth, and had as a necessary consequence the conduct of trade through "treaty ports" which limited contact with the outside world. Royal expeditions were the counterpart of the port of trade.

The raw materials native to Egypt, the products of her fields, her manpower and artisans, and her foreign trade, then, were all at the disposal of the pharaoh. This centralization of the economy made it possible for the Egyptians, even in their earliest days as a civilized and united people, to produce some of man's most stupendous works. The reign of Djoser, the first king of the Third Dynasty, was thought by the ancient Egyptians to mark an epoch, and clearly they were right, for his great step pyramid (*mastaba*) at Sakkara and the tomb complex about it is something unprecedented in earlier Egypt.

[10] Gustave Glotz, *Aegean Civilization* (New York: Alfred A. Knopf, 1925) pp. 188, 190.
[11] Emil A. Kraeling, "New Light on the Elephantine Colony," in *The Biblical Archaeologist Reader*, ed. G. Ernest Wright and David Noel Freedman (Chicago: Quadrangle Books, 1961), pp. 128ff.; Kees, *Ancient Egypt*, p. 192.

Earlier mastabas had been of brick with some granite and limestone for floors and the like, but Djoser's is wholly of stone. A maze of underground galleries reveals walls lined with blue faience tiles imitating matting and thousands of splendidly shaped vases and dishes of alabaster, breccia, schist, and other fine stones. The exquisite delicacy of some low reliefs of the king in ceremonial poses shows that the sculptors of the time had mastered their technique as well as the architects.[12] Here, then, is the first great monument of Egyptian centralization and the point of departure for Egypt's peculiar pharaoh-centered economy. The mastaba of Djoser led quickly to the tomb of Snofrue, the founder of the Fourth Dynasty, at Medum, and to the immense pyramids of his three successors, Cheops, Chephren, and Mycerinus, at Gizeh. Perhaps no later works were quite so stupendous, but the later pharaonic tombs have revealed awe-inspiring contents. In one after another, the reliefs on the walls show a remarkable effort and extraordinary competence, but the tomb of no really great and wealthy Egyptian ruler has been discovered unlooted. Most were sacked in pharaonic times—a reminder that all Egyptians were not pious. But the treasures of Tutankhamen, discovered in 1922 and now in the Cairo Museum, astonished the world though he was an insignificant person whose reign was far too short to amass a funeral treasure comparable to that of many pharaohs. The tomb of Sheshonk I (the Shishak of I Kings 14:25), discovered in 1938, was also intact and of immense splendor. In 1940 the tomb of Psusennos I (d. c. 1140 B.C.) was discovered at Tanis in the delta. The corpse lay in a quadruple series of sarcophagi: the outer two were of granite, the third of silver, and the fourth of silver overlaid with gold. One necklace of lapis lazuli and gold weighed more than 72 pounds.[13] Both of these last two pharaohs lived in an age of economic and military decline.

Such works as the pyramids, erected even before the Egyptians possessed the wheel, appear at first sight to have been a tremendous burden on the population and the economy. In some ways they may have been, but Herodotus' tale that the pyramids were built by huge bands of mistreated slaves is an anachronism. The ancient world did not yet know slave labor on a large scale. The pyramids were created by native, free laborers. The purpose of such tombs was to provide a house for the god-pharaoh so that he might reside in Egypt and care for his people after his death; we must suppose that the peasants who labored on them shared this theological view. Nor was the simple economic burden as great as might be supposed. The greatest need in putting up such a structure as a pyramid was an almost unlimited force of unskilled labor to transport the huge blocks of which it was composed from the quarry down the Nile to the site of the tomb and then to drag them up ramps and put them in place. Most economies today which we call underdeveloped have

[12] Gardiner, *Egypt of the Pharaohs*, p. 73.
[13] *The New York Times*, February 20, 1940, p. 23; March 5, p. 20; May 4, p. 6; Jack Finegan, *Light from the Ancient Past* (Princeton: Princeton University Press, 1959), pp. 110, 113.

great resources of untapped labor in seasons when there is little agricultural work to be done. During the flood the Egyptians can do none at all, and it was just during the flood that huge blocks could be floated to the sites of the pyramids on the edge of the desert to erect what the Egyptians judged a useful public work.

Such an economic picture is already familiar to us: a society highly integrated about a sacred center dominating the whole political union. There was no need for independent economic institutions, the merchant, the market, the independent artisan, the self-sufficient household; they would, indeed, have been felt to be socially dangerous and impious. Yet Egypt was no more unchanging than was Mesopotamia. The late third millennium (Dynasties VII–X c. 2200–2100), saw the decay of royal power and the development of political independence of the individual offices into which Egypt was divided geographically and administratively. The local monarchs who gained their independence from the pharaoh were undoubtedly in origin royal officials who had managed to make their offices hereditary. Each ruled his own region in tolerable independence and usurped the privileges of the pharaoh. During the Old Kingdom the highest and most coveted honor was the grant of a burial place within the temple complex about the pharaoh's tomb. Such burial gave hope of continuing service to the pharaoh after death and therefore of eternal life. Governors during the first Intermediate Period, however, no longer sought burial near the pharaoh. With extraordinary boldness they built tombs for themselves in their own names and sought to guarantee immortality by stealing the enchantments carved upon the pharaoh's tomb and imitating the dances and ceremonies of the pharaoh's burial service. Rather than being maintained by the court, artisans now served a multitude of local rulers and the arts declined temporarily into provincialism. This was a temporary aberration, however. The normal state of the world, to the Egyptian mind, was the union of the two lands under the pharaoh, and the rulers of the Third Dynasty, with their capital in Upper Egypt at Thebes, reestablished unity.

The great break in Egyptian history, one that might almost be called traumatic, came with the Hyksos invasion. The Hyksos were a mixed horde of Semitic and Hurrian tribes from Palestine and farther north, who broke into Lower Egypt about 1580 B.C. They never conquered the whole of the country or established unity among themselves, but they founded a number of states in the delta and raided the south, extorting tribute from the native rulers of Upper Egypt. The reaction came when the ruler of Thebes, Amosis (c. 1580–1557 B.C.), drove out the Hyksos and established the rule of his house over the whole of Egypt. The authority of the local nobles of Upper Egypt was ended and the old order reestablished. Amenophis I and Thutmose I in the latter sixteenth century fought in Palestine, but the reign of Queen Hatshepsut saw the establishment of Egypt's traditional relations with foreign powers. The great transformation in Egypt's political life came under her successor Thutmose III. Under him Egypt began a new career of imperialism and splendor that would last down to the end of the Bronze Age in the Near East in the eleventh century.

Thutmose brought back a rich booty from his conquests in Palestine. The Asiatic princes he conquered, although they were shepherd chiefs, possessed a cosmopolitan elegance. Captured cattle numbered some 2,000 or more on one expedition, goats some 2,000, and sheep some 20,000. There was also craftsmanship of high quality. The Egyptian government maintained a monopoly on the coniferous woods of Asia. For the first time, the Egyptians needed to develop a navy and transport to maintain these conquests and make these raids. The ports of Palestine were in their hands and ships brought supplies to their armies and took goods back to Egypt.

The economic results of the empire in Egypt were similar to those in Mesopotamia. It brought new wealth to the country, put a part of that wealth into the hands of private persons, and created new class lines. It also brought Egypt into closer contact with the rest of the Near Eastern world and, at least on a superficial level, created an international society of states and an international economic system.

Egypt's imperialism was directed chiefly toward Syria, Palestine, and to some degree toward Nubia in the south. Her purposes were not colonization and settlement, but booty and defense against the dangers of future raids like those of the Hyksos. Booty and tribute were delivered to the pharaoh to be distributed to his courtiers and generals, and no doubt by them to their attendants. The pharaoh appears, too, to have been in a position to conduct trade on a greater scale. It is often difficult to distinguish trade, conducted by treaties between heads of states, from the mutual assistance of allies, the tribute of the conquered, and the ransoms of threatened cities. But clearly the pharaoh's position in all these respects was stronger than before. That he did sometimes pay is certain from the precious and fine Egyptian goods found in the foundation of a temple at Byblos, which date from the reigns of Ikhnaton and his successor (first half of the fourteenth century).

The priesthoods of Egypt profited hugely from this new wealth and foreign tribute. Grateful pharaohs granted charters exempting the temples and their staffs from the duties which fell on other subjects, so the priesthoods were wedded to the conquests and further imperialism by self-interest. The temples of the Old and Middle Kingdoms had been relatively small and local in their influence; under the Empire some of them became huge and acquired vast estates. The greatest of them, by all odds, was that of Amon-Re at Karnak. The great hypostyle hall at Karnak is roofed by architrave blocks weighing sixty tons supported on columns eighty feet high [14] and is on the scale of the tombs of the earlier pharaohs. The Papyrus Harris gives a lengthy account of the possessions of the god: 2,756 statues; 86,486 tenants, servants, and slaves; 421,000 cattle, large and small; 433 gardens and orchards, and about 583,000

---

[14] Wilson, *Culture of Ancient Egypt*, p. 195.

acres of cornland; 83 ships; 46 building yards; and 65 townships or villages, seven of them in Asia.[15] The god also received large shares of the loot and was patron and senior partner in the exploitation of the gold mines of Nubia and the Sudan. In Thutmose III's thirty-fourth year, the god received more than 700 troy pounds of gold from these mines, in the next year about the same, and in the forty-first somewhat over 800 pounds.

From the point of view of the internal economy, this change is important. The great temple estates of the imperial period are the first properties that we see protected by privilege; their priests are the first Egyptians to have rights against the crown and property protected from the pharaoh's demands. And, indeed, they possessed such extensive properties as to become economic and political powers somewhat independent of the crown, carrying on extensive economic activities of their own. Egypt came to know an aristocracy independent of the royal household and administration.

> The royal monopoly over trade was . . . gradually broken by the progressive granting of trading concessions and especially by the steady transfer of real-estate [which provided the foundation for trading] to officials in the feudal period . . . and to temples; in this way independent economic entities were evolved. The cession by the king of transit dues and customs privileges also contributed to this development. Compromise arrangements were likewise made in this connection, but their results in detail are difficult for us to ascertain.[16]

There were other social results, too. The gap between the governed and governors was widened and the number of persons of middling position increased. A growing number of professional bailiffs and farm managers and probably an increasing number of clerks made their appearance. Originally the former might be slaves or hired servants, but they came to form a managerial class standing between the owner and the Egyptian peasant. The decline of the Egyptian into the oppressed and exploited *fellahin* of all later times was underway.

The peasant lost his place in the army as well. The spoked wheel and horsedrawn war chariot had appeared in the Near East by the eighteenth century B.C. and revolutionized warfare. The Hyksos conquered the delta with it, as perhaps the Hittites did Asia Minor. It was the instrument of communication and conquest that maintained all the later more durable empires: Hittite, Egyptian, Assyrian, Chinese (the Shang), and Persian.[17] But such an apparatus was expensive and difficult to use and maintain. The chariot itself was a complicated machine that could be produced only by skilled artisans; the warhorses were very expensive; and the men who fought on such chariots

---

[15] Translated in Breasted, *Ancient Records of Egypt*, Vol. IV, sections 182–396.

[16] Kees, *Ancient Egypt*, p. 140.

[17] On the spread and effects of the spoked wheel and war chariot, see McNeill, *The Rise of the West*, pp. 116ff., 167ff.

needed as much specialized training as a medieval knight. They could not be turned out in the few months of training needed by the modern state to teach a man to drive a tank. The result was a widespread use of mercenaries, often non-Egyptian. (Greek and Hebrew mercenaries will be seen serving the pharaoh in the last days of Egyptian independence.) The army was no longer a *levée en masse* of the peasantry, because the native militia could not acquire in spare time the skills necessary for the tactics of fighting in chariots. Soldiers and foreign mercenaries were often granted lands in Egypt to maintain them and they came to form a privileged class. An interesting relief shows a Syrian soldier sitting with his Egyptian wife while an Egyptian servant offers him a drink of wine.

Foreigners were making their appearance in Egypt in other roles as well. At Ikhnaton's capital of el-Amarna there have been found the remains of a fine house in the Aegean or Minoan style. People were included in the imperial booty and the number of slaves, mostly foreigners, greatly increased. Some such slaves, if they were attached to a great household or temple or if they acted as the farm manager of some military tenant of the crown, might be better off than the Egyptian peasant. They would, in fact, command the native fellahin. But others were in the lowest occupations. For the first time there are indications of the use of slave gangs: the mines of Sinai were exploited by Canaanitish slaves, and the Hebrew memories of forced labor in Egypt date from the Empire. Miserable themselves, they must have further depressed the native peasants by the cheapness of their labor.

In short, the economy of Egypt had been opened. The great and continuous egalitarian village stretching along the Nile had been transformed into a stratified, hierarchical society that could be held together only by rigid discipline. "In previous centuries Egypt had been an overgrown folk society; suddenly it became a cosmopolitan and urbanized society, diffused and heterogeneous, breaking with tradition and more strongly secularized." [18]

MINOAN AND MYCENAEAN CIVILIZATION

Egypt and Mesopotamia were the centers of the ancient Near Eastern world, but by the late second millennium, there were a number of other, peripheral civilized societies. The Hittites ruled an empire in Asia Minor and disputed Syria with the Egyptians, but the sources give us little evidence about their economic organization.[19] But a word should be said about the peoples of the Aegean. Before the Greeks, the center of civilization was on the island of Crete and the development of the state was closely tied to sea power and to overseas commerce. All over the Aegean the name Minoa survived into historical times—there is one in Siphnos, one in Amorgos off the coast of

[18] Wilson, *The Culture of Egypt*, p. 205.
[19] Oliver R. Gurney, *The Hittites* (London: Penguin Books, 1952).

Megara, one in Delos, one in Laconia, and others on the coasts of Syria, and in the west—no doubt marking former Cretan ports of trade.

Our sources from the Aegean are less satisfactory than those from Egypt or Mesopotamia. Before c. 1400 B.C. there are no written records that we can read, and though Minoan society did possess writing (the hieroglyphic and Linear A), remains are scanty. Even Linear B, which is Greek, provides only a limited kind of information for the period c. 1400–1200 B.C., though it is information very relevant to our subject. For the earlier period, then, we are limited to archaeological evidence.

The most striking difference between Minoan society and Egypt and Mesopotamia is the absence of temples. Minoan shrines are all of modest size. We cannot really say much about the role of religion in Minoan feeling and psychological experience from this evidence, but the temple clearly played no important part in the economy. The palace, and sometimes the large country house dominating a village, was the center of production and, it seems, of distribution. Society was integrated about the palace, of which the greatest was that excavated by Sir Arthur Evans at Knossos.

The Greek myth of the labyrinth is probably based on memories of Knossos. Rebuilt several times it became ever more splendid. Its frescoes reveal a sophisticated courtly life. But the palace was not only a center of political power. Its storehouses indicate that it was the center of a storage economy. Grain and olive oil were warehoused there and the finest artisan wares, metalwork and vases, were produced there. A "palace style" of pottery highly prized by princes was produced in the royal workshops at Knossos.

In the absence of political documents of any kind it is difficult to interpret the various levels of destruction and rebuilding at Knossos and other Aegean sites. The Late Minoan Period (c. 1600 to sometime before 1100 B.C.) saw the culmination of a long process of unification and centralization at Knossos. The island was held together by a regular network of roads protected by guardhouses at intervals. But in the last years of the fifteenth century the great palace was burnt and its reconstruction and continued occupation must be laid to Greek-speaking peoples. At the same time a number of independent palaces had grown to importance on the Greek peninsula. These Mycenaean sites have been shown by Michael Ventris's decipherment of Linear B script to have been Greek. At Thebes, Pylos, and Mycenae there were palaces similar to that at Knossos, though on the mainland they were fortified.

From the last phase of each of these sites and from Knossos, clay tablets written in Linear B have survived.[20] They are surely the most curious source materials in economic history, and it is important to understand just what they are and how they survived. Our entire knowledge of early Greek language and script consists of them. The Cretans and Mycenaeans, it is fairly certain,

---

[20] The basic work is Michael Ventris and John Chadwick, *Documents in Myceanaean Greek* (Cambridge: Cambridge University Press, 1956), which presents 300 selected texts of every known type.

did not bake tablets to produce a permanent record as the Mesopotamians did. The script used on the tablets is cursive and not, therefore, very suitable to writing in clay. It is a fair conclusion that some other writing material like parchment or papyrus was used for any permanent record. Unbaked clay was used only for temporary records, which were probably pulped regularly when no longer needed. It is an irony that the very last of the temporary records have lasted. No papyrus, no parchment, and not a single inscription comes down to us from the Minoan-Mycenaean civilization. But some of the tablets were baked by the very conflagrations that destroyed the palaces and probably cost the lives of their rulers. What have survived are some of the administrative records of the last few months of the palace economy at Pylos, which was destroyed about 1200 B.C. and at which some 12,000 tablets have been found; tablets were also found at Mycenae, destroyed about 1200 or a bit earlier; and at Knossos, destroyed about 1400. (Of these, only Knossos was rebuilt to prosper another 250 or 300 years.) How far back the conditions the tablets described may go we cannot tell, but they do reveal a developed scribal tradition and a fairly uniform administration of the economy for all of southern Greece. Since the area enjoyed a stable and uniform culture (revealed by archaeology) from about 1650 to about 1200 B.C., we may suspect that the origins of the system go back something like that far. The geographical extent of the culture is uncertain, but where Homer's account of the Mycenaeans can be checked, it is accurate and would include Thessaly, central Greece, Rhodes, and possibly, at the very end of the period, even Cyprus.

The palaces in which these tablets were discovered and are being discovered was not only the house of the king, but also the residence of a complex staff which ran the entire state and included a large body of artisans. Although there was no money, a system of controlled economics saw to it that necessary goods were produced and distributed. So the tablets from Pylos record the bronze allotted to each smith and include a list of the smiths who received none and so, presumably, were unemployed—at least by the state. Each smith must be supposed to have been responsible for manufactured articles equal in weight to the bronze he received. It seems certain that he was housed by the state and provided with a workshop by it, and we have records of the food allowances made him.[21]

Nothing in any of these tablets can, by any reasonable analysis, be made to read "buy," "sell," "lend," or "pay a wage." Nor did Ventris and Chadwick find any payments in silver or gold.

> [These omissions] reveal a massive redistributive operation, in which all personnel and all activities, all movements of both persons and goods, so to speak, were administratively fixed. Work was performed, land and goods were parcelled out, payments were made (i.e., allocations, quotas, rations) according to fixed schedules which were frequently corrected and re-established

[21] John Chadwick, "A Prehistoric Bureaucracy," *Diogenes*, XXVI (1959), 7–18.

(perhaps even annually). Such a network of centralized activity requires records—more precisely, records in the form, and in the minute detail which was on the tablets. But it can dispense with permanent records, and even, it would seem, with balance sheets and systematic summaries.[22]

In such a system and in the light of what we know of the system at work in the Near East, we should expect land holdings in payment for services. Artisans (called *demiourgoi* from *demos*), it seems likely, held in return for their services to the public, but the system of land tenure is not perfectly clear from the tablets. Such relations as payments from the land and its distribution might not appear in such records as these, for they would not need such frequent recording. It is clear however that at least some of the palaces were engaged in trade. Great stores of olive oil which caught fire in the last conflagration were found at Pylos. The amounts exceed the needs of the palace; the king must, then, have been in the business of exporting olive oil and perhaps other produce. Pottery in the palace style of Knossos is found outside Crete. The presence of such foreign products as ivory at the palaces proves that goods were imported. Indeed, these little kingdoms in the Aegean area, although they are organized along the same state-redistributive lines as the states of the river valleys, may be assumed to have devoted a much larger part of their energies to foreign trade and to have been specialists in it. The distribution of their ports of trade from Ras Shamra (Ugarit) in Syria and Cyprus to southern Italy indicates that they acted as middlemen as the Greeks would later for other peoples of the Mediterranean.

Yet the lords of the Mycenaean palaces were not able to create real cities about the palaces. Most of the population continued to live in purely agricultural villages and played little or no part in the higher culture about the palace and its advanced economy. When the palaces at Mycenae and Pylos were sacked and burnt about 1100 B.C., nothing replaced them.

The height of Minoan-Mycenaean prosperity came at the same time that the Egyptian, Mitannian, and Hittite empires of the Near East enjoyed their greatest prosperity. The age revealed by the diplomatic correspondence discovered at Tell el-Amarna in Egypt was the height of the Bronze Age political system and economy. Monarchs are in close diplomatic touch with each other and the political system begins for the first time to look full. There is no room for the independence of minor powers. All of Syria and Palestine, so often divided into petty city-states and kingdoms, is dominated by either the Hittites or the Egyptians.

To this political fullness corresponds what looks like the first international economy, the first faint adumbration of the economy of international ex-

---

[22] M. I. Finley, "The Mycenaean Tablets and Economic History," *EcHR*, 2d s., X (1957–1958), 135. There is dispute about some aspects of the landholding system. See L. Palmer, "The Mycenaean Tablets and Economic History," *ibid.*, XI (1958–1959), 87–96 and P. Vidal-Naquet, "Homère et le monde mycénien," *Ann. ESC.*, XVIII (1963), 711–2.

changes of the nineteenth century. The expansion of Mycenaean civilization led to a corresponding expansion of maritime traffic. In the records of the Assyrian merchant colonies in Anatolia which date from the twentieth century B.C. there is no evidence of Mediterranean trade, but the archives from Mari (c. 1850–1761) show that sea trade played a respectable role in its caravan business. Mediterranean goods were transported to this Mesopotamian city by way of Ugarit (Ras Shamra). "Objects of import are found increasingly in Egypt, Syria, and the Aegean after the nineteenth century. During the following centuries trade expanded more or less steadily, reaching a climax in the fourteenth century B.C." [23] This is, of course, the age of the el-Amarna correspondence. This maritime trade is on a scale without earlier parallel and appears to have been in the hands of outsiders—not of the empires, nor even of the merchants of Ugarit, but of the rulers of the Mycenaean palaces. We know, too, from the diplomatic correspondence found at both Tell el-Amarna and at the Hittite capital of Boghaskoy that international exchanges between kings and princes took place on a wider and more important scale. The pharaoh received gifts of iron from the Hittite kings and other princes in the north; in return they begged or demanded from him gifts of gold, which the Egyptians exploited in Nubia. Trade goods were popular, too. Scarab charms were exported from Egypt and imitated in cheap paste in Syria. They are found widely through the whole trade area. The Mycenaean kings were exporting oil and wine. There cannot have been a good market for them in the Aegean area and it may be supposed that some went to Egypt. At least on the highest, and perhaps most superficial level, the Near East was beginning to form an economic unity.

[23] William F. Albright, "The Role of the Canaanites in the History of Civilization," in American Council of Learned Societies Devoted to Humanistic Studies, *Studies in the History of Culture; The Disciplines of the Humanities* (Menasha, Wis.: George Banta Publishing Co., 1942), p. 24; Finegan, *Light from the Ancient Past*, pp. 171ff.

5 TRIAL AND PROOF OF THE BRONZE AGE ECONOMIC SYSTEM
The Iron Age Economy in the Ancient Near East

THE TIME OF TROUBLES AFTER THE AMARNA AGE

In many ways the age revealed by the diplomatic correspondence found at Tell el-Amarna (c. 1411–1375 B.C.) marks the climax of the first great period in human history. The entire Near East—Egypt, Syria, Mesopotamia, and Anatolia—was bound together in intimate diplomatic relations which maintained a balance of power among the great states and preserved each of them from attack intended to destroy them and to build a universal empire. With diplomatic exchanges among kings went economic exchanges. Some historians have gone so far as to say that for the first time the entire Middle East was bound together in a simple economic system of international exchanges. Such a statement may be misleading for we are accustomed to an immense scale of international exchange and to the possibility that goods in international trade may effect the lives of entire populations: for example, the citizen of Manchester may eat bread made from Nebraska grain. Nothing of the sort, of course, had developed in the Amarna age, but if the very limited scope and nature of international trade is kept in mind, the statement that an international and unified economy had developed is not wholly untrue.[1] The cities of Lower Egypt looking toward Palestine were cosmopolitan and polyglot, and the society of the Near East was prosperous as it had never been before.

A number of developments during the Amarna age, however, augured ill for the continuation of such prosperous and polished societies. The technical and social developments we have seen in Egypt did much to destroy the old unity of society. How large a part these internal strains played in the catastrophe that followed can hardly be made out. It is clear that the powers of attack had increased in the period, and it developed that civilized society was ill prepared to withstand them. The war chariot did much to give an

[1] Finegan, *Light from the Ancient Past*, pp. 127–38.

advantage to the attack and to increase movement, as did the camel, which had been known, apparently, early in the third millennium but then disappeared from view until the eleventh century B.C.[2] Its reappearance then gave a great advantage to the nomads of the Syrian desert. The nomads had, of course, always been a problem to Egyptians, Canaanites, and Mesopotamians; now with the camel they gained great mobility. In this age, the use of the camel appears to have been confined to those sheep herders of the tolerably fertile grazing lands of the steppe whom we have already seen. The next step would be the invasion of the high desert, which was for the first time made habitable by the camel. The ancestors of the Hebrews do not appear to have come from the high desert, but once settled in Palestine they would have to face camel-riding nomads from the desert.

The end of the second millennium, then, saw a series of upheavals and invasions which were to involve the entire Near East. It was a disaster comparable to that which befell the classical world in the fifth century A.D. and brought the civilized world of the West close to extinction (see Map VII).

The great expeditions of Ramses II in the thirteenth century B.C. were the last great effort of Egypt to exert foreign influence and build or maintain an empire. The invasions of tribes and bands whom the Egyptians called the "Sea Peoples" tore apart the entire political structure of the eastern Mediterranean and destroyed kingdoms and cities. Pharaoh Merneptah repelled the attacks of the Libyans and the "Peoples of the Sea" (who included what appear to have been Sardinians, Sicilians [Sicels?], Achaeans, and Lycians) in 1221 B.C. (Their attack on Egypt is distantly related to the Homeric war against Troy.) He was less successful in his troubles with the Semitic tribes to the east. Troubles in his reign in Palestine should be connected with the first appearance of the Hebrews there and perhaps with the career of Moses, about 1200 B.C. or shortly before the Hebrews entered Palestine from the east by way of Jericho. Archaeology can trace their advance by the successive destructions of Jericho, Bethel, Lachish, and Debir (Map V). But the conquest was slow, for the efforts of the Hebrew nations (called "tribes" in the English Bible) were not yet united. The Canaanite cities resisted, and the destruction was great. The Hebrew levels of the city sites clearly indicate a less civilized society, poorer in material goods, than the earlier levels they replaced.

Ramses III (1198–1167) repelled another wave of attacks from the Peoples of the Sea (who now included Homer's Danai), but the Philistines among them could not be prevented from settling, or were permitted to settle, along the coast of southern Syria, which henceforth was called Palestine after them.

[2] Abraham was not a camel-riding bedouin of the high desert but a sheep grazer from the steppe. The camels that Rebecca watered at Nahor and those that Jacob rode back to Palestine were almost certainly donkeys: Gen. 24:10ff. See: B. Brentjes, "Das Kamel im Alten Orient," *Klio*, XXXIX (1960), 23–52; H. von Wissmann, "Badw," *Encyclopaedia of Islam*, 2d ed., I (1959), 880ff.; and the *Chicago Assyrian Dictionary*, s.v. *gammalu, ibilu*.

The culture of the Philistines was Aegean and they were the possessors of superior iron weapons. Their command of iron technique later gave them a great advantage over the Hebrew nations from the desert.[3]

Indeed, the chief center of the disturbance seems to have been the Aegean. That the disruptive migration spread east as well as south is shown by the Thracian and Phrygian tribes that soon after 1200 B.C. completely destroyed the Hittite empire of Anatolia and the civilization of the Hittites with it. Politically the Hittites survived only as petty city-states south of the Taurus mountains in Syria. The Mysians, Lydians, Carians, Lycians, and Phrygians established themselves in the western part of the peninsula, while the eastern part sank into obscurity. There may, too, have been Achaeans among them, as there certainly were among those Aegean peoples who went farther afield. The Peoples of the Sea who raided Egypt first attacked the southern coasts of Asia Minor, Cyprus, and Syria, where the great port of trade for the west, Ugarit, was destroyed c. 1200 B.C. It was never rebuilt and the other little cities and large villages of Syria afterwards had to be heavily fortified. In the absence of any great powers endemic warfare became the general fate of Syria. This situation was made worse by the reappearance of the camel as a beast of burden and a mount. The first recorded raid upon the sown by camel-riding nomads from the desert was in the late twelfth century, but sometime before that the nomads of the steppe had probably learned to ride the camel and for the first time to inhabit and cross the wastes of the Arabian desert, to ride over long distances, and to surprise wholly unsuspecting victims asleep in remote villages. Thus the bedouin razzia was born, and year after year the wild Arabs poured over Palestine, forced the Israelites and others into the mountains and forest, and plundered their crops and livestock.[4]

At the center of troubles in the Aegean world, the transformation was far greater. The leadership of Crete in the Aegean ended with the final destruction of the great city and palace of Knossos, while the invasions of the Dorians (c. 1100 B.C.) overran almost all of mainland Greece, except the interior of the Peloponnesus and Attica. Even there the ancient social order was obliterated.[5] The Mycenaean connections with Cyprus, Ugarit, and southern Italy were lost. The Cypriot Greeks would for centuries be isolated from the home country, while the others went under completely. Unimportant Mycenaean settlements on the Aegean coast of Asia Minor, notably Miletus, however, were gradually reinforced by refugees from the peninsula. The destruction of Troy, recorded in the *Iliad* (probably level VIIa of the mound), was perhaps the last expansive effort of the Mycenaens; its destruction, at

[3] I Sam. 13:19–22; Finegan, *Light from the Ancient Past*, p. 128.
[4] Judges 6:3; William F. Albright, *The Biblical Period from Abraham to Ezra* (New York: Harper and Row, 1963), p. 41.
[5] Carl Roebuck, *The World of Ancient Times* (New York: Charles Scribner's Sons, 1966), pp. 117–9.

any rate, seems connected with the turbulence of these times. All the main centers of Mycenaean Greece were under attack in the latter part of the thirteenth century, and Mycenae, Tiryns, and Pylos had perished by about 1200 B.C. Athens, however, beat off the invaders and became a center of refuge and very probably the point from which the islands and the central stretch of the Aegean coast of Asia Minor (Ionia) were colonized. The collapse of the great citadels meant the end of the civilization and the cultural tradition of the Mycenaean world. Writing, fine craftsmanship, monumental architecture, and the palace-centered economy all disappeared. A dark age settled over Greece until the rise of the historical city-states in the eighth century, an obscurity broken only by the poems of Homer.

Mesopotamia weathered the great storm better than those regions that could be attacked from the Mediterranean, but the several centuries before the reign of Tiglath Pileser I (c. 1100 B.C.) are so obscure and devoid of great accomplishments in building as to suggest that Babylonia and Assyria were experiencing difficulties. The Arameans of the desert who established little kingdoms in Syria, like that founded about 970 by Rezon at Damascus, also invaded Mesopotamia. About 1176 Shutruk-nahunte of Elam raided Babylonia and carried off to Susa the stele, now in the Louvre, on which is inscribed the code of Hammurabi. It was a minor episode in the agony of that age.[6]

Assyria came forward only gradually to replace the earlier powers of the eastern part of the fertile crescent. The great invasions produced an almost totally new political map of the Near East. Egypt survived shorn of its foreign possessions. The empires disappeared for centuries and were replaced by tribes living in the heroic style, familiar to us from Homer's account and from the tales of Saul and David in the Bible, and by petty city-states (Hittite, Canaanitish, Philistine, and Aramaic). Only gradually were such small kingdoms as Solomon's built up, and his did not retain its unity even until the Assyrian conquests in the eighth century ushered in a new series of universal states: Neo-Babylonian or Chaldean, Mede, Persian.

But not only was the political map of the Near East transformed; her technology had changed in significant ways. It has long been customary among archaeologists to distinguish the first age of metals, the Age of Bronze, from the succeeding Iron Age. Because it requires a far greater heat to smelt and great technical skill, to temper, iron made its appearance late; or rather it was only gradually improved to take a sharp edge and thus become superior to bronze for most purposes. It was only in the violence of the great invasions that an iron metallurgy, itself one cause of that violence, made its full appearance in the Near East.

[6] The entrance of the Aryans into the Indus valley and the consequent destruction of the civilization of Mohenjo-Daro and Harappa cannot be dated with any certainty. It is often placed about the middle of the millennium, but there is no convincing evidence that it was not contemporary with the troubles farther west.

IRON METALLURGY AND TECHNIQUE

The economic effect of the introduction of iron was to gradually extend and cheapen production of goods. One of the chief reasons for this is that iron ores are widely distributed in the Near East and the Mediterranean and so often available at the surface that it was seldom necessary to mine them. Once the metal could be worked, it was readily available.

Iron tools are more efficient than those of bronze, for the greater hardness and tensile strength of iron make the tool longer-lasting and more versatile. An example of this advantage of iron over bronze can be seen in the sword. During the Bronze Age the sword had developed in efficiency, but its power and use were limited by the strength of the blade. The introduction of iron transferred this limitation to the strength of the human arm.[7] (This change from bronze to iron was to involve little alteration in the form of the sword, but probably a good deal in fighting technique.) The same thing was true of tools: no longer did the user have to consider the ability of the tool to withstand shock or the danger of bending. Efficiency is increased manyfold by this simple removal of the inherent weakness of the metal as a limit on the use of the tool or weapon.

Smelting copper results in a relatively pure ingot of metal. The same technique used on iron, however, results in a different product. A typical iron ore is put into a furnace in which the ore is interlaid with layers of charcoal and then fired and results in what is known as a bloom. A bloom is actually a collection of small particles of iron concealed in a mass of slag and cinders which looks like a dark, rock-hard sponge. The only way to reject the slag and to mold the iron particles together into a lump of raw iron is by repeated heatings and hammerings. The repeated heating and hammering of the iron bloom create a solid mass of iron known as wrought iron.

The discovery that a lump of wrought iron could be produced by hammering the red-hot bloom must have been slow in coming. As early as the first half of the third millennium pieces of man-made iron appeared occasionally in Mesopotamia, Asia Minor, and Egypt. At first the new metal, even when available, was no improvement over copper and bronze. The iron was not as easy to work, it required more fuel, and the cutting edge blunted more easily. The discovery of iron-working techniques was doubtless slowed by the fact that they could in no way be inferred from the properties of the metals already used by the smith (tin, antimony, arsenic, copper, silver, and gold). Only with steel plating may iron be used to its potential, and this was first achieved, apparently, by about 1400 B.C.

The smelting of iron ores on a large scale depended on the invention of a series of new techniques, tools, and processes. First there is correct slagging

[7] H. H. Coughlan, "Metal Implements and Weapons," *History of Technology*, I, pp. 601ff.

of the ore. This involves adding limestone or other flux to the ore in the furnace so that it will not be lost with the noniron residue (slag).[8] Second, the resulting bloom must be repeatedly hammered to get rid of the enclosed cinders and to consolidate the iron globules into a wrought iron bar. This required the development of tongs and hammers to manipulate the heavy, red-hot masses. Third, the wrought iron had to be converted into the more useful steel.[9]

This last step itself involved three techniques. The first is carburizing, the repeated reheating and hammering of the wrought iron while it is heated by charcoal. This adds sufficient carbon to the wrought iron to put a steel coating on it. The second is quenching: the structure of the red-hot steel is preserved by sudden cooling. Such hardened steel will hold an edge. Finally, tempering the hardness of steel by heating it for some time at moderate temperature and slowly cooling it enabled the ancient smith to obtain a tougher and less brittle tool, though at the sacrifice of some hardness. The regularization and interplay of these three techniques determined the success of the ancient smith. As he did not have modern methods of controlling temperature, we need not wonder that he often failed.

With such a metal it was possible to develop new tools, including drills, bits, augers, wedges, and true saws as well as a range of specialized hammers to suit the various trades. Most of our modern small hand tools had come into evidence by the Greek period. They include hinged tongs, frame saws, anvils for making nails, and blocks for drawing wire.[10]

The socket, while an admirable device in casting a bronze tool, is not well suited to an iron axe which cannot normally be cast but must be hammered into shape. But designs changed slowly and several examples of socketed iron axes are found. Iron improved the quality of the chisel, but its design was not changed. Chisels of tempered semisteel could be used against metal, as the cold chisel is today.

The drill, however, has a very different history and its cutting edge (as distinct from the edge of a chisel or point of an awl) appeared only in the Iron Age itself. The development of steel cutting edges into a drill depended upon carburized iron. The bow-drill (Figure 1) looks like a bow and arrow. The "arrow" however is a chisel or awl, with the bowstring looped around it. The awl hole is made by moving the bow back and forth, which makes the drill abrade the wood by circular motion. The carpenter's drill (Figure 2) relies on an entirely different principle. The cutting edges of the "S" drill cut the wood when the handle is turned. The center pin of the drill

[8] For a detailed discussion of Iron Age metallurgical technique, see R. J. Forbes, "Extracting, Smelting, and Alloying," *History of Technology*, I, p. 596.
[9] A limestone flux in the smelting of iron ore—i.e., limestone added to the ore and charcoal—facilitates the fusion of the iron particles into a bloom. Without the flux, the iron particles will not form.
[10] Coughlan, *History of Technology*, I, p. 618.

keeps the drill from "wandering." The drill makes a hole by its cutting edges, not by the abrasion. Steel-plate iron is necessary for this tool, bronze being too soft.

The Iron Age also witnessed marked improvements in the saw. Examples are known of Iron Age saws in which a correct set of the teeth allowed the saw a working clearance in its cut. This certainly increased its efficiency. Probably, however, the earliest iron saws had the "raked" teeth like those of the Stone and Bronze Ages which were little more than files (Figure 3). The teeth extended fully across the cutting edge of the saw, and the board was cut by abrasive action of the teeth. The iron saw is constructed on a different principle. On its cutting edge are two offset rows of teeth, one on each edge (Figure 4). Each tooth is triangular in shape, with each edge of the triangular tooth sharpened. The edge of the tooth cuts rather than rubs the wood; the space between the teeth permits the chips of wood to be removed from the cut by the motion of the saw. They are then deposited outside the cut without interfering with efficient operation. The set to the teeth keeps the cut area in the board slightly wider than the saw blade so that the board edges will not bind the saw on a deep cut. Only with the carburized, hardened, and tempered steel is the metal of sufficient strength, durability, and hardness to develop an efficient crosscut saw. An elementary form of saw with the teeth raked in one direction was also developed. The iron saw with raked teeth acts similarly to the saw with offset teeth, although the raked teeth cut only in one, not in both, directions, as does the saw with set teeth. The raked teeth of the iron saw are sharpened to cut chips of wood from the plank. The spaces between the teeth carry the chips of wood and deposit them outside the cut.

Hinged tongs are essential to the smith who forges at red heat. They must have been invented soon after the dawn of the Iron Age and are represented in a very modern form at a Greek smithy of about 500 B.C. By that time the Iron Age craftsman's kit of tools had been completed.

Considerable care was shown in choosing the best iron for the tools. Spartan iron from the Peloponnesus was the best for files, drills, gravers, and stone chisels. Chalybean iron was used to make carpenter's tools, and the development of iron tools made possible precision wood, ceramic, and metal work. The Bronze Age woodworker could accomplish almost any piece of work possible in later times. Sawing with copper or bronze saws was inefficient, laborious, and uncertain, but the cut piece could be subsequently finished with an adze or rasp. In the Iron Age, woodworking tools became more specialized. The axe and adze lost their status as ubiquitous carpenter's tools, because the carpenter now had one tool for each job.[11] The quality of work did not improve markedly, but speed increased and it became possible to make more use of unskilled labor.[12]

[11] Cyril Aldred, "Fine Wood Work," *History of Technology*, I, p. 689.
[12] We note in a later chapter that in the Greek agora in the fifth century sawyers with iron saws were hired as unskilled labor and spent all their day at sawing wood. Cf., too, Chapter VI on the improved efficiency of shipbuilding.

As important as the improvement of tools was their greater abundance. Compared to bronze, iron is cheap. It must not be thought that the average peasant was well equipped with iron tools, but for the first time the average peasant probably had some few useful metal tools. The results on farming, however, were not striking. At first this is surprising, for we are used to connecting the plow with metals. In neither of the great river valleys, however, was an iron edge to the plowshare of much use, nor was it in the highlands about the fertile crescent. In the wet muck of the valleys, a wooden edge would open the soil well enough to deposit the seed, while in the dry lands the chief problem was simply to scratch the soil sufficiently to prevent the escape of ground water by capillary action.[13] It is only on the heavy soils of northern Europe that the iron plow will have a decisive advantage.

This fact and the fact that the overwhelmingly greater part of the population was directly involved in cultivation accounts for the surprising fact that the introduction of an iron technology and the immense destruction of the social fabric in the great invasions did not result in any considerable innovation in the economic order. Among the Hebrews we can see something of the reconstruction of the ancient state-controlled distributive system and of how and why a barbarous people first entering the framework of civilized life came to adopt the economic organization of their predecessors.

THE IRON AGE ECONOMY OF THE HEBREWS

The Hebrew tribes came into Canaan at the end of the second millennium, principally in the second half of the thirteenth century, as nomads from the fringes of the desert, and first settled in the highlands west of the Jordan (Map V). Though these lands were perhaps better forested and hence moister than now, they were not truly a land of milk and honey. The Hebrews entered them because they were not so heavily settled as the more fertile lowlands, nor defended by fortified cities, and because they provided a refuge from other nomads behind them—the Moabites, Edomites, and Ammonites. Some of the Hebrew nations (tribes) may have had common traditions before entering Canaan, but they were not united. Late in the twelfth century they were attacked by the hordes of Midian and Amalek and the Bne Quedem from the desert; this is the first raid of camel-riding nomads of which we have record.[14] It was in the course of their struggles against such bedouin—the native Canaanites, and the rival newcomers on the coast, the Philistines—that the Hebrews came to form an amphictyony, a league for both religious and military ends.

When the tribes settled on the land, they appear to have broken up into clans (*mishpahah*), settled in typical large Mediterranean villages (which the

[13] Courtenay Edward Stevens, "Agriculture and Rural Life in the Later Roman Empire," *CEH*, I, pp. 96–7.
[14] Judges 6:30; Albright, *The Biblical Period*, p. 41.

authorized translation of the Bible often calls cities), and lived under what the English Bible calls judges (*sophets*). Social life centered in these villages and the old, basic framework of Deuteronomy is largely the law of self-sustaining villages: rules about cities of refuge, unknown murderers, rebellious sons, adultery, the levirate. This organization, based on the clan, survived to some extent under the monarchy and was still a living force on the return from the exile in the late sixth century B.C. (Neh. 7:5; Zach. 12:12–14). Archaeology shows that where Hebrew settlements replace those of the peoples they conquered, their villages are smaller and poorer; population seems to have declined; and there are no considerable buildings which might have been the homes of prosperous landlords. On the other hand the invention of cisterns made it possible to settle on new sites, so that hundreds of new settlements arose where there had been no Canaanitish villages. Examples from the neighborhood of Jerusalem are Gibeah, Ramah, Geba, and Michmas. Considerable woodland east and west of the Jordan was cleared and planted with vines and olives.[15] Here, too, archaeological evidence suggests an egalitarian society. Indeed, since all able-bodied men were—as is typical among the bedouin—warriors, the occupation probably involved an equal distribution of land among the conquerors.

But even in the earlier stages of occupation, there seem to have been forces at work to produce social inequality and the accumulation of wealth. When not simply slaughtered, the Canaanitish population was reduced to servitude, subject to public corvée labor and perhaps other obligations. Possibly, too, even from the conquest, there were special military "fiefs." The early economic and social classes are difficult to make out; there were no nobles or patricians, no plebians, no capitalists, and no proletariat, but there were persons of some wealth before the monarchy was established. Nabal, for instance, a stockbreeder in the highlands of Judah, possessed 3,000 sheep and 1,000 goats, and in order to appease David, his wife, Abigail, could send 200 loaves, 100 bunches of dried grapes, 200 fig cakes, skins of wine, bushels of parched grain, and dressed mutton (I Sam. 25:2,18). It was the monarchy which transformed the social structure, or at least gave direction to the transformation. At Tirsah, the modern Tell el-Farah near Nablus, the houses of the tenth century (the time of David and Solomon) are all of the same size and arrangement. Each is the dwelling of a family which lived in the same way as its neighbors. The contrast with the buildings of the eighth century on the same site is striking: the rich houses are bigger and better built and in a different quarter from that where the houses of the poor are huddled together. Between these two points a social revolution had taken place.[16]

The creation of the monarchy, for which the Hebrews are severely blamed by some of the conservative authors of the older parts of the Hexa-

15 *Ibid.*, pp. 46–7.
16 Roland De Vaux, *Ancient Israel* (New York: McGraw-Hill, 1961), pp. 68ff.

teuch,[17] was made necessary by the Hebrews' desire for more of their neighbors' land, their conflict with the Philistines (who possessed iron and controlled its sources), and the need for defense from camel-riding tribes behind them pressing in from the desert. Under Saul and David, the monarchy became the center of the nation's military effort. About the king a bodyguard of professional soldiers were gathered (his "servants" in II Sam. 11:1, his "mighty men" in II Sam. 23:16). They became the core of the army about whom the older levy of tribal foot soldiers gathered and appear to have been divided into several classes which cannot be made out clearly.

The change was connected, no doubt, with the need for chariots in war with more civilized peoples. The consequences among the Hebrews were similar to those among the Egyptians. The equipment was expensive—in Solomon's reign imported chariots cost 600 shekels of silver, war horses 150 (the shekel was a weight rather than a coin). The men who fought in chariots needed extended training and came to form a special military class about the king, who endowed them with lands.

With David, when the conquest was well advanced, the economy came to be centered about the palace. The court settled at Jerusalem, even then an ancient city. It was a conquest by David himself and unrelated to the older tribal system. It owed allegiance only to him and came to be inhabited largely by his personal retainers, "the slaves or servants of the king," and royal officers, and grew to be the largest center of artisans in the kingdom. At Jerusalem, too, the cult of Jehovah was centered. The blood sacrifice was forbidden in any other place, a rule which the author of Chronicles considered normative, although sacrifices had certainly been performed earlier at several other places. The Levites, on the other hand, were settled in many places about the country, a move which had the double advantage of weakening the influence of a traditionalist class and making religious practice throughout the country more uniform. Two things, however, David did not accomplish: the building of the temple at Jerusalem and the numbering of the people. This is to say that it was left to his son and heir Solomon (973–933) to complete the palace-centered economy.

Solomon's building of the palace and temple symbolized the completion

---

[17] Our sources in the Old Testament fall into two groups; Samuel and Kings; and Chronicles, Ezra, and Nehemiah. Samuel and Kings, in their present state are exilic or even postexilic. That is, they date from the fifth century. The division of Samuel and Kings into two books each is the work of a later editor. Chronicles, Ezra, and Nehemiah are the compilation of an author whose name is also unknown, but who may conveniently be called "the Chronicler." He wrote probably not before 300 B.C. They cover the period from Adam to the return of the exiles permitted by the Persian king Cyrus in 537 B.C. and cover the same period as the other great series of historical books (Genesis to II Kings), from the Creation to 561 B.C., but from a different viewpoint. Their main object is to give a history of Judah with special reference to the institutions of the Temple. The Chronicler used the earlier works, especially Samuel and Kings. The materials and sometimes the words of both authors are earlier; there are probably some later glosses in the text.

of the system. Both our sources give considerable information about their construction and furnishings (I Kings 5:1–8, 66; II Chron. 2:1–7, 22). He reorganized the defenses of the country after having expanded the kingdom by building fortified towns, towns to act as centers of storage, and "cities for his chariots," of which an example has been excavated at Megiddo (II Chron. 8:3–6). He also imported chariots and war horses from the north.

To maintain this system David had organized and Solomon continued an administration centered about the palace. The great offices and their holders are recorded: two secretaries, a recorder, the commander of the army, the king's friend, the major domo of the palace, the officer in charge of forced labor (corvée), and several priests (I Kings 4:2–6). The temple, it should be noted, was not an economically independent administrative unit drawing revenue from its own lands but was maintained from the palace. Its personnel was large, consisting of Levites to act as "officers and judges," gatekeepers, musicians, and guardians of the treasures.

The royal household and chapel were supplied by an organization throughout the country. Israel was divided into twelve parts which did not correspond to the ancient tribes, with a steward set over each. For one month of the year each was responsible for supplying the court (I Kings 4:7). There were also stewards over the king's property: tilled fields, vineyards, wine cellars, olive and sycamore trees in the Shephalah, stores of oil, camels, she-asses, herds, and flocks. "All these were stewards of King David's property" (I Chron. 27:31). Tribute was levied on a number of tribes along the desert margin of the kingdom (cf. the tribute in wool which King Ahab later received from Moab: II Kings 3:4).

Such an economy resembled in its broad outline the central storehouse economy of Egypt and Sumeria in its organization about the palace, but it was not so closely controlled. It was founded on obligations laid upon the Hebrews, both in services and in kind, and upon heavier tribute from the conquered. Only some phases of production were directly controlled by the king's servants and the palace: his herds, mines, and forests. Subject to tribute and the demands of military necessity, the villages and outlying tribes must have controlled and integrated their own economies. Generally this sort of change must have affected all of the empires of the ancient Near East. Politically, empire was superimposed upon local government. None of the conquerors of the ancient Near East possessed the means to administer all of their subjects directly. Old political institutions, therefore, were left intact, subject to service to the superstate. Generally the same was true of the economy. A new and higher level of integration was superimposed, but it continued to be a system revolving about the central storehouse and a status-distributive, input-output system.

As we should expect in such a system foreign trade was directed and controlled from the palace. The cooperation that Solomon received in the building of the temple from King Hiram of Tyre is famous. It involved not only the importation of cedar wood from the mountains of Lebanon but the borrowing of workmen skilled in wood and metals. The actual conduct of foreign trade, too, appears to have been in the hands of the Phoenicians, even of the commerce of the Red Sea. At the head of the Gulf of Aqaba, on the wadi Arabah (Map V), Solomon exploited copper and iron mines and founded an industrial town. Some of the smithies have been excavated. The furnaces are carefully set at an angle to get the full benefit to the strong north winds as drafts to their fires. At Ezion Geber nearby, a port was built and every third year a fleet, manned by sailors supplied by Hiram of Tyre, went to fetch gold, silver, ivory, monkeys, peacocks, and precious stones and woods (particularly woods suitable for musical instruments) from Ophir.[18] Ophir was probably Africa, for the queen of Sheba came by camel caravan from Southern Arabia, where the incense trees grew.[19]

Solomon also traded with desert caravans and may have been the first monarch to exploit the profits of the new trade carried by camel across the desert (I Kings 10:15). His agents bought horses in Cilicia and chariots in Egypt and then resold them both, if the common interpretation of I Kings 10:28–29 is correct. The same pattern of royal control continued after the division of the kingdom. Kings Jehoshaphat of Judah and Ahaziah of Israel joined together to build ships at Ezion Geber to sail to Ophir, but the ships were wrecked. King Ahab made a reciprocal commercial treaty with Ben-hadad of Damascus, by which he set up bazaars in Damascus and Ben-hadad in Samaria.[20]

Solomon's was a splendid empire, though small by earlier or later standards, and it has been enshrined in the memory of the Jewish people. But like most states created by barbarians in a civilized country, it did not long maintain its prosperity. Solomon's building program, his palace, and his administration weighed heavily on the Hebrews. Not only the subject populations (II Chron. 1:17–18), but the Hebrews themselves were required to labor on his buildings (I Kings 5:13). The building of the Temple was probably the justification for this innovation. These burdens were certainly the cause of the revolt of the northern tribes which split the kingdom after Solomon's death.

Like the imperial efforts of the Egyptian Empire, the palace economy created about it new social classes: a privileged priesthood; holders of grants

[18] I Kings 10:11–12. One is reminded of Herodotus' mysterious statement, at first sight unlikely, that the Phoenicians originally came from the Red Sea or Indian Ocean: VII. 89.
[19] I Kings 9:26–28; 10:1–3. Cyrus Gordon, *The Ancient Near East*, 3rd ed. (New York: Norton, 1965) ; Finegan, *Light from the Ancient Past*, p. 152; Nelson Glueck, "The Other Side of the Jordan," *The National Geographic*, LXXXV (January–June 1944), 233–56; de Vaux, *Ancient Israel*, pp. 78–9.
[20] II Chron. 20:35–6; I Kings 22:48–9. The Chronicler says that the ships were to go to Tarshish, but this is impossible, for, wherever Tarshish was (Tarsus in Cilicia, Tartessos in Spain?), it was certainly not in the Red Sea. The author of Kings says "ships of Tarshish to go to Ophir." It is at least possible that the author means a peculiar kind of ship.

of land from the monarchy; persons who could use their contacts with the court to gain land or profit from tribute and from the tasks imposed upon the subject peoples; artisans serving the temple and the court. The system of control and integration does not appear as strict as in the earliest stages of civilized life but closely resembles that of contemporary Egypt and Mesopotamia. Although they were a new and at first barbarous people among the ancient civilized nations of the Near East and although they showed great originality in the realm of the spirit, the Hebrews reconstructed the ancient redistributive system familiar throughout the Near East. In the organization of the economy, they showed no originality.

In only one respect did they do a new thing. For the first time there comes to us a voice of protest. Even in the Pentateuch there are reminiscences of the opposition to the establishment of the monarchy and such consequences of it as the census and taxation. Such innovations are thought contrary to the will of God, for they break with tradition and, therefore, with right order. There is perhaps something like them in the castigation of the rich and of those who have put together estates and oppressed the people in Lagash against which Urukagina took action.[21]

In the prophets the poor for the first time found a voice:

> Hear this, you who trample upon the needy, and bring the poor of the land to an end, saying, "When will the new moon be over, that we may sell grain? And the sabbath, that we may offer wheat for sale, that we may make the ephah [measure] small and the shekel great, and deal deceitfully with false balances, that we may bury the poor for silver and the needy for a pair of sandals, and sell the refuse of the wheat?" [22]

In the concept of a just god the prophets made an appeal against those who were at ease in Zion and who sold the poor for a pair of shoes. Such a concept—that the economic order was subject to divinely ordained moral rules—originating as far as we can see with the Hebrews,[23] was as important for

---

[21] Above, p. 43. Deimel, *Orientalia Commentarii de rebus Assyro-babylonicis arabicis, aegyptiacis*, etc., II (1920), 3–31; *ibid.*, V (1922), 1–25.

[22] Amos 8:4–6.

[23] The peculiar Hebrew view of economic behavior was as closely connected with their religious views as was that of the earlier peoples of whom we have spoken. To be sure, the demand for economic and social justice did not come from the priesthood maintained and privileged in the established order but from the prophets. But the prophets appealed to a god very different from that known among the pagans. The greatest originality of the Hebrews was not their monotheism (which developed only late and slowly), but their conviction that God was not to be found in nature, in anything that one might see or feel or smell or taste. Rather he transcended the created universe, and just as God was absolute, so his moral law could be. When the prophets appealed to a transcendent god, they appealed also to a transcendent moral law divorced from nature and even, at its extremes, from tradition. Such a law was valid not because it was convenient or profitable, not even because it produced human happiness, but because it was laid down by a transcendent god. See William A. Irwin in *The Intellectual Adventure of Ancient Man*, ed. Henri Frankfort, pp. 233ff.

the future as the beginnings of analytic economic thought in Greece. The normative rules of economic behavior transmitted from Judaism to Christianity and the European culture were so solid that nineteenth-century industrialism, capitalism, and free trade could not eradicate them.

EGYPT IN THE IRON AGE

Elsewhere, too, the Bronze Age distributive (nonmarket) economy was reconstructed on an Iron Age technology. In Egypt the system of the late Bronze Age survived, first under native pharaohs and then under foreign conquerors. But Egypt was a broken reed. She was unable to reestablish her domination in Palestine and to prevent the establishment of Solomon's monarchy in the tenth century. Subsequently she was conquered by the Assyrians and the Persians. There were probably two or three reasons for her declining strength and independence. Egypt lacks any local source of iron, nor are sources conveniently available, and thus Egypt could not develop an iron economy to compete with her northern neighbors. She lacks good pasture for horses, even though she had been successful at the tactics of chariot fighting under the Empire. Nor was her enviable isolation such an advantage in the growing maritime life of the Mediterranean. She did not, and perhaps could not, take the lead in Mediterranean commerce. Finally, the Empire had bequeathed to Egypt a great burden in the immense temple estates, which appear to have made little or no contribution to Egypt's conduct of foreign affairs and to have imposed a greater burden on the rest of the country.

So tenacious, then, were the old centers of their ancient civilization that after the confusion of a heroic and barbarous age, most of the regions of the ancient Near East managed to restore the ancient economic system and apply it to the new technology, and so to produce a tolerably stable social order, though one which seems, at first sight at any rate, less firm than the old one. The Hebrews in Palestine introduced remarkable innovations in religion, but their social order and their economic system, when once they settled as peasants on the land and erected a state in the monarchy of David and Solomon and their successors, appears to have been modeled on the ancient royal and temple economies of Babylonia and Egypt.

THE PHOENICIAN INNOVATION

Only on the extreme periphery of the civilized world was the old system too weak to weather the storm. No great state and no equally highly developed economy appears to have replaced the Hittites in central and eastern Anatolia, while the Aegean world foundered in the chaos of the Greek heroic age so brilliantly but imperfectly revealed to us by Homer. Yet it was just in these regions of western Asia Minor, the Aegean, and the Greek peninsula, where

civilization was most sorely tried and indeed destroyed, that the great innovation of the market followed the revolution of an Iron Age technology. We
shall look at that innovation in the next chapter. It is our business here to
view the first people to make any serious innovation in the economic order
as a result of the great invasions and the introduction of iron, the Phoenicians.

The Canaanites, overcome by the invading Aramaeans, Philistines, and
Hebrews, were driven from most of Syria and Palestine to a narrow strip of
sea coast. From roughly the eleventh century on they may be called Phoenicians. Having lost some nine-tenths of their land, they were forced to undertake an intensification of their mountainous hinterland. Here the discovery
of plaster made with slaked lime made possible cisterns impervious to water
and habitation in places before empty and would also make possible the
colonization of waterless islands all over the Mediterranean. The vast forests
of Lebanon and the discovery of iron there enabled the Phoenicians to build
ships and arm the sailors of the coastal towns: Sidon, Tyre, Beirut, and
Aradus.[24] The disappearance of the Mycenaeans from maritime trade in the
twelfth century opened the way for these cities which were independent until
the Assyrian attacks in the ninth century and managed even to maintain
their independence for some time thereafter. Some of them, indeed, proved
their value to the inland empires of the Assyrians and Persians sufficiently to
be allowed considerable self-government and economic freedom even after
their conquest. There can be little doubt, however, that their early independence was necessary for the formation of new economic habits and patterns
which permitted the organization of their policies to plant colonies and extend their trade throughout the Mediterranean.[25]

The chronology proposed by Albright for this development is reasonable,
although it cannot yet be thought established. The Phoenicians were in
Cyprus, at Citium (see Map VII), perhaps as early as the late eleventh century; probably their next establishments were in western Sicily (first on such
islands as Malta and Motya, which were relatively safe from native attacks
and which the techniques of cistern building made more attractive than they
had earlier been). A colony and iron foundry at Nora in Sardinia seem to
have been flourishing in the early ninth century so that its foundation should
probably be pressed back several generations. Utica in Africa was presumably
earlier than Gades and Tartessus in Spain, which the Phoenicians possessed
by c. 950, the time of Hiram I of Tyre and Solomon. Carthage was founded
at the end of the ninth century. But the foundation of Carthage marked the
beginning of the decline of Phoenician domination, as the colony [26] must
soon have begun to rival the mother city, and Greek colonization in Italy and

[24] Albright, *Studies in the History of Culture*, pp. 32–4.

[25] The ancient use of the word "colony," both Phoenician and Greek, is rather different
from the modern. A colony was an independent city, linked to the mother city by ties of
affection and of religion, but not ordinarily dependent politically.

[26] Albright, *Studies in the History of Culture*, pp. 43–6.

Sicily began to compete commercially. The end was marked by the Neo-Babylonian (Chaldean) capture of Tyre in 572 B.C. The Phoenician cities remained important until the conquests of Alexander, but they no longer played a great part in the western commerce.

Unfortunately we know very little of the economic organization of the Phoenician cities. (Even their political organization is obscure.) They have left no records comparable to the cuneiform tablets of Mesopotamia or to the literary tradition and inscriptions of the later Greeks. At Tyre we hear of kings, like Hiram, and at Carthage of *suffetes* (the word is the same as that which the English Bible translates as judges; the Romans equated them roughly to their consuls). Such kings as Hiram were themselves merchants. This, of course, is not unique. It appears something of an extension and an extreme development of those gift exchanges we saw among the monarchs of the Amarna age. The pharaohs and the kings of the Hittites sought by these exchanges to enhance their prestige by possession of exotic goods and to gain those necessities their own lands did not produce, while the Phoenician cities, in fact, produced very little and their whole existence, or at least their prosperity, depended upon commercial activity. The role of the Phoenician cities, then, was that of the older ports of trade like Ugarit in Syria, for the great continental states still avoided direct contact with the outside and the opening of their economies to uncontrolled outside mercantile activity.

But the Phoenicians' activity differed from that of the older Syrian centers in several significant ways. For one, they were more successful in maintaining their political independence. Consequently the state was probably better able to support its citizens' economic activity abroad and to organize trade in less traditional ways. Perhaps this is the reason that the Phoenicians were able to adopt and popularize a revolutionary innovation, the alphabet. They were not its inventors but they appear to have been the first people to use it widely, and many other peoples, like the Greeks, adopted it from them. Consider its advantages and disadvantages. It had no traditional, sacred associations and so was not suitable to sacred writing or to such uses as Egyptian hieroglyphic for the decoration of temple walls and tombs. A society dominated by a priesthood, then, would resist it. But it was relatively easy to learn and, from the point of view of merchants, this was a great advantage. They could learn it themselves and do their own writing or they could hire clerks more cheaply to write for them or train slaves to do it. In more traditionally oriented societies, where the convenience of commerce did not dominate social life, the professional and more or less hereditary class of clerks would resist such a transformation, as they did in Mesopotamia. In the Phoenician cities commercial convenience was triumphant.

This independence was long maintained. They fortified themselves against the land and the sea, and even under the Assyrians and the Persians kept considerable local autonomy. The Persians never built or manned a fleet but depended upon the Phoenicians. The Phoenicians in return remained loyal to the Great King, and perhaps Alexander the Great's most difficult accomplishment was the siege of the island on which Tyre stood.[27]

The Phoenicians were also far more venturesome and active than the inhabitants of the older centers such as Ugarit. This was true not only when the state backed such enterprises as the founding of colonies. The Phoenicians acted as intermediaries in other peoples' commerce. Homer retains the tradition that they traded in the Aegean. The "chief trader" of the Assyrian king Nebuchadnezzar II bore the typical Phoenician name of Hanno. The Phoenicians traded in the grain of Egypt. They crossed Israel and Judah to the Red Sea and dominated foreign trade among the Jews, leaving only the barter of local farm goods to the peasants.[28] There was as yet no Jewish merchant class.

The Phoenicians acted as middlemen and perhaps exploited the resources of backward peoples. Their own land supplied few goods of value in trade. The most famous are the cedars and the shellfish called the murex, that supplied a brilliant red (purple, violet) dye.[29] Heaps of shells or vats have been found near Tyre and Sidon and on Cape Bon in modern Tunisia, near Carthage.

The dye was very expensive and much desired. It gave rise to an export of cloths. Flax and cotton were imported from Egypt, wool from Mesopotamia, and improved weaving techniques were developed by taking advantage of and combining the methods of both countries. The Phoenicians also produced some exceptional furniture from their fine woods at a time when more elaborate and plentiful furniture was gradually coming into use. The Assyrian palaces were far more elegant and elaborate in this respect than the Sumerian had been. Phoenicia also produced "objets de Paris": ivory carvings, small metal objects, and semiprecious stones for jewelry and trinkets. Some were almost like the trade goods distributed by nineteenth-century Europeans in Africa, others far better. But it was not by the production of such goods that the Phoenicians and their colonists in North Africa carried on a trade which must have been larger than that of Ugarit, and which spread over a greater sphere than that of the Minoans and Mycenaeans. Their commercial prominence was rather based on their role as intermediaries and entrepreneurs.

[27] The part taken by the Phoenicians in the naval operations of the two Persian campaigns against Greece is described by Herodotus, vii–ix passim. Some investigations of the ports have been undertaken: A. Poidebard, *Un grand port disparu, Tyr. Recherches aériennes et sous-marines* (Paris: Librairie Orientaliste, Paul Geuthier, 1939) ; and A. Poidebard and J. Lauffray, *Sidon, amènagements antiques du port de Saïda, étude aérienne, au sol, et sous-marine*, 1946–1950 (Beirut: Ministry of Public Works, Republic of Lebanon, 1951).
[28] Isaiah 23:1–11.
[29] D. Harden, *The Phoenicians* (New York: Praeger, 1962), p. 146: "The murex, when it is dead and putrefied, secretes a yellowish liquid which provides—according to the strength used—tones ranging from rose to dark violet; for the darker tones exposure to the sun is necessary. The method was to break the shell, extract the fish and deposit it in vats, where the dye liquified out." Cf. Arist. *Hist. Anim.* v. 15.

Yet the Phoenicians did not radically break with the economic organization of the past, nor were they numerous and powerful enough to act as a leaven in the Near East as a whole. The economic order, and consequently the social order, was to be transformed by a people who had passed into barbarism during the great invasions and who only slowly emerged from it during the Phoenician economic ascendency: the Greeks.

6 THE APPEARANCE OF THE MARKET AND MONEY IN GREECE BEFORE THE FIFTH CENTURY

MEDITERRANEAN GEOGRAPHY

In spite of the successful reintegration of the status-distributive economies of the ancient Near East at the end of the second millennium, a new, looser economy appears to have been made possible by the middle of the first millennium. It was directed largely by the market rather than by an integrated social order of status relationships. This was due to the different geographical situation and profound changes in technology. The geography of the Mediterranean, to which the scene now moves, did not call for the great bureaucratic social control of agriculture necessary in Egypt and Mesopotamia, based as they were on irrigation and drainage. Agriculture here was based on rain water, needed less social control, and thus allowed more individual initiative.

Since goods could be moved to a great variety of places by ship, the Mediterranean presented the emerging Greek societies of the Iron Age with far wider opportunities for long distance trade than the ancient Orient had enjoyed: in Egypt and Mesopotamia bulky goods could only be moved up and down river. Full advantage of the versatility of the great sea's ports and routes had to wait until the Iron Age. Only in the Iron Age did anything comparable to the volume of Greek seaborne commerce appear, but once the necessary technology developed, the Greeks were not alone in taking advantage of it. As Map VII shows, they had a rival—and one slightly in advance of them—in the Phoenicians. Iron effected trade and its organization profoundly in two respects. First, it brought about a revolution in ship-building. Even if the earliest part of the first millennium saw no major improvements in navigation or in construction—which is not certain—the use of iron tools must have made ships far easier to build and hence far cheaper (to use modern terminology) than they had ever been when made with tools of bronze and stone.

The second reason for the new scale of commercial life in the Iron Age is that a much larger part of the population began to want products that it could not make itself. In the Bronze Age economy, as we have seen, the city and the artisan had had little to offer the peasant that he could possibly afford. Manufacturing had been organized about the court and the temple and maintained by levies on the peasantry—whether taxes or rent—for which little economic return was made. But iron was cheaper than bronze, and iron tools, weapons, and armor were objects desired by every peasant, merchant, and artisan, as well as by rulers and priests. Hence the first half of the first millennium B.C. saw the opening of new economic possibilities and the possibility of new economic organization.

The next major innovation after the revolution brought about by the invention and spread of iron in the new physical and social environment of the Mediterranean—and in a sense dependent upon it—was the invention of the market based upon household production. This innovation made possible, indeed made inevitable, profoundly new economic and social forms which it will be the major concern of the rest of this book to discuss. But as these developments took place in a different geographical situation, it will be necessary to speak first of the geography of the Mediterranean [1] and then of the social order of the Greeks and some of the other peoples who inhabited it.

If one excepts certain areas under peculiar conditions: Egypt, of course; the Po Valley in northern Italy, which receives perennial streams from the Alps and thus has a significantly different hydrology; and the two great plateaus of Castile and Anatolia, whose barren uplands are entirely un-Mediterranean, the geography of the great inland sea is homogeneous; as one moves from southern Spain to Syria there is no basic change comparable to the difference, say, between London and Moscow on the great plain of northern Europe. The climate is so uniform and so characteristic as to give geographers the term "Mediterranean climate," which is applied also to a few other regions: southern California and the Central Valley of California, central Chile, and small parts of South Africa and Australia.

The cycle of weather is distinctive and in many ways favorable to human habitation. In the winter the Mediterranean lies in the path of the dominant water-bearing westerlies coming across the Atlantic. Blocked by the Castillian plateau and the Atlas Mountains, they enter through the straits of Gilbraltar and the gap between the Pyrenees and the Cévennes of southern France. Because of the difference of temperature between the warm waters of the Mediterranean and the cooler hinterlands, the region produces local cyclones and wind eddies which subject the sea to sudden squalls during the winter and closed the sea to ancient mariners during the winter months (see discussion below and Map VIII).

Considerable winter rain results, rising to a height in October and March, but sufficient in all the winter months. Rainfall, however, tends to be errati-

---

[1] The best survey of the subject for the historian is Cary, *The Geographic Background of Greek and Roman History*. See also John L. Myres, *Geographical History in Greek Lands* (Oxford: Clarendon Press, 1953).

cally distributed, for the sea was formed by the folding of mountains and everywhere the small plains are separated and interrupted by abrupt heights. Rain-bearing winds meeting these mountains are forced up, cool, and deposit their moisture on the windward side. Some regions, therefore, like the western slopes of southern Italy, have sufficient rains to maintain dense hardwood forests, while others, like the depression in which Athens is placed, are peculiarly dry.

The Mediterranean escapes the numbing effect of long northern winters —and incidentally has a low fuel bill, which is fortunate, for her forests are very limited. She escapes, too, long periods of dark and depressing gloom. Although the weather can be erratic and even dangerous, there are no prolonged fogs and clouded skies. The remarkable clarity of light upon the accidented landscape can be seen in paintings from the Tuscan renaissance to the landscapes of the Provençal Cézanne but is perhaps most striking in Greece.

When the Atlantic gales cease in April, the immense heat of the Sahara sucks up air from the north, and the Mediterranean comes under the influence of winds from the Eurasian land mass, which contain little moisture. Day after day the sky is almost clear and the sun's rays beat down almost horizontally. The mean temperature is 76° at Rome in July and 80° at Athens, which is dreadfully hot and makes one shudder to think of those few districts where it rises to 90°. The winds, however, are generally cool, except in hot spots like the Athenian hollow which they do not reach, and the air is dry, so that the heat is not so enervating as it is in moist tropical climates.

From the farmer's point of view, the chief disadvantage is the summer drought. Of the thirty inches of annual rainfall, more than twenty come in the winter. Most of the Mediterranean has no rain for several months in the summer, just at the time when growth would otherwise be best. This shortcoming can rarely be corrected by irrigation. Egypt from the beginning of history and the Po Valley from a much later date are exceptions, for both the Nile and the Po receive their waters from mountains outside the Mediterranean hydraulic system. Irrigation on a much smaller scale has been practiced elsewhere, as by the Moors in southern Spain, but few streams are suitable for irrigation on a large scale, as many go dry in the summer. Even such considerable rivers as the Tiber lose a great part of their volume during the drought, for the mountains are not sufficiently high to retain their snows through the summer heat, nor are their soils and forests heavy and dense enough to store great amounts of water. The limestone mountains of the Mediterranean are permeable. Water runs easily into and through them until it meets a layer of less pervious rock, when it will run between the two layers until it bursts out of the mountain side in a gushet. Artesian wells, therefore, are numerous and delightful, and were praised by the classic poets:

O fons Bandusiae, splendidior vitro.

THE PATTERN OF SETTLEMENT

The hydrology and the topography of the middle sea combine to force a certain typical pattern of settlement. The Mediterranean area is generally rugged, much cut up by small mountain ranges and by barren areas. The typical cultivable areas are small plains, the typical settlement a large village located by a source of water. The isolated farmstead, typical in America and common in some parts of northern Europe, is unusual in the Mediterranean. These villages are much the same, as respects a pattern of settlement from Mediterranean Spain all the way along the coast to Syria. They are the Latin *vicus* or *villa*, the Greek *kome*, and what the Bible calls "cities" or "towns" in the King James and some other translations. In archaic Greece and later in a much wider sphere under the political influence of Rome, it was possible for some three or four such villages to join in a political or even in a physical union giving birth to the classic polis, but in some districts like Palestine the city was never typical. Both the city, in this sense, and the large village were typical of the Mediterranean for almost the whole course of historical time. Only the modern innovations of piped water and a national police have begun to break up the ancient pattern of settlement.

Except for its abundance of excellent building stone (limestone and marble chiefly), the Mediterranean is not well supplied with minerals. Neither coal nor oil were important in the ancient economy. The supplies of gold and silver, although famous, were not plentiful; few mines had a long life. Copper and iron were more abundant and during classical antiquity appear to have been adequate to demand. Tin was the most important metal permanently deficient. It is a measure of the ancient world's modest requirements in metal that Spain had much the same reputation among the Greeks and Romans as a source of metals that the New World had in the sixteenth century.[2]

The sea supplied fish, which appear to have been a more important element in the common diet than meat. The Mediterranean is not a major fishing ground. It lacks such shallow spawning grounds as the Newfoundland shoals and Dogger Bank, and many of the most valuable and numerous food fish—cod, herring, and sole—are excluded by the warmth of the water. The large tunny was the only important food fish that traveled in great schools and gave rise to anything like the mass fishing and salting enterprise that developed in the Baltic and North seas during the Middle Ages. Local catches brought in the various *frutti di mare:* cockles, mussels, octopi, and squid, still much prized by natives, if not by their foreign guests.

[2] O. Davies, *Roman Mines in Europe* (Oxford: Clarendon Press, 1935).

The plant life is peculiar and tolerably uniform and is, of course, determined by the climate, which does not wholly suspend growth in the winter. The long, clear summers favor the growth of fruits, but summer droughts deny water to garden and grain field just when it is most needed. In the mountain regions above 3,000 feet the vegetation (thickets of deciduous trees and summer pasture) is much the same as in Western Europe north of the Alps. Below 3,000 feet the full effects of the summer drought are felt. From 1,500 to 3,000 feet is the region of the *maquis:* scrub evergreen, laurel, junipers, gorse, thyme, and acanthus. (The agave and cactus, now common, are New World imports.) These badlands cannot be brought into production but are not wholly profitless. Aside from their herbs, they support great numbers of bees and hence provide honey. This was perhaps less important to the Mediterranean than to northern Europe, for Mediterranean fruits, especially the grape, are extraordinarily good sources of sugar, but honey was the chief sweetener before the Arabs introduced the cultivation of sugar cane in the Middle Ages. Today—and probably in ancient times as well—this region's strongly scented flowers support a perfume industry.

The lowlands, however, support most of the population and produce the basic crops on which the population lives. Their soils consisting mostly of light clays and marls rich in plant food are easily worked. Oats, which require a damp, cool summer, are rarely grown; maize and rice thrive today in the wetter areas but were unknown in antiquity. Wheat and barley were the major grains. The season of work in the grain fields differs greatly from that familiar to Americans and northern Europeans. Plowing and sowing come in the fall, the harvest in the spring.

Ancient works on agriculture by Hesiod, Xenophon, Cato, Varro, Columella, the elder Pliny, and Palladius provide a far better picture of the agricultural regime than we have of any other aspect of the classical economy, and doubtful points can often be filled in from modern information, since the climate has not altered and in many places the methods of the peasant have not changed radically.

Besides wheat and barley for bread and porridge, the grape and the olive are the basis of Mediterranean agriculture. The grape, of course, can be produced in a wide district north of the typical Mediterranean clime, but the range of the olive is an excellent measure of the true Mediterranean. Wine played an important part in the diet as well as in conviviality. The olive was the chief source of fats in a diet which had little meat, milk, or butter. It was also used for washing, for lye soaps were not much produced until the Middle Ages.

Other orchard products were important: the pear and the cherry were introduced from Persia and Iran and the apple from northern Europe, but citrus fruits were probably unknown. It is sometimes thought that the golden apples of the Hesperides were oranges, but whether or not this is true, the widespread cultivation of citrus fruits waited until their development by the Arabs in North Africa and Spain.[3]

Such a regime has certain peculiar social advantages worth pointing out. In the northern regimes of agriculture more familiar to most readers, work tends to accumulate in back-breaking loads in the spring and fall. It is urgent to get into the fields as soon as they are dry enough to plow; it is urgent to harvest the crop before a frost and before it is lodged by wind or hail. As late as the eighteenth century, the statute of apprentices of the city of London required that all apprentices—butchers, bakers, costermongers, clothiers—go out to help with the harvest. The Mediterranean regime, on the other hand, spaces work rather nicely. Work on the three basic crops—grain, olives, and grapes—comes at different times and there are rarely such periods of crisis as the northern spring and fall. Throughout the year there are days on which peasants need not tend to business. The short interruptions made it possible for the Greek and the Roman peasant to walk to town to attend to public affairs; this was perhaps a necessary prerequisite to the development of the classical ideal of citizenship. On the other hand, the fact that agricultural work continued throughout the year made chattel slavery more profitable, or at least more economically tolerable, than in northern Europe or the great river valleys where it appears never to have played an important part in agricultural exploitation. In these areas it was probably simply too expensive to maintain a slave through the long winter idleness and the slack periods of the summer.

Such is the geographical setting of classic civilization and such the agricultural regime to which it was subject. It will be seen that conditions were sufficiently different from those dominant in the Near East as to lead one to expect a different sort of economic growth, and perhaps this new setting was as important as the introduction of iron in producing an economy less subject to social controls, an economy of the market. There was, for example, in most of the Mediterranean no need for the extensive organization of drainage and irrigation which forced governments in Egypt and Mesopotamia to regiment their peasants. During much of the agricultural year, there was no serious farm work to be done, though the work was surely laborious at times. In this seasonal leisure for the peasant, the Mediterranean stands in contrast both to the great river valleys of the earlier civilizations and to the later developments

[3] It is worth noting here how many of the plants now so common to the Mediterranean as to be thought typical were unknown to the ancients. Oranges, lemons, and mandarines were brought from the Far East by the Arabs; cotton, of which much of the best is today grown in Egypt, was known to the Assyrians, but not much cultivated until Moslem times; the cactus, agave, and aloe were brought from America, as were the potato, tomato, and tobacco; the eucalyptus came from Australia; the aubergine from India; maize from Mexico; the pimento from Guyana. The peach reached the Mediterranean from the mountainous regions of China by way of Iran in classical times. The Greeks and Romans had not the green bean. Rice was not widely grown until Moslem times.

in northern Europe. Seasonal idleness in the great river valleys had produced the great public works, the ziggurats and pyramids. They would have no parallel in classic antiquity until the Roman Empire learned to marshall the immense manpower of its army and of captive slaves. On the other hand, the Mediterranean seasons appear to have made it possible for the Greek peasant to take part in the social and political life of the community, in fact to become a citizen.

The original advantage of the river valleys over the neolithic upland agriculture dependent upon rain had been a superior surplus product. If any other ecological region could produce a similar or superior surplus without the immense mass labor and bureaucratic rigidity of these civilizations, it should possess the basis for a comparable or superior economy. It would appear that the Iron Age technology made such a development possible, first in Aegean Greece and then in the Mediterranean generally, and that the market supplied the more flexible means of distribution and exchange compatible with the lesser degree of social control demanded by the agricultural system.

In theory it should be possible to work out a typology of the chief types of agriculture in human history, since they depend upon the climate and the plants and animals available. From such a typology one could explain much about the differences among human societies, for the greatest elements of the economic and social order are necessarily dependent upon its agricultural pattern:

1. The river valleys of the Tigris, Euphrates, and Nile produced a dense, contiguous population over a considerable area, used the plow, and demanded major water works. The plow made agriculture dominantly men's work and required draft animals. The presence of waste country nearby also contributed to the major part that animals played in these civilizations. The need for irrigation and drainage produced a centralized government and a bureaucracy.

2. The Mediterranean and northern Europe, though in different degrees, knew seasonal labor. Like the Near East, their chief food was small grains and the chief tool the plow; animals played a great part.

3. Tropical agriculture was not seasonal, at least in the sense it is in temperate climates. It depends far more on tree and root crops and has no use for the plow. The garden rather than the field dominates it. There is a description of such a garden, one in Guatemala, in Edgar Anderson's *Plants, Man, and Life*, pp. 136ff. The radical differences in the problems faced by tropical farmers have at times made fruitless the efforts of experts from the United States and Western Europe to advance backward economies.

(We might note in passing that, while millet culture was introduced into the narrow best of the Sudan, the moderately watered zone south of the Sahara desert, at least by the second millennium B.C., true tropical agriculture in African forest regions had to wait upon the introduction of products from abroad, for none of the important forest food crops is indigenous to Africa. The most important crops in these areas today are maize and cassava, both of which came from America in the sixteenth and seventeenth centuries. Earlier the main crops had been borrowings from southeast Asia: the banana, the Asian yam, and the coco yam. Since none appear to have arrived before the beginning of the Christian era, there was a time lag of some two or three thousand years between the development of the forest and that of the savannah. See Oliver and Fage, *Africa*, pp. 27–8.)

4. The maize-bean culture of Mexico and the southwestern United States was based on garden-sized plots: beans, maize, and other plants were sown in the same hills. The plow was unknown, and there were no draft animals. Domesticated animals played a small role in farming.

5. Many of the same characteristics were true of the farming of Peru, which was based on the potato.

6. The rice-growing agriculture of southeast Asia is more akin to the tropical garden than to the field system of Europe and North America. The plow is not used, though oxen do tread the wet fields. Animal husbandry, milk, cheese, and meat play a small role, and the entire development of milling and bread making, which in the West played a part in the development of technology, the accumulation of capital, and the division of labor between the sexes, among other things, is absent.

MEDITERRANEAN ECONOMY

The great migrations of peoples in the late second millennium, which we have connected with the introduction of an iron-based technique of warfare, involved the devastation of the older Mycenaean Greek civilizations of the islands and the peninsula by Dorian tribes from the north. We have seen that the central regions of the civilized world survived these invasions more or less intact or were able to reconstruct something much like their old economic and social order. But the Hittite civilization of Anatolia and the Mycenaean-Minoan culture of Greece and Crete disappeared. The Greece which Homer reveals to us is a heroic society of clans and tribes living under petty kinglets or chiefs, whom his imagination and the collective memory dress with a legendary grandeur and wealth borrowed from Mycenae and Knossos.[4] Under these chiefs, the Hellenes created on their islands and in the many little plains of the mainland a multitude of tiny states which developed into *poleis* (singular: polis), a word we awkwardly translate as "city-states." Hampered and limited at every turn by a clan nobility which controlled the greater part of the population and the land, these kings were unable to reconstruct a system of social and economic control comparable to that revealed by the Linear B tablets found at Pylos and other earlier Greek sites. On the contrary, in the formation of the polis the aristocrats disembarrassed themselves of their hereditary kings or reduced their powers to those of religious

[4] Interestingly enough, he remembers, too, that the Mycenaeans fought with bronze rather than iron weapons.

offices. (The only important exception was Sparta, and even there royal power was much limited.) The Greeks to the north, in Thessaly and Macedonia, continued to live in tribal groupings under kings, which by the time our continuous literary record opens distinguished them sharply from the peoples about the Aegean. Everywhere about the sea, the aristocracies created public offices and magistracies to replace and to divide the royal power.[5]

Under such uncentralized and divided political regimes the iron technology and the relative ease of transport by sea during the summer appear eventually to have made it possible in Greece for the peasant to enter the system of exchanges as a member of a family or clan rather than of a status-oriented distributive system.[6]

During the first settlement of the Dorians in Greece, landed property undoubtedly was the possession of the clan rather than of the individual. The clan chief who exercised control over the whole number of his relatives controlled the clan's land as well, but it did not strictly belong to him. It rather belonged to the whole lineage, the living and the dead in their graves, and to the family symbolized by the fire kept burning on the family altar.[7] Family property was inalienable: the land itself, the graves of the ancestors, the altar, the images of the gods of the family (what the Romans would call *lares* and *penates*), and the sacred utensils.[8]

Such clans later broke up into nuclear families and property eventually became alienable, but the primitive system gave rise to a household system of production that survived through the classical period—not only among the Greeks, but among the Italians and Romans, and many other peoples of the Mediterranean sphere. The Homeric poems give much evidence of the largely self-sustaining household economy among the kings of Greece and the poems of Hesiod reflect the same system among the commons a bit later. The family, of course, ate the food of its own lands; its flocks supplied wool which was

[5] There is an excellent statement of this political development in H. D. F. Kitto, *The Greeks* (Baltimore: Penguin Books, 1951), pp. 64–78.

[6] There is much talk about individualism in certain periods of history: the Italian Renaissance, the late Roman Republic, and the fifth century in Greece. It is all rather loose and hardly comparable to the individualistic economic activity of the nineteenth and twentieth centuries. Men acted far more as part of a kinship group and in the interests of a family. The most striking and easily attainable proof is usually that marriages were arranged by relatives and generally made on economic grounds.

[7] See the brilliant, too systematic, reconstruction by Numa Denis Fustel de Coulanges, *The Ancient City*.

[8] We do not, of course, know conditions and practice in detail. By inalienable, we presumably mean that the land could not be sold away from the clan in the ordinary course of affairs; it was not on the market, just as the Masai and the Fulani do not sell their cattle in the ordinary course of affairs and do not raise cattle for the market nor take advantage of the fluctuations of the market, though they sell cattle, women, and children when forced by economic crises. See Paul Bohannan and George Dalton, *Markets in Africa. Eight Subsistence Economies in Transition* (Anchor Books; Garden City, N.Y.: Doubleday and Co., 1965), p. 17; and Marguerite Dupire, *ibid.*, pp. 94ff.

spun by the women, free as well as slave. Skill at the spindle and loom was the pride of many noble and even royal women, like Penelope. The hero Odysseus made his own bed and was able to build ships. In the common necessities, then, the family was self-sufficient. It is not hard, under such economic circumstances, to understand why the Greeks thought that almost the worst fate that could befall a man was exile. To be homeless was, in simple fact, to be without the common resources of life.

Some goods, however, could not be produced in this way, for they demanded greater skill than the making of cloth or furniture. Among the Homeric population was a class of skilled craftsmen, the demiourgoi, who worked for the public; smiths were the leading members of this class. Like the early modern tinker or the contemporary knife sharpener, they moved about from place to place seeking work and doing it on the spot. They were not, however, subject to the indignities and penury of exile, for their services were in demand and they were members of powerful gilds or mysteries. Their products must have included many common and necessary items of iron: cooking utensils, bits and bridles, some farm tools, knives, and common weapons. But they also included things of great artistic and intrinsic value: armor, swords, and spears for the nobles; and cauldrons and tripods (in which wealth was sometimes reckoned). The smiths were, no doubt, paid in one manner or another, but their occasional presence did not constitute a market for labor, and the goods they made did not move from one man to another by sale. They would ordinarily pass from father to son, but they might also be prizes in contests and gifts as well, of course, as booty in war. They were treasures which illustrated a great family's eminence and honor.

The entrance of such small, independent, and uncontrolled household groups into the distributive system seems to call forth a system of exchanges which, if it becomes complex enough and deals with considerable enough things, cannot easily be carried on by casual barter.[9] They seem to call for the creation of a market and a medium of exchange, namely coins. But the evolution from the heroic age of Homer to the market economy of fifth-century Athens was long. The crisis of the archaic age involved not only much social strife and structural change in society, but the creation of new attitudes towards wealth and measure.[10]

[9] Under exceptional circumstances, this may not be true. The Hudson's Bay Company's business with Indian trappers was a matter of barter without money, but the conditions were unusual.

[10] Historians are prone to lament the obscurity of the periods in which they are interested and to lament generally the loss of information about the past, while laymen perhaps doubt that enough has been buried. Yet if we wish to understand the economic development of the Western world, we must confess that the obscurity of early Greek history is especially regrettable. Homer wrote at an uncertain date about the Mycenaean society which had passed away long before his birth. Our first Greek historians were Herodotus and Thucydides, both of whom lived in the fifth century and neither of whom was much interested in earlier times. The modern historian must make do with what they tell of earlier times, with the

THE ARCHAIC CRISIS

By the late seventh and the sixth centuries, the traditional aristocratic governments of the more advanced Greek city-states which had replaced the Homeric monarchies faced a social crisis in which the ancient solidarity of the clan was breaking up and the land was more and more engrossed by noble families. The peasants who lost their land were reduced by debt to a status approaching that of serfdom or were sold as slaves beyond the frontier. At one time, when the origins of coinage were put at an earlier date than they are today, this crisis was sometimes attributed to the introduction of money. It may, in fact, be due, at least in part, to the growth of trade with the East for luxury goods and to the aristocrats' desire for such goods and the prestige that they brought. We know from the designs upon pottery that the growth of trade in the seventh century brought a considerable oriental influence to Greece. It is, then, a fair surmise that the Greeks were beginning to import luxuries from the East. There is also evidence that Greek craftsmen were beginning to produce fine wares for the aristocracy. (Again pottery is our most impressive evidence.) There was developing something of a courtly way of life which can be seen in the fragments of the early poets and most clearly in the latest aristocratic poets who protested the much later change to democracy, Theognis of Megara and Pindar.

---

archaic poets (most of them very fragmentary), and with what little material archaeology can provide. Since ancient writers are generally so little interested in economic matters, in production (except for agriculture), or in trade, we are dependent upon what the spade can give. For the development of commerce and the movement of goods, this means chiefly identifying the origin and dates of pottery and coins. Pottery was itself an object of trade and was the common container of wine and olive oil shipped from one district to another, for the glass bottle and the barrel are both later inventions (from the point of view of the economic record, unfortunate ones). Apart from being breakable, pottery is practically indestructible. Shards are found in large quantities on most ancient sites. Coins can be excellent for dating and for some other purposes, but it is more difficult to understand what economic reality is behind the isolated find of a coin or even of a coin hoard than a wine jar.

Perhaps the best general guide in English to the history of classical Greece is still J. B. Bury, *A History of Greece to the Death of Alexander the Great*, now to be read in the third edition by Russell Meiggs (London: Macmillan, 1959). The standard American college text is somewhat shorter: G. W. Botsford and C. A. Robinson, *Hellenic History*, 4th ed. (New York: Macmillan, 1956). Most recently, see N. G. L. Hammond, *A History of Greece to 322 B.C.* (Oxford: Clarendon Press, 1959).

A beautiful and lucid characterization of the city-state and what it meant to the Greeks of the classical period will be found in Kitto, *The Greeks*, pp. 64–79. The culture and social life of aristocratic Greece is brilliantly pictured in Henri Irenée Marrou, *History of Education in Antiquity*, trans. George Lamb (New York: Sheed and Ward, 1956), chap. i–iii, a work whose interest is considerably greater and broader than its title suggests.

This aristocratic society centered in towns rather than on country estates and found an income in kind more desirable than dependents and followers. One result was that it used its monopoly of state offices to turn the common land of the clans into the private property of the family or even of the individual heads of aristocratic families. This is a process which, in one fashion or another, can be found at many times in human history: the breakup of the solidarity based upon real or fictional kinship and of the common property of the kin, F. Toennies's movement from *Gemeinschaft* to *Gesellschaft*, the transformation that Sir Henry Maine traced from status to contract in civil relations. If the parallel is not pressed too hard, it can be said to have happened again in the course of the Middle Ages, when feudal lords found that efficient farming and the production of a surplus to sell was becoming a more effective way of gaining prestige and holding political power than simply having a numerous following housed in the manor and fed by the produce of the fief, and indeed that without wealth in money a numerous following could not any longer be maintained. This process can be examined in the brilliant invective that Karl Marx launched against the enclosures in Scotland in the eighteenth and nineteenth centuries, by which the Scottish clan chieftains assimilated themselves to the property-owning, sheep-raising, rent-collecting English aristocracy by the expulsion of those clansmen unnecessary to efficient market farming.[11] The result in Greece was that the ties of blood and of the family religion no longer held men in their clan groupings.[12] Society was divided into the possessors of land and a dependent or even landless peasantry. Debt and debt-slavery became the crying issues of the day.

THE COLONIAL MOVEMENT

Greece was in fact creating for herself a surplus population due in part to social pressures,[13] to which the commonest reaction was colonization. Many

[11] *Das Kapital*, 3 vols. (Chicago: Charles H. Kerr and Co., 1906–1909), Vol. I, Pt. vii, Ch. 28, pp. 850ff.

[12] See the very interesting, though no doubt too schematic, analysis of the evolution of property in the ancient world in Fustel de Coulanges, *The Ancient City*.

[13] Historians are prone to explain any social strife and any movements of peoples to population pressure. In the sparse soils of Mediterranean, population pressure can be quickly felt, but the reader should note that the term is not a rigorous one. It may simply imply that people do not undergo the hardships of migration except under some kind of compulsion, which is true, but in fact explains nothing, unless it is the known by the unknown (a favorite occupation among social scientists generally and perhaps particularly among historians). It is theoretically possible, of course, to have some kind of absolute population pressure where the birth rate is in excess of the death rate and the population subsists at the wolf point at which life can barely be sustained, and where it is literally impossible to modify the technology in any way to support a greater population. Such conditions, if they have ever existed, must be most extraordinary. The term "population pressure" usually conceals some state of society, some arrangement of the economy, which makes a part of the population economically useless to the dominant class.

cities of the Aegean sent out bands of their citizens to found new cities on
the central sea wherever they found resistance weak enough. Such settlements
might be purely agricultural or they might have commercial aims. Generally
these new cities, although we call them colonies, were complete and independent poleis, although they might be founded with the commercial and political
interests of the mother city in view. Occasionally the tie with the mother city
was more than religious and sentimental.[14]

The colonial expansion of the Greeks lasted from the middle of the eighth
to the middle of the fifth century and was generally directed to three areas:
the western Mediterranean, the northern Aegean and the Black Sea, and Egypt
and Africa.[15] The modest city of Chalcis, which dominated half of the island
of Euboea, led the movement westward with the foundation of Cumae about
760. Cumae, strengthened by immigrants from Athens, founded Neapolis
(Naples) and was the mother city of a host of other towns: Himera, Rhegium
(Reggio) on the Italian side of the Straits of Messana and Zancle on the
Sicilian side. Later Zancle was reinforced by refugees from the Spartan conquest of Messenia and the town became Messene, which gives the modern
Messana. A single city like Chalcis, especially when—as we shall see—she was
also busy elsewhere, could hardly have supplied men for so many considerable colonies. Such cooperation as Athens' at Naples and such reinforcements
as the Messenians at Zancle were the general rule. Chalcis almost appears as
an entrepreneur of colonization. The same may have been true of the little
city of Phocaea [16] and the great commercial center of Miletus.

The Achaeans founded a town at Sybaris in the instep of Italy, a place

[14] See the discussion of Ionian and Greek colonization in the Aegean, Propontis, and Black
Sea in Carl Roebuck, *Ionian Trade and Colonization*, Vol. IX of the "Monographs on
Archaeology and Fine Arts Sponsored by the Archaeological Institute of America" (New
York: Archaeological Institute of America, 1959); and John Boardman, *The Greeks Over-
seas* (Baltimore: Penguin Books, 1964).

[15] The chief works on Greek colonization: Jean Jannoray, *Ensérume, Contribution à l'étude
des civilisations pré-romaines de la Gaule méridionale* (Paris: E. de Boccard, 1955); F.
Villard, *La céramique grecque de Marseille (VIe–IVe siècles). Essai d'histoire économique*
(Paris: E. de Boccard, 1960); F. Benoît, *Recherches sur l'hellénisation du midi de la Gaule*
(Aix-en-Provence: Editions Ophrys, 1965); J. Bérard, *La colonisation grecque de l'Italie
méridionale et de la Sicile dans l'antiquité. L'histoire et la légende*, 2d ed. (Paris: Presses
universitaires de France, 1957); T. J. Dunbabin, *The Western Greeks. The History of
Sicily and South Italy from the Foundation of the Greek Colonies to 480 B.C.* (Oxford:
Clarendon Press, 1948); G. Vallet, *Rhégion et Zancle. Histoire, commerce et civilisation
des cités chalcidiennes du détroit de Messine* (Paris: E. de Boccard, 1958); V. Pârvan,
"La pénétration hellénique et hellénistique dans la vallée du Danube," *Bulletin de la Section
Historique de l'Académie Roumaine*, X (1923), 23ff.; and the works of C. Roebuck cited
elsewhere. There is also a valuable annotated bibliography of works and articles published in
the U.S.S.R. between 1940 and 1962: E. Belin de Ballu, *L'histoire des colonies grecques du
littoral nord de la Mer Noire*, 2d ed. (Leyden: E. J. Brill, 1965). The chief ancient authority on Western civilization is Thuc. vi. 2–5.

[16] This is noted below in discussing the Ionian long distance trade with the Tartessians in
Spain for tin, copper, and bronze.

which could command the route for transshipping goods across to the Tyrrhenian Sea, and even the Dorians of the Peloponnesus founded one colony,
Tarentum (Tarento) in the same gulf.

In the year 733 B.C. Corinth sent out a colony to Sicily which founded
the greatest of all the western cities, Syracuse. En route, the expedition
stopped at the island of Corfu and founded a settlement there too, the city of
Corcyra. Clearly Corinth had commercial aims in view: Thucydides shows
that she attempted to keep some control over Corcyra and thus to guarantee
and protect her western trade. Indeed, Corinthian products dominated the
western markets until the rise of Athens' export business.[17]

The Greeks had thus settled the peripheries of southern Italy, which
received the name Magna Graecia (Great Greece), and on almost the whole
coast of Sicily. But beyond these regions the Greeks ran into stronger opposition. The natives of southern Italy do not appear to have presented much
opposition, and Syracuse was able to reduce the native population of her
territory to serfdom. But the extreme western end of Sicily was held by Carthage, and that colony of Phoenician Tyre was tenacious of its fortresses of
Lilybaeum and Motya, for they guaranteed control of the narrows of the
Mediterranean and excluded the Greeks from the most direct route to Spain
and the Atlantic, as well as the coast of Africa itself. This was to remain
Carthaginian territory, for the northern route to the far west was held by a
people capable of powerful resistance, the Etruscans. The origin of this people
is shrouded in mystery. Their language, of which a few examples remain on
tombstones, cannot be related to any other family group.[18] But their origin
does not concern us as much as their strength and prosperity. They were an
urbanized people, whose towns centered in modern Tuscany, which takes its
name from them. North of the Campania of Naples and Cumae they closed the
western coast of Italy to Greek colonization. Not only Tuscany itself, but
Latium, the region about and south of Rome, was closed to the Greeks, and
at the battle of Alalia about 535 B.C. the Etruscans made common cause with
the Carthaginians to prevent a settlement of Phocaeans on Corsica.

The ultimate group of Greek cities in the west was, then, isolated. In
southern Gaul the Phocaeans had established, about 600 B.C., a colony at the
fine port of Marseilles, the nearest harborage to the mouth of the Rhône. From
Marseilles a string of little cities stretched along the Riviera: Nice in the
Maritime Alps, Antibes, Cannes, down to Ampurias (Greek *emporion*) in
Spain. But south of the Ebro River the Carthaginians excluded the Massiliots

[17] Pottery is our chief source concerning trade routes and goods traded over long distances
in the ancient world. For a brief summary of its importance as a source for economic history and the succession of styles which permits dating, see Roebuck, *The World of Ancient
Times*, pp. 221–3. The dates of the colonization of the eastern Mediterranean must be placed
chiefly by the dates of the pottery found in the lowest levels; that of the western colonies
in Italy and Sicily is helped by some information given by Thucydides.
[18] The recent discovery of a bilingual inscription awakens hope that the language may soon
be understood.

from Spain and the sea route to the Atlantic was closed. The battle of Alalia really marks the end of Greek colonization in the west. The spheres of the Greeks, the Phoenicians, and the Etruscans had been marked out (see Map VII). In fact the division was to remain definitive until the conquests of the Romans, although this was not yet clear in the fifth century, when a struggle for control of the western seas took place between the Greeks and the Carthaginians in Sicily.

Contemporary with, and even a bit earlier than, the expansion to the west was the colonization of the north. The settlement of the northern coast of the Aegean dates from this period, and here again Chalcis took the lead, as the name of the Chalcidian peninsula suggests: Olynthus and Torone were colonies of Chalcis; Mende, Methone, and Scione of her neighbor Eretria; and Potidaea of Corinth. The chief occupations in this rough country were agriculture and fishing, but later timber and the gold of Mount Pangaeus would provide revenue. From these little cities, Macedonia would receive her initiation into Greek life and training, but Macedonian power prevented the settlement of the shores of the Thermaic Gulf into which the Vardar River empties,[19] while to the east of the Chalcidice, Thracian tribes made settlement impossible.

However, the Greeks, led by the great commercial city of Miletus, did settle the Hellespont and the seas behind it. Miletus is said to have had eighty colonies in the region. The cities along the Hellespont and the Bosphorus and the Propontis between them flourished on the great schools of tunny fish, their own agriculture, and on some trade with the natives of their hinterland, although such towns as Byzantium and Perinthus on the European shore and Sestos in the Chersonese had unpleasant neighbors in the wild Thracians. The Black Sea proper was Miletus' great venture. Here the most important cities were Olbia, Panticapaeum, and Sinope: Olbia at the mouth of the Bug; Panticapaeum in the Crimea; and Sinope on the northern shore of Asia Minor.

The third area of Greek colonization in the Mediterranean was the southeast. Along the coast between the Carthaginian area on the west and Egypt proper on the east, a number of cities were founded, the most important of which was the Dorian Cyrene in modern Libya. To the east, colonies were founded along the south coast of Asia Minor and an emporion located at Al-Mina in Syria.

In Egypt and Syria, of course, colonization in the ordinary sense was impossible, but the Greeks did establish contacts. About the middle of the seventh century the Ionians had gained a knowledge of Egypt, probably as the result of mercenary service there under Pharaoh Psammetichos I, to whom King Gyges sent some troops. Gradually a regular line of traffic from Ionia

---

[19] The authors cannot claim perfect consistency, but an attempt has been made to use the modern name whenever the ancient is not much more familiar. Since one never says Roma for Rome, there seems no reason to say Massilia for Marseilles or Axios River for the Vardar.

to Egypt by way of Rhodes and Cyprus was established, and shortly before 600 B.C. the port of Naucratis was founded. It was not a colony in the ordinary sense, nor a polis. Egypt was a highly centralized monarchy. No Greek community could be established in Egypt without the pharaoh's consent, and Naucratis was certainly founded by his charter. It enjoyed treaty privileges and something of what modern diplomacy would call extraterritorial rights. The Greeks in it did not compose a citizen body but were organized about several national shrines and several common shrines as well. Some were merchants who presumably remained citizens of their poleis in Greece. Craftsmen settled in the place as well and seem to have been permanent residents producing Hellenic goods for Egypt. Naucratis was in short a port of trade, an emporion.[20] Naucratis appears to have been something rather new to Egypt. A map makes it appear that Egypt opens upon the Mediterranean, but in fact the seacoast is a dense swamp which cuts the country off from the sea and from maritime trade. What limited commerce had been carried on earlier had been the work of Egyptians and the monopoly of the pharaoh. Now there were Greeks resident in Egypt, both as mercenaries and as merchants, and while the commerce and the status of the resident aliens was doubtless strictly controlled by the state, the scale of imports and exports must have been considerably greater than ever before in the past. The system of relationships found in Egypt is already familiar to us under the name of the port of trade, although it is probable that the Greek merchants at Naucratis were acting in an individual capacity and more freely in respect to their home governments— though not in respect to their host—than had any of the earlier merchants in foreign trade we have seen at Mycenaean Al-Mina or at the Assyrian colony in Anatolia in the second millennium.

The economic consequences of Greek expansion, as far as they can be grasped, differed in different regions. The chief consequence in Italy and Great Greece, in the Chalcidice, and the region of the Hellespont, the Propontis, and the Bosphorus was at first to expand the area of the traditional Greek economy—the small-scale agriculture of barley, wheat, the olive, and the vine —and its attendant independent artisans. But even in these areas, it is clear, there was a demand for the finer manufactures of the Aegean area. Much Corinthian pottery of the orientalizing animal figure type, for instance, is found in the Greek cities of the west and in Tuscany.

But in Gaul to a very modest extent and in the colonies of the Ukraine, Olbia, and Panticapaeum, for the first time we see clearly another development. North of the Black Sea stretches the vast eastern extension of the great plain of northern Europe, a land which European geographers call steppe, but which Americans would recognize as prairie. The grain production of this land in the nineteenth century and today almost rivals that of the American

---

[20] See Carl Roebuck, "The Grain Trade Between Greece and Egypt," *Classical Philology*, XLV (1950), 236–47; "The Organization of Naucratis," *ibid.*, XLVI (1951), 212–20; and *Ionian Trade and Colonization*, pp. 69, 134ff.

Midwest. Here the little, more and more crowded cities of the Aegean world found an adequate source of their staple food. (Egypt and the virgin fields of the west, too, would come to contribute to the Greek table.) The Aegean offered luxury goods in return. Most of our evidence about the movement of goods in the classical world comes from finds of pottery. Pottery itself could be luxury product, and the Aegean early produced beautiful vases in great demand among the barbarian princes, the Scythians of the steppe. In demand, too, were wine, olive oil, and scents that could be shipped in pottery; arms; and luxurious and splendid metal tableware. It may be assumed that wool cloth was also a part of the trade, though the evidence that survives gives no proof of it.

Such vases and Greek arms and other metalwork are found in the graves of Scythian princes. From the point of view of the Scyths, this trade must have resembled the ancient pattern of ports of trade. The Greek cities on the coast, which certainly could not have been established in the face of concerted opposition by the inhabitants of the interior, served as ports of entry to these states centered away from the sea. In the Black Sea such ports were Apollonia and Mesembria in Thrace; Istria near the mouth of the Danube; Tyros at the mouth of the Dneister; Olbia at the mouth of the Bug; and in command of the mouth of the Dnieper, Odessa on the coast between them; Chersonessus and Theodosia in the Crimea; Myphaeum, Hermonassa, and Phanogoria at the straits that lead from the Black Sea into the Sea of Azov; Tanais on the inner sea at the mouth of the Don (see Map VII). We may surmise that such towns traded with the interior tribes according to a system of regulated exchanges established by treaty. Control was in the hands of the chieftains and kings. The trade was carried on in their interest. Just as we have seen that in the Bronze Age economy the city had nothing much to offer the peasant that was within his conceivable power to purchase, so the peasants of the steppe could hardly aspire to the consumption of anything that the Greeks might bring. Wine, olive oil, and even ordinary Greek pots arriving from the Aegean were luxury goods. Thus the princes must have organized the steppe to produce a surplus for export: the peasant had no interest in producing grain to send to Greece.

The chieftains, however, greatly desired the luxuries that the Greeks brought. In an age far closer than ours to that of the Scythian chiefs, Aristotle still defined wealth as a number of different things, where we would probably say that it was simply one—money.[21] He includes the possession of splendid objects, preferably objects inherited from ancestors and surrounded by the aura of the actions of the ancients. Or turn to Homer again, and think of the prizes he describes at the games. Some are weights of gold or silver (very small weights to our mind), and some are slaves; but others are splendid objects—tripods, armor, or weapons. Herodotus tells us that Polycrates, the tyrant of Samos, valued above all his other possessions a great emerald signet

[21] Arist. *Politics.* i. 8, 9.

ring, and Herodotus thinks it worth recording the name of the man who engraved the emerald: Theodore, son of Telecles, a Samian.[22] Herodotus gives
the name of the maker, but he sets no price to the ring. Such things really no
more have a price than do paintings by Titian and Rembrandt. We have
today only a faint echo of this in our feeling about family heirlooms. In the
Aegean, even by the sixth century, the sense of what constituted wealth certainly was changing. But among the barbarians of the north, it would not yet
have changed at all; indeed it would not for centuries to come. The possession
and display, then, of Greek vases and metal bowls, of Greek armor, weapons,
oil, and wine would do much to enhance the prestige of the Scythian chief.[23]
(Coins, when they later appeared, would be treated as jewelry and served the
same function.)

But such objects would do more: they would help him build a state. The
great problem of a chieftain who wished to get and maintain power among
a primitive people was the establishment of some permanent authority over
the families, bands, or tribes that belonged to his people. If the chieftain
could command foreign goods, he was in a far better position in this respect.
Even in so late and advanced a society as the feudalism of Western Europe, a
lord was judged largely by his gifts. The greatest man was the greatest gift
giver.[24] Since the possession of such objects did as much to raise the reputation of the lesser heads of families, bands, and tribes as of the chieftain, they
served to keep these persons in line and, therefore, to maintain the loyalty of
the kinship groups.[25]

Thus there was a basis for trade with the Scyths in the absence of markets

---

[22] Herod. iii. 41.

[23] On the Scythians, see E. Minns, *Scythians and Greeks in South Russia* (Cambridge:
Cambridge University Press, 1913), which is especially valuable on the archaeology and
grave finds; M. Rostovtzeff, *Iranians and Greeks in South Russia* (Oxford: Clarendon Press,
1922), and more recently the relevant parts of A. L. Mongait, *Archaeology in the USSR*,
trans. M. W. Thompson (Pelican Books; Baltimore: Penguin Books, 1961). The first two
works are dated and the third sketchy, but there is nothing better to recommend, for the
Russians since the Revolution have gotten into the bad habit of writing scholarly works
in their own language instead of French. Yet since the Second World War they have produced marvels of systematic archaeological exploration that put the Western states to shame:
see S. Frederick Starr, "Archaeology in the Soviet Union," *Yale Review*, LIV (1964),
311–20.

[24] See, for example, the characteristic attitude in the highly romantic thirteenth-century
Fall of the Nibelungs, prose trans. Margaret Armour (Everyman's Library; London: J. M.
Dent and Sons, 1908), pp. 25, 65, 68, and passim. The attitude toward wealth as accumulated
treasure of prestigious objects is seen here as well as it is in Homer.

[25] Such is a part of the general thesis of F. J. Teggart, *Rome and China, A Study of Correlations in Historical Events* (Berkeley: University of California Press, 1939). The thesis
of this curiously organized book may be reduced to this: that whenever the chieftain's control of external trade broke down or the transit trade ceased to yield him revenues, his
barbarian state broke up and a period of unrest on the steppe ensued. The presentation is
unnecessarily elaborate and Teggart does not make clear the nature of wealth among the
barbarians, but the basic thesis is probably sound. It accords with everything else we know
about the organization of such peripheral peoples.

or money, and colonization was not simply an expansion of the old Greek economy. In the west it was chiefly that, but also something more, while in the greater part of the Black Sea region, it does not really appear that the Greeks were able to establish Greek life and training as they had known them in the Aegean. (Perhaps one reason was that it was too cold for the gymnasium and the open-air assemblies about which Greek life was ordered.) Like Naucratis, such places as Olbia and Panticapaeum retained the character of ports of trade, of an establishment dependent upon distant commercial and economic contracts. The Aegean, in short, was beginning to specialize in manufactures and the finer and more difficult agricultural goods (oils and scents, wine, and probably wool cloth) and to depend upon backward lands for grain.

THE ORIGINS OF COINAGE

From the time of Homer until the time of Aristotle, when the money economy and related institutions were firmly established, two significant developments occurred. First, the concept of real wealth and of the natural leadership of the tribe by clan chiefs changed to concepts of money wealth and government taxation and leadership by formally chosen state officers. Second, with the origin of the concept of money wealth, a money economy developed. The government could augment its revenues by imposing taxes and developing ports for merchant transactions, as did Corinth and Miletus.

Coins first made their appearance on the margin of the old civilized world; not in Greece itself, but rather in Lydia, the kingdom of Croesus, in western Asia Minor.[26] It is a country which seemed to the Greeks rich in gold and silver. Electrum, a natural alloy of the two, was panned from the river Hermus near the capital of Sardis. Here the idea first came to men that since they were universally desired and since they were used to reckon the values of other goods, precious metals could be portioned out in lumps of uniform size and that these lumps could be stamped with seals which would indicate their value and guarantee their passing as currency, at least for certain purposes, and, therefore, that such coins could be used not simply to figure values, but as an actual means of exchange to pass from hand to hand. The first coins were issued about or shortly after 650 B.C.[27] These coins were of electrum, a mixture of gold and silver.

[26] Herodotus i. 94: "So far as we have any knowledge, [the Lydians] were the first nation to introduce the use of gold and silver coins, and the first who sold goods by retail." Modern historians have not been able to improve much on Herodotus. Assyrian inscriptions indicate that under Sennacherib (704–681 B.C.), small coppers were coined, but we know nothing about their use. They would have preceded the Lydian coinage but do not appear to have led to permanent innovation or given rise to the later money economy of Mesopotamia, which was imported from Greece and Macedonia.

[27] The chief means of dating the invention of coinage is from the estimated date of a hoard deposited at the temple of Artemis at Ephesus. This date has recently been lowered to about

It is natural for modern men to suppose that such coins were issued as a means of exchange, and it seems certain that very soon, at any rate, they were so used, for Sardis was not only the home of the world's first coinage but also possessed the first marketplace of which we hear.[28] Archaeologists have been unable to discover any sites in the ancient cities of the Near East which might have served the purpose. We are surprised to discover that Herodotus was probably correct in one of his most improbable statements.

Still there are difficulties about the function of the earliest coinage. The coins are large; they might be suitable for foreign trade—Lydia may have had considerable foreign trade—but they do not seem suitable for the retail transactions of a marketplace. Then, too, it is difficult to imagine an oriental despot of Gyges' sort making such an innovation in the interests of retail merchants. Indeed, it is difficult to imagine such a government's doing anything which did not bring itself some advantage. An acute and painstaking analysis of the coins themselves by the Swedish numismatist, Sture Bolin, has made clear the advantage to the government (and, as will be seen later, has also thrown much light on the whole history of ancient coinage).[29] There can be little doubt that the king of Lydia possessed either a monopoly on mines or imposed a substantial tax on their workings as well as on the panning of gold and electrum from the rivers. It had long been supposed that the earliest coins were of electrum because it was a natural product of the rivers. This supposition was natural enough, even though it was known that the technology of the ancient Near East had long been able to refine very nearly pure gold and silver. By careful weighing and tests for specific gravity, Bolin established two remarkable facts: first, the proportions of gold to silver in the coins was never the same as that found in natural supplies of electrum in Lydia itself or in other places nearby; and second, the proportions varied greatly from coin to coin. Since the Lydians could have attained great exactness, it is clear

---

600 B.C. The Lydian invention of coinage is necessarily older, but earlier estimates of 700 B.C. or even earlier probably must be lowered considerably: G. K. Jenkins, "Greek Numismatics," *Historia*, II (1953–1954), 214.

Ancient coins were in high relief and were struck by dies made with cutting tools. Casting was confined to Roman bronze pieces too large to strike and to a few barbarian coinages. Medieval coins were in low relief, and the engraved striking die was replaced by a punch. Apart from bricks made in molds, coins, whether struck or punched, were the first product made in series on a mass scale and they remained the only one until the industrial revolution of the late eighteenth century.

[28] Herod. v. 101: "As the fire raged, the Lydians, and such Persians as were in the city, inclosed on every side by the flames which had seized all the outskirts of the town, and finding themselves unable to get out, came in crowds into the market-place, and gathered themselves upon the banks of the Pactolus. This stream, which comes down from Mount Tmolus, and brings the Sardians a quantity of gold-dust, runs directly through the market-place of Sardis, and joins the Hermus, before that river reaches the sea."

[29] Sture Bolin, *State and Currency in The Roman Empire to 300* A.D. (Stockholm: Almquist and Wicksell, 1958).

that this discrepancy was intentional. The government, rather than issuing coins of a guaranteed value, was deliberately disguising the value of the coins. There can be no doubt that it was overvaluing them. That is, all coins passed for having the value of those with the highest or very nearly the highest proportion of gold to silver. The Greek poets of the period in several passages show much interest in touchstones for the purity of the precious metals, but until the discovery of the principle of specific gravity, there was really no way of checking on the government, provided only that it did not adulterate enough to make the coins noticeably pale. Thus the king's purpose in creating coinage was to impose a secret levy on his subjects. What still remains obscure and hypothetical is the exact function of coinage in the Lydian economy.

Miletus, a Greek city on the Aegean coast of Asia Minor, and the island state of Samos early followed the Lydian example of coining. King Pheidon of Argos was once credited with having introduced the use of coins to peninsular Greece in the early seventh century. (He is credited in the sources with a modification of the system of weights and measures.) But this date is probably too early, perhaps by a century. The dates are currently the subject of much controversy, but it seems that late in the seventh century, after c. 620, under the tyrant Cypselus, Corinth followed the Asiatic example and began the issue of her famous "colts," coins named for the head of Pegasus which appears on them. Aegina, too, was a major commercial center and early produced a distinctive coinage. So did the two chief cities of Euboea, Chalcis and Eretreia, until finally "all the states of Greece gave up the primitive custom of estimating value in heads of cattle, and most of them had their own mints." [30] Sparta was an exception; she continued to use iron spits for her rare monetary transactions.

But the ancient Orient did not follow suit. Only early in the fifth century did King Darius of Persia begin to mint coins, the famous gold darics, and it does not appear that coins in the Persian Empire filled the same functions as in Greece, for Herodotus tells us that the Persians even in his day in the middle of the fifth century, had no markets. Later we shall have to consider the function of Persian coins.

Greece lacks good supplies of gold, which it is found only on the islands of Siphnos and Thasos, and so used a silver coinage. By the fifth century the whole of Greece—the Greek homeland on the peninsula, the islands, and the cities on the Ionian shore, the area of the city-state—appears in some sense to have been on a money standard and to have made extensive use of coins. By that time, too, they were used for commercial purposes.

But is it any longer clear to what use the Greeks *first* put coins, when they borrowed them from the Lydians? At first historians naturally assumed that they were designed for both long distance "wholesale" and local retail trade, and hence for the conveniences of exchanges by a newly appeared class

[30] Bury, *Greece*, p. 113; see G. F. Hill, "Coinage," *CAH*, IV, pp. 124–36.

of professional merchants. Neither the nature of the earliest Greek coins nor their distribution bears out this view, nor does what we know of the social structure of the archaic Greek state. It seems unlikely that the state would have issued coins for such a purpose. If they were intended for local retail trade and a provision market, there should have been an early development of fractional coinage. In fact, there was not, so that local retail trade must be ruled out as a primitive function of coins. Nor does the distribution of silver drachmae support the supposition that they were used for payments in trade between city-states. Rather their distribution as revealed by coin finds is extremely limited. The coins of the Greek cities of southern Italy barely pass into Sicily or those of Sicily into Italy. The coins of the greater commercial cities do not have a distribution proportionate to their trade. It is rather the coins of cities with silver mines that are most widely distributed. It looks, then, as though coins were an object, not a means, of trade in the earliest period of coinage.[31]

MARKET DEVELOPMENT AT ATHENS

The outcome of the new economic organization of coinage, distant commerce in specialized goods, and the open market was of most consequence in Athens, which in the fifth century came to dominate the Aegean economy and consquently the economy of a much larger area. Fortunately the economic and political development of Athens is also the best understood, thanks chiefly to the information Herodotus and Thucydides give about her history before the fifth century. Athenian political development was slower than that of many cities. She played no important part in the great movement of colonization, was slow to coin, and was tardy in accepting a tyranny. One factor was probably her great size: Attica hardly seems large to the inhabitant of a modern nation, but by Greek standards an area which probably came eventually to support some 350,000 persons was an immense state. Only Acragas, the modern Girgenti, and Syracuse in the west were ever comparable. Such a state was built upon a different scale from the other cities of old Greece. Unification, therefore, came more tardily; the effects of an excessive population, too, may have been felt more slowly.

The first popular agitation against the old aristocracy of the Eupatrid families that we hear of in Athens came in the latter part of the seventh century—a relatively late date. A noble named Cylon attempted to make himself tyrant of Athens. After he had won prestige in the chariot race in the Olympic games and had married the daughter of Theagenes, the tyrant of Megara, he seized the Acropolis with a small group of clansmen. But the people followed

---

[31] See Vidal-Naquet, "The Function of Money in Archaic Greece," Appendix B; Ed. Will, "Les origines du monnayage," *Revue numismatique*, 5th s., XVII (1955), 15; Roebuck, *Ancient Times*, p. 94, note.

the legal *archon*, Megacles, the head of the powerful Alcmaeonid clan, and Cylon and his supporters were massacred. His failure is evidence that at this date the ties of blood and clan loyalty were still strong enough at Athens to prevent the creation of an impersonal state or the tyranny of a single man over the clan chiefs.

But the commons were certainly not content. It seems strange to us at first sight that their first successful demand should be directed to the law. They demanded that it be written down, though certainly most of the commons of Athens were illiterate. But the law had hitherto been quite literally unknown to the commons; it was the monopoly of the aristocrats, who alone had learned it from their fathers and hence alone could act as judges and advocates in court. Since the commons did not know the rigid and traditional formulas in which cases had to be couched, they might easily lose their cases on what we would call procedural grounds and generally they were obliged to proceed at law by means of an aristocratic patron. It may safely be supposed that the aristocrats were no more reluctant to use their monopoly of the courts and of their exacting ritual than were the landowners of seventeenth- and eighteenth-century England to use their power in Parliament and as Justices of the Peace to appropriate and enclose common land. Popular agitation finally led to the appointment in c. 621 B.C. of Draco to set down in writing the law that already existed.[32]

Draco's committing the laws to writing certainly helped the commons, but it hardly solved the outstanding social problems of Athens. A generation later, in 594, another extraordinary magistrate, Solon, was elected to reform the laws and the political constitution of the state. His activities are a bit better known, and it is clear that he undertook to reform the economy as well as the constitution. The city was still under the control of the clans or leading families. The development of trade and commerce had created a taste on the part of the leading men for luxuries that could be acquired only by the exploitation of the poorer classes. The beginnings of the use of money made the situation worse. Many of the poorer classes got into debt and some sold their families and even themselves into slavery outside Attica to pay their debts. Others tilled their farms as sharecroppers (*hektamoroi*) of richer persons to whom they were hopelessly in debt. Many of the leading men must have realized that the common people had been pushed to the point of revolution.

It does not seem to have been Solon's intention to give the demos a part in the government. Rule was to be left as always to the aristocrats, but it was

[32] It is possible, of course, that Draco innovated to some degree, but we can no longer really judge. It is unfortunate from the economic historian's point of view that the only parts of his code which have survived deal with homicide. Blood offenses were to the Greeks religious matters involving ritual pollution (cf. Aeschylus' *Eumenides*), and the law of murder and manslaughter consequently remained so conservative that the lawyers of the fourth century still cited Draco on this, but on no other subject. To the demand of the Athenian commons that the law be written, compare that of the Roman plebs which produced the XII Tablets centuries later.

his intention to so arrange the government as to protect the commons from injustice, and for this purpose the institutions of the polis were modified. Protection against injustice, however, meant first and foremost protection against the poverty that aristocratic expropriation of the soil and the growing population was producing. It, therefore, meant economic reforms. Solon outlawed debt slavery by making it illegal for freeborn persons to pledge their bodies or those of their wives and children against a loan. Public money was even used to buy back from abroad those Athenians who had been sold into slavery. Since Solon did not, however, redivide the land and since Athens appears to have taken small part in the great movement of colonization, these measures did little to alleviate the basic causes of social trouble. Other states sought a solution in colonies and the redivision of the land. Though both were popular neither provided an enduring solution to the economic problems faced by the archaic Greek city-state. The sending out of colonies reduced the population and therefore weakened the state. The division of land necessarily divided the city between those who lost and those who gained and yet satisfied the poor only until the population again grew a bit. Solon's greatest accomplishment and the most decisive proof of his creative genius is found in those economic innovations which opened the way for a far-ranging revolution in the world's economy. These innovations led to the first full institutional expression of an economy suitable to the Mediterranean Iron Age.

While he refused to redistribute the land, Solon did cancel or reduce debts. This was called the *seisachtheia*, the "shaking-off of burdens," and probably involved chiefly the freeing of the land from obligations we would call mortgages. Seisachtheia made it possible for the remaining small farmers to hold onto their farms, if—but only if—some means could be found to make them profitable. (We use the modern term, although the Athenian peasant was not, of course, thinking in terms of profits and of bookkeeping.) [33]

Solon was most original in commercial and monetary reform and his reforms of foreign commercial relations greatly helped the dependent farmers, though to what degree they were intended to do so is not clear. To facilitate trade with other maritime cities and establish Athens' independence of her chief commercial rivals, Aegina and Megara, Solon coined money on a new standard. Probably Athens had not earlier struck coins but chiefly used those of Aegina and Megara; she had used the Megaran standard of weights. When she did begin to coin she adopted the lighter standard of the cities of Euboea.[34] Athens was not on good terms with either of her near neighbors,

[33] Land was not distributed to the poor, nor were the conditions of sharecropping changed, so that the condition of the hektamoroi was improved only by their safety from slavery. They may, indeed, have found it more difficult to borrow money from private persons.

[34] The Euboean standard was lighter than the Aeginetan, so if debts contracted in the old coins could be paid in the new, indebtedness of all kinds must have been considerably reduced. One hundred of the new Attic drachmae were equal to seventy of the Aeginetan. On the origins of the Athenian tetradrachma, G. K. Jenkins, "Greek Numismatics," *Historia*, II (1953–1954), 214–6.

and the new standard seems to have invited her into the distant fields of commerce beyond the sea where Euboean Chalcis and Corinth had led the way.

That the reform looked in this direction is clear from two related measures. Solon induced foreign traders to settle at Athens or in the Piraeus, the port of the city, and offered citizenship to those who did. This does not seem a radical measure to modern eyes; we are used to the idea that one who lives in a land is a member of its society, that the state is determined by its territory and that membership—at least after a term of probation—comes with residence in the territory. Such was not the Greek view. The state was not simply an area. Its membership was made up of a number of clans with blood ties to each other. We know that these relationships were often fictitious, and sometimes the ancients themselves knew as much, but real or fictitious kinship was important because citizenship involved participation in the state religion. The religion of the state, for example, the cult of Athena at Athens, was in a sense a composite of the cults of the clans.[35] Only members in good standing could participate.[36] Thus down at least to the fourth century, there were very real religious barriers to entrance into the political community. Solon broke through them in order to make Athens commercially great. At the same time, he forbade the export of the agricultural produce of Attica with the single exception of olive oil. The reason, no doubt, was to protect the poor by keeping down the price of bread,[37] for, in Solon's time, Athens was not yet importing much grain, although her land was not good and particularly was not very suitable to the cultivation of cereals.

Athens could export a little olive oil and some pottery. Soon some wine might be added to the list. The commercialization of Athenian life, then, had not gone far during Solon's archonship. Nor did his political reforms as a whole endure. His term of office was followed by a social struggle among three parties at Athens: the party of the plain, which presumably was dominated by the landed aristocrats; of the hill, which should have represented the poor farmers and the shepherds; and the party of the city, presumably craftsmen and traders. Conquest abroad was one means of keeping down social tensions at home. The island of Salamis was taken from Megara, but its settlement by Athenians did not long relieve social pressures at home, and the political struggle led shortly to the tyranny of Pisistratus, the leader of a popular or democratic party.

[35] See generally Fustel de Coulanges, *The Ancient City*. There are interesting parallels in the ancestor worship of the Chinese: Marcel Granet, *La civilisation chinoise* ("L'évolution de l'humanité"; Paris: Albin Michel, 1948).

[36] Herodotus v. 72: For when [Cleomenes] first went up into the citadel [the Acropolis], meaning to seize it, just as he was entering the sanctuary of the goddess, in order to question her, the priestess arose from her throne, before he had passed the doors, and said, "Stranger from Lacedaemon, depart hence, and presume not to enter the holy place—it is not lawful for a Dorian to set foot there."

[37] Such provisions shock the modern reader, nurtured willy-nilly on the theories of Adam Smith, but they were common enough almost everywhere in Europe up to the time of the French Revolution.

Pisistratus broke the power of the Eupatrids and saved the small Athenian farmer. During his long tyranny from 561 to 527 he introduced a number of reforms which were largely designed to accomplish this aim. What was peculiar about Pisistratus' reforms is that as a result of them the Athenian economy—an economy of small farmers—came to be organized largely about the marketplace and international exchanges. No doubt the growing importance of the commons in the sixth century B.C. was largely, perhaps ultimately, based on the increasing importance of *hoplites* in the armed forces and their growing superiority to the aristocratic cavalry. A hoplite was a heavy-armed soldier, one with a full panoply of helmet, breastplate of iron or leather, greaves, sword, and spear. By the time of Pisistratus such soldiers, trained to fight in the line, had become very much more important than cavalry and certainly more important than light-armed troops.

The domination of the battlefield by such soldiers had political consequences, for no Greek city ever attempted to supply arms to its citizens. A man's arms were his own property. The city classified its citizens according to their wealth and required that each member of each census class provide himself with the arms that a man of that grade could be expected to afford. Hoplites corresponded roughly to the solid middle-class peasantry. When such troops came to the fore in battle, every city necessarily gave men of the middle class a considerable voice in the government. They no doubt used this voice to defend their own interests.

There were still a number of possible roads open for a Greek city. Sparta provided herself with an excellent hoplite force, the best in Greece, by the conquest of Messenia and the creation of a very peculiar, archaic social system which ended her commercial and economic progress. Athens took a very different path; perhaps it was at first unique.[38]

We have seen how an economy can be organized that does not make use of the market as a price-fixing mechanism that distributes goods and forces people to economize or at least teaches them how they can do so. (The reader is reminded of the technical definition of "economize" on p. 31.) Under such circumstances—and they appear to be the commoner circumstances—the state must organize production and distribution. Such an organization will involve people's giving and receiving, producing and consuming, according to their status. (The only other possibility that we can discover is that of a primitive, almost self-sufficient economy as that of the neolithic village, but both Athens and Sparta before the sixth century were much too complex for that.) Let us turn the question around now: Can an advanced economy be organized except around and by a political authority? The idea that it could seems not to have occurred to the Spartans; at least,

---

[38] The chief literary sources for the early history of Greece are two passages in Thucydides (i. 2–21, 89–117), several in Herodotus (v. 39–97; vi. 52–93, 125–131), and Aristotle, *The Athenian Constitution*. There are descriptions of the Spartan constitution in Xenophon and Plutarch, and the fragments of the archaic poets add something, as do many passages in Aristotle's *Politics*.

if they saw the possibility among the Ionian Greeks in such cities as Samos and Miletus, they rejected it. The Athenians under Pisistratus however developed, for the first time that we can see at all clearly, a complex economy that did not revolve about distributive relations organized according to status.[39]

A large number of Pisistratus' noble opponents left Athens on his coming to power. Some of their estates may have been distributed among the poor,[40]

---

[39] Note that even so extensive a commerce abroad as Miletus maintained with the Black Sea or Marseilles with the interior of Gaul does not necessitate a local market economy.

[40] Hammond, *A History of Greece to 322* B.C., pp. 79–85 and 180–195, contrary to most historians, doubts that the Pisistratids confiscated the estates of the nobility. No ancient authority attributes such an act to them, and the exiled nobles remained wealthy, some returned at various times, and at least some of those who returned entered into their old estates. This is surprising. We think in terms of a modern society and expect that the Pisistratids would do what the Communists did: liquidate the enemy class. The matter in practice, of course, was a bit more complicated, but the bourgeoisie and the nobility of Russia were "liquidated," in theory at least, as soon as they were expropriated, for from that moment they ceased to exist as bourgeois, as a possessing class. In fact the system worked very well, if one wants the ends that Lenin and his heirs did want. Even the French Revolution, which was in a way much more moderate and did not manage to destroy the aristocracy as a class, at least managed to destroy noble property on the night of August 4, when it abolished what the lawyers and politicians of that age called "feudalism," that is, the certain kinds of property and certain rights in property which descended from the ancient rights of the lord of the manor.

We are not certain why the Pisistratids did not do the same, but it may be worth speculating. Late in the previous century, Cylon had attempted to establish a tyranny and been prevented by the clans following their noble leaders to Athens to besiege him in the Acropolis. That is to say, at that date (623?), the ancient organization about kinship and the ties of family religion still took precedence in men's minds over the struggle between the peasant and the aristocrat. Certainly since that time the class struggle had become sharper in many places and minds, but there is nothing about Athenian history in the interval that proves with much certainty that the situation had changed completely. (The simple existence of the Pisistratid tyranny is the commonest proof, but we must not argue in a circle.)

Now suppose that the Pisistratids had not, in fact, expropriated the estates of the exiled nobles, even of those who went into exile. They can only have failed to do so because it was either extremely difficult or impossible. It would have been impossible in practice, if the peasants retained their clan loyalties. If their peasants remained loyal to the Alcmaeonids and other nobles, the expropriation of their property could have been accomplished only by putting a great number of peasants off the land. The strength of the state and its internal peace would hardly permit that.

The one conclusion that accords with all the evidence, then, is that the development of the state was uneven and that the Pisistratids presided over an uneasy compromise. Some of the nobles may have lost the loyalty of their clans and suffered the expropriation of their lands which, we assume, would then have been distributed by the tyrant. The new holders would certainly be staunch supporters of the tyranny. But many more peasants were in rather more doubt. They were willing enough to see the aristocrats expelled from the government and to see it no longer the instrument for the aggrandizement of the interests of the great families, but they were, nevertheless, held to their natural leaders by ancient ties of loyalty and religion. Not yet were these directed solely to the polis. That revolution

who thus became landowners, peasant proprietors, owing only the land tax
of one-tenth of their produce to the city. It is uncertain whether this tithe
was first levied by Pisistratus or was older, but it did provide the means of
loans to these newly established proprietors. Pisistratus himself possessed
mines on the Strymon in Macedonia. Perhaps at this time the silver at Laureion
came to be more efficiently exploited. At any rate it seems clear that the state
possessed greater revenues in his day than it had before and that much was
used to benefit the peasantry. The need for such loans is greater than it
would at first appear, for at this time Attica began more and more to specialize in the production of olive oil. It takes an olive tree some twenty years,
a human generation, to come to its full maturity and production. (Small
wonder then that the olive branch became a sign of peace among the Greeks;
trees are so easily killed by girdling them that the olive plantation could
prosper only in peacetime.) The new produce was slow in coming to fruition
and the peasant getting into the business of producing olives and olive oil
needed loans to tide him over.

We may be safe in assuming also that such specialized crops were necessary to create an independent peasantry. An agricultural regime based on the
cultivation of grain had given rise to aristocratic estates in Attica. It is doubtful that the small family-sized farm could make a go of it on such a basis,
although of course much grain continued to be raised. Specialization in olives,
however, implies that the Athenian farmer was producing for export.[41] This
export gave rise to a new organization of the economy. Such specialization
and export had, of course, appeared before. It was clear from the records in
Linear B found at Pylos and dating from the twelfth century B.C. that olive

---

would be achieved only by Cleisthenes at the end of the century, with the cooperation of
many of the returned exiles after the fall of the sons of Pisistratus in 510.

If this view is correct, the Pisistratids held power by an odd and perhaps awkward
coalition of interests. They were supported by many foreign powers, by the mercantile and
artisan population of Athens and the Piraeus, by any peasants who actually received land
from their hands, and by the more or less passive consent of a much greater part of the
peasantry. The doubtful attitude of this last element explains why the return of the aristocrats and the overthrow of the tyrants was always a real possibility and how it could in fact
be attempted several times.

[41] By the fifth century efforts at intensive agriculture were being promoted by handbooks
on plants and cultivation—Charmantides of Paros, Apollodorus of Lemnos, Androtion of
Athens, and certain parts of Xenophon's *Oeconomicus* and Theophrastus' *History of Plants*.
The rotation of crops improved; the two-field system of rotation was giving way to a three-
field scheme which allowed for winter grain, summer grain, and fallow, while the fallow
itself was replaced by a crop of vegetables or fodder, including lucerne, introduced from
Persia: Luigi Pareti, Paolo Brezzi, and Luciano Petech, *The Ancient World, 1200* B.C. to
A.D. *500*, trans. Guy E. F. Chilver and Sylvia Chilver, Vol. II of *The History of Mankind,
Cultural and Scientific Development*, sponsored by the International Commission for a History of the Scientific and Cultural Development of Mankind, UNESCO (New York: Harper
and Row, 1965), p. 384.

oil was produced there in greater quantity than was necessary for local consumption. However, its export was in the hands of the king who received it as tribute laid upon the land as a *quid pro quo* of holdings. The state did play some part in the foreign commerce of Athens in the sixth, fifth, and fourth centuries, but it is, however, abundantly clear that the organization of the economy under the Pisistratids was not in any way a return to the earlier system, whose very existence the Greeks had long forgotten.

That the tyrant undertook the promotion of foreign commerce seems clear from the war for Sigeum. Sigeum was a Lesbian fortress on the shore of the Troad, guarding the entrance to the Hellespont. Some forty years before Pisistratus' seizure of power, Athens had occupied this place, no doubt as a counterpoise to Megaran interests in the Black Sea trade. It seems that the place slipped out of Athenian hands again during her internal struggles. Pisistratus recaptured it, and the value he set upon a place that controlled relations with the Black Sea can be seen by his installing one of his sons as governor. It was Athens' first exploit in distant seas and her first act of maritime imperialism.

A more important achievement followed, one which was not the work of the tyrant, but oddly of his chief political rival. Miltiades, son of Cypselus, a member of the noble family of the Philaids and one of the leaders of the party of the plain, established Athenian power in the Thracian Chersonese.[42] Miltiades was probably glad enough to get away from Pisistratus and so accepted the invitation of a native tribe, the Dolonci, to bring an Athenian settlement and aid them against their neighbors to the north. Pisistratus must have been relieved to see such a dangerous subject go. Miltiades ruled the Dolonci as a Thracian king and the Athenian settlement in the Chersonese as a tyrant.[43] To protect the peninsula from the north he built a wall across its neck from Cardia to Pactye, waged war with the Greek city of Lampsacus, and established friendship with the king of Lydia. The Ionian cities had preceded Athens in the colonization of the Black Sea and the Propontis and, no doubt, in trading with the natives of these shores, the Thracians and the Scythians. But Athens took the field under Pisistratus and was to outstrip all her rivals. By the end of the Pisistratid tyranny, c. 510 B.C., the Athenians were overtaking the Corinthians and the Miletans, too, who were hampered by the Persian conquest of Asia Minor.

Thus under Pisistratus Athens followed a commercial path that we can more vaguely discern was taken earlier by the Ionian cities of Asia Minor—Ephesus, Phocaea, Miletus, and Halicarnasus—and by Corinth and Aegina. It would perhaps be best not to press yet the ultimate consequences of this

---

[42] Herod. vi. 34–40. "Chersonesos" is simply the Greek word for peninsula.

[43] "The Tyrant of the Chersonese was freedom's best and bravest friend./That tyrant was Miltiades. Oh, that the present hour would lend/Another despot of that kind. Such chains as his were sure to bind."—Byron, *Don Juan*.

and to present its final crystallization into a new, complete economic form and organization, but rather to trace the further economic innovations at Athens.

Pisistratus, like many other popular tyrants, undertook a program of building and public entertainments or civic education. The great Panathenaic festival had been remodeled shortly before his seizure of power, if it had not been founded then. Pisistratus made more splendid this festival of athletic and musical contests, whose central act was the procession to the temple of Athena on the Acropolis to present the goddess with a robe woven by the hands of Athenian maidens. He rebuilt the original temple and surrounded it with a Doric colonnade. Earlier architects and sculptors had used the marly limestone of the Piraeus, but those of Pisistratus' time introduced the use of harder marble.[44]

Pisistratus began an even greater work than the house of Athena. On a site which now stands in the Zapeion gardens, he began a great temple to Olympian Zeus. So immense was the scale of the undertaking that neither Pisistratus and his sons nor Athens at the height of her prosperity under Pericles could finish it. It was finally finished by the Roman Emperor Hadrian in the second century A.D.[45]

More important to us than even the Panathenaic festival was another work of the tyrant. At the foot of the Acropolis Pisistratus built a new house for the god Dionysus, and there instituted a new festival, the Great Dionysia, in honor of the god, which completely overshadowed the old festival of the wine press. Within a generation the dances of this new festival would develop into Attic tragedy and give rise to the theatre which we recognize as the distant foundation of our own. Like so many others in the Mediterranean world who desired the name of a benefactor, Pisistratus built waterworks, an aqueduct which carried waters from the upper stream of the Ilisus to the city.

Both the splendid celebration of festivals and the new buildings called for the work of artisans and craftsmen. So did the export of farm products, wine, and olive oil. The potter, living in the city, whether a freeborn citizen, a metic (resident alien), or a slave, produced not only the luxurious vases that caught the fancy of barbarian chiefs, but also the plain amphoras in which oil and wine were shipped. Such persons were not part-time artisans and merchants. Neither the scale of production that developed after the fall of Pisistratus' sons, Hippias and Hipparchus, nor the skill demanded of metal-

---

[44] This is not the Parthenon whose ruins are seen today. That work was built in Pericles' time, served during the Middle Ages as a Christian church dedicated to another virgin, and was blown to pieces by a Venetian bomb during a war with the Turks, who used it as an ammunition depot. Pisistratus' structure was to the north of the later Parthenon, by the site of the old royal palace.

[45] The cathedral of Cologne, which is one of the largest, although certainly not one of the best of the Gothic cathedrals, was begun in the thirteenth century, but its spires were not completed until the nineteenth. Work on many of the greatest of the French cathedrals— Paris, Amiens, and Rheims—has, strictly speaking, not yet been completed, for their spires— certainly envisaged by the original architect—have never been added.

workers, potters, and the painters of the pots permitted peasant production. How, then, were these artisans and merchants to make their livelihood and provide themselves with food? The answer was the produce market, a place where farmers came to sell food retail, even food ready to eat. Here the landless craftsman and merchant could buy his daily bread with the wages he received. He did not need the sort of allotment from the state or temple that supported the craftsman of the Sumerian temple, for his coin was freely taken. But notice that without the institution of the provision market, coins would have been worthless for he could not get his daily bread by means of foreign trade. Notice too that the provision market could not have functioned if the peasant had not willingly brought in his produce for sale. This willingness implies that he received a *quid pro quo*, that the market was producing things he desired and could afford. The Athenian agora is the first such market about which we have much information.[46] The marketplace we have seen at Sardis must have resembled it, and it can hardly be doubted that such markets existed in some of the Ionian cities at an earlier period than at Athens. Archaeological excavations reveal two agoras at Corinth, one of which should have been devoted to retail sales.[47]

Probably by the end of the sixth century the marketplace was a regular feature of the Greek city-states, with the notable exceptions of Sparta and the small Dorian cities of Crete.[48] Thus at Athens—and presumably elsewhere— the small peasant was saved from the moneylender and the great landowner by the presence of a local market on which he could sell goods and of long-distance trade for which he could provide bulk products. An uncontrolled system of production for export was made possible by the presence of a pro-

[46] The student should be reminded of the distinction between a market and a fair. A fair will be a meeting at which professional merchants buy and sell and exchange goods with each other at a prearranged time and place. As such, it is likely to be an annual, semiannual, or quarterly event. A market in the first instance is a place where people can buy food for consumption and where farmers can sell it. As such, it will generally be frequent, perhaps weekly, but the earliest Greek markets appear to have been held daily, i.e., to have been perpetual.

[47] It seems likely that Corinth had such a market under the tyranny of the Bacchiadae family (c. 750–610 B.C.). She took a toll on goods passing across the Isthmus of Corinth and, we are told, fought the first sea battle in Greek history with her colony of Corcyra in 640: Kathleen Freeman, *Greek City-States* (New York: W. W. Norton and Co., 1963; originally published 1950), p. 88.

[48] The peculiar Dorian constitution usually left business in the hands of the *perioeci* and excluded them from citizenship. Crete after the Dorian invasions was certainly backward. The earliest inscription there in the Greek alphabet is the earlier code of laws from Gortyna, which is dated to the early sixth century. From this it appears that fines were reckoned in cauldrons or tripods rather than in coins, which were first minted in Crete only at the beginning of the fifth century. Still, the best known archaic site, Lato, in the east of the island, has an open agora with a portico along the west side. This place could have served as a market as well as a meeting place for the citizens on political matters: John D. S. Pendlebury, *Archaeology of Crete* (New York: Biblo and Tannen, 1963), pp. 329–30, 339.

vision market which made it unnecessary to create an elaborate system of controls and allotments to maintain artisans of the sort that we have seen in Mesopotamia and at Mycenaean Pylos. For the first time in history, there appeared an urban class that made its living on the market, that needed to buy and sell in order to live. If this innovation did not first take place at Athens, it is first truly visible to us there; it developed its greatest political and social consequences at Athens, those found in Athenian democracy and Athenian imperialism; and it was through Athens that this innovation reached the rest of the Mediterranean world.

7 ARISTOTLE AND THE MARKET

Before the late fifth or early fourth century in Greece, we find no efforts in literature to analyze economic activity, except for advice about how to farm well, such as that given by Hesiod. But in the late fifth century Thucydides was able to make a profound economic analysis of Greek history, and Socrates, who himself left no writings, appears to have considered the problems of wealth getting: two of his students, Plato and Xenophon, wrote about the matter. Even more important, in the fourth century, Aristotle, who began his teaching in Athens about 355 B.C., devoted considerable attention to the analysis of economic activity. There are doubtless a number of reasons in Greek intellectual development that account for this, but one appears to be that until the market made its appearance, economic activity had never been sufficiently separated from other human activities to attract particular attention. Even the most important area of economic activity, agriculture, was so embedded in religion and tradition that rational thought about improvement was almost impossible.[1]

We can see little of the early development of Greek economic thought. The archaic poets were puzzled by some of the characteristics of money and speak of efforts to distinguish pure gold from alloys.[2] By the fifth century systematic handbooks on agriculture were appearing, and a real part of economic life was isolated and rationally treated.[3] But only with the development of the market could the segment of human activity concerning economics be sufficiently cut off, so to speak, from other activities that attention was drawn to it as a discrete activity to be analyzed. With the establishment of the market as an economic institution it is possible, at last, to attempt a modern market analysis of ancient economic activity.

---

[1] Contrast, for example, the life of an ancient peasant family with that of a modern American factory worker. The peasant's religion was tied completely to his plowing and reaping, as were his sports and his holidays. The entire family devoted all its attention and efforts to agriculture (though not all its time to labor). The modern factory worker leaves his home to work. His family has no part in his economic activites and may never see them. When suburban children are asked at school what their father does for a living, they often do not know and have to inquire at home, usually of their mothers. Labor is separated from the rest of life and consequently is a suitable subject for analysis.

[2] Bolin, *State and Currency*, p. 22.

[3] The earliest to survive is Xenophon's *Oeconomicus*. See above Ch. VI, p. 117, note 41.

The market is one of the common ways of organizing society for pro- duction and distribution. Market institutions are not necessarily basic to a society. We have seen that they are not necessary at all. Furthermore, a market may not be the way in which people go about accumulating wealth. The market may be, and by the fifth century had become, one of the ways in which a particular society acquires the production that it needs and allocates that production among the various groups in the society. *The market is simply a rationing device.* The significant difference between a market operation and the other methods of rationing is that the latter deal with real wealth, while markets deal with money wealth. Other methods of rationing deal directly with the actual things that are distributed. In market operations purchases and sales are usually made for money, not directly for other commodities or services.

A market may be dscribed in two ways, by its institutions and by its functions. As a group of institutions or elements, the market may be defined by looking at its component elements: private property and inheritance, money wealth and income, the profit motive, standardized commodities, and an exchange of price information within geographic limits. The mere exist- ence of these elements, however, is not enough to create a market. A society might possess all the necessary institutions without in fact having anything that functions as a market.

It is necessary, then, to consider what the market does. A market is a series of transactions by buyer and seller where prices measure the scarcity of a commodity on the market. A high price indicates that the quantity of a given commodity on a market is low when measured against buyer demand; low prices indicate that the quantity is great when measured against buyer demand. The market exists for a specific quantity of a specific product at a given time. The term "free market" is perhaps redundant. In the sense that the word "market" is used here, an unfree or controlled market is impossible. It is an essential point of market trading that the political authority of the society (government, temple, gilds) gives up control of production and dis- tribution to this impersonal mechanism. The market mechanism of exchange must determine the use of resources regardless of the status of the individual participants to the transaction, regardless of the relation of the individuals to the transaction and to each other. Transactions on the market must result in prices which measure only the scarcity of standardized commodities in a given market at a given time. Even politically powerful interests and corpora- tions must agree to accept the market decisions whether or not the outcome of a particular market transaction favors a person of high status. In short, market trading does not exist unless the elements within the society univer- sally agree to accept the market as the method of allocating resources and commodities.

Clearly a society may have markets for some products and not for others. Grain can go on the market in a social order which prohibits entirely the alienation of land from the clan by sale. In most societies some things are not directly marketable: for example, public office in the United States.

PRIVATE PROPERTY AND THE MARKET

Probably all societies have some concept of private property, though in some it is very limited. A considerable domain of private property is necessary before a market economy is possible. The social institution of private property is simply the legal acceptance of two propositions: (a) that people have the right to use their own resources (time, money, chattels, land) as they wish, subject only to limitations safeguarding other peoples' property and rights; and (b) if property is lost or stolen, the government and law will aid in returning property to the legal owner. Private property, then, involves more than mere physical possession. It involves a social, and hence a legal, sanction to use property and to transfer title with considerable freedom.[4] Clearly no market can occur unless the transfer of property is accompanied by a transfer of title or ownership.[5] Such transfers of title must be sanctioned and guaranteed by the government.

The peculiar character of a society is largely determined by its ideas of property. An owner of property is less concerned with property itself than with its use. A coin, a spear, a wife, a slave, a herd of cattle, a plot of land, a first mortgage, a bottomry loan, and a right to contract are all property. A savage claiming a share of a crop or part of a catch, a lord of a fertile field, a sea captain with his cargo, and a speculator selling futures are all men of property.

Since the nature of property and its permissible use characterize a society, the sanctions attached to the ownership and use of property characterize its economic system also. For an economic system to be a market system, exchanges of private property must be accompanied by simultaneous exchanges of legally recognized rights in property and its use. No market could operate if litigation or quarrels over the legal title of the property could not be settled.

Private ownership of property, then, is an essential condition of the market, but its existence does not guarantee that a market will exist or that contractual exchanges will occur. To be sure, in the absence of private prop-

[4] Yet many limitations are possible without making the market impossible: Christian teaching about usury did not prevent the development of a medieval money market, and the medieval system of fiefs did not prevent the eventual development of a market in land.
[5] "Ownership" is said for convenience, but it is meant here to cover any number of rights of possession such as usufruct and servitude in Roman law, and tenures in feudal law. In both of these ownership in the strict sense remained vested in a third person. The possessor need not be a single human being but may be a corporation such as General Motors or the Archbishopric of Chicago. English and American law call both "persons." In other societies the owner or possessor may be the family, clan, a saint, or a god.

erty in the ancient Near East and early medieval Europe, we find a distributive economic order. Is there, then, some relation of cause and effect between private property and the operation of a market? It seems that insofar as there is monolithic ownership and control of property (as in the Sumerian temple communities, or with the god-king pharaoh of Egypt) there can be no development of a market. Where private property was so limited, there could be no market trading. While there could be a considerable development of governmental status distribution and some marginal barter, there could not develop a price-making market. Hereditary private property did develop in the ancient Near East before Greek influence was felt but did not give rise to the market. That development took place in the area of the Greek household economy and was thence transported to the Near East by the conquests of Alexander. By 330 B.C., however, the Near East was ready to receive and to use this institution as it could not have a thousand years earlier.

A type of private property developed in Greece which appears to be a prerequisite to the origin of markets in Greece and thus warrants our somewhat more detailed consideration. The Dorian invasions destroyed the Mycenaean civilization and with it the status-distributive economy which had been ordered about the royal palace. In the Homeric age, when we can again see clearly something of the Aegean social order, property in land was in the hands of clans and clan chiefs. In the archaic period private property in land emerged out of this society.

The old Anatolian system of large estates worked by serf labor that existed before the arrival of the Ionians continued to be employed there. But while the nobility of the Ionian invaders may have gained large land holdings by right of conquest, or by marriage into the Anatolian landed aristocracy, all of the settlers were not nobles. Small free holdings undoubtedly were allocated from the conquered land. While there is little explicit evidence to support this view of the small free holdings, two considerations do tend to support it: the Homeric reflections in the *Iliad* of the social and economic conditions in Ionia, and the evidence of the emergence in the Ionian cities by the seventh century B.C. of a hoplite class (the heavily armed infantry drawn from independent farmers of average means). Since we are in fact dealing with an agricultural community, the basic form of wealth was land. By Hesiod's time property in land was heritable, divisible, and probably alienable. By the sixth century B.C. there is ample proof that property in land was in fee simple, that is, private individual ownership without obligation or condition.

While it is possible to have control of the products of the land without owning the land itself and to have a market for produce without a market for land, private property in land was probably conducive to the development of the market in archaic Greece for two reasons. Ownership of the produce followed from ownership of the land, and the peasant owner of the hoplite class was no longer a member of a large, self-sufficient economic unit. He had to look beyond the farm for his needs. Two conditions of market operation were thus met: private property in kind and the need for exchanges. These conditions might arise in a society which was not dominated by private property in land, but in Greece private property in land seems to have preceded the market.

REAL AND MONEY INCOME

Transactions in distributive economies invariably take the form of commodities of real value. This is so even when transactions are in value of standardized weights of a precious metal. Market transactions are usually exchanges of a commodity for money. Often the money is not present except as an I.O.U. or credit instrument. There is an essential difference, however, between real wealth and money wealth and between real income and money income. The profit motive attaches only to money wealth or income.

One of the first writers to focus directly on this distinction between real wealth and money wealth was Thucydides. He contrasts the Peloponnesian War with the war carried on by the Greeks against Troy and discovers a difference in wealth between the two periods. In the earlier period the wealth of the community was reckoned in land, the products of the land, the quantity of arms, treasure, utensils, metal in general, and the possession of large houses and slaves. In the latter period the Greeks, especially the Athenians, possessed wealth in the form of coin which could command all forms of real wealth.

The cause of the length of the Trojan War was not, according to Thucydides, so much the lack of men potentially available as a lack of money. The impossibility of marshalling resources by purchase with money on a market limited the Greeks to an army which could live on the Trojan countryside while at war. When the Greeks arrived and prevailed in battle initially, they seemed not to have used their whole force. They had to farm in the Troad and to pillage the countryside in order to obtain supplies.[6] Because the Greeks had to divide and scatter their forces in this fashion, the Trojans were able to hold the field against them for ten years. The main reason given by Thucydides for the insignificance of the effort against the Trojans was the lack of money and the lack of a market in which to buy supplies. But by the time of the Peloponnesian War, the economy had progressed so far that a distinction between real and money wealth could be made and could become a tactical factor in the conduct of the war.

The immediate cause of the Peloponnesian War was a conflict between Corinth and Corcyra. The Athenians came into the conflict on the side of Corcyra; Sparta came to the aid of Corinth. The main motives of the

[6] Thuc. i. 3–12; cf. John H. Finley, Jr., *Thucydides* (Ann Arbor: University of Michigan Press, 1942), ch. iii.

Athenians were that the island of Corcyra off the western coast of Greece (Epirus) was an admirable stop on coasting voyages into the western Mediterranean and to Italy and the value of Corcyra's navy.

Thucydides puts into the mouth of a Spartan king a speech stating that the type of power of Sparta and most of her Peloponnesian allies is in real wealth. The Spartans have never engaged in the commercial market activity. The Athenians, he argues, are experienced in seamanship and are better equipped with respect to public and private real and money wealth, while the Spartans have neither money in the treasury of the state nor would they find it easy to raise money from private resources by taxation, for the Peloponnesians, apart from the Corinthians, have never engaged much in market or trading activity.[7] They do not have money available, for money wealth involves not simply coin or the medium of exchange, but market operations by which the money may be turned into goods and supplies. Pericles, in considering this same question before the Athenians, notes that the Peloponnesians (with the exception of the Corinthians) tilled their land with their own hands. They had little money, either private or public.[8]

In other words, according to Thucydides, the strength of the Athenians lay not so much in their real wealth as in their commercial orientation and the money wealth and the market operations with which they were familiar. By the time the Peloponnesian War began there was, then, a clear recognition of the distinction between money wealth and real wealth and the role that money wealth played in commanding real wealth.

PROFIT MOTIVE

With Aristotle wealth and profits take on a precise meaning. Since Aristotle began his teaching in Athens about 355 B.C., he is dealing with the Athenian market at a relatively sophisticated stage. This is significant because he is familiar with market developments following the Athenian defeat in the Peloponnesian War, and thus, assuredly, with Athens' need to attract commerce and wealth simply through the development of the market apparatus. Aristotle, then, is talking about this relatively late stage of the economic development of the Athenian community.[9]

When speaking of possessions Aristotle notes two uses for property, a proper use and an improper or secondary use. The first or proper function is the value of a thing in household use. The secondary use is its value in exchange. This distinction may be made of all possessions, for the art of exchange extends to all property or possessions. The value in exchange arises out of the natural and proper value in use.

[7] Thuc. i. 80–5.
[8] Ibid. 141–44.
[9] Aristotle Politics 1256ª–8ᵇ.

Aristotle notes there are two types of exchanges. One involves exchange with another person for the necessities of life. This sort of barter is not part of the wealth-getting art and is not contrary to nature, because it is necessary for the satisfaction of men's natural wants, since the household cannot be self-sufficient. The other method of exchange is more complex and grew out of the simpler. When citizens of one country became more dependent on those of another and imported what they needed and exported what they had too much of, money came into use. Because the necessities of life are not easily carried about, men agreed to employ something which was instinctively felt to be intrinsically useful to the purposes of life, such as iron, silver, and the like, as a measure of value. In time a stamp was put upon the metal to save the trouble of weighing it. This is money.[10]

When the use of money as coin had been discovered, the simple barter of necessary articles gave way to a second type of transaction which is the art of getting rich. This is termed retail trade, which aims at the accumulation of coin. The art of getting wealth, which consists of household management, has a natural limit in the satisfaction of the members of the household. The basic purposes of the household are the health, safety, and welfare of its members. Money is useful to this end because it facilitates barter. In retail trade, however, the end is the mere accumulation of coin by means of exchanges. Although man does not desire unlimited quantities of consumer goods, there is no natural limit to his desire for money, since money commands all goods and can be hoarded for the future.

Many men, Aristotle believed, confused money and real wealth. The cause of this confusion is that wrong-headed men believe that the purposes of household management may be served by seeking and increasing bodily pleasures. Since the enjoyment of bodily pleasures depends upon property, their aim becomes the unlimited acquisition of property, including money. When this occurs, men try to change every art into the art of getting riches, and consequently they transform the art of household management into the art of retail trade. But this is an unnatural perversion and the two should be distinguished. The profit motive attaches not to wealth but to the accumulation of riches or coin which is accomplished in a market distinct from the state and the household.

But Aristotle failed to analyze the market as a price-setting mechanism. The reason for this failure is probably to be sought less in a failure of his acumen than in the stage of development of the market in the Aegean at that time, in the limited scope and magnitude of market operations, and in the Greeks' moral insistence upon a proper limit to real wealth and the dangers of an unlimited pursuit of coin.

---

[10] For a critique of Arisotle's theory of the origin of coinage, see Vidal-Naquet, Appendix B, and Ed. Will, "De l'aspect éthique des origines grecques de la monnaie," *Revue historique*, CCXII (1945), 209–34.

EXCHANGE OF INFORMATION

The position of Corinth on the gulf and on the isthmus joining the Peloponnesus to central Greece was an ideal location for both land and sea communication. Travelers had to pass through Corinth, and thus the Corinthians became a rich and powerful people. When navigation grew more prevalent among the Greeks, the Corinthians acquired ships, swept the sea of piracy, and offered a market by sea as well as by land. They raised their city to a great power by means of the revenue thus obtained. By the time of the Corinthian mercantile development a separate word distinguished merchant vessels from warships. The Corinthians had developed a significantly modern plan for the harbor: the basin itself, docks and storage facilities, and provisions for constructing and repairing ships.

One of the elements necessary to a market is adequate information about the goods and services demanded and available for sale and their prices. The slow and limited means of communication in the ancient world made specific locations necessary (a need that is felt even today). From the time such information becomes available the market no longer exists simply because it happens to be in the path of travelers or trade; it attracts people who desire information about goods, services, and prices. The Corinthian market became a central point not only for travel and exchange of goods but was perhaps the earliest international center for market information.

A single center for information about international market exchanges is a necessity for any trade area. Consequently when Athenian commerce took the lead in the early fifth century B.C., Athens and the Piraeus took over Corinth's function as a center for information and attracted business which would not otherwise have had to come to Athens. The international information center has a particularly strong attraction for banking and persons involved in the money market. It may be surmised that this attraction was at work in Athens at least from the early fifth century, but we have almost no information until the fourth century B.C. It should be noticed that this special function of the market as an information center does not work in the local provision market. There, information about goods and prices is simply a natural outcome of trading activities and does not attract further business.

Prices measure market conditions. Standardized goods are a necessary condition of a regularly functioning market. Without standardized goods buyers cannot bid for specific types of goods and prices cannot measure market conditions. Unless the goods and services on the market are standardized, the price will measure the quality as well as the scarcity of the product. To give an example, if a talent of silver is the standard of value and products are not standardized, then a high price for a cow, say 1½ talents of silver, may mean that the cow is of excellent quality or it may mean that cows are in short supply relative to demand. To be sure, products such as cows cannot be perfectly standardized, but they usually can be graded into classes acceptable to trade. Products such as grain and olive oil are more easily given standardized grades. In barter transactions products need not be standardized, for real goods are exchanged for real goods. Barter transactions do not create prices. Price is the way in which buyers and sellers read the conditions of supply and demand in the market. This is a basic distinction between market and barter transactions.

Clearly, one of the keys to understanding the nature of a market involves the knowledge of and the communication of supply-and-demand conditions among the various buyers and sellers. The essence of market transactions requires that the prices of earlier transactions be known in the accomplishment of current transactions. It is only by a knowledge of the prices of prior transactions that one learns the conditions of supply and demand in a given market. Thus the prices of previous transactions must impinge upon—in fact must help determine—the prices of current transactions.

Here we have one of our key differences between a market and a port of trade. Exchanges in a port of trade may be so infrequent as to permit no continuity; they nearly always take place at predetermined rates of exchange set by tradition or treaty and are influenced by the political relations of the parties. Information about such prices communicates nothing to the participants. The very essence of market transactions is a sufficient sequence of prices so that the prices of prior transactions will affect subsequent transactions—e.g., that higher prices will induce traders to bring in a greater quantity while lower prices will reduce the supply brought in or induce larger purchases. It is only through the knowledge of prices of prior transactions that one is able to communicate to buyers and sellers the conditions of supply and demand of goods and services on the market.

MONEY AND THE MARKET TRANSACTION

Trade is the movement of goods from one market to another. It will be convenient at this point to make a distinction between the trader and the merchant and to say that: (a) traders move goods from one point to another in response to political commands,[11] while (b) merchants move goods from one place to another because prices differ in different markets; seeking a profit, they cause the market to operate. In nonmarket trading, unlike market trading, there is no risk of loss on a transaction.

The point we wish to emphasize is the relationship of money to prices in the exchange of standardized commodities and services on the market. *Money is an arbitrary measure of value, a unit of account.* In this sense coin does

---

[11] The reader may wish to refer to Chapter 3, "The Economy in Primitive Sumeria."

not have to exist in order for money to be used or to be a unit of account. As long as all persons involved agree that this designated unit shall measure the value of all commodities and services traded on the market, money exists as a unit of account. If, however, free exchanges are to be made—that is, exchanges without the intervention of political power—money must be a circulating medium of exchange. The usual term applied to money as a circulating medium of exchange is currency or coinage. As a medium of exchange, money is defined as something that people accept not for its inherent value in use but because of what it will buy.

A market is made up of buyers and sellers attempting to accomplish their respective aims. A market transaction is a choice by a buyer of the product of a seller and the arrangement of acceptable compensation to the seller for the goods or services sold. The transaction normally implies the exchange of commodities or services at suitable prices. The price is the value of the commodity or service in terms of the standard of value. The elementary step, then, is not necessarily coinage but the willingness of both participants to a transaction to agree that the value of the commodities or services involved shall be measured in terms of a third idealized and arbitrary commodity. This is money as a unit of account and a standard of value. The next step is relatively easy and simply requires that the standard of value shall no longer be a commodity of real wealth like an ox or a talent of silver but shall be stamped onto an ingot or plug of metal and guaranteed by the state. Merchants need no longer weigh the metal disks; they need only count them. The value need not have a one-to-one relationship to the quantity of precious metal in the plug or ingot itself. Such a plug or ingot of metal passed in exchange is a coin. Coins are in fact money as a medium of exchange.

The use of coins broadens the choices of both buyer and seller. In a barter transaction a seller of sheep who wants a cow is limited to trading with a man who has a cow and wants sheep. When coins become a medium of exchange the limits are removed. The seller of sheep may sell sheep to anyone in the market who wants sheep and can pay for them and with his money he can buy cows from anyone who has cows to sell.

The final development in the idea of money is to be found in the Athenian market development of the fifth and fourth centuries B.C. When money loans were developed, money became an instrument of credit. As an instrument of credit, money becomes a standard of deferred payment. Thus coin fulfills all four of the recognized functions of money, by operating as a standard of value (unit of account), as a storehouse of value, as a medium of exchange, and as a standard of deferred payment.

At the same time that money becomes a standard of deferred payment, it also becomes something quite different—it becomes capital or a factor of production. Production is usually defined as the combination of the basic factors—land, labor, and capital—into the creation of a finished product. With the development of banking and loans, money becomes a basic resource, a way of saving, of directing investments, and of mobilizing and allocating factors of production to given ends. (In this respect it comes to fill a function that political power exercised in the earlier status-distributive economies.) At this point a market develops for the purchase, sale, or rent of money as a factor of production. It will return interest to its owner. Interest is payment for the use of money as capital: it is rent for money.

It is essential to keep these distinctions in mind. Money as a standard of value (unit of account) does not need a physical existence: neither coins nor currency are necessary. Money as a medium of exchange is a physical presence —a coin or bit of stamped paper which will be accepted in exchange for commodities or services. Money as a factor of production need not necessarily exist as a physical presence but may appear as a substitute (a draft, letter of credit, or I.O.U.) expressed in terms of the unit of account. Thus even in the fifth and fourth centuries B.C. the Athenians made bottomry loans in which no currency changed hands, but in which credit instruments mobilized money to develop commercial ventures.

Aristotle regarded money solely as a medium of exchange (coin) and thought it was justified only because it eliminated the inconvenience of barter. Other uses for money were unnatural:

> There are two sorts of wealth-getting: . . . one is a part of household management, the other is retail trade. The former necessary and honorable, while that which consists in exchange is justly censured; for it is unnatural, and a mode by which men gain from one another. The most hated sort, and with the greatest reason, is usury, which makes a gain out of money itself, and not from the natural object of it. For money was intended to be used in exchange, but not to increase at interest.[12]

The Athenian businessman regarded money in another light, as a factor of production that was essential to production and distribution. This focus led to the conclusion that money was a part of the process of production and distribution, as in the Athenian bottomry and *respondentia* loans. If so, money, like any other factor of production, should earn income, the return being interest. The interest paid to the lender or owner of money is compensation to the lender for: (a) the inconvenience to the lender by reason of his foregoing present use of the money, (b) the risk of loss, and (c) the lender's share in the income and product created by the use of the money in production.

Characteristic of the bottomry loan is that the lender provides capital in the form of money to the borrower to purchase objects exposed to risks in overseas commerce. The borrower shall repay the sum only if the objects to which the loan was applied arrive at their destination. If they are lost at sea, the borrower is released and need not restore the sum borrowed. Minute pre-

---

[12] Aristotle *Polit.* 1258ª–8ᵇ, trans. W. D. Ross.

cautions were taken to protect the lender, and moneylenders did not hesitate to invest relatively large sums in this type of loan.

Thus money by the fourth century B.C. was no longer merely an instrument of direct exchange between buyers and sellers. It had finally taken on the characteristic of a basic resource to be used in the process of production and distribution. Despite the philosopher, the Aegean and Mediterranean businessman knew the value of money as capital and its role in commercial and production operations.

8 THE MARKET AT ATHENS

By the time of the Persian Wars at the opening of the fifth century B.C., an economy organized about the market had appeared in the Aegean world and in some regions connected with it. This new system was far freer of political control than any earlier one. Its center was at Athens which came to dominate and integrate the new system and where the economic institutions necessary to a market and money economy developed during the next two centuries. Athens made the effort to take advantage of the political consequences of the new system in the creation of a democracy and an imperialistic empire. This effort was defeated in the Peloponnesian War (431–404) by economically conservative Sparta and her allies, several of them commercial cities jealous of Athens' success and damaged by it. Consequently the Greeks themselves never found political institutions suitable to their bursting economic energies. That task was left to the Macedonians following the conquests of Alexander the Great at the end of the fourth century.

Long before the Macedonian conquests, however, the system was expansive. It behooves us, then, to follow the invention of market institutions at Athens and attempt a description of the working economy. This market economy remains the prototype of the most advanced levels of the ancient economy down to the fifth century A.D. The Athenian market economy was the model that the Macedonians introduced into the ancient Near East. Indeed, this expansion involved moving Macedonia itself out of the patriarchal system into a market and money economy. This chapter will attempt an account of the period of Athenian hegemony; the next will give an account of the economy after Alexander.[1]

As early as the eighth century the older aristocratic economy was being supplemented and broken by a new system. The household economy, which had once been served by wandering artisans, the demiourgoi, came to demand products by sedentary artisans. The development can be traced to some degree in the pottery discovered in excavations. With the introduction of oriental

---

[1] Perhaps the best standard and introductory works on the economic history of fifth-century Greece are Gustave Glotz, *Ancient Greece at Work, An Economic History of Greece from the Homeric Period to the Roman Conquest* in *The History of Civilization*, ed. C. K. Ogden (London: Kegan Paul, Trench, Trubner, 1926) and Alfred Zimmern, *The Greek Commonwealth. Politics and Economics in Fifth-Century Athens*, 5th ed. (London: Oxford University Press, 1952).

styles a number of centers, like Miletus, Samos, and Lesbos, grew up which distributed to considerable areas. By the middle of the seventh century the distribution of Corinthian pottery in the oriental style reveals a great change in the productive and distributive system in the Aegean. Other centers disappeared and from about 650 to 575 B.C., Corinthian pottery was exported to all parts of the Aegean, except Miletus, which continued to command her own area, and to the Black Sea, Syria, Cyrene, Carthage, and above all to the western colonies in Sicily and southern Italy. Only Rhodes retained a part of the international market. Then a generation after Solon's reforms a much superior Athenian ware, the black-figure style, surged ahead. It was followed after the Persian Wars by the new red-figure style,[2] whose distribution was also very wide.

Pottery was, as far as we can trace, the most centralized and commercialized product of Greek industry, although the reader should keep in mind that the literary sources say little about economic matters and that pots, or at least identifiable potsherds, unlike other manufactured products, are indestructible. Other manufactures were certainly produced at particular centers. Athens specialized in armor and in luxurious silver work. Megara produced common clothing; Pellene, plushy cloaks; Miletus, military cloaks; Argos, cauldrons; and Chalcis, swords. Corinth continued to produce blankets, long garments with fringes, and linen cloth. Cos was famous for fine cloth, and Tarentum and Patrae for linen. Chios, Miletus, and Cyprus produced hangings, embroidered garments, and carpets. Syracuse in Sicily sold woolen textiles in many colors.

Raw materials and some manufactured goods came from outside the Greek sphere. Metals and metalwork came from Etruria in Italy and metal probably from Spain through the mediation of the Carthaginians. Egypt, when trade was not interrupted by a Persian embargo, sent not only grain, but papyrus, linen, glass, ointments, and ivory and frankincense that she imported from the south. In addition to grain, the Black Sea sent fish, iron, chestnuts, and almonds from Sinope; hemp and wax from Phasis; and hides and cattle products from the Crimea. The Aegean was short of wood and especially needed good shipbuilding timbers. A great part of the need was supplied by the ports of the Black Sea. Sicily sent not only grain, but cheese, hides, pigs, and timber. From the north end of the Aegean came wood, flax, pitch, livestock, grain, gold, and slaves.

It should be noticed that this list is a bit peculiar both from the modern point of view and by comparison with the trade we have seen in the ancient Near East. A good part of the trade was, as we should expect, in luxuries, such as special clothes. But a certain number of absolute necessities are involved, of which the most important is grain. For the first time, it seems, a

[2] R. M. Cook, *Greek Painted Pottery* (London: Methuen, 1960) for the styles. A considerable number of the Athenian painters and potters are known whose work can be identified.

large area was truly dependent upon imported food. Grain was supplemented by less essential fish and pork. (Little beef was eaten except in connection with the sacrificial feasts on the greater holidays.) A number of useful, almost necessary, goods, like papyrus and ship timbers also came from abroad. Thus the Aegean system was essentially dependent upon imports (and consequently on exports). Foreign trade was thus not simply a matter of importing luxuries for the temples, the gods, the aristocratic landowners, and the possessors of political power.

In the latter part of the sixth century Greece had experienced a considerable, though moderate, increase in precious metals: gold and silver from Thasos, the Thracian coast, and Siphnos; silver from the Athenian mines at Laureion. Then between the First and Second Persian Wars in 483 B.C. or a few years before, the Athenians made a great new strike at Laureion. It was not the first mining there, but it brought in immensely greater quantities of silver than before. In a few years the state accumulated 100 talents as its share. The increase in bullion did not cease here. Soon the king of Macedonia would receive even more: a talent of silver a day from the mines of the Strymon. The gold of Mount Pangaeos was attracting the Athenians. Late in the fifth century Persian gold would enter Greece as subsidies for political ends. King Philip of Macedon in the fourth century would draw 1,000 talents a year from the workings of Mount Pangaeos.

Athens took her place at the center of the system. Under the government of the Pisistratids the Athenians began to learn the value of sea power and the new democracy learned to use the new system of exchange to gain naval hegemony. Themistocles persuaded the Athenians to use their new wealth from Laureion to build the fleet which defeated the Persians at Salamis in 480 and saved the freedom of Greece. In the Greek world, as Thucydides so clearly saw,[3] command of the sea meant empire, both political and commercial. It was her fleet which enabled Athens to take up the championship of the Greeks in the place of the traditional and hitherto undisputed leaders of Greece, the Spartans. After the second Persian invasion Athens marshalled the island cities, formed them into a league, and liberated the cities of Asia Minor. The league, first established at Delos but transformed into an empire with its center at Athens, gave Athens a money income from tribute. Hence, control of the navy was essential to her commercial domination. Not herself particularly rich in raw materials, Athens became the center of the new commercial system that had been growing up since the eighth century. Athenian pottery dominated every market. Its production depended upon Attica's possession of fine potter's clay and worked in well with her export of olive oil and wine in which she had tended to specialize since the reforms of Solon. But such production and the possession of the mines of Laureion were hardly sufficient to make Athens the center of the commercial system. Athens was

[3] Thuc. i. 12–4, 140.

also the single international market, and she held this position on account
of her navy and her ability to protect seaborne commerce from other powers
and from pirates. She was even able, in spite of the inveterate localism of
Greek life, to produce rules for the conduct of commerce and courts to decide
commercial cases between citizens of the different cities of her alliance. Hence
Athens became the nearest thing that the fifth and fourth centuries knew to a
nineteenth-century London. She was the center of international exchanges,
the best place that merchants of all nations could get information about the
state of the market, the banking center, the seller of maritime insurance,
and the general clearinghouse for debts.

Much of our information about the organization of trade and industry
comes from the orators of the fourth century.[4] There is reason to believe that
fourth-century industry was more highly developed than in the fifth century.
Some concerns were larger, wealthy entrepreneurs were wealthier, and banking and credit were more developed. Yet the best we can do is to develop
something of a composite picture.

Household production certainly survived, but the rule of production for
the market was the small shop. Occupations were becoming more specialized
than before. There were leather workers with shops which specialized in
saddles, harnesses, shoes, or even in particular kinds of shoes. In potteries,
shaping, firing, and decoration had been separate occupations from the sixth
century; but in the fifth shops began to specialize in certain shapes. In the
building industry some progress of specialization can be seen between the
Erechtheum accounts of 421–407 B.C. and those of the buildings at Eleusis in
the 320s.[5] Among cabinet workers, some confined themselves to beds, some
to chairs, some to boxes. Employment by private persons of free citizens for
wages was uncommon and seems to have been avoided. There is little evidence that the average Athenian despised handwork, but much evidence that
he heartily disliked working for another man, especially on a regular basis.
To be subject to another man's orders was fit only for a slave. It is not
surprising, then, that slaves were widely used. They were also remarkably
cheap compared to those later times about which we have any information.
We cannot estimate the average number of slaves in an Athenian shop: perhaps most had none or one. But some shops were fairly large. Since half the
black-figure vases of Athens that have signatures come from five masters and
another quarter from ten more, we can conclude that in Pisistratus' time there
were a few factories of considerable size that managed to reduce costs by
large investment and concentration of production. They were not large by
later standards but controlled a considerable proportion of production. There
are some definite figures from the fourth century. The bed factory that
Demosthenes the orator inherited employed 20 slaves, his arms factory 32 or

---

[4] The corpus of Attic orators consists of the speeches of Antiphon, Andocides, Lysias,
Isocrates, Isaeus, Lycurgus, Aeschines, Demosthenes, Hyperides, and Dinarchus.
[5] Glotz, *Ancient Greece at Work*, pp. 226–7.

33. A shield factory bequeathed to Apollodorus had twice the output of Demosthenes' and may, therefore, have had twice as many slaves. The largest of which we know is the shield factory of Cephalos of Syracuse (a metic settled at Athens) in 404 B.C. which employed 120 slaves. Some of the owners of these shops had capital to enlarge them if they wished, but it is of interest to note that Demosthenes' father preferred to possess two factories producing different products than to enlarge one.[6]

Megara specialized in the production of rough woolens traded to barbarians for slaves, and this production in the middle of the fourth century produced the greatest fortune in Greece, although Megara was a small city. Phocis was a land of free labor until the Holy War ended in 346; then it began to be a center of great industry. A single entrepreneur, Mnason of Elateia, is said to have imported 1,000 slaves, who must have been mostly for industrial purposes.[7]

Only the mines employed labor on a much larger scale. The reason apparently lay in the market. Some producers could produce without a specific order: when the Thirty Tyrants confiscated the factory of Lysias, they found, along with great stores of metals, 700 finished shields. Some pottery was produced for an anonymous market, but the craftsman found no advantage in producing without ceasing and in sinking much capital in the shape of stock, and much pottery was produced on order because the demand was restricted.[8] Rather than concentrate in a single operation, the really wealthy preferred to spread their investments. Only the mines at Laureion could produce indefinitely without ruining the market or tying up capital in unsold produce. The land at Laureion appears to have been privately owned, as were the shops for working the metal and extracting the ore. But it seems that from the time of Pisistratus the state reserved mineral rights. The state never worked the mines directly, however, but rather let them out to private, generally small, entrepreneurs. The register of mines published by Oikonomos from an inscription

[6] The question of slavery in classical antiquity has been much discussed. We have the most information for fifth- and fourth-century Athens and for the late Roman Republic, and hence controversy has centered there. Since Marx and Engels maintained that the ancient economy was a "slave economy," the argument has revolved about whether slavery was the "basis" of the more advanced stages of the classical economy. (It certainly was far less important in less polished times.) The question, however, is futile unless some specific meaning can be given to such a concept as "base" and, like the arguments about whether the ancient economy had a "capitalistic phase," is best avoided. From the point of view taken in this work, slavery can be considered as one aspect of labor as a market commodity. It was an element in capitalization, but since it involved the use of force as well as the free play of the market, it necessarily led to what modern analysis would call economically irrational results. On the controversy about ancient slavery, see George Thomson, *Studies in Ancient Greek Society*, II (London: Lawrence and Wishart, 1955), pp. 196–205; Moses I. Finley, ed., *Slavery in Classical Antiquity* (Cambridge, Mass.: Heffner, 1960).

[7] Julius Beloch, "Grossindustrie in Altertum," *Zeitschrift fuer Socialwissenschaft*, II (1899), 23, citing Isocrates, fr. 117; Xenoph. *Mem.* ii. 7. 6, and Timaeos fr. 67.

[8] Glotz, *Ancient Greece at Work*, p. 272.

is certainly incomplete, but it reveals some 35 concessionaires. Some of the exploitations at Laureion were on a large scale, or a number may have been joined in the hands of one man. Nicias hired out 1,000 slaves to Sosias, a metic, for work in the mines; Hipponicus hired out 600; Philomenides 300. When the Spartans, during the Peloponnesian War, occupied Deceleia, they are said to have released 20,000 slaves from the workings.[9]

This hiring-out of slaves is worth a word. It was common to hire slaves from their master for the harvest, oil pressing, and other periods of intensive farm work. The state employed seventeen public slaves at the constructions at Eleusis, but many of the workers there and at the Erectheum were slaves on hire from their masters. Such a tactic made possible a more continuous employment of slaves, and some Athenians lived on the wages earned by their few slaves.

Sources of slaves were birth, war and slave raids, chiefly upon barbarians, and the loss of civil status due to debt (except at Athens). Cimon threw more than 20,000 prisoners on the market after the Eurymedon campaign. Chios, Ephesos, Byzantion, and Thessaly were the great markets of supply, but almost all sales seem to have gone through the Athenian market, where there was a monthly fair in the agora. Part of the cargoes went to the mines, and surplus imports were reexported to Sicily. The price of a slave was probably about equal to the ransom of a prisoner, which in the sixth century had commonly been two minas (200 drachmae); by the beginning of the fourth century it had risen in Sicily to three minas, and later it oscillated between two and five, settling at the latter, higher figure after Alexander's conquests. Late in the fifth century, male barbarian slaves cost about 105 dr. and Thracians about 167, while well-trained Syrians might run to 240 and even 300 dr. The cost of women varied, depending upon their intended occupation. In the fourth century mine workers cost 184 dr. or perhaps 154; their life expectancy was short. Field workers sold for as low as 125–150 dr. Skilled workers, of course, were worth much more: cabinet workers, 2 minas each; an armorer from 3 to 6 minas. Prices were more variable in the fourth than in the fifth century, a measure of the increase in skills and specialization.[10] It can be seen that slavery at Athens was concentrated in industrial and commercial occupations, and Glotz is probably correct in judging that slavery appeared in Greece as a concomitant of trade and industry, its prevalence varying according to their development. There were a few grand households with large numbers of slaves in the fifth and fourth centuries and some Italian Greeks appear to have had large numbers of slaves, who probably were employed in agriculture, but such were not found at the center of the commercial system in the Aegean where the greatest fortunes were not in land or in manufacturing, but rather in commerce. Sosias employed a thousand slaves in the mines of

[9] See C. N. Bromehead, "Mining and Quarrying," *History of Technology*, I, pp. 1ff.
[10] Glotz, *Ancient Greece at Work*, pp. 189, 194–5.

Laureion, but Pasion, the metic banker, realized his business for a capital of 60 talents, which may have given him an income of 40,000 dr.

In placing orders for public works, about which we have a good deal of information from inscriptions, the state regularly split up the work into units that could be handled by persons of very modest capital, whether it was a matter of supplying goods or of doing work. "The work on the Erechtheion was the occasion of a vast number of small payments. The largest sum mentioned in the Eleusis accounts of 328 B.C., amounting to 7,087 drachmae, was paid for binding the windlass with iron, i.e., for an indivisible operation"; another came to 2,600 dr., after which only one or two items rose above 500 dr.

In Athens, too, we see something of the economic institutions that developed in a market economy, and probably in large part they were developed there, though there was certainly an early market at Corinth and probably others in the Ionian cities.[11] The first thing that strikes a student who has viewed the economies of the Near Eastern states is the remarkable freedom that commerce enjoyed. Customs tariffs were moderate and levied for income rather than protection, as would be expected in an international emporion. Special judges, the *nautodikai*, judged disputes between traders, cases of transport, shipbuilding, and dockworkers, and by the fourth century rules had been established to guarantee judgment within a month, a promptness which, if it were met, would be the envy of the modern litigant. There were ten market commissioners (*agoranomoi*)—five for the Piraeus and five for the city. Their duty was to see that all articles offered for sale in the markets were pure and unadulterated. The same number of commissioners of weights and measures (*metronomoi*) were to see that sellers used fair weights and measures. These officials were elected by lot.[12] The market in the city, the agora, was the great retail market, whose function we have seen above. Its hours were fixed by regulation. Places were assigned to various goods, and the holders of stalls paid a rent to the city.

The one great exception to the freedom of commerce was the corn trade. Grain was stored in a special warehouse at Piraeus. It was the duty of the superintendents of the mart to compel merchants to bring up into the city two-thirds of the corn which was brought by sea to the corn mart. The corn commissioners (*sitophylaces*) were to see that the unprepared corn in the market was offered for sale at reasonable prices and that the millers sold barley meal at a price proportionate to that of barley and the bakers sold bread at a price proportionate to that of wheat. The law also required them

---

[11] It is not certain that something more cannot be learned about the earliest Greek markets. Classical historians do not seem to have dealt with their origin as a specific problem. Archaeology and inscriptions may eventually throw some light on the distribution of markets and of market institutions in the Aegean world, if not upon the very origins of the institutions themselves.

[12] Arist. *Res. Athen.* 51.

to set the weight of loaves. The reason for the state's concern for the grain trade is obvious. No city could leave its provision in necessities to the chances of the market; in times of dearth the government was, indeed, forced to take far more active measures to ensure a supply of grain. The same thing was certainly true of other Greek cities: aristocratic governments might act to reduce popular discontent; democracies reflected the desires of the consumer, and in Athens did so intelligently. Still, to judge by rather parallel situations among the city-states of the Middle Ages, it may not be bold to suggest that manufacturing and mercantile interests, which employed labor, had a great interest in keeping down the price of grain and thus encouraging immigration. At any rate, if Athens' policy were successful, and it seems to have been moderate enough in its demands on the grain merchants, the price of grain would have been unnaturally low at Athens. It was for the grain trade that Athens secured for herself by treaty a privileged position on the grain markets of the Cimmerian Bosphorus, priority of loading, and exemption from the export duty in the fourth century.

The harbor at Piraeus replaced the open roadstead at Phaleron, and its works appear to have been provided by the state. There were wharves, slips, and arsenals for the fleet; moles; and five porticoes for warehousing all goods but grain. The Piraeus was built by Hippodamus of Miletus on the checkerboard plan, which became almost standard thereafter in the Hellenic world. In it were found those necessities for a transient and mercantile population that have ever since marked seaports: hostelries and inns, taverns, and houses of dubious reputation. They were run by private persons, not the state.

While the state seems to have provided adequately for the needs of sea travel and the conduct of commerce at the port, it was not so attentive to land-bound trade. One great shortcoming of state activity was roads, which certainly were very inadequate. Another was the absence of a public post even for government business. There seem to have been no regular private letter carriers and deliveries. This lack was not made up by such messenger services as fourteenth-century Italian merchants maintained to inform themselves of market conditions abroad, though information did, of course, move about the great ports by word of mouth.

The other functions of the Athenian government in relation to business were simple. Athens in the fifth and fourth centuries B.C. kept no official record of the ownership of and transfer of land and thus had no basis for the evaluation of property for taxes. Private commercial documents were not registered with the government or by authorized notaries nor was there a record of obsolete legislation. The state's function was limited to the enforcement of contracts by suits brought before a court by private persons. Courts accepted the testimony of witnesses rather than documents, or only documents substantiated by the testimony of witnesses. References by earlier Attic orators to written agreements, except wills, are rare, and the deposit of contracts and wills with public officials or in public offices was extremely unusual: for the two centuries between 400 and 200 B.C. only three cases are known. Written contracts however were commoner for maritime transactions than for land.[13]

The corporate structure of business appears to have been remarkably simple, indeed almost lacking. There were no craft gilds of which we have any record and the forms of organization are simply the shop handed down from father to son, the *societas unius rei*, and the partnership, although it is possible that the state permitted some further corporate development for the farming of the customs.

Commerce showed little of the specialization of industry; the merchant traded in anything and everything. In the fifth century the ship owner and sea captain (*naukleros*) were usually the same man, who moved about in his ship—or his partner's ship—from port to port. While he might intend to go to the Crimea for grain, this was only because he knew in a general way that there was demand for grain in the Aegean area. On the way out and back he would be likely to trade in other goods.

In the fourth century the *phortegos,* who carried his goods on another man's ship, came to the fore. Aristotle is careful to distinguish the two and to distinguish them both from the local agent with whom they dealt at the other end, whose work is called *parastasis*.[14] This shift suggests a growth of capital and a concentration of it in the hands of persons who could afford to forego the profits of undertaking travel themselves. The use of factors resident abroad and of regular newsletters giving information about the state of market do not, however, seem to have been common. Merchants in the classic period must have worked very largely in the dark. Consequently windfall profits must have retained an important place in trade.

Everything, then, indicates that the age before Alexander saw concentration of wealth, complication of the instruments of business, and—if the matter may thus be put—a readiness for industrial and commercial expansion on a large scale.[15]

---

[13] Moses I. Finley, *Studies in Land and Credit in Ancient Athens, 500–200* B.C. *The Horos-Inscriptions* (New Brunswick, N.J.: Rutgers University Press, n.d. [1951]), pp. 14ff., 19, 21, 27.

[14] Zimmern, *Greek Commonwealth,* pp. 321–2.

[15] On Greek business methods, see the rather technical work of Fritz Pringsheim, *The Greek Law of Sale* (Weimar: Hermann Boehlaus Nachfolger, 1950). Its legalistic orientation and vocabulary make it difficult for the economic historian to use. It is to be hoped that the economic implications of such studies will gradually be worked out and explained in a less technical vocabulary.

9 THE HELLENISTIC ECONOMY FROM ALEXANDER THE GREAT TO THE ROMAN CONQUEST

THE OLD ORDER

The development of the Greek economy met a check to further growth in the fourth century. As Thucydides so clearly saw, the failure of Athens in the Peloponnesian War foreclosed the possibilities of wider political unity and hence of greater economic growth and integration. Neither Sparta nor Thebes, both of which bid for the hegemony of Greece in the fourth century, could provide the political unity which would have permitted an expansion of the new market economy, because neither was the center of a market-oriented system on an international scale. After her defeat, Athens again emerged as the chief commercial center of Greece and organized much of the economy of the Aegean and its periphery about her market. But wider growth, dependent upon greater political unification, could not be achieved in the face of Greek disunity and the hostility of Persia. Asia and Egypt were not open to the Greek market practices until the conquests of Alexander the Great opened the Persian Empire—or at least the western parts of it—to the methods and organization of Hellenic economic integration.

In fact what we see happen from the fourth to the second centuries B.C. is the rise of a number of peripheral powers on the model of the center: Macedonia, the Hellenistic kingdoms, and Rome. This was both a political and an economic process which has been more often studied from the political point of view. As far as our sources permit, we shall try to view it as an economic process. (The reader should, however, keep in mind that ancient sources deal far more with politics, and we shall sometimes have to talk about political development when we should like to talk about economic development.) This process of imitation of a central area by less developed peripheral states and economies is a recurrent one in history. We have already seen one instance in the imitation of the Sumerian state-ordered status-distributive system by the northern Mesopotamian, Syrian, and Anatolian states. We shall see a third example at the opening of the modern age, when the national monarchies of northern Europe imitate the political and economic organizations of the Renaissance Italian city-states, and a fourth in our own age, when the peripheral states of Russia and the United States come to overshadow western Europe by imitating much of her productive and distributive organization. Such imitation, of course, involves innovation as well. The most striking element of such innovation is the greater size of the peripheral states. The old center will long remain the most highly organized part of civilization and will possess the greatest store of wealth and culture and the greatest pool of human skills, but it will eventually be overborne by the sheer size of its imitators.

In the course of the fourth century the kings of the old tribal monarchy of Macedonia created a military state built on a far greater scale than the poleis of old Greece. This state-building was largely the work of Philip II (359–336 B.C.). The picture of the earlier Macedonian state gleaned from the pages of Herodotus and Thucydides is of a tribal confederation whose monarch maintained some sort of leadership through tribal loyalties. He sought the loyalty and cooperation of other tribal chiefs by maintaining himself as the chief gift giver, the fount of honors and splendid works of craftsmanship, those splendid objects and heirlooms which Aristotle so significantly included in his list of kinds of wealth. Its economic order, then, was much like that of the Scythian tribes we have already described. Such a monarchy was much dependent upon subsidies from abroad. It seems odd at first sight that in the fifth century, Athens, even while she was engaged in a struggle with most of the independent states of Greece, could control the much larger state of Macedonia and that Macedonia could not intervene against Athenian control of the cities on the Macedonian coast. Having no commercial economy, Macedonia lacked money. The kings depended upon subsidies from abroad to raise support among the tribesmen. Without these it was impossible to call out the militia or even to prevent civil strife. But the fourth century saw an economic transformation.

King Archelaus (413–399 B.C.) had built roads and, following the example of Greek tyrants, made his court at Pella a center for artists and poets and a city on the model of the Greek polis. Philip II reorganized the army on the model of the Theban phalanx and it was about the army—rather like modern Prussia—that the Macedonian national monarchy was reorganized. The reorganization of the peasant army and the establishment of military discipline called for the institution of regular pay. This made the peasant soldier dependent upon the king rather than his "natural" leader, the tribal chieftain. Philip seized the great fortress of the Strymon, the city of Amphipolis, and converted the Thasian settlement of Crenides into a great fortress, which he called Philippi after himself. The gold mines of Mount Pangaeus on Macedonia's eastern frontier were thus secured and miners were brought over from the island of Thasos, where gold had long been exploited. The yield of the gold mines soon reached 1,000 talents a year (some 8,000 lbs. avoirdupois). No Greek state was so rich. With these means Philip united the hill tribes and made the highlanders into professional soldiers, kept always under arms. "A professional army with a national spirit—that was the new idea." [1]

With this instrument Philip's son, Alexander, imposed order on Greece and conquered the world empire of the Persians. The results of these conquests in the economic sphere were revolutionary. They introduced money exchanges and the market economy into the parts of Asia Minor as yet untransformed by the Hellenic economy, as well as Syria, Palestine, Egypt, and Mesopotamia. Alexander's conquests, of course, extended further to the east, as far as Iran and the Indus Valley. These Asian conquests and the new Greek kingdom of Bactria had important consequences in the history of art *and* civilization but need not be considered here.

Yet it is possible to believe that the economic changes of the late fourth and third centuries were not simply the result of the Macedonian conquest and the migration of Greeks to the east. There seem also to have been forces at work that made the ancient Near East ready for such a change. It may, then, be best first to look for signs of change in the old economic patterns of the territories Alexander conquered, signs that the ancient status-distributive system was breaking down or was ready for transformation and that the ancient Near East was ready for a market economy.

In some sense the restoration of the status-distributive system after the introduction of iron and the great invasions of the late second millennium had never been perfect. The vast size of the states that then developed, especially the Persian Empire, made a tight system of economic integration impossible. A system of exploitation and tribute could be imposed upon smaller and more coherent states, like Israel or Egypt or the Mesopotamian cities, which retained a status-distributive system, but the Persian Empire as a whole could hardly enjoy such economic coherence.

Iron had made cheaper production and easier artisanship possible, opening new possibilities for the distribution of goods. In the original status-distributive system of the Sumerian city-state there had been little demand on the part of peasants for the products of the town. Exchanges between primary producers and the city could not maintain the economy. But iron tools and weapons were relatively cheap and were useful to the peasant. At least some possibility appeared that craftsmen might maintain themselves by exchanging their products for the products of others, e.g., peasants and shepherds. The Iron Age economy of the ancient Near East, however, does not seem to have exploited this possibility to any considerable degree nor to have provided the market institutions suitable to it.

The Persian kings, to be sure, did mint coins, the gold darics. There

[1] Bury, *History of Greece*, pp. 686–7. With this accomplishment of Philip it is interesting to compare the work of contemporary statebuilder, Mausolus of Caria, *ibid.*, pp. 688–94. The Carian "peripheral" state, too, had to adopt to the new economy and did so by building a navy and attempting commercial exploitation. It is indicative of the times but did not, of course, produce the immense consequences that the Macedonian reform did.

seems to be no evidence, however, that they were used for market exchanges or were regularly circulated in trade. The government rather hoarded them against emergencies and used them to buy off barbarians, to bribe Greek politicians, and to pay for Greek mercenaries.[2] Some coins seem even to have been minted for this express purpose. A coin of the Athenian type, but with the portrait of Tissaphernes, satrap (governor) of the Anatolian coastal provinces, is thought to have been minted at Miletus in 421/11 B.C. for payment to the Spartan fleet in the Peloponnesian War. At the same time certain other "satrapal" coins were issued: one seems to have been struck at Colophon or Iasos about 400 B.C., again by Tissaphernes, in connection with a campaign against the rebellious Ionian cities; another such issue was made by Pharnabasus for the payment of Conon's fleet in 395/94.[3] Thus the Persians were issuing coins in order to subsidize the enemies of Athens during the latter stages of the Peloponnesian War, and thereafter they continued to intervene in Greek politics in the same fashion. During the fourth century stories were freely circulated about the subsidizing of barbarian kings and the bribery of Greek politicians by Persian gold. In short, Persia was finding that military and political ends required the adoption of some new economic forms.

But the introduction of coins into the Near East was also in some way connected with trade. Corinthian coins are found chiefly in the west, in Italy and Sicily; those of Athens traveled to Egypt and the Levant. Many hoards of the late fifth and fourth centuries show that there was a very substantial supply of Athenian coins. A hoard of some 10,000 Athenian tetradrachmae was discovered at Tell el-Mashkouta in Egypt. Further evidence of the penetration of Greek coins deep into the Persian Empire is provided by a Babylonian goldsmith's hoard.[4] In Egypt and Babylonia such coins must have been treated as bullion. But how did they get there? They can hardly have been booty, for the hoard in Babylonia was in private hands and Egypt is not likely to have profited from a Persian victory over the Greeks. It is more likely that they are to be connected with trade. By the end of the fifth century, the activity of local mints around the Levantine coast from Pamphyria to Phoenicia had greatly increased and there is a corresponding decline in the number of Athenian tetradrachmas of the fourth century. This change was probably hastened by a shortage of Athenian silver during the later part of the Peloponnesian War, especially after the disruption of mining operations at Laureion in 413.[5] Generally, it seems that the Phoenician and Greek com-

[2] Xenoph. Anab. i. 1. 10. The standard work on the Persian Empire in English, A. T. Olmstead, History of the Persian Empire (Chicago: University of Chicago Press, 1948), has several chapters on the economy.

[3] Jenkins, Historia, II (1953–1954), 214–6.

[4] Ibid., pp. 219–20. The indispensable work is S. P. Noe, Bibliography of Greek Coin Hoards, 2d ed., Vol. LXXVIII of "Numismatic Notes and Monographs" (New York: The American Numismatic Society, 1937).

[5] Colin M. Kraay, Greek Coins and History, Some Current Problems (London, Methuen, 1969), pp. 47–9.

merce on the Mediterranean by the fifth and fourth centuries far surpassed in quantity and value any trade that had preceded it. At least during the periods of Egyptian independence from Persia, Egyptian grain was sent to Athens and other Greek cities through the fondaco of Naucratis. This was, to be sure, state-controlled treaty trade rather than a free market operation. But it differed from that we have seen before in several ways: from the Greek side the trade was in private hands and its products were destined for the market in Greece; on the Egyptian side the trade was still controlled by the pharaoh, but its regularity and size differed from the earlier trade to Punt and Byblos for luxuries. Egypt was exporting a staple and bulky necessity—wheat. In return she continued to receive silver, for which there had long been a demand in Egypt, but the silver was now received in the form of coins. What difference this may have made in Egypt is unknown—probably none, except the introduction of an idea. We cannot guess to what degree the demands of the Greek market may have influenced production and investment in Egypt. Both Mesopotamia and Egypt lacked mints until Alexander's conquest.[6] Greek trade with Syria and the interior was funneled through a similar port of trade, Al-Minah, where Greek merchants were settled, and Greek coinage was imitated by Byblos, Sidon, and Tyre from the middle of the fifth century and during the fourth and by Carthage perhaps as early as the late fifth. In the fourth century, the Jewish temple state imitated Athenian drachmae.

There are tantalizing hints of change in areas less exposed to the activities of Mediterranean traders. In the Mesopotamian cities the ancient temples and their priesthoods show a curious development. We hear of persons holding office in the temple for a part of a year and even for a few days and of the sale of temple offices. What seems to be involved is something like an annuity. The officeholders had divided their property among their heirs, and this property included temple offices and the right to the income attached to them. (This income was chiefly in kind rather than in metal.) Two sons might divide the income, each taking the office and perquisites for half the year. Division went much farther, and such incomes were bought and sold.

Banking, and hence the allocation of investment, had largely passed from the temples into private hands. From Nippur we have the accounts of a private bank, Murashu Sons. The archives of another banker, Egibi, have also survived.[7] The ancient formulas remained, but the reality had changed. The economy was no longer so completely controlled by state and temple. Clearly

---

[6] *Ibid.*

[7] A. T. Clay, *Business Documents of Murashu Sons of Nippur Dated in the Reign of Darius II, 424–404 B.C.*, Vol. X of *The Babylonian Expedition of the University of Pennsylvania. Series A: Cuneiform Texts*, ed. H. V. Hilprecht (Philadelphia: Department of Archaeology and Palaeontology of the University of Pennsylvania, 1904) ; *Legal and Commercial Transactions Dated in the Assyrian, Neo-Babylonian, and Persian Periods* (Philadelphia: Department of Archaeology and Palaeontology of the University of Pennsylvania,

by the Persian period, the ancient integration of the Sumerian city-state was a thing long past.

These are hints that the Persian empire failed to integrate the economy satisfactorily. We may suspect that there was considerable dissatisfaction on economic grounds, not from the always oppressed poor, but from persons of some wealth and position who saw new possibilities which the economic system did not permit. Be that as it may, the conquests of Alexander the Great ushered in a new spirit of enterprise and daring and a new order of economic institutions.

THE ECONOMIC EFFECTS OF ALEXANDER'S CONQUESTS

The empire of Alexander, although its unity was maintained for only a short time after his death in 323, managed within a few years to create a new and vaster area of active commerce which united the Mediterranean to the Near East in a more intimate fashion than had the old ports of trade. It also extended commercial contacts farther to the East. Alexander's military campaigns beyond Persia were also campaigns of exploration. He extended his conquests to the foot of the Hindu-Kush Mountains and established a city, another Alexandria, to connect perhaps with the caravan trade to China. The expedition to India more clearly involved commercial objectives. He entered India from the north and sailed down the Indus River. From its mouth he led his troops along the dreadful desert coast of Baluchistan, while his admiral, Nearchus, sailed back to the mouth of the Tigris and Euphrates. (That the march turned into a disaster need not concern us here.) On his arrival at Babylon he made plans to clear the river of fish weirs and to establish a port for the Indian trade. At the time of his premature death, plans were under way for either the conquest of Arabia—which would certainly have proved impossible—or, more likely, for its circumnavigation. Such an expedition would have opened the way for sea traffic from India and Mesopotamia to the Red Sea and Egypt. The new city of Alexandria-by-Egypt would have been the terminal point of this route, all the stages of which could have been in the hands of Alexander's subjects. The Egyptian Alexandria was to be the point of contact between this eastern system and the commerce of the Mediterranean. The reopening of the ancient canal from the Red Sea to the Nile would presumably have provided an all-water route.

1908); *Legal Documents from Erech Dated in the Seleucid Era* (Philadelphia: Privately printed, 1912); A. T. Olmstead, "Materials for an Economic History of the Ancient Near East," *Journal of Economic and Business History*, II (1930), 234; G. Cardasia, *Les Archives des Murasû, une famille d'hommes d'affaires babyloniens à l'époque perse, 455–403 av. J.-C.* (Paris: Imprimie nationale, 1951).

The site of Alexandria is remarkable. It is built on a spur of rock jutting out from the western desert, as near the delta as possible, but not in it. It thus avoided the floods of the delta to which it was connected by a canal. Before Alexander it had been the site only of a miserable fishing village. The ports of Egypt had hitherto been on the Nile at the eastern edge of the delta facing Palestine and Syria; stations for coastal trade had always turned east. Now for the first time the port of Egypt was directly on the Mediterranean and turned toward the Aegean.

Had Alexander lived to rule his empire and to maintain its unity, his scheme might have born fruit more fully and quickly. In fact the exploration of the Arabian coast never took place and the carrying trade from India to the Red Sea and Egypt remained for the time in the hands of the southern Arabs. There is some reason to believe that northern explorations were also planned. It was commonly believed that the Caspian Sea was connected with the ocean and that a route might be found to the north of Europe. But Alexander's death and the confusion and civil wars that followed it cut short such efforts, and the further development of the north was long delayed.

The Persian king had minted coins, but his great wealth was in hoarded bullion. A large chamber at the head of the Great King's bed was called the "cushion" and is said to have contained 5,000 talents of gold; a small chamber at the foot of the bed, the "footstool," to have held 3,000. In all, 120,000 silver talents are said to have been confiscated at the Persian capital of Persepolis.[8] This immense wealth was coined and distributed by Alexander, largely in payment to soldiers—including some native soldiers—and probably, too, in payment for labor on the great public works and programs of city building. Thereafter coins were in circulation throughout all the areas of the former Persian Empire. (Something of the consequent inflation of prices in Greece can be traced.) In Alexander's own lifetime the most important mints were at Amphipolis in Macedonia, Babylon, Tarsus in Cilicia, and Alexandria-by-Egypt. That at Alexandria continued to operate under the Ptolemies. In the Seleucid state each of the eastern provinces was served by a single mint: Seleucia-on-the-Tigris served the province of Babylonia and also such general purposes as military commitments; the mint of Susiana was at Susa; of Persis at Persepolis; of Media at Ecbatana; of Bactriana at Bactra; and there was probably one more at either Hekatompylos or Artacana in Parthia. The western parts of the empire had mints in Mesopotamia, Syria, Phoenicia, and Cilicia.[9] A single standard of weights, however, did not endure. The Attic standard dominated the Aegean, Asia Minor, and Seleucid Asia, while the Phoenician system was adopted by the Ptolemies for Egypt and her Palestinian and Mediterranean dependencies and by Carthage in the west.

The presence of coins alone would not have revolutionized the Near

[8] Olmstead, *History of the Persian Empire*, p. 250, citing Diod. xvii. 71. 1; Curt. v. 6. 9. See also W. W. Tarn, *Hellenistic Civilization*, p. 250.
[9] Jenkins, *Historia*, II (1953–1954), 221ff.

Eastern economy, but Alexander and his successors (except the Ptolemies of Egypt) also founded many cities on the Greek model. Some areas in the eastern parts of the empire were urbanized for the first time. Elsewhere some of the cities were new and wholly Graeco-Macedonian, while others were established alongside older native cities. Alexander hoped and planned to use natives in the government of his empire and to bring even the Persians into partnership, but his successors did not carry through this policy.

After Alexander's death his immense empire fell to a number of rival generals: Ptolemy in Egypt; Seleucus and his successors in Parthia, Babylonia, and Syria; Bactria under Euthydemus in the east, Pergamum, and a number of native states in Asia Minor. The kingdom of Macedonia fell to the descendants of Antigonus, while many of the old city-states in Greece banded into the Aetolian and Achaean Leagues. Some cities, such as Athens and Sparta, were sufficiently strong to maintain their formal independence and some real freedom of action. The rivalries and wars of these states, however, did not destroy the economic unity which had begun to form under Alexander. The wars of these rivals were bitter and even more expensive. In the successor states, the government and the army long remained in the hands of Greeks and Macedonians and the cities were dominantly Greek. A place like Alexandria had a Greek community and a separate native one, as well as a Jewish *politeuma*. Typically, each ethnic group lived in separate quarters. Some ruling elements in the native population might be Hellenized, and the towns were always dominated by persons of Greek culture. The peasants remained what they had been, speaking their native languages and maintaining much of their older social institutions. There would be an enduring tension in the Hellenistic and Roman worlds between these two elements.[10]

These Greek settlers introduced all of the institutions of the polis that were necessary for Greek life and training: the assembly,[11] theater, gymnasium, military training for citizens, and the market institutions we have seen at Athens. Most of these new cities, like the old ones of the Aegean area, were small and their market transactions largely local. But in the grain trade and in the production of special manufactures, chiefly luxuries, they played into an international scheme of trade that pivoted about international emporia:

[10] In Ptolemaic Egypt the Graeco-Macedonian monopoly of rule endured down to the Syrian wars with the Seleucids. The crisis came with the Battle of Raphia (217 B.C.), when the government had to call upon the native Egyptians for service in the army. Henceforth some promotion had to be offered the natives. Earlier only the temple aristocracy had survived to some degree and under strong government control. The breach was, of course, never truly healed, as any reader of the Gospels can sense, and even in the fourth and fifth centuries A.D. the rise of Christian heresies and of Christian literatures in Coptic and Syriac may be manifestations of this social condition. Down to the fourth century A.D. the literary culture was wholly Greek.

[11] An exception at Alexandria-by-Egypt should be noticed. The Ptolemies were reluctant to grant the corporate rights of Greek political institutions to their capital, and the great numbers of Egyptians and Jews complicated the picture.

Seleucia-on-the-Tigris, Alexandria, Antioch in Syria (which replaced the old port of Al-Minah), Rhodes, and later Delos.

Thus the new Hellenistic market economy created a far larger area of trade in which the market replaced the port of trade and for the first time really integrated the ancient Near East with the Greek world. The Mediterranean was on its way to becoming the "Middle Sea," the center of a commerce which sent out branches into the western Mediterranean, the Black Sea, the Indian Ocean, and the subcontinent of India itself. We want to trace, as well as is possible, the purely economic results of this transformation, the relations of the new economy to the state, and to see something of its effect in the creation of a profoundly new social order.

Private wealth appeared on a new scale. The richest man in Athens during the Peloponnesian War appears to have been that Nicias who led the expedition against Syracuse. His wealth can be estimated very approximately. It is modest when set against the wealth of some men in the Hellenistic age. When Alexander turned eastward for his Mesopotamian campaign, he entrusted the finances of Egypt to one Cleomenes of Naucratis. About 330 B.C. Cleomenes planned and brought off a brilliant coup by cornering the wheat market. There was general famine in Greece, while the harvest in Egypt had been good. Cleomenes used his political position to stop the export of wheat, which caused the Egyptian price to fall and that in Greece to rise even further. While the Egyptian barns were full, the Athenians were paying 32 dr. the medimnus. Cleomenes then bought up the Egyptian harvest at a price good enough to command the sale of the whole crop and organized its export on a large scale. In every port he had his agents provide information by private mail on prices and sales. Being informed of all demands and fluctuations, he was able to export without hesitation to the markets where prices were best.[12] His profits were enormous.

It should be noted, however, that the result was achieved only by the use of political authority. Indeed, the great fortunes of which we know were nearly always founded upon political connections rather than manufacturing or commerce. Trade seems to have been more likely than manufacturing to produce a considerable accumulation of money.

At the same time in the great eastern empires the moral limits upon avarice declined or disappeared. Avarice is no doubt universal, but it is not uniformly tolerated by all societies. Though modern Western society may look upon it as a social virtue, within the ancient polis the opinion of neighbors and the imposition of public burdens had limited accumulation. Now only the prince's envy and favor could curb ambitions of the wealthy. At the same time the citizenry lost control of the highest level of political affairs. The government of the Ptolemaic and Seleucid kingdoms and of the smaller Hellenistic kingdoms was the affair of the monarch. A morality and society of

---

[12] Glotz, *Ancient Greece at Work*, p. 364; Pseudo-Arist. *Oeconomica* ii. 2. 33.

private life developed and with them a taste for luxury on the part of the wealthy and a new literary genre whose object was to picture private life. It is best seen in the "Characters" of Theophrastus, which are sketches of human types, and in the surviving fragments of the playwright Menander.[13] Persons in such a society could and did devote themselves more whole-heartedly to accumulating money wealth.

TECHNOLOGICAL DEVELOPMENTS

There was some technological advance during the three centuries after Alexander. Hellenistic science deserves admiration; it was in this period that the Greeks achieved their highest development in mechanics, medicine and *materia medica,* astronomy, and mathematics. The most famous center of such studies was the Museum at Alexandria. Founded and subsidized by the Ptolemies, it was not a school, but a kind of institute of advanced studies where professors were paid to think, write, and edit earlier texts. Medical care among the upper classes may have improved somewhat; the pharma-copeia expanded, which must have had some slight effect on commerce and agriculture. The distillation of alcohol seems to have been discovered, although no practical consequences followed. There was perhaps some commercial value to geographical studies. But by and large scientific thought did not yet have any contribution to make to technology or the economy.

It is best to view the modest advances of technology in the Hellenistic period in connection with the market. In agriculture essentially the same methods were used as in the classical period in Greece, but that age had seen some rational differentiation of plants and their adaption to different kinds of soil. The demands of the towns for food seem to have pressed farmers into innovations of planting and manuring which made possible a threefold rota-tion.[14] The great number of Greek settlers in the East no doubt learned much from the natives about husbandry; they also introduced Greek methods and were less bound by tradition. Suitable varieties of plants and animals were transferred from one part of the world to another. Alexander himself had a lively interest in botany and zoology and, when on campaign, is said to have corresponded with Aristotle and to have sent him specimens. Sugar and cotton were grown in a small way, probably for the first time in the Mediterranean area. Sugar comes from India (the Greek word for sugar, *saccharon,* is de-rived from Sanskrit). Cotton may have been grown earlier in Assyria, but the Greeks seem to have learned of it on Alexander's expedition to India.[15]

[13] To our mind, perhaps, the surviving fragments do not bear out the ancient critic who asked, "Ah, Nature, Ah Menander, which of you the plagiarist?" but he probably reflected contemporary opinion.

[14] Xenoph. *Oeconomica* 16. 12–5.

[15] Perhaps earlier: F. E. Zeumer, "Domestication of Animals," *History of Technology,* I, 373–4.

It was grown in Ptolemaic Egypt and in Roman times spread from there to Malta, Asia Minor, Syria, the Persian Gulf, and Arabia. Neither of these products affected the economy as strikingly as they would in modern Europe,[16] though it is not quite clear why their culture was not more successful. The peach, cherry, and apricot also come from the East and were introduced into Italy by Lucullus in the first century B.C. It is likely that they too were spread by the Hellenistic Greeks.

The shaduf had been used for irrigation in Egypt since the second millennium B.C.

> It is usually made by erecting two pillars, some five feet or more high, joined near the top by a short beam. Over this a long pole is balanced, which has at one end a vessel to hold water and at the other a counterpoise. A man standing at the water's edge fills the receptacle by dipping, raises it, and empties it into an irrigation channel. With this device a man can raise about 600 gallons to a height of six feet in a day.[17]

Later a continuous chain of buckets seems to have been devised to water the Hanging Gardens. The ox-driven waterwheel, which uses gears to link a vertical shaft to a horizontal wheel, made its appearance about 200 B.C. This mechanism can water a half-acre in a day. With such a device gardening could be extended considerably in Egypt and perhaps in some places a second crop of grain be raised.

Hellenistic experts produced a number of treatises on agriculture which were useful to owners of large estates who had capital to invest. They are all now lost, but much of their content survives in the Roman manuals of Cato, Varro, and Columella, who copied from them. They seem to have been much concerned with increasing production and sale for the market. The development of such large-scale farm production for the market will come to a climax in Roman Italy during the late Republic.[18]

The advances in the mechanisms to process agricultural goods for the growing market were perhaps more considerable. Donkey-driven mills had been used to crush ore at the mines of Laureion in Attica in the fifth century. By about 300 B.C. their use was applied to grinding corn.[19] The earliest method of grinding corn had been the wooden pestle and mortar. By c. 2500–2000 B.C. the Egyptians were using the saddle quern. The pushing mill appeared in Greece by the fifth century. Its great advantage is that corn can be fed into it continuously.[20] The rotary quern was still rare in Greece in the

[16] Patterson, "Spinning and Weaving," *ibid.*, II, p. 199.

[17] T. K. Derry and Trevor I. Williams, *A Short History of Technology from the Earliest Times to A.D. 1900* (New York: Oxford University Press, 1961), p. 52. Cf. Strabo xvii. 30.

[18] F. M. Heichelheim, "Agriculture," *Oxford Classical Dictionary*, ed. Max Cary et al. (Oxford: Clarendon Press, 1949), s.v.

[19] Derry and Williams, *Short History*, p. 249.

[20] R. J. Forbes, "Food and Drink," *History of Technology*, II, 107–8 (illustration).

third century B.C., but it had spread through the Mediterranean and to Gaul and Britain by the first century. All these are really instruments for women to use at home. The donkey mill, on the other hand, gave rise to the miller's profession, although it was used on the farm as well as in town. Professional miller-bakers had made their appearance in Italy by about 170 B.C., earlier in the east.

There was a parallel development in presses for squeezing grapes and olives—important work in the Mediterranean. The earliest method was presumably to trample grapes with the feet. The squeeze bag must have come into use later. By the second millennium B.C. the Aegean world used a beam press with a lever fixed into a wall or between two stones to press down upon the squeeze bag. This device could be improved by a windlass and pulley to force down the free end of the lever. Screws to force down the lever appear to have been invented in Greece in the second or first century B.C. and to have been introduced into Italy in the late first century. (By A.D. 50, at the latest, some presses omitted the lever and used the screw to press down directly on the mass of fruit.) [21] An olive mill was used to separate the pits from the meat without crushing the meat. The oil was then extracted from the meat in much the same way as juice from the grape.

These devices played into the increase of commerce in two ways. They gave rise to the miller's profession. The squeezing of grapes and olives, of course, had to be done on the farm and did not give rise to a new profession in the strict sense, although in first-century Italy entrepreneurs with gangs of hired workers moved about from farm to farm doing the job. It is more important that these devices made possible the production and preparation of much larger surpluses from the farm. Great quantities of grape juice or olive oil could be sent out to the city markets or into international commerce directly after the harvests. [22]

There was a corresponding improvement in transport by sea. A new, heavier warship, far larger than the classical quinquereme, made its appearance about 258 B.C. at the Battle of Cos between Antigonus of Macedonia and Ptolemy II of Egypt. Like the Roman ships after them, Hellenistic ships were sturdy and large enough for the needs of the time. Indeed, some of them were larger than any practical need demanded. A transport built about 230 B.C. for Hiero, tyrant of Syracuse, could carry 60,000 bushels of grain, 10,000 jars of salt fish, 600 tons of wool, and other freight amounting to 600 tons, as well as provisions for the crew. Few cities would permit it to enter their

[21] *Ibid.*, pp. 112–8.

[22] Parenthetically it might be added here that the Greeks had from the seventh century made wide use of the lathe and of turning in the making of furniture. In the Hellenistic period they spread its use to Egypt and elsewhere: C. Aldred, "Furniture: To the End of the Roman Empire," *History of Technology*, II, 222–3. Since the use of rotary mills and the water wheel also became common at this time, it seems that men were getting a new and more sophisticated idea of tools.

ports.[23] The wreck of a Rhodian ship off Grand Couglone near Marseilles, dated about 250 B.C., shows that the hull was sheathed in lead plates as a protection against the Mediterranean shipworm (*Teredo navalis*), which was still attacking British ships operating in the Mediterranean in the eighteenth century.[24] Such protection seems to have been standard on large transports.[25] The cost of shipping goods, then, is thought to have declined decidedly between the early and the middle third century.[26]

Large and seaworthy as they were, ancient ships had inadequate rigging. It is almost certain that they could do more than simply run before the wind, but their square sails did not permit them to beat against it except in the most limited sense, and hence they had to await a favorable wind. Cities that depended upon imported grain might face famine in bad weather.

At the same time that ships were getting better, there was an improvement in harbors. In the fifth century Hippodamus of Miletus had rebuilt the Piraeus of Athens, and something is known of the harbor facilities of Carthage in the Punic period. Before the Emperor Claudius built the artificial harbor at Portus at the mouth of the Tiber, however, the greatest achievement was probably the port of Alexandria and the Pharos, which Sostratus of Cnidos designed about 280 B.C. It was the first real lighthouse and stood at least 85 feet high.

There were, then, some substantial technological advances, but they were not of the sort to change the relations of industry to commerce or the social dominance of the landowner over the town and the commercial classes. Hellenistic scientists understood the principle of steam power, but their world lacked coal or vast supplies of wood for fuel, so that it was never used in production but only for toys and religious mystifications. The application of the ass or slave to the rotary mill and the wheel for raising water were the only improvements in power.

BANKING AND BUSINESS ORGANIZATION

More profound and important than purely technological changes were changes in techniques of business, control, and administration. Both in government and private business the clerical profession made advances. In fifth-century Athens, commercially and economically the most advanced of the Greek city-states, all offices had been open by lot to all citizens and no

[23] Tenney Frank, *Economic Survey of Ancient Rome*, 5 vols. (Baltimore: Johns Hopkins University Press, 1933–1940), I, 105–8, gives a translation of Athenaeus' account of this ship. Frank's *Economic Survey*, to which several scholars contributed, will be cited hereinafter as *ESAR*.

[24] T. C. Lethbridge, "Ship-Building," *History of Technology*, II, 569.

[25] Paul MacKendrick, *The Mute Stones. The Story of Archaeology in Italy* (New York: St. Martin's Press, 1960), p. 104.

[26] Larsen, *ESAR*, IV, 407–8.

account taken of professional or technical competence, except for the selection of generals. Democratic doctrine held that all citizens were competent to handle any of the city's affairs, so that the treasurer's only training was the management of a private household. In the fourth century the need for expertise was more strongly felt and the Athenians elected and reelected the same man to be treasurer. He became something like a permanent and professional civil servant. All Hellenistic kings and governments had such officials. Some of their wisdom—or chicanery—is to be found in the second book of the *Economics*, wrongly attributed to Aristotle.[27]

Literacy was widespread, so that men were prepared for clerical operations on the basic level. Government officials and businessmen were almost always able to write and read their own correspondence. The use of the abacus became habitual. Without the zero, written sums are extremely difficult, and neither the Greek nor Roman system of numbers was convenient. It is surprising that the superior Mesopotamian number system was not adopted, but the abacus came to the rescue. On it addition and subtraction are easy, and this simple tool remained in habitual use until the sixteenth century, by which time almost everyone used "Arabic" numerals. But while addition and subtraction are easy on the abacus, even fairly simple multiplication and division remained so difficult that professional abacists had to be called in.

It is in the light of these more general conditions that the progress of banking, of commercial management, and of government control should be seen.

Warehousing—the practice of storing real wealth in barns and treasuries in order to keep it for various purposes at a later date—is as old as the history of civilization. Storage of grain might take place not only on the farm, but in temples of the gods and the palace of the king, lugal, or pharaoh. Closely related was the hoarding of gold and silver in the form of jewelry and other artistic objects. Until the seventh century B.C. saving and, therefore, exchange were primarily in real wealth, in useful goods. Banking is warehousing of money instead of real goods. Greece was an innovator in the development of the banking function.[28] Egypt would learn of it only with the Macedonian conquest.

When the Greeks adopted coinage from Lydia, the first and most obvious depositories of the new form of wealth were the temples of the gods. They were the traditional repositories of precious goods and they were better guarded than other places. (Herodotus repeatedly describes the treasures of

[27] Edited with an English translation by E. C. Marchant in The Loeb Classical Library (Cambridge, Mass.: Harvard University Press, 1923); text with an extensive commentary in French by B. A. van Groningen, *Aristotle, le second livre de l'Economie* (Leiden: A. W. Sijthoff, 1933).

[28] William L. Westermann, "Warehousing and Trapezite Banking in Antiquity," *Journal of Economic and Business History*, III (1930–1931), 30–54.

Apollo's temple at Delphi.) In the fifth century the goddess Athena received one-sixtieth of the tribute paid Athens by her allies in the Delian League. Pericles borrowed money from this temple treasure and repaid the goddess at low interest. The Parthenon and the temples of Delphi and Olympia developed into simple deposit-loan banks. In the second century B.C. the temple at Delos continued this function and made private loans on a modest scale as well, but by that time the temple bank had been overshadowed by private banks.[29]

Private banking evolved from the moneychanger (*trapezites*). His primitive function seems simply to have been to know the value of foreign coins and the proper exchange rates and to make the exchanges. There were, after all, a great many different coinages in circulation in Greece and they were on several different standards. The two chief ones were the Aegintan and the Euboeic, which Athens borrowed and which is, therefore, often called the Athenian. While the coins of some cities were sound, those of others were more or less debased. On the simplest level exchanges would be freely made and, allowing for the moneychanger's commission, such exchanges should have reflected the metallic contents, weights, and relative purity of the gold, silver, and bronze in the coins. In fact, however, it soon developed that two sorts of coinages were in circulation: silver in international exchanges and bronze circulated locally. (Gold coins were exceptional and played no essential role in trade.) From some uncertain date the state itself set the standard of exchange in its territory; that is to say, it established a relation between silver and bronze coins. This official rate probably overvalued bronze. At least this was true later in the exchange of local Greek bronze coins for Roman silver and it was true in the Ptolemaic state.[30] Certainly the exchange rate was artificial and did not correspond exactly to the ratio of uncoined silver to uncoined bronze. These trapezite bankers probably also lent money on pawn. By the fourth century and probably already in the fifth century B.C., private banking had largely ousted the temples from the private sector of business, although the temples continued to serve public functions.

Modern readers are used to considering banking functions that operate under the direction of a central authority, like the Federal Reserve system or the Bank of England, that has the power to print money and to control its issue. If a modern bank gets into trouble, it can simply call on its Federal Reserve District Bank for temporary aid until it can readjust its position. Earlier banks were of a rather different sort.

In antiquity and in the Middle Ages there was no central banking authority. The amount of money available for use was determined by the amount of precious metal available and by the government's coining of it, not by a central bank. Banks did not control or manipulate the money supply.

[29] Larsen, *ESAR*, IV, 337–48.
[30] Bolin, *State and Currency*, pp. 238ff.

They simply accepted coin on deposit from a customer. Thus banks in ancient times acted as warehouses for coin under the order of a customer. These deposits were held at the pleasure of the depositor. It does not seem that they earned interest. Money on deposit could either be withdrawn as cash or transferred by the bank to the account of another customer. This kind of in-bank transfer reduced the amount of cash withdrawals to a small fraction of the total deposits. (We have no evidence of the use of interbank letters of credit in the fifth or fourth centuries B.C.) Subject only to demand withdrawals, then, the banker could use the surplus funds any way he desired. The economic significance of banking, even on this limited scale is clear: money could be collected into a single fund and used for whatever purpose the banker desired. Banks therefore acted as a means of directing surplus funds into investments. This should have had a different impact on the nature and type of investment than would have prevailed without banks.

The earliest considerable information we have about Greek banking, credit, and risk operations stems from operations centering about the Athenian grain trade in the fourth century B.C.[31] Since Athens depended on imported grain, a type of public control regulated grain prices and the margin of profit was limited. Private methods of financing trade and industry were just being invented. In trade and industry the dominant forms of organization were the proprietorship and the partnership. Thus the problem for the banker as a custodian of deposits was to place the funds in ventures that would be relatively secure and still return a profit to the banker-lender.

Two of the loan practices of the Athenians, related to the foreign seaborne grain trade, were the lending of money on ships (bottomry loans) and the lending of money on goods (respondentia loans).[32] Rates were normally the result of several factors: the cost of money (normally 12 to 18 percent per annum) ; the length of time of the loan; whether or not the loan was secured; and the marine risk. Marine risk—e.g., the risk from piracy, bad weather, and shipwreck—would vary from season to season and from year to year. On a particular voyage (most loans were for a single voyage) the rate was 22½ percent if the ship sailed before, and 30 percent if the ship sailed after, a particular date in the fall. The difference of 7½ percent was due to increased marine risk in the winter season. (The normal period of increased risk was from mid-September to early June.) Thus the Greek interest rate appears to be a combination of a loan charge (interest) and a risk charge (insurance), but Greek banking did not make this distinction specifically. Because of the considerable sums needed, and because of the specialized and technical information needed, the bankers directed the investment of capital into commercial ventures.

---

[31] George M. Calhoun, "Risk in Sea Loans in Ancient Athens," *Journal of Economic and Business History*, II (1930), 563.
[32] *Ibid.*, 561ff.

An analysis of the functions of banking shows that it serves several functions: the accumulation of wealth in money; the transfer of wealth by means of letters of credit and checks or bank drafts; and the allocation of funds for investment. The transfer of funds from place to place was possible at least by the first century B.C.: when Cicero wished to send money to his son at school in Athens, he did so by letter without actually shipping coins. The extent to which Hellenistic banks served these functions is uncertain. Since the bank is, in fact, the money market, our ignorance means that we do not really understand to what degree these functions were functions of the money market and to what degree they remained functions of the household economy or of state control.

The means of saving seem to have been limited. It must have been particularly difficult to find profitable investments for small savings. The continued practice of hoarding all through antiquity is proven by the frequent discovery of coin hoards. Many are found in the houses of Pompeii, which was buried by volcanic ash from Vesuvius in A.D. 79 and which generally resembles the Hellenistic cities now under discussion. Hence the business community had only limited capacity to marshal its resources for investment. The soldier saving to purchase or equip a farm on discharge and the widow with a small legacy set aside for a minor child were not likely to find a safe investment bringing in a modest profit. Indeed it was not until the 1860s in the United States that a mechanism was developed that could continually and effectively tap the $1.00 or $5.00 or $10.00 that a working man might desire to save.

Nor does the system seem to have marshalled private savings for the state. The state could tax; cities often received bequests from wealthy citizens for particular purposes, and most possessed lands whose income was devoted to special funds for temples and festivals. But the state's credit was not generally good, and private banking does not seem regularly or willingly to have served the state. There was no regular public debt, and in times of emergency the state had recourse to extraordinary and ingenious expedients, most of them bordering on fraud or violence. Many of them are recounted in the second book of the *Economics*, wrongly attributed to Aristotle, but in fact dating from the Hellenistic age.

THE ECONOMIC INTEGRATION OF PTOLEMAIC EGYPT

The economy of Ptolemaic Egypt was the most highly integrated in the Hellenistic and Roman worlds; administrative techniques were probably more developed there than elsewhere.[33] Egypt can hardly be thought typical, for

---

[33] General references for Graeco-Roman Egypt: W. W. Tarn and G. T. Griffith, *Hellenistic Civilization*, 3d ed. (London: E. Arnold, 1952); M. Rostovtzeff, *The Social and Economic History of the Hellenistic World*, 3 vols. (Oxford: Clarendon Press, 1941) and "Ptolemaic

the Greek polis with its free market institutions played only a subordinate part there. Besides Alexandria there was only one such Greek city. But the Egyptian economy is by far the best known, for diggings in the past fifty years or so have produced a great number of public and private papyri dealing with business and government as well as with literature and religion. They are a unique source for Hellenistic and Roman history, having no parallel in other regions, where only a very little archival material has survived in the form of inscriptions. For all their generosity, however, the Egyptian sources are unbalanced. Papyri survive only in the dryness of the desert and on the borders of the sown. They reveal only the life of Upper Egypt: "To describe the Ptolemaic system is to describe a body without a head, for all threads ran to Alexandria, and of the central bureaux there nothing is known; the extant information comes from the country." [34]

Taken from a certain point of view, the whole of Egypt appears to be the household (*oikos*) of Ptolemy, the successor of the pharaoh. He was, indeed, the god Pharaoh in the eyes of the native Egyptian. Egypt was exploited as his private estate. The *dioecetes*, one of the most important men of the state, was in charge of finance. From the second century at least he was assisted by the Director of Accounts of Extraordinary Receipts and by the Director of Accounts. The *nomes* (local administrative districts) were governed by *nomarchs*. Alexander probably had retained the native officials; but Ptolemy I instituted a military occupation, and a *strategos* or general was placed in each nome. The nomarch fell into second place, and his duties became chiefly financial. In the second century he seems to have disappeared altogether. The nome was divided into smaller districts called *toparchies*, usually under a *toparch*, and these into the smallest administrative districts, the village or *kome* with its lands, under an official called the *komarch*.

But alongside this political administration was the administration of the oikos. Alongside and subordinate to each strategos there was a royal scribe (*basilicogrammateus*), who acted as a controller and was responsible to the dioecetes. Beneath him in the smaller districts were the *topogrammateus* and the *komogrammateus*. They made out all the documents (tax rolls, reports on the crops, and so forth) which were used to establish the survey and to govern the exploitation of the country. Together they formed a body of paid,

Egypt," *CAH*, VII (1928), 533ff. The papyri, our chief source, are still being intensively studied and much progress can be hoped for. The English reader can get a good view of their value and range from Allan Chester Johnson, *Roman Egypt to the Reign of Diocletian*, Vol. II of *ESAR* (Baltimore: Johns Hopkins University Press, 1936); and A. S. Hunt and C. C. Edgar, *Select Papyri*, Vols. I and II (Loeb Classical Library; Cambridge, Mass.: Harvard University Press, 1932–1933). There is a good general introduction to papyrology with adequate bibliography in E. T. Turner, *Greek Papyri, an Introduction* (Princeton: Princeton University Press, 1968).

[34] Tarn and Griffith, *Hellenistic Civilization*, p. 186. The description of the Ptolemaic economy in this section is largely drawn from this book.

professional civil servants and a bureaucracy which followed established prece-
dents and had regular rules for promotion.

This bureaucracy presided over the management of Egypt, Ptolemy's
household. The native fellahin were kept on the land and forbidden to leave
without permission, although they were not the slaves of private persons and
not exactly slaves of the king. In theory all land belonged to the pharaoh and
was his to do with as he pleased. The only exceptions were the old Greek
settlement at Naucratis and the few new Greek cities. The landed nobility was
abolished, and the native temples greatly reduced. Four sorts of titles of land
were created:

1. The king's land in the narrow sense, "land in hand," which was
farmed by the king's peasants. Rents were paid in both kind and money.
These peasants not only could not leave but could be forced to extend cultivation to the waste and conscripted to work on canals and other public works.
They could also be turned out of their farms. Hence they were little different
from serfs and were protected only by the need for their services and by
petty bribes they paid to lesser officials. The extent of royal land is uncertain,
but it was certainly considerable.

2. "Land in grant," either to a native temple or to a Greek or Macedonian soldier. Some of the produce of temple land was used to maintain the
cult and the priests, but what remained went to the king. Soldiers usually
paid a light rent, but they were under an obligation of military service.
They were usually settled in Greek villages rather than scattering among the
native population. By 218 B.C. their *cleruchies* had become heritable, and
later they also became alienable, although in theory, of course, grants made
in return for military service should not have been.

3. "Gift land" meant an extensive estate comprising one or more native
villages with their land and the services of their peasants. Such an estate was
conferred on a high official, who thus became the superior of the village
authorities. One object, of course, was to reward and pay the servants of the
state, but another was to get the land fully developed through the recipient's
agency. The king could resume the estate at any time.

4. "Private land" seems originally to have been confined to house, garden, and vineyard. But sometimes the king gave perpetual use of some land
(such as waste or escheated cleruchies) in order to insure development.
Probably the occupiers of private land manned the lesser state offices, of
which there were an infinity.

All corn land paid a rent to the king. The peasants were left only enough
to live on until the next harvest. Even the seed corn was taken from them,
stored by the administration, and supplied at the next planting season. The
government thus had control of what crops were to be sown. The vast surplus
that Egypt produced was sent first from the village barn to the barns in the
nome (district) capital, and thence to the royal barns at Alexandria to feed
the city or be exported. Ptolemy thus became the greatest corn merchant the

world had seen, and it was through the government that the household economy of Egypt entered the Mediterranean market.

Other production was also controlled. The raising of sheep and weaving
of wool seem to have been relatively free; Egypt was not good wool country
and could not expect to export much. But linen weaving was largely controlled. Of both fibers the state took what raw material it needed to produce
cloth in its own factories for the court, the administration, and the army.
But the royal factories also produced linen cloth for export, and Egypt was
the chief Mediterranean source of linen cloth.

The greatest royal monopoly was oil. In Egypt the olive was scarce and
grown only for the fruit, but other plants—sesame, croton, linseed, safflower,
and gourd seeds—gave oil. The king determined how much land was to be
planted in these and took the whole of the produce at a fixed price. The
harvest was processed by state serfs and distributed by licensed retailers at
prices fixed by the state. This, of course, guaranteed the government any
return it wished. Among the Greek population there remained a demand for
olive oil. Imports of it were taxed at levels that prevented competition with
the state-controlled local products.

There were further state monopolies: mines, quarries, saltworks, natron
(which gives soda for soap), and perhaps fulling works. The state also
licensed fishermen and beekeepers and took a quarter of their catch. In some
way, not altogether clear, baking was also a state monopoly. Some other
trades and businesses—perhaps all others—called for licenses.

The king claimed all pasture land and possessed large herds of cattle.
Royal peasants, after they had reaped their corn, were required to grow a
green crop on which they fed the royal cattle. The administration also owned
large flocks of pigs and geese, which were let out. No tree could be cut in
Egypt without the king's permission, for it was rooted in his soil.

The papyri reveal, too, innumerable taxes on production. One-sixth of
the produce of vineyards was paid in kind, while the tax on orchards and
gardens was paid in money. All in all, it was a pretty thorough job. An army
of scribes and petty administrators directed the system and produced mounds
of records which would make a modern bureaucrat feel at home, except for
the absence of duplicating machines.

The Greek helpers of Alexander introduced the coinage system into
Ptolemaic Egypt. When Alexander died and Ptolemy took control of Egypt,
he began for the first time to pay the obligations of the Egyptian state in
money. The need to pay in money brought with it the need to make transfers
and hence a peculiar system of state banks. Since, however, the chief income
of the state was in agricultural produce, not in coin, it was necessary to
retain the existing warehouse system. Consequently the Ptolemaic royal treasury consisted of two parts, a system of warehouses and the bank. Warehouses
handled receipts and payments of taxes, loans, and credit in kind; the bank
handled taxes in coin and monetary transactions. The dual system permitted

deposits and withdrawals of grain from and to various accounts. It also permitted a real payment of grain to private persons and transfers from money
to grain accounts and vice versa. All of the financial accounting systems of
the private Greek bankers recur in the Ptolemaic system and the Roman
administrators would later copy the Greek models.

The lines of the classes were kept clear, so that everyone did what was
for the best and kept to his place. Greek officials and merchants (who were
very much the same men), the soldiers, and the surviving Egyptian priests
were at the top. They were divided from the mass of little persons by the fact
that, except for the Egyptian priests, they lived under Greek law. The vast
body of the Egyptian fellahin were at the bottom and their condition was
wretched. The state was well run in early Ptolemaic times and there was no
desire to oppress the Egyptian, on whom the whole system rested. But the
system was stricter than anything he had known before, and the native could
have no hope of rising in the social hierarchy. Nothing in the system was
designed for his welfare, and no attempt was made to give him a Greek education. Some Egyptians did eventually gain wealth and position, but they did
so by Hellenizing. The two nations lived separately, one above the other. The
only recourse left to the Egyptian peasant was *anachoresis*, "withdrawal."
Sometimes whole villages went on strike and took asylum in a temple, acting
simply out of despair or in hope that some minor imposition might be lifted.

The purpose of the system, then, was not to provide for the inhabitants
of Egypt. It was not even designed to exploit the Egyptians for the benefit of
the Greek administrative class. The monarchy depended upon the talents and
services of that class and had necessarily to provide for it a more plentiful
substance than for the fellahin. But they were not much freer and their
freedom in fact consisted only in a greater variety of choices in the service
of the king. Their advancement in the system depended upon their service.
The entire system of exploitation, by which Egypt was made a milch cow,
was directed to enabling the Ptolemies to play a role in the politics and
warfare of the Hellenistic kingdoms, to fight off the Seleucids in Palestine in
the long series of Syrian wars and, ideally, to dominate Cyprus, the southern
coast of Asia Minor, the Aegean, and Cyrene. It was to these purposes that
the immense surpluses of Egypt were put. Looked at internally the system
was what the Greeks would call a household economy. Within Egypt, markets
and money exchanges played a subsidiary role in the storehousing of wealth
in kind. But this accumulation in kind had not been adequate for the purposes of foreign policy since Pericles proposed his imperialistic policy to the
Athenians at the beginning of the Peloponnesian War and pointed to Athens'
great advantage in ready money that commands goods and services of all
kinds. To be sure, the cities of old Greece were often short of grain, and the
Ptolemies' possession of barns full of it could be used to bring direct political
pressure, as could an embargo against a hostile city. But Egypt lacked certain
materials needed for the army and navy. She produced no iron or tin and

probably not enough copper. Elephants and horses, necessary for the advanced military tactics of the Hellenistic age, had to be imported. Perhaps her greatest need was ship timbers, for Egypt has no useable forests. These needs directed Ptolemaic foreign policy. She sought to control Cyprus, which produced timber and copper, and Cyrene from which she could get horses. The trade to the south, both up the Nile and by the Red Sea, was developed in order to import elephants and luxuries for resale. Probably some iron came from Meroë and gold from Nubia. But autarchy and self-sufficiency were not adequate. Coin was necessary to pay mercenaries, and navies were very expensive in money. Hence the accumulated surpluses of Egyptian wealth had to fit into the Hellenistic market system to earn money for Ptolemy. Egypt was the estate which provided him an income.

THE INTERNATIONAL MARKET SYSTEM

We know much more about the organization of the Ptolemaic household economy in Egypt than about the Hellenistic international market system. Cities and provinces specialized more and more in goods for which they became famed. Although this specialization is an expansion of that of the Hellenic age, it has some peculiarities. Because there was no real development of greater efficiency in production, no economies resulting from capital investment developed which would have made goods manufactured in one place cheaper than those made elsewhere. Increased size and organization of producing establishments did little to increase efficiency. Certainly no investment in cost-lowering machinery could compensate for the cost of transport, even though shipping costs fell somewhat in the first half of the third century B.C. The improvement of lighthouses and harbors, the increase in bottomry loans, and probably a lower cost of insurance all contributed to the great expansion of Hellenistic trade, but nothing developed that even remotely resembled the economies of the modern factory.

Goods in circulation tended to be of three sorts: goods that could be produced only in few places, like papyrus and metals; the necessities of life, such as grain, which could be grown almost everywhere but were regularly imported by the larger cities from a few places like Pontus and Egypt; and specialized manufactures, developed largely from local materials, but commanding the market on account of the skill and fame of the artisans of certain cities. Such goods were likely to be luxuries far more expensive than home-produced cloth or pottery. (This is the opposite of modern industrial specialization: automobiles today are made in Detroit and exported throughout the nation, because it is cheaper to make most cars in one place; Phoenician purple cloth was prized everywhere because it was more expensive than any other.)

Rather than a concentration of the production of cheap goods and the exploitation of more efficient productive methods, the conditions of production in the Hellenistic age and generally throughout ancient history caused a dispersion of production toward the consumer. Thus in the Hellenistic era Athens lost the greater part of her market for pottery and wine. The production of pottery moved to more provincial centers and its artistic quality declined. Attica seems to have kept command only of the market for luxury wines, while Syracuse took over much of the Adriatic market.

In such circumstances the market demand for goods, even though larger than ever before, continued to be restricted. The common man rarely used foreign goods, unless he lived in one of those cities which depended upon regular imports of grain. The increase in the use of slave labor during the Hellenistic period tended to depress wages. At least the cost of day labor appears to have been lower in the third and second centuries B.C. than it had been in Periclean Athens. The common man's diet continued to be simple, and the other basic necessities of life were not so great as in the north. There was little expense for heating; housing could be kept very simple. Hence there was almost nothing comparable to the modern mass market. The chief customers for the specialized products of the Hellenistic towns—foreign cloth, pottery, incense, and spices—were an urban class living on rents from the country and, in the kingdoms, on government employment. Such persons can be called "bourgeois," but the term is rather misleading. Most were generally burghers in the strict sense that they were citizens of the city in which they lived, although a merchant might well be a metic, a resident alien. They controlled the land, the chief means of production and source of wealth. They certainly organized farm production for the market, for sale in the local town or even for export abroad. Such management entailed investment, and insofar as this is true, this "middle class" were entrepreneurs. But it appears to have been a rare city in which this middle class were dominated by persons who made their living by capital investment in and management of commerce and crafts and by persons in the liberal professions, by those persons whom Marx called the "bourgeoisie."

A system of market exchanges demands one or a few central markets of money and information, a place that will function as a general clearinghouse. Athens had performed this function in the fifth and early fourth centuries, but after Alexander she lost her commercial preeminence and gradually— although only gradually—began her decline to the quiet university town of Roman times. Her place in the Aegean was taken by the island of Rhodes, ideally situated for contact between Greece and Egypt and the East. When Alexander opened the East and destroyed the city of Tyre, Rhodes found the way open to becoming a mercantile republic, comparable in many ways to medieval Venice. It withstood siege and pressure from the great monarchies, compelled the Byzantines to abolish the toll which they had levied on ships sailing through the Bosphorus,[35] fought King Eumenes when he tried to close the Black Sea, and kept the sea safe from Cretan pirates. Her money largely replaced that of Athens in international commerce, and as early as 306 B.C. she had made a commercial treaty with the distant power of Rome. The wreck of a Rhodian merchant vessel which went down about 250 B.C. has been discovered off Marseilles. Rhodes' success was splendid; her goods and connections are found everywhere, and the customs duties, which were 2 percent, brought the city a million drachmae a year, which would represent a movement of imports and exports of 50,000,000 dr. per annum.[36] Rhodian wealth was certainly great, for she must have also profited from "invisible" imports: the profits of banking and the carriage of goods in Rhodian bottoms between other ports.

A more graphic idea of her wealth and an idea of her importance to states involved in trade comes from the year 224 B.C., when Rhodes was destroyed by an earthquake. So important was her function as an international market that the kings of the East and West showered her with gifts for rebuilding.[37] Hiero and Gelo, tyrants of Syracuse, sent: 75 talents of silver in two installments for the gymnasium; some silver cauldrons and their stands, and some water vessels for religious purposes; 10 talents for sacrifices, and 10 talents to attract new citizens, intending that the whole should amount to 100 talents; they also gave immunity from customs to Rhodian merchants in their ports. Ptolemy of Egypt sent: 300 talents of silver; one million medimni of corn (i.e., about 171,000 lbs.); ship timbers for ten quinqueremes and ten triremes, consisting of 40,000 cubits of squared pine planking; 1000 talents of bronze coinage, 3,000 talents of tow, 3,000 pieces of sail cloth; 3,000 talents for the repair of the Colossus, 100 master builders with 350 workmen, and 14 talents yearly to pay their wages; 12,000 medimni of corn for their games and sacrifices, and 20,000 medimni for victualling ten triremes. King Antigonus sent: 10,000 timbers, 5,000 rafters 7 cubits long, 3,000 talents of iron, 1,000 talents of pitch, 1,000 amphoras of unboiled pitch, and 100 talents of silver. His queen gave: 100,000 medimni of corn, and 3,000 talents of lead. The Seleucid kings: lifted import duties in their domains for the Rhodians; gave ten quinqueremes fully equipped, 200,000 medimni of corn, 10,000 cubits of timber, and 1000 talents of resin and hair.[38] Nor were other princes of Asia Minor behind hand. Recovery was rapid.

The two other great commercial centers of the Hellenistic world were Alexandria and Antioch in Syria. Their greatness was largely due to their positions as capitals of great empires, but it must be supposed that they also played something of the same role in integrating the market as did Rhodes.

[35] Polybius iv. 46.
[36] *Ibid.* xxx. 31. 10–2.
[37] *Ibid.* V. 88–9.
[38] *Ibid.* The Attic talent was almost 37 kg.; her medimnus was about 52 liters. The liter is a bit more than a quart; the kilogram is 2.2 lbs. avoirdupois.

Antioch and the other cities of the Levant continued to be starting points and terminals of the caravan trade into Asia. The sale and distribution of goods coming by sea from Africa and India took place largely at Alexandria. The Sabaean power of South Arabia broke up. This state had blocked direct contact between Egypt and India and acted as middleman. When this state broke up, the way was open for direct contact with the East by water. Under Ptolemy VII (c. 120–117), an Indian sailor, the sole survivor of a shipwreck, was picked up in the Red Sea by Egyptians. He guided Eudoxus of Cyzicus on the first European voyage to India. They coasted, but gradually the monsoons were discovered and voyages across the Indian Ocean became possible. Pepper had been known to Aristotle's pupil Theophrastus, but only as a medical drug prescribed in minute quantities. In 89 B.C. a man in Athens had two quarts of it.[39] This transit market, like the export of Egyptian goods, was no doubt strictly regulated by the Ptolemies, who sought the advantages of monopoly, but as a center of international banking and information about goods and prices and as an emporion, Alexandria can have been little, if at all, inferior to Rhodes.

The successor of Rhodes was the little island of Delos. Its history is peculiar. In the third and early second centuries Delos already enjoyed a considerable importance as a center of trade, but her great age came after the Battle of Pydna, by which Rome became supreme in the Aegean world. Until the Third Macedonian War (171–167 B.C.) Rhodes had enjoyed the favor and protection of the growing Roman power, but in that war the two allies had a falling out and Rome established Delos as a port free of harbor dues. Rhodes was destroyed as a naval power; she lost her carrying trade and the business of her harbor, Polybius reports, shrank catastrophically.

One result was the growth of piracy. Rhodes had policed the seas as Britain would in the nineteenth century, but Delos and her nominal owner, Athens, were too feeble to do so. Rome, on whom the task properly should have fallen, neglected it until the expedition of Metellus in 68–67 B.C. suppressed Cretan piracy and made that island a Roman province and the expedition of Pompey in 67 B.C. destroyed the pirate nests along the southern coast of Asia Minor.

Delos is a small, barren island, producing nothing important for international trade. Excavations on the island have revealed much about the plan of the city and the port, as well as a considerable body of inscriptions relative to economic affairs.[40] The buildings along the waterfront of the harbor are arranged to allow easy communication between the warehouses and the docks, though not between the warehouses and the interior of the city. Such a plan

[39] Tarn and Griffith, *Hellenistic Civilization*, p. 24ff. Description of Alexandria, Strabo xvii. 6ff.

[40] On the publcation of the inscriptions and their content, see Larsen, "Roman Greece," *ESAR*, IV, 334–5. There follows a good and detailed presentation of what is known of the economy of the island, to which this account is much indebted.

reveals that Delos was a transit center where foreign goods were exchanged largely by foreigners from all over the Mediterranean and beyond. The presence of immigrants and merchants from Arabia, Alexandria, and especially from Syria suggests trade in spices, unguents, and glass. There were close commercial relations with Macedonia, which supplied forest products and probably grain. The grain market, on which private merchants and even cities bought and sold, was largely supplied from the Black Sea. Yet even Numidia may have been exporting wheat by the second century, for her king is known to have taken a friendly interest in the welfare of the Delians.

Slaves were a very important commodity. Strabo says that Delos could admit and send away 10,000 slaves in one day, but there is no reason to take the figure seriously. Like so many large numbers in ancient literature, it probably means "a great many." Yet Delos does seem to have been a clearing-house for the growing slave trade, which was fed by piracy and Rome's wars as well as by the more regular trade from barbarian lands. Slavery may not have been increasing in the Hellenized East during this period, but there was a growing demand for slaves on the part of Roman aristocrats, who used gang labor on their great estates in Italy. This trade would account in part for the prominence of Roman merchants at Delos, although they were also found in other parts of the Aegean.

As might be expected, Delos was a banking center and a place to get credit for commercial enterprises. The temple there made loans, but its capital was limited and private banks were more important.[41] The accounts of the temple treasurers have survived, and they reveal much not only about the temple's finances, but about the related finances of the city and of its grain fund. Probably every city government of the Hellenistic period considered that it was the city's business to assure adequate grain for its citizens. The board in charge of the grain fund at Delos managed to keep the price steady and probably to keep it low. The interests of grain-producers would count for nothing in the politics of such a city, but the interest of merchants would count for a great deal. As hirers of labor, they would be especially concerned that grain prices be stable and, if possible, low, for low prices mean—or can mean—low wages, urban growth by immigration, and hence an ample supply of labor.

CONCLUSION

Such an account of the functioning of the market in the Hellenistic economy as is given above is clearly inadequate in many ways. The sources do not answer many questions about the organization and methods of business, banking, and credit. The almost complete lack of statistical information is a

---

[41] *Ibid.*, pp. 357–61.

serious loss. The market was clearly an established institution throughout the Greek world and it controlled a part of production. That is to say, market prices determined to some degree how capital would be invested and what goods would be produced in some sectors of the economy. But we can gain only a vague notion of how large this sector was and how large a part of labor and investment was determined by political authority and by the surviving and still important household production. Some farm produce, for example, went to the market, and this was not simply a surplus of good years. Both the owners of estates and peasant households were planning production to earn money on the market. But both were also producing for household consumption (the old "subsistence economy") and both were required to pay rents and taxes. When such rents and taxes were required in coin, the taxpayer had to plan production to earn money by sales. Rents and taxes in kind might also control production in a different and more direct way, as they did in Egypt.

Even though the whole role of the market in agricultural production cannot be measured, some things are obvious: the luxury trades were more largely market-ordered than was the production of cheap, durable goods and necessities. The purchasing power of the city workman and of the peasant landowner, tenant, day laborer, and slave was very small; that of individual landowners and officials was considerable, but their numbers were limited. Cloth was produced at home both for the home and for the market. Cheap pottery, brick making, and tile making were in the hands of specialists producing for the market. Even cheap cloth for the clothes of slaves might now be purchased. However, in the absence of a radically new and more efficient technology, internal development soon reached a limit and, in some places, there may even have been a decline.

Greece certainly lost relative importance, but there is no convincing evidence of positive decline before the Roman civil wars.[42] Although Rome's power in the eastern Mediterranean in the first century was unchallenged, she hesitated to occupy and govern. She was determined only that no other power which might endanger her should do so. Considerable distress resulted from the decline of the Seleucid kingdom, and the degeneracy of the later Ptolemies resulted in a far less efficient exploitation of Egypt. It is not certain, however, that this was a disadvantage to the native peasantry. As the Hellenistic age advanced, the clear progress of its earlier stages was not continued. Further intensification of the system seems to have become impossible. There was only the possibility of geographical expansion, which, in fact, did take place wherever political and geographical circumstances permitted.

India was too far by sea to be integrated economically with the Hellenistic system and Bactria was even farther, considering the heavier costs of land transport. The inhospitable coasts of West Africa offered few possibili-

---

[42] See the discussion of the decline in population (Appendix C).

ties, although the Ptolemies explored it and directed what trade there was through Alexandria. In the Black Sea conditions were more favorable. The demand for wheat stimulated agriculture in the river valleys of the steppe and the Greek cities of the coast grew considerably during the Hellenistic period.

But the Hellenistic economy found its greatest field for expansion in the western Mediterranean. Here the eastern cities found more than grain and metals and an outlet for their manufactured goods. Something more profound took place: Italy and the rest of the western shores of the sea developed the same sort of economy as the east. The story of the introduction of the Hellenistic economy into the western Mediterranean is not simply the story of traders and Greek-Phoenician emporia. The west did not develop a colonial economy of the sort that grew up in the Black Sea; its economic development was inextricably tied up with the fortunes of Rome and her Empire. The exceptional importance of this development requires that it be traced in some detail and its peculiarities be defined.

10 THE WESTERN MEDITERRANEAN AND THE ROMAN REPUBLIC

The climax of ancient economic development took place in the Roman Empire, which during the last two centuries before the Christian era came to include the Hellenistic world. Indeed, the economy of the Empire may be considered a continuation and expansion of the Hellenistic economy. The Hellenistic economy found the greatest room in the western Mediterranean for that territorial expansion which took place on a lesser scale elsewhere. Much of this expansion took place within, and was given form and structure by, the expanding Roman state.

By the fifth century B.C. the Greek market economy had been established in Sicily and southern Italy by the foundation of Greek cities: Syracuse, Taormina, Cumae, Naples, Sybaris, Croton, and others. These cities were tied to the economy of old Greece as markets for manufactured goods and as suppliers of raw materials, especially grain. Farther afield, the Greeks had established colonies on the southern coast of Gaul and on the northern part of the Mediterranean coast of Spain. Of these the chief was Marseilles (Massilia), founded by the Phocaeans about 600 B.C. From it a number of other poleis and emporia were founded from Nice on the east to Emporion in northern Spain. These places acted as ports of trade in connection with the tribes of the interior. Their position was comparable to that of the Greek cities of the Black Sea coasts. Further Greek settlement in the western Mediterranean had been prevented by the considerable power of Carthage and the Etruscan cities of northern Italy. The Phoenician colonies of North Africa were in many ways comparable to the Greek colonies in Sicily and Italy. Those in what is now Tunisia and western Algeria were true city-states dominating and cultivating the land about them. Landowners were influential in the government of Carthage, the greatest of these cities, down to its last days. Just as the Greek cities of Sicily came eventually to be dominated by Syracuse, the Punic cities of Africa were dominated by Carthage. She and her dependent cities established emporia along the coasts of Africa, in southern Spain, western Sicily, and on Corsica and Sardinia, trading by treaty with the natives of the interior. The Carthaginians do not appear to have been major producers themselves; at least, few Carthaginian products have been definitely identified by archaeologists. But Carthage imported products from the East and from Greek cities: wine came from Sicily and Campania and the island of Rhodes; oil from Acragas in Sicily. Etruscan metalware was probably distributed by the Carthaginians, as well as Corinthian pottery, statuettes, and jewelry from the Greek world. To the western barbarians she offered many "objets de Paris," paste goods, glass beads—the sort of thing that was called "trade goods" in Africa in the nineteenth century. In return she received and reexported both luxuries and necessities. Caravan traffic developed by way of the oases across the Sahara to the Sudan and central Africa. Some gold came up this way, and probably ivory and slaves. The traffic must have been limited, however, for the camel had not yet been introduced to Africa. (There was an advantage to this, for it robbed the desert tribes of that mobility in attack which would make them so dangerous in the late Roman period and the Middle Ages.) Skins and all manner of wild animals captured alive were exported: lions, panthers, antelopes, and elephants. Some of them may have come from the south, but the lion and elephant still inhabited North Africa. The great age of the Spanish mines lay in the future, but the Carthaginians supplied tin and lead to the eastern Mediterranean. Some of it probably came from Brittany and Cornwall.[1]

The only indigenous peoples in the western Mediterranean to show much urban development were the Etruscans, the center of whose civilization was in modern Tuscany, but whose influence at one time extended south into Latium and Campagnia and north across the Apennines into the Po valley. Their civilization is known chiefly from the splendid tombs of their aristocrats and from Etruscan influence on later Roman civilization, particularly religion. The Etruscan cities were dominated by a landed aristocracy whose estates were probably worked by serfs, but the internal distributive system is entirely unknown. Greek goods were popular, and by the fifth century Greek influence on Etruscan art and probably on other aspects of the civilization was strong. Since there is no evidence that Etruscan merchants moved about the Mediterranean, it is to be supposed that the Carthaginians and the Greeks of southern Italy acted as intermediaries for Greek imports. This trade was carried on by barter until about 500 B.C., when Etruscans began to use the coins of Ionian cities. Within a generation they were minting their own.[2] Identifiable Etruscan products are not frequently found in other parts of the Mediterranean, but iron was mined at Elba and Etruscan metalware was exported.

Carthaginians and Greeks, then, played the role of intermediaries and established ports of trade for the exchange of eastern products in the western Mediterranean, but a true market economy was established only in southern Italy and Sicily and perhaps in Punic Africa. In Mauretania, most of Numidia, Spain, Gaul, the Po valley, and the mountains of Italy, the general level

[1] Jules Toutain, *The Economic Life of the Ancient World*, pp. 192–7.
[2] Roebuck, *Ancient Times*, p. 425.

of economic organization was much the same as that of Greece in the Heroic Age. There is no evidence that this economy would of itself have evolved into a market economy. The market had originally developed in the Aegean, an area of easy maritime transport, under the peculiar social and political conditions provided by the polis. It had been adapted to the highly developed storage economies of the Near East by Alexander's conquests, but nothing as yet indicated that it might be a suitable system of economic integration for the large land masses about the western Mediterranean or even for Italy as a whole. The Roman conquest created an economic unity out of this vast region and endowed it with the institutions of a market economy. This was a major accomplishment, one of the most important aspects of the Roman achievement and one which had abiding consequences in world history.

EARLY ROME

Nothing about its primitive condition suggests that Rome was fitted for such an economic role.[3] In the sixth century B.C. she seems to have been dominated by kings of Etruscan origin. The Roman literary tradition—by no means trustworthy for this earliest period—probably suppressed an Etruscan conquest. These kings undertook public works of surprising magnitude. By c. 500 Rome had a number of temples in the Etruscan style, decorated with terra cotta friezes and large cult statues. Even more impressive were the city's sewers and the drainage projects undertaken by the kings.

But the expulsion of the kings (the traditional date is 509 B.C.) brought an end to such projects. The senatorial aristocracy which dominated the early Republic had no such tastes. With the court gone, there was little demand for Greek or Etruscan products. Rome subsided into a subsistence economy dominated by peasant farms and the modest estates of the squires who sat in the Senate. Production was confined mostly to self-sufficient households, of which even the greatest were modest. Consul and slave alike wore homespun, and women of every rank made cloth for their household. Rome's household economy was perhaps more homely than that of Homeric Greece but contrasts sharply with what we know about the temple and royal economies of the earliest stages of civilized life in Sumeria and Egypt. How very modest this society was and how profound was its economic egalitarianism are evident from the census classes established in the middle of the fifth century:

---

[3] The two histories of Rome most widely used in American schools are Arthur E. R. Boak and William G. Sinnigen, *A History of Rome to* A.D. *565*, 5th ed. (New York: Macmillan, 1965); and M. Cary, *A History of Rome down to the Reign of Constantine*, 2d ed. (London: Macmillan, 1960). On economic history, two general surveys: Tenney Frank, *An Economic History of Rome*, 2d ed. (New York: Cooper Square, 1927); and Tenney Frank, ed., *Economic Survey of Ancient Rome*.

First class: Property above the value of 100,000 asses of bronze
Second class: Property above the value of 75,000 asses of bronze
Third class: Property above the value of 50,000 asses of bronze
Fourth class: Property above the value of 25,000 asses of bronze
Fifth class: Property above the value of 12,500(?) asses of bronze

(The last figure is a bit uncertain. The *as* was originally a Roman pound of bronze; its weight as a later coin was much reduced.) From the modern point of view and from that of the later Roman, the narrow spread from rich to poor and the fineness of the divisions are surprising. The property which made a man rich is even more surprising. Tenney Frank has calculated that twenty *iugera* of land were enough to qualify a citizen for the first class; [4] the iugerum is only about five-eighths of an acre.

The earliest craft gilds of which any record survives confirm this simple picture. They were composed of the goldsmiths, carpenters (or rather, builders in general), dyers, shoemakers, tanners, bronzesmiths, potters, and flute players. (The last performed at funerals and religious ceremonies.)[5] There must have been other crafts and trades: butchers, boatmen, fishermen, and some kind of merchant. The last may not have formed a gild because they were foreigners. The economic and artisanal functions of these gilds are not clear. They should not be equated with those of the Middle Ages, which played so large a part in government and did so much for the economic advantage of their members. The ancient states never allowed gilds such freedom and influence.

The size of the household as an economic unit was probably fairly large. The authority of the father, his *patria potestas*, extended over his wife, his unmarried daughters, his sons, their wives and children, and his slaves. Only on the father's death were the sons emancipated to exercise the same authority over their own families, and only then was property divided. While the father lived he had complete control of his sons' property and of any *peculum* he allowed his slaves to accumulate.

The curious institution of clientage and patronage also served to encourage the extended family. One freeman, the patron, might possess under Roman law certain rights and authority over another freeman, the client. Liberated slaves, for example, passed into the clientage of their former owner, though all clients were not freemen or their descendents. This relationship was personal and binding. It was also economic. Clients were expected to attend their patrons to the forum, support them in politics and at elections, and, if necessary, support them with their goods and chattels. In the early period the patron was expected to represent his client at law, perhaps to set him up in business, and certainly to further his prosperity by the use of

[4] Frank, *ESAR*, I, 20ff.
[5] Jean P. Waltzing, *Etude historique sur les corporations professionelles chez les Romains,* I (Louvain: C. Peeters, 1895), 62–7.

influence. Such relations, spreading from the greater to the lesser families of Roman society, must even at an early time have done much to modify the isolation of the self-supporting household, and the whole Roman *familia* formed an economic unit larger than the word "household" suggests to modern ears. Indeed, these bonds were probably weakened by the development of a money economy, although they were perpetuated by the peculiar style of Roman politics and would have important effects on Rome's later economic development.

From an early period, this system of self-supporting households was supplemented by *nundinae*, public meetings held every eighth day. If we are right in thinking that early Rome knew little of a market economy, we must suppose that these assemblies were not originally comparable to the provision market at Athens. They may have been political and social assemblies with no economic function. Much later the elder Pliny recalled a time when the Romans had had no markets.[6] But some barter in kind among the peasants would naturally have taken place. Gradually the nundinae grew into local markets for the exchange of rural goods, and even later, it must be assumed, for the sale of farm goods to merchants for resale in town. Whatever the early functions of the nundinae, the household economy does not seem to have been transformed into a market economy by a gradual growth of local trade in farm goods.

Nor did the direct workings of a growth of international commerce transform the Roman economy. The city of Rome has never been an important center of trade. She is not a seaport and would lack a good harbor near the mouth of the Tiber until an artificial one was created in the early imperial period. Rome stands at a place where the Tiber can be easily crossed, and the name of the crossing, the *via Salaria*, indicates the early movement of one essential product, salt. But the river was not an important traffic route, and ancient roads were an unsatisfactory means of moving goods. Perhaps no major city in Western history has had so little commercial and economic importance as has ancient, medieval, and modern Rome.

Having no commercial aspirations, the early Republic got along well with Carthage. A treaty dated 508 B.C.[7] established friendship between the Romans and their allies and the Carthaginians and their allies. Under this treaty, the Romans are not to sail to the coast of Africa west of Carthage, unless driven by the weather or fear of enemies, and then are not to trade there. (They are free to trade at Carthage and in Libya and Carthaginian Sicily.) The Carthaginians shall do no injury to the coastal towns of Latium which are allied to Rome, nor build forts or hold towns in other parts of Latium. Slave raids against towns not allied to Rome seem to have been permitted. A second treaty from the year 348 B.C. further limited Roman activity in Spain, Corsica,

6 *NH* xix. 51–7.

7 Polybius iii. 22. 1–13. The date has been disputed, but most scholarly opinion seems to accept it: Frank, *ESAR*, I, 6–7.

Sardinia, and Libya.[8] Clearly at this time the Romans had no commercial interests of any importance.

The choice of Rome's site was strategic, not economic: Rome was at first a northern outpost of the Latins against the Etruscans, and the site later proved to be an admirable one for the domination of the Italian peninsula. In central Italy the mountains lie along the eastern coast and traffic through them is difficult. A city that controls the Tiber can dominate all movement by land from north to south. It would eventually be true that all Italian roads led to Rome. The Romans' motives for conquering Italy were the desire for safety from her neighbors and greed for their land. Perhaps the political ambitions of some leaders also played a role even at an early date. Rome's early conquests did not involve changes in economic organization. But when the conquest of Italy south of the Apennines was complete, Rome's power drew her into the wider struggles of the third century. It was largely the military needs of the expanding state which destroyed the primitive homogenous community and introduced a more complex economy.

ROME ENTERS THE MARKET ECONOMY
THROUGH STATE ACTIVITY

Even from the end of the fifth century, some changes may be observed. Rome conducted a long siege of the nearby city of Veii. Because the siege was protracted, the Romans are said to have introduced regular pay for their citizen-soldiers. At about the same time (c. 420 B.C.), a new office was created, the aedileship. Two aediles were elected to supervise the markets and public works and for other duties. This was a plebian office. The patrician fathers and landowners were not much interested in it, but its existence does suggest an urban population interested in commerce of some sort, perhaps in a provision market. The significance of these actions is hard to judge, for as yet Rome did not mint coins. It is particularly unfortunate that the date of Rome's first coinage is uncertain and much disputed. The tendency of recent scholarship has been to reduce the date. It seems that minting was postponed until Rome made her first contact with the more advanced Greeks of Campagnia. A bronze issue is perhaps connected with Rome's alliance with the city of Naples in 327 B.C. But the date is doubtful and the issue is extremely rare and must have been very limited. Silver coinage was delayed until 269 B.C. and perhaps until a good deal later.[9]

[8] Polybius iii. 24. 1–13; Frank, *ESAR*, I, 35–6.

[9] Harold Mattingly, *Roman Coins from the Earliest Times to the Fall of the Western Empire*, 2d ed. (Chicago: Quadrangle Books, 1960), p. 4; Bolin, *State and Currency*, pp. 131ff.; C. Nicolet, *Ann. ESC.*, XVIII (1963), 433–4. No certain date is yet possible. Note Nicolet's remark: "Or, il est incontestable que dans l'Antiquité, sauf exception, ce sont les besoins de l'état (et, le plus souvent, ses besoins militaires) qui déterminent une politique financière et monétaire destinée essentiellement à les satisfaire à court terme" (*ibid.*, p. 436).

The real transformation of the Roman economy must be dated from those wars which took Rome outside the peninsula, especially the Pyrrhic and First and Second Punic Wars. During the Pyrrhic War (282–272 B.C.), Roman troops fought in the extreme south of Italy, for the first time against Hellenistic armies. Because the enemy possessed the elaborate tactics and siege equipment of the East, Roman troops had to campaign for ten years and at considerable distance from their sources of supply. It was, in short, a kind of war new to the citizen militia of the Roman state. It is possible, then, that the first issue of silver coins should be connected with this war. Earlier Roman wars would not have cost much in the way of money, nor would soldiers on campaign have spent much. But to maintain armies in the south of Italy, the Romans, like the Greeks before them, would have found it necessary to pay their soldiers in money and to negotiate with local towns and villages for markets on which to buy supplies.

As far as we can see, however, the major changes came with the First and Second Punic Wars (264–241 B.C. and 218–201 B.C.). The great struggle between Rome and Carthage began in the Greek city of Messina on the Sicilian shore of the straits between Sicily and Italy. Social strife in the city had led Agathocles, tyrant of Syracuse, to invite mercenaries from Italy to garrison the town. After his death these *Mamertines* or "sons of Mars" took over the city, killed the male citizens, married the women, and settled down to a life of piracy, collecting protection money from ships passing through the straits. It was in the interest of the commerce of both Carthage and Syracuse to destroy them. In 265 Hiero, the new tyrant of Syracuse, attacked and defeated the Mamertines, who saved themselves for the moment by inviting help from Carthage. Since the straits were a valuable prize to the Carthaginians, they kept a garrison in Messina. The Mamertines then invited Rome to help them against the Carthaginians. What interest Rome had in the affair is not clear, and the Senate appears to have been reluctant to accept. It cannot be thought that an assembly of country squires from northern Latium had any interest in the traffic that passed through the straits, but popular leaders pushed a resolution through the assembly to send help to the Mamertines. Several political purposes may be conjectured for their action. It seems most likely, however, that the interests of the allied Greek cities of southern Italy were the chief motive. Unlike Rome, they could not afford to have Carthage control all traffic between the eastern and western halves of the Mediterranean as well as the coastal trade of Italy itself.

When Rome sent two legions to southern Italy, the Carthaginian commander at Messina, on his own authority, withdrew his garrison and allowed a small Roman force to take the city. The government, however, allied itself with Syracuse, rushed troops to the island, and blockaded the harbor. The Romans then made the decisive first step on a course that was to lead from the isolation of a subsistence economy in Italy to a Mediterranean empire. Although she had no fleet except a small force of twenty outmoded triremes and the naval aid of her Greek allies in southern Italy, she put an army into Sicily and set out to fight a war for possession of the island. The war took twenty-three years and forced major changes in the Roman state. If Rome were to fight on an island against a great naval power, she must possess ships. Using the skills of her Greek allies, Rome built a fleet modeled on the Carthaginian quinquireme. This was a strong, heavy vessel in which each oar was pulled by five men. To enable soldiers to board enemy ships, the Romans fitted out each ship with a "beak," a sort of gangplank with a great spike at the end with which could be made fast to the deck of an enemy ship so that the marines could board it. Naval warfare quickly developed on a scale unparalleled even in the Hellenistic East. The first Roman war fleet, numbering about 140 ships, put to sea in 260 B.C. and speedily demonstrated the value of the beak in an impressive victory near Mylae. Fifty Carthaginian ships were taken and their prows sent to Rome to decorate the forum. Four years later a large expedition of 250 warships, 80 transports, and about 100,000 men won a victory off Cape Ecnomus in eastern Sicily and landed in Africa to ravage the open country.[10] These early victories however were followed by disasters at sea, the loss of whole fleets and the armies on them, and by fierce fighting in Sicily. No decisive victory was won and the combatants settled down to a long war of attrition.

Such unprecedented military and naval efforts and the long course of the war began a revolutionary change in the Roman economy that by the end of the next century resulted in the social crisis inaugurated by the tribunates of Tiberius and Gaius Gracchus in 133 and 123 B.C. The war forced the government to undertake activities it had never before attempted, to reorder economic institutions for these activities, and hence to create new social classes and to alter the relations of old ones.

THE APPEARANCE OF A BUSINESS CLASS AT ROME

At first the means were crude. When the treasury was empty and a fleet needed, patriotism supplied the place of public wealth. Either single or by a kind of limited liability corporation of several citizens (*societas*), contributors undertook to build and outfit a quinquireme on the understanding that they would be repaid from booty if the expedition were successful. By this means a fleet of two hundred quinquiremes was quickly prepared.[11] In the Second Punic War a corporation, apparently on a more regular basis, was used to carry supplies to Spain. The arrangement does not appear to have been a success and probably was not repeated.[12] Some profit was to be made in loans to the government to be repaid after the war. An important change

[10] Roebuck, *Ancient Times*, pp. 460–1.
[11] Polybius i. 59.
[12] Livy xxiii. 48. 9–49; Frank, *ESAR*, I, 84–6.

seems to have come in 179 and 174 B.C., when the censors began letting out contracts to corporations of partners whose liabilities under the contract were limited and who consequently enjoyed a privilege which Roman law did not extend to purely private partnerships. Such societates thereafter became a regular institution of the Roman public economy. Their members were usually drawn from the equestrian class, that is, those members of the first class of the census who had not sought a public career and hence were not in the Senate.[13] The censors of 179 were particularly interested in harbor and retail facilities. They also established several new customs stations. Contracts were let for the *pons Aemilius*, the earliest stone bridge that can be dated. (Its arched superstructure of stone was added in 142.) Thereafter building probably increased fairly regularly. The immense work of the Marcian aqueduct was contracted for in 144. There were quarrels between the censors, Senate, and knights over contracts, and possibly the magistrates for a time took direct charge of public works. Some roads were built and repaired by contractors, others by the army. The same was true of waterways, drainage, and some other public works. It seems probable that the mines of Spain, which the state at first exploited after the defeat of Carthage in 201, were let to private contractors in 179. These equestrian companies, too, acted as publicans for the collection of some taxes: the tithe and pasture tax of the public land in Italy and the *portoria* or customs of several harbors in Sicily and Spain. They were not worth a great deal before about 150, when the annexation of Macedonia and Africa greatly increased their values.[14] Equestrian companies however were forbidden to bid on the tithe of Sicily, which was used largely for the army. Then in 133 the kingdom of Pergamum was annexed as the province of Asia, and the corporations could and did bid on Asiatic taxes. By about 100 B.C. the customs probably yielded something like ten million denarii to the state and gave a profit of one million to the contractors. The taxes of Asia brought about an equal sum, and probably much greater incidental profits from bribes, extortion, and usury.

As early as the middle of the century Polybius could write:

> For contracts too numerous to count are given out by the censors in all parts of Italy for the repairs or construction of public buildings; there is also the collection of revenue from many rivers, harbors, gardens, mines, and land —everything, in a word, that comes under the control of the Roman govern-

[13] The *equites* were at no time during the late Republic or Empire a social class devoted exclusively to public contracts and commercial affairs, though they entered politics and, therefore, the literary texts as such. Prosopographical studies of the inscriptions, however, reveal clearly that all through these periods by far the greater number possessed no income except from land, which, of course, remained the overwhelmingly most important source of wealth: C. Nicolet, *L'ordre équestre à l'époque républicaine (312–43 av. J.-C.)*. (Paris: E. de Boccard, 1966), pp. 283–313.

[14] Frank, *ESAR*, I, 150–5.

ment: and in all these the people at large are engaged; so that there is
scarcely a man, so to speak [he means a man of property], who is not interested either as a contractor or as being employed in the works. For some
purchase the contracts from the censors for themselves; and others go partners
with them; while others again go security for these contractors or actually
pledge their property to the treasury for them.[15]

The fortunes of the equestrian contractors started from very tentative beginnings in the First Punic War and grew little until the early second century.
In the first half of the second century they increased regularly, though moderately, until they were considerably advanced in the middle of the century
by the acquisition of new provinces; the annexation of Asia in 133 ushered
in greatly increased fortunes in the next fifty years. The tribunate of the
younger Gracchus in 123 would show that the equestrians had become a
power in Roman politics.

At the same time, smaller profits were accruing to men of lower status.
Inscriptions from the port of Delos record that southern Italians from the
middle of the century and Romans from the Gracchan period, who were con-
nected with the government and tax system, were oppressive and resented.
When Mithridates of Pontus invaded the province of Asia in 88 B.C., the
Greeks rose up and slaughtered some 80,000 Roman citizens in a single day.
By that time citizenship had been extended to all freemen in Italy and the
distinction between Romans and southern Italians can no longer be made.
In public building and the erection of fine private houses, Pompeii in the
period between c. 150 and 80 B.C. appears to have been in advance of Rome,[16]
but it is clear that Roman contractors were extending their operations beyond
Italy and that they were entering banking, moneylending, and other commercial pursuits. Their factors followed and even accompanied the Roman armies.

Depending, as it did so largely, upon state contracts and war, equestrian
wealth increased with the increasing wealth of the state. From the time of
the Punic Wars booty, indemnities, and tribute began to play an important
part in Roman public finance. Polybius reports that when the Romans took
the town of Aspis in Africa in 265, they captured more than 20,000 persons,
whom they enslaved and shipped off to Italy. The figure need not be taken
literally, but the number must have been great. In Italy slaves must have been
sold to repay those who had invested in the war and to provide the state with
exchangeable wealth. On other occasions booty might contribute to the development of the money economy in a slightly different way. On the sack
of a city or defeat of an army, booty was pooled, and its distribution was
generally a prerogative of the commanding general. He might reserve a part
for the state, keep part for himself and his officers, and distribute a part to
his army. But much of such booty cannot have been in usable form. Slaves,

---

[15] vi. 17, trans. Shuckburgh.
[16] Frank, *ESAR*, I, 282.

furniture, and fine cloth were of no use to soldiers on campaign or of much use to the treasury. They had to be turned into coin.[17] Captives might be ransomed by their relatives, but the army was followed by sutlers who would buy up the booty and sell it elsewhere.[18] They might also get back a good part of their money from the common soldiers by selling them necessities and catering to their pleasures.

The treasury also profited directly from indemnities imposed upon defeated enemies. From that imposed upon Carthage in 241, the state paid off the debts it had incurred from its citizens. Rome began also to receive tribute. During her Italian wars she had taken defeated peoples into her military confederation but had not exacted tribute. Possession of an island like Sicily, however, demanded keeping a standing army there, and a tribute was imposed to maintain it. The subject cities and peoples of the island paid a tithe of grain and other produce, and customs dues were collected. The tithe of grain seems to have been consumed by the army rather than sold for income, but a money income was realized from the customs. Rome's public receipts would increase with the addition of new provinces. In 238 B.C. Sardinia was seized and eleven years later Corsica was added to the new province. After the Second Punic War, in 197, Spain was organized into two provinces: Hither Spain in the Ebro Valley and Farther Spain in the Guadalquivir. For fifty years thereafter, there were no new provinces, for the Senate was reluctant to impose direct rule on the East. Only in 148 was Macedonia organized as a province. Two years later after the Third Punic War the region about Carthage—roughly modern Tunisia—was made the province of Africa. In 133 the last king of the Attalid dynasty of Pergamum willed his kingdom to the Roman people and this rich region became the province of Asia.

Provincial tribute had to be spent largely within the province to maintain armies there and on the frontiers. The booty that victorious generals displayed in their triumphs was brought to Rome and, in the second century, was deposited in the treasury. Fairly comprehensive figures have survived, although they cannot be complete and are not perfectly trustworthy. After the First Punic War Rome imposed an indemnity on Carthage of 3,200 talents of silver, to be paid in ten annual installments. (The talent weighed about 37 kilograms or almost sixty pounds. In coined money this silver could make nearly 2,000,000 den. a year.) In 238 an additional 1,200 talents were added to the Carthaginian tribute. Other indemnities, booty, and ransoms collected between the close of the First and the opening of the Second Punic War (between 241 and 218) must have amounted to something like 3,600 talents, making a total of 8,000, from which over 40,000,000 den. could have been coined.[19]

---

[17] Onasander's advice that all booty should not go to the soldiers, but that sometimes the general should take all or part of it to sell to meet public expenses: 35. 1–4.

[18] Compare Herodotus' account of the origins of the wealth of the Aeginetans from the booty taken at Plataea in 479: ix. 80–1.

[19] Frank, *ESAR*, I, 75.

In the next fifty years extraordinary state income increased. The indemnity imposed upon Carthage in 201 was more than twice as great as the earlier one: 10,000 talents to be paid over fifty years. Booty from the eastern wars brought in 31,735 pounds of gold; 669,113 of silver; and 5,787,000 den. Income from the Spanish mines, which were exploited by the state until 179, and from booty in Spain amounted to 6,316 pounds of gold; 350,352 of silver; and 1,738,000 den. (What the state received from the mines later is unknown.) Booty from campaigns in Gaul and Istria added another 2,000,000 den.[20] In sum, metal to the value of 183,500,000 den. must have come to Rome in the first half of the second century. Much of it was quickly coined. For the latter half of the century our information is far less complete.

THE WEALTH OF THE ARISTOCRACY

If these activities brought opportunities to a business class headed by members of the equestrian order of the city of Rome, it brought far greater profits to the senatorial aristocracy which controlled public office and the distribution of the profits of war. It was precisely in the period when the eastern wars were raging between c. 200 and 146 that certain members of this class established their huge fortunes. Direct profits from war were used to lay the foundations of great fortunes in Italian land. New economic conditions in Italy also played an essential part.

The campaigns of Hannibal in Italy, especially in southern Italy, caused immense devastation. At the same time, because great numbers of Roman and Italian peasants were out of the peninsula on campaigns for years on end, their farms fell into decay. The state also expropriated much land from those cities in the south which went over to Hannibal. The number of citizens declined greatly during the war: from 270,713 in 233 B.C. to 214,000 in 204, just before the end of the war.[21] At the end of the war, the Romans undertook the reconquest of Cisalpine Gaul and founded colonies of ex-soldiers there. Other veterans seem to have chosen to live at Rome. The government, then, had much land but few takers. It therefore let any amount of land at a low rent to citizens who had the means to get it back into production. Thus the rich, especially the senatorial families who had war profits to invest, began to establish great estates (*latifundia*). Conditions in the second century proved propitious to the development of these villas for market production.

---

[20] Frank, *ESAR*, I, 127ff. Cf. Henry C. Boren, "The Urban Side of the Gracchan Economic Crisis," *American Historical Review*, LXIII (1957–1958), 890–9. The reader should compare these considerable sums with the fantastic amounts listed below from the height of the Republican plundering of the world in the middle and late first century.

[21] All the surviving census figures will be found in Frank, *ESAR*, Vol. I. The decline in 204 may be partly due to the censors' failure to register citizens who were on campaign outside Italy.

The wars Rome was waging produced immense numbers of slaves and greatly lowered their price. Indeed, some of Rome's manoeuvres in this period seem to have been designed to provide cheap slaves. In 169 by a ruse recalling the massacre of Glencoe, Aemilius Paullus fell simultaneously upon all the towns and villages of Epirus and made a haul of 150,000 prisoners, who were sold off into slavery. Since Epirus had rendered no effective aid to Rome's enemy, Perseus of Macedonia, this kidnapping expedition strained to the utmost the ancient usages of war.[22]

Production by such means was cheap, and the market was improving. The towns were growing. (Rome itself probably lagged behind the development of urban industry and luxury in the south of the peninsula.) Some of the new estates developed ranching rather than grain culture, and gangs of armed slaves on horseback, true cowboys, rode over great ranges. The import of grain from overseas had not done anything to damage the market for Italian grain. The use of slave gangs in agriculture increased beyond measure and the second century saw a series of great servile rebellions: conspiracies of slaves in Etruria were suppressed in 198 and 196; in 185 the shepherd slaves of Lucania were so lawless that the praetor Lucius Postumius had to campaign against them; and after the great Servile War of 134–132 B.C., 4,000 slaves were executed at Sinuessa in Sicily alone. A consular army had to campaign four years against a second servile revolt in 103 B.C., and the great Pompey himself campaigned against the slaves under Spartacus who seized Mount Vesuvius.

That this development of latifundia was connected with the development of the urban market for farm goods is evident from the first Roman handbook on estate management, the elder Cato's De agricultura, written about 160 B.C. Cato attempts to figure costs and set them against market prices. His basic principle is to buy as little as possible and sell as much. He specifies the number of slaves necessary for grain fields and vineyards of a certain size and calculates that for the reaping or vintage it is cheaper to hire seasonal labor than to maintain that number of slaves all year. Contractors seem to have let out slaves for such purposes, but also freemen of the neighborhood were hired. Clearly Cato is calculating costs and planning production for the market. The villa does not simply sell off the accidental surplus of good years.

This growing market should be connected with the introduction into Italy of new milling techniques from the East and, somewhat later, of improved olive and grape presses. The donkey-mill came into Italy in the early second century and the profession of miller-baker made its appearance.[23] Thereafter, and certainly by the first century, city dwellers customarily bought their bread. The screw press for squeezing olives and grapes seems to have come to Italy only in the late first century. Cork stoppers for wine jars ap-

[22] Cary, History of Rome, p. 208.
[23] Pliny NH xviii. 107.

peared. The market appears to have been good in the second century. As population recovered from the losses of the Second Punic War, demand increased. From sometime toward the middle of the century grain prices seem to have increased. While this must have caused widespread distress, it was profitable to the efficient farmer.[24]

Everything, then, accorded to make market farming on a large scale profitable. Private wealth was not yet on the immense scale of the first century but was growing. Aemilius Paullus on his death in 160 left property worth 370,000 den., while the elder Scipio (d. 184) must have been worth some 1,000,000 den., for he promised dowries of 300,000 den. for each of his daughters. Fortunes were much larger by the end of the century. When he died in 129, Scipio Aemilianus left only 32 pounds of silver, but his brother Allobrigicus was the first person at Rome to own a thousand pounds of it. By 91 B.C. Livius Drusus, a tribune of the people, possessed ten thousand.[25]

It need surprise no one but the stubborn moralist (of whom the Romans produced more than their proper share) that such new wealth at the top of the social scale produced a taste for luxury. Some, like Cato, might be rich and live meanly, but not most. The Romans began to appropriate the culture of the Hellenistic East, Roman literature was born of imitations of Greek models, and both the rich and the urban poor began to adopt a new style of life:

> The first of the Scipios [the conqueror of Hannibal] opened the way for the world power of the Romans; the second [his brother, the victor in Asia] opened the way for luxury. For, when Rome was freed of the fear of Carthage, and her rival in empire was out of the way, the path of virtue was abandoned for that of corruption, not gradually, but in headlong course. The older discipline was discarded to give place to the new. The state passed from vigilance to slumber, from the pursuit of arms to the pursuit of pleasure, from activity to idleness.[26]

There is both rhetoric and moralism in this, but Polybius, who was a contemporary and a Greek, ascribed a moral decline to the extravagant habits young men brought back from the war against Perseus of Macedonia (168 B.C.); Cato the Elder observed the change; and long afterwards Pliny the Elder, with the advantages of hindsight, subscribed to their view.[27]

The service of this new luxury was largely performed by Greeks and

---

[24] Heichelheim, "On Ancient Price Trends from the Early First Millennium to Heraclius I," *Finanz Archiv*, n.s., XV (1955), 507: there was a sharp rise in grain prices from 138 B.C. or slightly earlier throughout the Mediterranean, and from c. 160–140, "for two decades or so the overwhelming majority . . . had to live close to . . . starvation."

[25] Pliny *NH* xxxiii. 141, 147.

[26] Velleius Paterculus ii. 1. 1.

[27] Polybius xxxi. 25. 4–8.

orientals who spoke Greek. They came to Italy as slaves, artisans, merchants, doctors, rhetoricians, and schoolteachers. The Latin language was flooded with Greek words. There were a far greater number of them than familiarity with the classic authors would suggest, for many were rejected from the polite language of Cicero's age and others probably were confined to the urban commons. But Plautus' vulgar comedies already reveal a great number of them, and Plautus died in 184 B.C. There are nautical terms: for example, *prora* (ship's prow), *nauta* (sailor), *carina* (keel), *pausarius* (rowing master), *cymba* (boat), *gaulus* (merchant vessel). Others dealt with business and finance: *danista* (moneylender), *logista* (accountant), *trapessita* (money-changer or banker), *syngraphus* (written contract), *exagoga* (export).

In addition to words dealing with medicine, grammar, and education, many words came in dealing with technology and town life: *machaera* (sword), *pessulus* (bolt), *platea* (square or street, from which comes our word "place"), *macellum* (provision market). There are many Greek words for plants and cultivated crops: *cupressus* (cypress) and *ceras* (parsnip). They are particularly numerous for wine vessels and household equipment: for example, *ampulla, cantharus, patina, cista, culleum,* and *marsuppium.*

"But it is especially in the sphere of pleasure, luxury, extravagance, and debauchery that the Greek made his contribution to Roman life and language." The craftsmen listed by Plautus suggest the high degree of specialization the new luxury produced: *phrygio* (embroiderer in gold), *patagiarii* (border) *diabathrarii* (makers of slippers), *strophiarii* (makers of stays) and *zonarii* (girdle-makers), *molocinarii* (dyers with mallows), and *murrhobathrarii,* who scented shoes with myrrh. Latin also derived fashionable adjectives and adverbs from Greek, as we do from French, and had its equivalents of *chic* and *soigné.* Most ornaments and cosmetics had Greek names: *fucus* (rouge) and *schoenus* (cheap perfume).[28]

By the second half of the second century, then, the economy of Roman Italy had been radically transformed. This was not simply the result of market activity, although market activity played into the change. It was largely the result of the profits of empire. Opportunities for great wealth and the exploitation of the Empire depended on possession of political power at Rome. Such power was largely in the hands of a small inner circle of senatorial families who regularly held high office, gained great wealth as a consequence, and invested their wealth in Italian land worked by slaves and producing for the market. There was also an outer circle of senatorial families, not themselves influential enough to gain high office independently, but useful to the great families in their rivalries with each other and receiving political patronage as a consequence.[29]

[28] Greek words and usages in Republican Latin are treated by L. R. Palmer, *The Latin Language* (London: Faber and Faber, n.d.), pp. 81ff.

[29] Mattias Gelzer, *The Roman Nobility,* trans. Robin Saeger (Oxford: B. Blackwell, 1969), deals chiefly with the legal status of the nobles, but its definition of the class has important social, and therefore economic, implications.

A group of men from the first, or equestrian, class of the census was interested in state contracts, tax collecting, trade, moneylending on a large scale, and probably in city real estate, whose value was rapidly increasing. Most persons of the equestrian class were, no doubt, still estate owners as eager to accumulate farms as were the senators, but an important group owed its wealth to different sorts of activities. Neither as a class nor as individuals did they equal senatorial wealth; their positions depended upon state contracts and, therefore, upon the Senate, and especially upon those few families that led the Senate. These men towered above the citizen peasantry and the men who lived by petty market transactions and production for the market: millers, bakers, and shopkeepers in the towns; small traders and merchants from southern Italy and the eastern Mediterranean.

The yeoman farmers, the solid peasantry of old Italy, were declining. Some hung on by working a bit of land and earning seasonal wages on the great estates. Others, near towns and on good roads, must have been able to take advantage of the growing urban market which was dominated by the production of the latifundia. Others were moving north to the newly opened lands of the Po Valley in Cisalpine Gaul. At the same time the numbers of landless men were increasing and the poor were swelling the populations of the cities of Italy, especially Rome. They depended upon their political influence in the assemblies, where they more and more openly sold their votes, and upon the patronage of the great houses. For most of the profitable professions and crafts were filled by immigrants from the East: slaves, freedmen, and resident aliens. Of these, many belonged to the great houses, but others provided goods and services for the urban market.

This structure must have been reproduced on a modest scale in the allied cities of Italy, whose common citizens fought in the Roman armies and traditionally received a smaller part of booty and smaller allotments of land in new settlements than did Roman citizens, and whose leading citizens might envy the opportunities of their Roman counterparts.

In a sense, then, the whole structure of Roman society worked for the exploitation of the Empire by a handful of families which had traditionally held high office. The desire of other citizens and of the allies—of every class with some political power—to share the profits of empire led to the great crisis of the Roman state. The situation was complicated by the introduction of the market economy, by the social mobility which it encouraged, and by the luxuries for which it created a taste. That the appearance of so many new elements in Roman society should cause political difficulties and a social crisis should occasion no surprise. We should rather wonder that stolid Roman self-discipline postponed the crisis to so late a date as 133 B.C.

11 THE ROMAN CRISIS

In the year 133 B.C. Tiberius Gracchus, a member of the old senatorial aristocracy whose family had for generations held high office in the state, carried in the Tribal Assembly, against the opposition of the Senate and by unconstitutional means which threatened violence, a law for the redistribution of landed property in Italy. His act inaugurated a century of constitutional crisis and civil discord which destroyed the Republic and led to the monarchy of Augustus (27 B.C.–A.D. 14). This prolonged crisis was largely the outcome of the development of the market economy in Rome and the vast wealth which the empire brought in. To put the matter better, the crisis was the result of the inadequacy of Roman political institutions to cope with the new social and economic conditions.

Since Marx we have been taught that revolutions arise from class antagonisms and particularly from the rise of new classes which, having gained economic power, attempt to seize control of the state. In Marxian thought a revolution—the French revolution is the classic example—is the act by which a newly arrived class takes violent control of the state and its apparatus of power. Marx went on to argue that a new class was the result of new "relations of production." That is, the sources of its wealth differentiated the new class from the previous possessors of political power. The French Revolution was a "bourgeois" revolution and brought to power persons whose wealth came from trade and manufacturing rather than land. Now the movement we see in the last hundred years before Augustus has been called a revolution [1] and it certainly contained revolutionary elements. Marx's analysis however was drawn largely from the experience of Western Europe in the eighteenth and nineteenth centuries and we must see if it can be applied to the development of Rome in the hundred years before Augustus.

Certainly dissatisfied classes had been created by the market economy during the latter half of the third and the second centuries B.C. The repeated revolts of rural slaves reveal the desperation of one class. But their position was quite simply hopeless. Their numbers, but not their economic power, were growing, so that they were no real threat to the political power of the landed aristocracy. Amelioration of their condition would come only with a rise in the price of slaves, a more enlightened self-interest on the part of landowners, and the appearance of Stoic humanitarianism. It is worth noting that, except for gladiators, the urban slaves did not revolt. Their conditions of

[1] See Ronald Syme's important work, *The Roman Revolution* (New York: Oxford University Press, 1960).

life were probably much better: their hopes for their own or their children's futures were much brighter, and their chances for emancipation much greater as freedmen came to play an important role in commerce.

Free landless peasants presented a greater danger to the existing social order. They were citizens either of Rome or of some allied Italian city. In the course of the second century the population of Italy recovered from the losses of the Hannibalic War and again began to grow.[2] The land of Italy was largely in the possession of the aristocracy: the senators and knights of Rome and the officeholding class of the allied cities and tribes. An agitation developed for the redistribution of that public land which the Senate had entrusted to the wealthy when others could not be found to exploit it after the Hannibalic War. The agitation for redistribution in the 140s and 130s B.C. found considerable support among the aristocracy itself—not, it is thought, on humanitarian grounds, but for military reasons. The course of the wars in Spain, especially the contest against the city of Numantia, revealed incompetence among the Roman aristocracy and a decline in the value of Italians as soldiers. In returning from a tour of duty in Spain, Tiberius Gracchus is said to have passed through Etruria and to have observed there the great estates worked by slaves. From the point of view of the aristocracy, slaves have one great fault: they cannot be used to fight wars. Moreover, unless balanced and awed by a large free population whose political interests are joined to those of the slaveowners, they can be dangerous. In 135 the servile population of Sicily had arisen *en masse*. Their number was estimated at 60,000, which would be some fifth of the whole number of Roman citizens; a consular army was needed to suppress them. There were lesser outbreaks in southern Italy, and in the new province of Asia a social revolution broke out in 133 B.C. It must have looked as though the whole world were in revolt against Roman misgovernment.

Tiberius, therefore, returned to Rome to promote a program which would deal with three pressing social problems: military failure, the landless citizen, and the danger from slaves. When the Senate refused to act on his proposals, he stood for the office of tribune and announced that he would propose a land law. The present holders of public land would be permitted to retain 500 iugera apiece and an additional 250 for each of their first two sons. Any one family's holding would be limited to one thousand iugera. To placate the nobles, he proposed that these lands be freed of the small quit-rent paid the state, which said in effect that they should pass from public to private ownership. Holdings in excess of one thousand iugera were to be repossessed by the state and distributed to landless citizens in parcels of a size to make family farms. These new allotment holders were to pay a small quit-rent and

---

[2] The figures, which fell from 291,000 in 225 B.C. to 214,000 in 204 B.C., grew to 337,000 in 164 B.C. and 318,000 in 136 B.C. We do not know how much of this increase was due to natural growth and how much to the admission of new citizens.

were forbidden to alienate their plots, at least for a term of years. A commission was appointed to carry out the transfer of lands.

In proposing the bill, Tiberius omitted the usual prior consultation with the Senate, which might be expected to reject it.[3] On the day of the vote rural voters in great numbers flocked to the city to attend the Assembly, but the aristocrats induced the tribune Octavius to impose a veto. Tiberius persuaded the Assembly to remove Octavius from office, although such impeachment was unconstitutional. He then carried his bill into law. The land commission included Tiberius himself, his younger brother Gaius, and a prominent senator, Claudius Pulcher. By a subsequent enactment this commission was invested with judicial power to decide all disputes arising from the redistribution.

An attempt by the Senate to sabotage the commission's work by refusing funds was circumvented by another breach of the constitution. Tiberius proposed that the income from the new province of Asia, bequeathed to the Roman people by the last king of Pergamum, should be diverted to the use of the land commission. The Senate capitulated and made funds available. The commission set to work, especially in the outskirts of the central and southern Apennines.

To protect himself from indictment on leaving office and his legislation from nullification, Tiberius offered himself for a second tribunate. In doing so, he raised yet another constitutional issue. Whether such reelection violated any statute is uncertain, but it clearly violated established usage. Tiberius' election might, perhaps, have been defeated by constitutional means, but the heat of the conflict had raised tempers. Led by the former consul, Scipio Nasica, a group of senators attacked Tiberius in the Forum and clubbed him to death before his friends could come to his aid. The Senate instituted quasi-legal proceedings against his principal supporters. The consul P. Popilius was directed to hold an inquiry, which proved to be something of a bloody assize against the reformers. Scipio Nasica was discreetly removed from danger and accusation by an honorable diplomatic mission to the new province of Asia. It is with surprise that we learn that the work of the land commission continued, but boundary stones have survived to prove it did. Licinius Crassus took Tiberius' place and even P. Popilius cooperated.

The work of the commission increased the dissatisfaction of the Italian allies. Many cities and peoples which were members of the Roman military league had long been content to retain their own customs, laws, and magistrates, but as the advantages of empire increased, they pressed for an extension of citizenship. Not all the occupiers of public land who were brought under the scope of the agrarian law were Roman citizens; some were prominent citizens of allied states. As the Gracchan commissioners approached the limits of the land which they could profitably take from Roman holders, they

[3] For a contrary opinion, see Cary, *History of Rome*, p. 283.

began to seize land held by noncitizens. Hence the latter increased their agitation to extend the franchise. The censors of the year 125 relieved the pressure for a time by an unprecedented liberality in recognizing claims of Roman citizenship: the census roll leapt from 318,000 to 394,000; but it was becoming clear to the more perspicacious Roman politicians that a general settlement could not be long postponed. Settlement was delayed, however, until it became involved in the increasingly complicated social and political conflicts of Rome itself.

Ten years after Tiberius' death, his brother Gaius stood for office. The legislation that he proposed during his tribuneships of 123 and 122 B.C. extended much farther than than of Tiberius and was far more damaging to senatorial authority. The work of the land commission was resumed, and colonies were planted at Tarentum, Capua, and probably other cities of Italy. He proposed roads to help farmers in the marketing of their produce. More shocking to conservative opinion, he proposed a colony on the territory of Carthage, which had been destroyed in 146 and whose land had been cursed. In these measures, of course, he was continuing Tiberius' program to maintain a healthy peasantry. But he set out to attract other supporters as well.

To the urban plebs he offered a rational plan to maintain a stable, low price of grain by building state granaries and by overseeing its import. Such measures had long been taken by the Hellenistic cities of the East. They were certainly necessary measures for any large city in ancient times. Under ancient agricultural conditions the price of grain was likely to vary greatly from year to year and even from season to season. Crops varied greatly from year to year; shipping was irregular; the common man had no means to store a supply bought when the price was low. While the promise of cheap or free grain was eventually used to buy votes, it is likely that Gaius' law freed the commons in a measure from the largesse, and hence the political influence, of the great houses. Opposition to his program continued down to Cicero's time,[4] but the practice continued all through the late Republic and the whole course of the Empire.

Both the rural and urban poor must have been attracted by proposals that the state should furnish clothing to soldiers at public cost and that no one under seventeen years should be enrolled in the army.

A proposal to extend the franchise and citizenship rights to the Italians did not appeal to the narrower interests of the Roman commons and was rejected by the Assembly, but two acts attracted the new business class of Rome to Gaius' faction. One was a bill concerning the letting of taxes for the province of Asia. Tax contracts for the older province of Sicily were carefully controlled to protect the provincials' interests. They could not be bid on by societates and they were auctioned in Sicily, not at Rome. For Asia the

[4] Cicero De off. ii. 72; Tusc. Disp. iii. 48.

collection of taxes was to be sold at Rome to Roman knights, who were permitted to form societates for the purpose. The income from the taxes of Asia can be estimated at roughly 10,000,000 den. per annum, after the publicans had deducted their tenth for collection. The contracts, then, brought the Roman equites about a million denarii a year. Bribery and undue exactions soon increased the profits of the knights and their factors, while the Asiatics suffered severely.

A second law that Gaius offered to attract the equites is more complicated to understand.[5] He proposed that the juries which heard charges of misconduct against officials at the end of their terms of office should be drawn from the equestrian class of the census rather than, as formerly, from the Senate. The specious argument in favor of the change was that the senators had been too lenient in judging their own colleagues. This was true, but the proposal was not so innocent. The very contractors whose conduct in the provinces it was the duty of the governor to control might now judge him on his return. A vigorous and upright governor who protected the legitimate interests of provincial taxpayers might discover that such conduct had become dangerous. This legislation, then, created a new constitutional class of quasi nobles and gave it the political means to exploit the provinces. By threats to ruin senators' careers it could also bring pressure on the Senate in the matter of state contracts. The consequent rivalry between the equestrians and Senate would become murderous; Gracchus himself said that he had "thrown daggers into the Forum." [6]

After this the growth of the wealth and activities of state contractors and related businessmen appears to have been rapid. The expansion of Roman equestrian business in the East, as revealed by the inscriptions from Delos, dates from the passage of this law, for much Roman business with Asia seems to have passed through the free port of Delos and to have had its headquarters there.[7] So rapid was this expansion that in 89 B.C. at the outbreak of the Mithridatic War, the native population is said to have set upon and slaughtered 80,000 resident Romans in the Aegean area and the province of Asia.

If not so numerous elsewhere, Roman businessmen spread widely during the first century. They are first mentioned in Alexandria in the Gracchan era. In the early years of the first century B.C. there were groups of Roman merchants (conventus civium Romanorum) in the cities of Africa, and in 69 B.C., before the conquest of Celtic Gaul, Cicero could say—with some rhetorical exaggeration—that not a penny changed hands in Narbonese Gaul without

---

[5] A translation is found in A. H. M. Jones, ed., *A History of Rome Through the Fifth Century*, I (*Documentary History of Western Civilization*; New York: Walker and Co., 1968), pp. 119ff.

[6] On the legislation between the murder of Gaius and the appearance of Marius, see Frank, *ESAR*, I, 247–55; and Cary, *History of Rome*, pp. 297–8.

[7] Frank, *ESAR*, I, 244–5; on publicans in Asia, Broughton, *ibid.*, pp. 535ff.

being recorded in the accounts of Roman traders, colonists, tax farmers, cultivators, and graziers.[8]

Out of the Gracchan era, then, there emerged two parties or factions: the *optimates*, who represented the senatorial interest, and the *populares*, headed for the most part by members of senatorial families but composed of the interests which Gaius had formed into a political alliance. During the ensuing years, the same issues remained predominant, and the only new element was the change of senatorial tactics. Optimate politicians tried at times to ruin popular leaders by outbidding them in the Assembly. One measure lifted the rule that Gracchan allotments be inalienable and permitted their sale. The measure was popular among the recipients and perhaps inevitable, but the result was that land began once again to move from the peasantry to the latifundistas.

Marius introduced a new element into the stuggle. In the war against the Cimbri and the Teutons, in 105 B.C., he enlisted persons without property, members of the proletariat class of the census, as infantry in the legions. Such men came to look to their general for their futures. They desired booty, wages, and allotments of land on the expiration of their terms. It comes as a surprise to the modern reader to learn that, in the whole course of the struggle down to the triumph of Augustus, neither the Assembly nor the Senate made any effort to form a permanent fund for discharged soldiers or any provision for giving them land. The reason was probably the inadequate organization of public finances and the lack of anything like an annual budget. To do so might have neutralized the growing political influence and activity of the armies.

The Senate was losing control of the generals. In the past that control had been based largely upon the *auctoritas* of the Senate, and in particular upon the general habit of leaving to the Senate appointment to commands. But Marius, a parvenu without noble ancestors, had received his command not from the Senate, but from an act of the people in the Assembly. After his time ambitious men more and more appealed to the Assembly for commands and the troops to carry them out. The Assembly, regularly attended only by those who lived in the city, was no longer representative of the Roman people, and it was often influenced by bribes and threats. Violence in the city had become a regular element in Roman public life in the last years of the second century. With the generals free of civil authority and with the armies looking to their generals for grants of land, the central issues of power passed from the civil government to the generals and the land question passed from the Assembly and Senate to the armies. That land, especially Italian land, was central is clear from the careers of all the great commanders of the last century B.C.: Marius, Sulla, Pompey, Caesar, Antony, and Augustus. But since

[8] Cic. *pro Font.* 11–2.

the land of Italy was occupied, each military settlement involved the dispossession of a great number of citizens. Virgil was only the most famous of those who lost their property but he was more fortunate than most, for his genius moved Augustus to compensate him.

Still, after Marius' military reforms, the small landowners were better off because they could no longer be taken from their farms to serve unwillingly in the army. Transfers of title continued. Sulla made some 12,000 allotments of Italian soil; Caesar some 80,000; and Augustus, 17,000. Many of these family-sized allotments seem to have been sold to persons who were putting together great estates. Others seem to have continued to be worked by their former owners in return for a rent. There is not much evidence for the continued growth of great estates after the Gracchi, and perhaps the work of the land commission and the expropriations of the armies balanced the purchases of the great. Certainly the great landowner did not disappear. During the civil war between Pompey and Caesar in 49 B.C., one of the wealthiest senators, Domitius Ahenobarbus, could promise to each of his soldiers four iugera from his private property.[9] Had they been made, these grants might have come to some 72,000 iugera or 24,000 acres. There is no reason to suppose that these grants would have beggared Ahenobarbus.

Rural discontent seems to have declined after Sulla's time. This is suggested by the failures of Lepidus and Catiline to muster forces in rural Italy to overthrow the aristocratic regime. After the Social War (91–88) Rome extended citizenship to the Italian allies. There was considerable emigration to the provinces, and much provincial land passed into the hands of Italians. Marius settled soldiers in Africa and probably in southern Gaul about Narbonne. Caesar paid off most of his troops with Gallic or Spanish land; in 43 B.C. the Senate directed the foundation of a colony at Lyons in Gaul. (It became the capital of the Gauls.) Caesar made civilian settlements at Carthage, Corinth, and in Spain, and after Actium Augustus founded numerous colonies. Thus as time progressed, the settlement of the agrarian crisis in Italy was made more and more at the expense of the provincials.

But if the land question became to some degree less pressing in the course of the century, the social problems raised by vast new wealth became overwhelming. In the course of the first century wealth poured into Rome at an unprecedented rate. The annexation and exploitation of Asia after 133 B.C. had opened new opportunities to both the equites and the politicians. The senatorial aristocracy thereafter had been reluctant to annex more territory or even to meet the obligations entailed by their political domination of the Aegean region. The opening of the free port of Delos in 168 had done much to ruin Rhodes and with her ruin went the navy that had kept the eastern seas safe for merchants. In 69 B.C. pirates sacked the harbor of Delos and

[9] Caesar *BC* i. 17.

ruined the commerce of the island forever. In the following years their depredations along the coasts of southern Italy posed a threat of famine at Rome. Over the objections of the older senatorial interests, Pompey was given an extraordinarily broad mandate to eradicate the pest. His resources were adequate, his success complete and swift. His command was extended to Asia Minor and Syria and he was given authority to make a general settlement in these regions. Before Pompey's victory in the East, the state is said to have had an income of some 50,000,000 den. per annum; to this Pompey added 35,000,000. At his triumph in 61 B.C. he gave 50,000,000 den. to the state; he, his two quaestors, and 18 legates appear to have divided some 25,000,000 among themselves, while the common soldiers received 1500 den. apiece.[10]

Caesar, however, was the ugliest example of provincial looting for personal gain. "He went to Spain heavily in debt in 61 B.C. [Appian says he owed 25,000,000 sesterces [11]] and created wars that cleared him of debt." He is said to have received a bribe of 6,000 silver talents in 59 B.C. for carrying a law that recognized Ptolemy XI Auletes II as king of Egypt and ally of the Roman people. Auletes, as worthless a monarch as the house of Ptolemy ever produced, was eventually placed on the throne by Roman politicians. To bribe Roman politicians, when he was cut off from the revenues of Egypt during the years 58–57 B.C., he had had to borrow from the Roman financier Rabirius Posthumus. It was a risky operation, so the rates must have been usurious. Roman looting of Egypt, then, began even before the country was annexed.[12]

Caesar gathered immense wealth during his campaigns in Gaul (59–50 B.C.). The Senate of the Venetii was put to the sword, and the commons were all sold as slaves. The whole city of the Aduatici in Belgium was sold in one lot. Numbering nearly 53,000 and selling at 250 den. apiece—a low figure— they would have brought 13,250,000 den. A later historian says that in all Caesar took more than 400,000 captives who would have brought him some 100,000,000 den. But Caesar raised four legions without the authorization of the government and presumably had to pay them until the year 56, so that in 49 B.C. he was actually in debt to Cicero's friend, Atticus.[13]

No one could equal the depredations of Pompey and Caesar. But even among such rivals, Lucullus, a far less successful commander, was famous for his luxury, and Crassus seems to have been richer. There were opportunities open to all who were fortunately placed. Cicero passed for an honest man and spoke for decency and humanity in 70 B.C., when he represented the Sicilians against their former governor Verres. The case made Cicero's name in Roman politics, and the grateful province payed the costs of Cicero's curule

---

[10] Frank, *ESAR*, I, 322–3. He estimates that in 80 B.C. the annual public income must have been some 40,000,000 den.

[11] Appian, *BC* ii, 8.

[12] Edwyn R. Bevan, *House of Ptolemy. A History of Egypt Under the Ptolemaic Dynasty* (Chicago: Argonaut, 1968), pp. 352–3, 355–7.

[13] *BG* ii. 33; iii. 16; Frank, *ESAR*, I, 324–6.

aedileship.[14] Caesar's chief-of-staff and his chief engineer grew wealthy in Gaul; the opportunities of lesser men for lesser profits may be left to the reader's imagination.

Such rapacity could not be endured forever, for it beggared the provinces and tore apart the political structure of Rome. Caesar's short dictatorship failed to settle the political crisis, and it was left to Augustus, after his victory at Actium (31 B.C.) the sole Roman to possess an army, to bring a final settlement. For two hundred years thereafter the Mediterranean world was to enjoy substantial domestic peace; foreign wars were not to be a great economic burden, once Augustus had established the Rhine and Danube rivers as the European boundary of the Empire.

At the beginning of this chapter a number of questions were posed about the social structure of Roman Italy in relation to the developing market. The almost incredible wealth that the wars of the previous fifty years had brought into Italy had made it, and Rome in particular, a kind of economic center for the market integration of the whole Mediterranean world. Although she was never a center for the redistribution of goods in long distance trade, Rome became the banking center of the Empire, replacing such centers as Rhodes, Delos, and Alexandria. International banking developed considerably. There were still no savings accounts receiving interest, but special drafts on account could be sent throughout the Roman world and credit established in distant cities. (The general letter of credit or check was unknown.) That branch of the money business of which we hear most, however, is simple moneylending by banks, by private persons, and by private persons through banks. The depredations of the Roman governors and troops had brought the cities of Asia to such a pass that they were forced to borrow from Roman moneylenders, including senators, at rates as high as 12 percent per month. At Rome indebtedness was high among politicians, and a considerable cabal of bankrupt nobles was behind the conspiracy of Catiline in 63 B.C. Such borrowing as this was not, of course, for purposes of capital investment and brought no increase in production. Nor do the debts of the cities of Asia or of Ptolemy Auletes in any way resemble the funded debts of modern governments. The cities entered into such arrangements only in great and pressing need, the terms were extremely harsh, and the creditors lent only when they had advantages of political pressure and power to guarantee repayment. None of the advantages of public debt as they have developed in Western Europe since the late Middle Ages appear to have come into play, nor do ancient governments appear ever to have operated with standing public debts as a normal part of fiscal policy. (The advantages of such a debt are real. A funded debt permits

---

[14] One is reminded of George Washington Plunckett's distinction between honest and dishonest graft. Honest graft is seeing your opportunities and taking them, like learning that the city is going to lay out a new subdivision and quietly buying up property. Dishonest graft is like what that rotten Philadelphia gang did when it sold the lead off the courthouse roof. The distinction is real, if not idealistic.

the state to tap more of the community's resources than do taxes alone and to do so quickly in an emergency. It permits the state to build a clientele of creditors who will, of necessity, support and defend the liable government.)

The profits of empire, of course, increased the market in Italy and at Rome. There was a continuous growth of luxury trade and an increase in the public grain dole of the city itself. Under Augustus the system would be regularized and public granaries built. Ostia had been sacked by pirates in about 68 B.C., but under Augustus there was a vigorous building: a theatre and a great colonnade, where representatives of overseas trade could rent offices. Major improvements of the harbor, however, would await the reigns of Claudius and Trajan. At Rome itself, too, the great extension of the forums and markets was delayed until the imperial period.

The influx of precious metals and money from the provinces, then, paid for the imports of manufactures and to a considerable degree Italy remained an economic parasite on the empire, just as the city of Rome itself was supplied without returning goods in exchange. But there was also a considerable market development in Italy. Varro's book on agriculture, which was published in 37 B.C., is a guide to profitable estate farming for the market and lays a good deal more emphasis than Cato did on the raising of such luxuries as birds and fish. At the same time the pleasure villa and the villa which supplied the master's table with luxuries from its fish ponds was developing. Yet Italy was also developing industry of its own. The best known is *terra sigillata*, a red-glazed pottery decorated with designs embossed by molds. Its production began at Arezzo in Tuscany shortly after 30 B.C., and it quickly captured a considerable market outside Italy and has been found even in India.

These advances certainly created a profound change in the tenor of Italian life and society, but they were not sufficient to create a new class that could command the state. Merchants and artisans were persons of little consequence, and most merchants and all artisans persons of little wealth. Commercial families which attained great wealth (we know only one from the imperial period) sought to put their money into land, a safer and more respectable investment. That equestrian class which did business for the government and profited so greatly in the provinces and had so disturbed the state between the Gracchi and Sulla rather mysteriously fades from view as an independent political interest. In the early Empire the sort of affairs that they had handled are largely in the hands of provincials and freedmen. The reasons why the equestrian monied class faded away are obscure. The horrors of the Sullan proscriptions are only a first cause. It is strange that later in the century they are seen operating more or less harmoniously with the senatorial government. Quarrels were common enough: the equestrians never forgave Lucullus, who as governor reduced the debts of the Asiatic cities, and they transferred his command to Pompey. But in Cicero's career we can see the sort of cooperation that could develop between even an honest man pursuing a public career and a man like Atticus who pursued wealth. The two classes had learned to keep their quarrels within limits. The conspiracy of Catiline appears to have scared everyone who owned property. His plans for the murder of many men of wealth and the abolition of debt caused Cicero to attempt a union of all "good men" (*boni homines*), by which Cicero certainly meant everyone with property. His attempt did not save the Republic, as he hoped it would. But the Republic was destroyed by men like Pompey and Caesar and Antony, with armies at their back; it was not destroyed by social revolutionaries like Catiline.

Thus the new force that the development of the market economy let loose in Italy was not a "bourgeoisie," but the military, which represented a land-hungry peasantry. The question which loomed largest in men's minds was the land question. During the civil wars many Italians, like Virgil, lost their property to returning soldiers. After the defeat of the senatorial clique headed by Brutus and Cassius, Antony took the eastern command and left the young Augustus in Italy with the unpopular task of finding Italian land for their veterans. The task was done, but the confiscations do not appear to have been on so large a scale as were some earlier in the century. On his victory over Antony, Augustus' soldiers forced him to assign to them some of the lands in Italian cities that had favored Antony. But he favored the settlement of colonies of soldiers in the provinces in Africa, Sicily, Macedonia, both Spains, Achaia, Asia, Syria, Narbonese Gaul, and Pisidia.[15]

Thus, in an obscure way that we cannot wholly understand, the land question was settled, largely at the expense of the provincials. While the allotments to soldiers must have done much to reinforce the moderate peasantry, it did not destroy the great estates, nor does it appear to have seriously damaged the accumulation of great riches. By the time of Augustus' victory many of the old Republican senatorial families had been ruined and Augustus himself would ruin more, yet the private wealth of both new and old senatorial families continued to be enormous, as is clear from any number of examples in Pliny's *Natural History*. Augustus himself raised the census rating for a senator from 800,000 sesterces to 1,200,000.[16]

Augustus wisely saw that he could not destroy the influence of the Senate in the Roman state, but he could master it. That body continued to enjoy immense prestige and great privileges, but individual senators were dependent upon the emperor not only for their advancement in public office, but for their very lives. This is a reflection of the economic fact that the emperors did not attempt to abolish great wealth in land. Under Nero six persons were said—probably with great exaggeration—to have owned half the province of Africa. But the political power of the very rich was limited. The emperors did not look to the senatorial class for support, but farther down the social scale. The

---

[15] *Res Gesta divi Augusti* 16, 28.
[16] Suet. *Aug.* 41.

great outpourings of loyalty to the dynasty came from the commercial classes of Italy, from freedmen who could gain some social status from enrollment in the colleges of Augustales, from the urban poor who were fed by the public dole (*annona*), and from the provincials who were immensely relieved by the end of anarchy and misgovernment.[17] None of these, however, had sufficient weight in the state to maintain the new order. The moderate land-owners of Italy, whom Augustus made secure in their possession, and the military colonists of the provinces profited most from the settlement and assured its continuity. The veterans who had gotten a bit of money and a bit of land to be tilled with a slave or two, their officers who had gotten more and held office in the country towns of all the western parts of the Empire and in some parts of the East, and the local gentry with whom they assimilated were the supporters of the military regime which posed as a restoration of the aristocratic Republic.

---

[17] Gagé, *Les classes sociales*, pp. 138–43, 169–73, et passim.

12 THE HEIGHT OF THE ANCIENT ECONOMY

Augustus' campaigns in the Balkans permanently established the northern boundaries of the Roman Empire—and hence of the civilized world in the West—along the Rhine and Danube rivers. The project of conquering Germany to the Elbe was given up. The line between the sown and the desert served as a frontier in Africa, where the desert peoples would not present a formidable threat until the appearance of the camel in the Sahara during the third century. Essentially these boundaries would survive until the early fifth century. The additions that were made were peripheral: Mauretania and Britain under the Emperor Claudius; the *agri decumates* to defend the angle between the upper Rhine and the upper Danube in 83 A.D., and Dacia under Trajan in 107. In the East Rome for a time continued to make use of such clientele kings as the Herods of Judea. One by one these petty kingdoms were given a regular provincial administration in the course of the first century. In the East, however, Rome faced a powerful and civilized neighbor in the Persian state, first Parthian and then Sassanid. While Rome always dominated Syria and Asia Minor, her influence and control in Armenia and northern Mesopotamia varied from period to period. Economically the most striking feature of the Empire, of course, is that it found its unity in the Mediterranean. But if the Empire provided a political unity and the possibility of economic unity, the social and economic conditions of the provinces varied greatly at the outset of the Empire and continued to do so during all its history.[1]

SURVEY OF THE PROVINCES

Before Caesar's conquest Gaul north of the Roman province had already passed from a hunting or grazing economy to a thoroughly agricultural

---

[1] General works on the Roman Empire's economy, aside from T. Frank, *ESAR*: M. Rostovtzeff, *The Social and Economic History of the Roman Empire*, 2d ed., rev. P. M. Fraser, 2 vols. (Oxford: Clarendon Press, 1957); Courtenay Edward Stevens, "Agriculture and Rural Life in the Later Roman Empire," *CEH*, I, 92–125; Charles Parain, "The Evolution of Agricultural Technique," *ibid.*, pp. 126–79; Frank William Walbank, "Trade and Industry Under the Later Roman Empire in the West," *ibid.*, II (1952), 33–85.

country whose population depended upon the cultivation of grains.[2] Society was dominated by a chariot-driving, warrior nobility who controlled the land and reduced the peasantry to a status approaching serfdom. Coins were minted in imitation of the Macedonian coins of Philip II,[3] and their use was common enough that Caesar reports that their accumulation was necessary for warfare on a large scale.[4] Foreign traders, Greeks from Marseilles and Romans from the province, had penetrated independent Gaul and created among the aristocracies of most tribes a demand for wine and other Roman luxuries.[5] The social order of southern Britain was similar, though more backward.

The possessors of land, at least those who had not opposed the Roman conquest, may be assumed to have kept their possessions and their dependent peasants. Under the Roman Peace the government encouraged this aristocracy to move from the countryside to the chief town of each tribe, while at the same time the old strongholds were moved from defensible heights to low ground to become a center of assembly and communication. Thus each native tribe became assimilated to a Mediterranean city-state. (The names of such modern French cities as Paris and Rheims are the names of pre-Roman tribes.) Most such towns were small. Le Mans, with a population of four or five thousand, must have been typical of the sort which had only local importance, though the cities which gained commercial or wider political importance were larger.[6] These new cities were endowed with constitutions on a Roman model, and their aristocracies were assimilated with the magisterial class of Roman municipality. The nobles rapidly adopted Latin speech, Roman education, and a taste for Roman manufactures.

It must be assumed that during the period of independence the aristocrats had taken their toll from the peasantry largely in goods and services. The imposition of Roman tribute necessarily forced them to seek rents in money and to dispose of rents in kind on the market. The growth of the towns produced some sort of a local market for agricultural goods, as did the presence of the army on the Rhine. The change, however, seems to have produced hardship. In the light of the size and potential wealth of Gaul, the tribute

[2] On the origins and early development of agriculture in Europe, see V. Gordon Childe, *The Dawn of European Civilization;* and Marc Bloch, *Les caractères originaux de l'histoire rurale française,* I, 2d ed. (Paris: Armand Colin, 1955), p. 1.

[3] Their artistic history is traced by André Malraux in the second chapter of his *Voices in Silence.*

[4] *BG* xi. 2; cf. v. 12; i. 4.

[5] *Ibid.* i. 1; ii, 15, et passim. A few tribes systematically excluded them.

[6] On the Gallo-Roman city, see Albert Grenier, *Manuel d'archéologie gallo-romaine,* 4 pts. in 7 vols., supplement to J. Dechelette, *Manuel d'archéologie préhistorique, celtique et gallo-romaine* (Paris: A. Picard, 1931–1960). The speed of the Romanization of the upper classes is illustrated by the great villa discovered in 1960 at the village of Fishbourne near Chichester, Sussex. This hundred-room palace built by the British king, Cogidubnus, was begun within a generation of the Roman conquest but is wholly Roman.

which Caesar imposed does not seem to have been excessive, but it created difficulties. At any rate, Tacitus attributes the widespread Gallic revolt of A.D. 22 to indebtedness, apparently the debts of local aristocrats to Roman moneylenders.[7]

The admirable river system of Gaul (the Rhône, Garonne, Loire, Seine, Scheldt, Meuse, Moselle, and Rhine) made possible the development of relatively cheap transport and of internal exchanges. Inscriptions attest to gilds of river boatmen and shippers. Very considerable prosperity followed, but of these rivers only the Rhône flows into the Mediterranean. Consquently, Lyons became the chief city of Gaul. Farther north the army on the Rhineland frontier produced intensive economic development there. Traders and artisans settled near the fortified, permanent camps: such cities as Cologne, Bonn, and Strasbourg owe their early development to these forces. But since the other rivers turned to the Atlantic, the Channel, the North Sea, and the Low Countries, their fuller development would have to await the development of Atlantic and northern commerce and the intensive settlement of the Low Countries in the Middle Ages.

Agriculture in the north was probably relatively backward. It seems that the Gauls made considerable use of plows with iron cutting edges, unlike the Hellenistic Greeks and Romans. But generally the Romans developed Mediterranean agricultural methods in Gaul. The cultivation of the olive and the vine was extended or introduced, and the soils that could be tilled with a light plow were exploited. In northern Gaul and Britain this meant that the Romans settled largely on the uplands and neglected the heavier and moister soils of the river bottoms, which required heavy plows, great ox teams, and extensive drainage. These lands were conquered for agriculture only slowly in the course of the Middle Ages. Consequently in Roman times development was fuller in the south than on the great plain of northern Europe, and the north tended to be peripheral to ancient economic development.[8]

To the eastern provinces the Augustan peace meant a restoration of prosperity. Both the Roman conquests and the civil wars had caused immense damage to the prosperity of Greece and the Aegean. Before Pompey's conquest the contests of the last Seleucids and the wars of such native dynasties as the Macabees had thrown Syria into confusion. The Ptolemaic state economy in Egypt seems to have suffered a profound breakdown under the last

[7] *Ann.* iii. 40.

[8] On the Romanization of Gaul, see Franz Cumont, *Comment la Belgique fut romanisée*, 2d ed. (Brussels: Maurice Lamertin, 1914) ; Camille Jullian, *Histoire de la Gaule*, 8 vols. (Paris: Hachette, 1908–1926) ; and the work by Grenier cited above. On the Romanization of Britain, which of course dates only from the conquest of Claudius' reign, see R. G. Collingwood and J. N. L. Myers, *Roman Britain and the English Settlement*, Vol. I of the *Oxford History of England*, ed. G. N. Clark, 2d ed. (Oxford: Clarendon Press, 1937). On the Danubian regions: Vasile Pârvan, *Dacia* (Cambridge: Cambridge University Press, 1928). The Augustan colonization of this region was from Italy and consequently the regions to the south of the Danube came to speak Latin.

monarchs, who not only fought civil wars but had to buy off the Romans in an effort to prolong the monarchy's independence. The rapacity of late Republican tax collectors and governors appears to have had particularly severe consequences in the province of Asia.

The extent of this economic dislocation is difficult to estimate. The troubles did not all come at just the same time. It has been argued that the prosperity of Greece never fully recovered from the Mithridatic and civil wars. Certainly it never recovered its relative importance in the commercial life of the eastern Mediterranean. Athens declined to the rank of a university town, although Corinth, refounded as a Roman colony, gained considerable commercial importance. The cities of Asia showed great mercantile resiliency and played an important part in the trade of the early Empire.

The status of Egypt within the empire was peculiar. Even after its annexation by Augustus in 30 B.C., Egypt remained a land somewhat apart. It was not, strictly speaking, annexed to the Empire but became part of the patrimony of the imperial house. Its taxes went into the emperor's private treasury. Unlike other provinces which were governed by senators, it was governed by an equestrian prefect appointed by the emperor. Senators, indeed, were forbidden to enter it without special permission, and special licenses were necessary for natives to leave the country. Although the old royal monopolies were replaced by a system of taxation in money and kind on agricultural artisans,[9] Egypt's economy continued to be isolated by the circulation of a special coinage. This coinage was overvalued so that it would not leave the province, and an *agio* was paid when it was used to buy coins of the Empire or of Alexandria.[10] Within Egypt goods were bought and sold in this coin, at least at retail, and wages were paid in it. This special status of Egypt is largely explained by political as well as economic considerations, if, indeed, the two can be separated. Since Egypt was responsible for the greater part of the public corn supply of the city of Rome, loss of control of, or disorder in, the province was especially dangerous.

The Augustan peace restored the commercial cities of the East to their former function of producing specialized products for an international trade. They did so now, however, in the more peaceful and unified world of a universal empire and catered to a greater luxury trade. Their products moved free of protective customs, for the harbor dues exacted were hardly enough to maintain port facilities, and the low customs barriers between provinces or groups of provinces hardly impeded trade at all. Augustus himself performed the great service of a sound improvement and a more regular and numerous

[9] Axel W. Persson, *Staat und Manufaktur im Roemischen Reich*, Vol. II of the "Publications of the New Society of Letters at Lund" (Lund: Carl Bloms Boktryckeri, 1923), pp. 36–7. The license tax on crafts appears to have been peculiar to Egypt. Elsewhere trades were free.

[10] On the working relationship of the local bronze of eastern cities to Roman silver, see Bolin, *State and Currency*, pp. 238ff.

issue of Roman coinage than had the late Republic. The emperors reserved to themselves the right to mint silver, though the Senate and many cities in the East were permitted to mint bronze. The silver content of imperial silver coins held steady until a deliberate reduction was made under Nero. Thereafter it remained fairly stable until the Marcommanic War of Marcus Aurelius. Roman silver provided the great instrument of trade outside the local markets of individual cities and was even the instrument of foreign trade.

EASTERN TRADE

The Augustan age saw the opening of the Far East to commerce with Rome.[11] It seems to have been Alexander the Great's intention to connect the mouth of the Tigris-Euphrates with the mouth of the Indus by a sea route, but his Seleucid successors were unable to accomplish this. The Egyptians, under the last Ptolemies, pushed discovery and exploration in eastern waters. With the establishment of the Roman peace, a new epoch opened in the eastern trade. The scale of luxury set by the Roman aristocracy and the general level of prosperity under Augustus and his successors led to an increased demand for luxuries which spurred the avarice of merchants. The coasting voyage direct from the Red Sea to India was expensive and dangerous. The Arabs of Yemen, who desired to maintain their place as middlemen, were hostile, and the coast of the Indian Ocean between the Persian Gulf and the mouth of the Indus was barren and dangerous on account of piracy. Again and again merchant ships were required to pay tolls or protection money to local shieks and chieftains.

It seems to have been under Augustus that a Greek sailor from Egypt by the name of Hippalus discovered the monsoon winds. From May to October the prevailing winds across the Indian Ocean blow from the southwest and are remarkably steady; from November to March, the counterwinds blow from the northeast. Hippalus discovered that, once having sailed the length of the Red Sea and come into the Indian Ocean, he could sail directly to India out of sight of land and out of danger from pirates. He reached the mouth of the Indus in northwest India, but it was the goods of southern India which were in especial demand: jewels and spices, especially pepper. By c. A.D. 50 merchants were sailing directly to Musiris (the modern Cranganore), the greatest mart of southern India. Ships regularly left Egypt in July and started their return trip in December. The carriage of goods from

[11] Sir Mortimer Wheeler, *Rome Beyond the Imperial Frontiers* (Harmondsworth: Penguin Books, 1955) ; E. H. Warmington, *The Commerce Between the Roman Empire and India* (Cambridge: Cambridge University Press, 1928) ; Max Carey and E. H. Warmington, *The Ancient Explorers*, 2d ed. (Harmondsworth: Penguin Books, 1963) ; M. P. Charlesworth, *Trade Routes and Commerce of the Roman Empire*, 2d ed. (Cambridge: Cambridge University Press, 1926).

India to Egypt took about sixteen weeks under this system, and the trade flourished and grew for some two hundred years. The Romans sent wine, copper, lead,[12] and even such rather ordinary pottery as terra sigillata to India. Fewer eastern goods are found at Mediterranean sites, and yet it is certain that the balance of trade was unfavorable from the Roman point of view, for Roman coins are found in many Indian sites (the Indians imitated Roman coinage), and the elder Pliny complains of the loss of bullion from the Empire in payment for useless eastern luxuries: cloth, jewels, and spices.

Roman traders probably did not regularly enter the interior of India, but they established permanent trading stations along the coast which had all the appearance of provincial towns of the Empire with a forum or agora and little temples to the Roman gods. In the second century Roman subjects from these emporia pushed on into the Bay of Bengal and to southeastern Asia, the region of the Mekong River and even to the Gulf of Tonkin, so that direct contact was established with Chinese merchants. Chinese records speak of ambassadors from the Roman emperor in the second and third centuries. (They were probably only merchants who passed themselves off as official representatives.) The ports of the west coast of southern India maintained their dominant position until the trade disappeared in the third century as a result of the declining prosperity of the Empire. (The latest Roman coins in India date from Caracalla.) The Empire in turn was visited by some Orientals. A Buddhist tombstone has been discovered at Alexandria, but most of the carrying trade from India to Egypt appears to have been in the hands of Roman subjects from the Eastern provinces, especially Greek-speaking Egyptians. The same seems to have been true of the growing cinnamon trade with the Somali Coast. Cotton from Ethiopia appeared, while frankincense had long come from Arabia Felix (Yemen).[13] Alexandria, of course, was the port which received, warehoused, and distributed these goods throughout the Empire. Rome herself was the chief luxury market.

It is more difficult to establish a certain chronology for the establishment of regular trade by the silk route across central Asia. The Han dynasty had unified China and by 101 B.C. had conquered the oases of Sinkiang and even reached the Jaxartes River. Here contact could be made with merchants from the Near East and even from the Roman Empire, as long as the routes were protected by the Kushan and Parthian kings, who enjoyed a regular tribute from the trade. The route ended on the Upper Euphrates in the Roman province of Syria, and the Syrian ports delivered Chinese silks to the vanity of Roman ladies and gentlemen. Thus for the first time direct contact was established between China and the Near East and even eventually with the Roman Empire. This route was, of course, more uncertain than the sea route

[12] Pliny *NH* xxxiv. 163.
[13] *Ibid.* xii. 63; xiii. 90.

in the south for it depended upon order in central Asia. It was also far more dear, for land transport was costlier than water transport and tolls must have been paid, as they were at the Roman boundary. But for the first time in a tenuous way and at the rarified level of the most extravagant luxuries, the great mass of Eurasia became something of an economic unity for two hundred years.[14]

ITALIAN PRIMACY

During the early Empire Italy held a central position in the economy of the Mediterranean world. The city of Rome, of course, enjoyed a highly privileged position, having by far the greatest concentration of wealth. Much of it was in the hands of the senatorial aristocracy, which resided at the city. In the course of the next two centuries this class was recruited increasingly from the provinces, but it settled at Rome and there, of course, created a great market for luxuries. During the Empire a great series of markets and shopping areas were built in the city, of which the greatest was that complex of a forum, libraries, a column, and a market which Trajan built with the booty from his Dacian War. But our fullest information about the luxury market comes from an earlier period and is found in the elder Pliny's *Natural History*. Pliny describes the qualities of spices and medicines and gives their prices in some detail. The products of the East were not the only ones that supplied Rome. Geese fattened for *foie gras* were driven to Rome all the way from the Morini in northern Gaul, while the most prized goose down came from the German provinces. Oysters came from the Bay of Biscay and mushrooms from Bithynia. In Nero's reign a Roman made the voyage to the Baltic coast to obtain amber, which the Romans had previously received only through intermediaries.[15]

There were also imports of a less elegant sort. The obligation to feed the great population of Rome fell upon the emperor, who continued to supply free grain, as had the Republic, but did so in a more orderly and rational way. The greater part of public grain came from Egypt and the province of Africa. It seems that in Augustus' time Egypt contributed 20,000,000 *modii* and Africa 40,000,000.[16] Residents of other cities occasionally received benefactions from wealthy citizens or were relieved by private generosity in times of want, but no other people enjoyed so regular a provision as those citizens at Rome on the list for the annona. By the end of the second century their number appears to have been some half-million persons. To provide for these

[14] This development is put in a broader context by McNeill, *The Rise of the West*, pp. 316–60.

[15] *NH* x. 53, xii passim, xxxvii. 45–6.

[16] Haywood, *ESAR*, IV, 43: modius (corn measure) = about 1 peck or ¼ bushel.

distributions public granaries were built at Rome. Claudius began the construction of a safe harbor at Ostia and Trajan built one at Centumcellae, both impressive works lately revealed by archaeology. On the basis of the density of the buildings excavated and the makeup of the apartment buildings it is possible to estimate roughly the population of Ostia, whose only purpose was to supply Rome. Its population seems to have to been about 27,000 persons at its height in the second century. The same author suggests that the population of Rome itself was probably somewhat less than a million.[17] (Rome was the largest city of the Empire, followed by Alexandria, Antioch, and Carthage, probably in that order.)

Italy imported other goods, of course. Hides came from Gaul. Spain was the chief western supplier of metals. Cinnabar from Almaden was worked by a societas on lease from the government, which set an official price of 70 sesterces a pound (at Rome apparently). Lead, which the Romans used plentifully for building and water pipes, was mined on a large scale. One mine in southern Spain was at first let for 200,000 den. a year and then for 255,000; another rented out for 400,000 den. Since lead sold for seven denarii per pound at Rome,[18] we can arrive at some idea of the size of the operations: 57,000 lbs. would have to have been sold to pay the rent of 400,000 den. and an uncertain amount more to cover costs of production, transport, and profit. Much, but not all, Spanish lead came to Italy. Iron must have been imported from Gaul, Noricum, and Illyricum. That great amounts of wine and olive oil were imported is proven by potsherds found at Monte Testaccio at Rome. The ancient pottery that composes that hill came largely from Spain. A great part of these imports was paid for by provincial tribute to the government and by rents to rich Italians from their estates in the provinces.

Italy also exported goods, chiefly to the undeveloped western provinces. Italian pottery, the dark red ware called terra sigillata,[19] for a time dominated the market for modest tableware and encroached on the eastern market, where it is found outside the Empire at Seleucia-on-the-Tigris and even in India. Italian agriculture, especially the olive, vine, and fruits, appears to have been prosperous in the first century. Italian land escaped taxation. Senators were required to invest a large part of their fortunes in Italian land, and the market for Italian produce, both in Italy itself and in the provinces was good, so that capitalistic farms on a large scale, worked by slaves, continued from the late Republic. Italian wines improved and replaced eastern wines on the luxury market in Italy.[20] Cultivation of the medlar and cherry tree spread, and the pistaccio was introduced.

[17] James E. Packer, "Housing and Population in Imperial Ostia and Rome," *Journal of Roman Studies*, LVII (1967), 80–95. Other educated guesses vary from a quarter of a million to well over a million.
[18] Pliny *NH* xxxiv. 161.
[19] Frank, *ESAR*, I, 375; Grenier, *ibid.*, II, 540ff.
[20] Pliny *NH* xiv. 59–96.

TECHNICAL INNOVATION

This review of the economic order of the Empire indicates that the ancient economy was brought to its height by the imposition by the Roman state of universal peace and a rational political order. It did not involve any profound technological innovation. The age did, however, see some advances. Some were spread as a result of the conquest of Gaul. There Caesar had discovered superior draft horses and an extraordinarily sophisticated kind of war chariot. Traces, to steady the body of a chariot, may have been a Gallic development. The fact that many Roman vehicles bore Celtic names suggests some other improvements from this quarter, although generally improvements in wagons and carts did not keep pace with the progress of Roman roads.[21] The wider use of iron plowshares in the western provinces may been due to Gallic influence. They are to be connected with the heavier frames used for northern plowing, though the subject is most obscure. The use of the barrel, probably also a Gallic innovation, became common in the imperial age. From the other direction, the camel of the Near East spread to North Africa by the third century and in late Roman or early medieval times it carried goods in Spain and even in southern Gaul.

The most striking innovation in manufacturing was the appearance of free-blown glass and of glass blown in molds. Glass had been known for a very long time, but the Egyptians had only carved or ground it to make vases, beads, and small ornaments. Now small glass bottles and flasks for unguents and perfumes appear in Augustan archaeological sites. The technique of glass blowing seems to have been invented in Syria. The speed with which Syrian artisans carried its production about the Empire is remarkable. It seems to have been produced in Italy within about a generation of its invention and thence was carried to the Alps and the Rhineland.[22] Goblets and drinking glasses, some of extraordinary workmanship, appeared on the tables of the rich. Simple bottles for unguents and perfumes, however, were common and cheap enough for middle-class use. Indeed, the modest luxury of the new glass industry just fit the market demands of that class of comfortable landlords which benefited most from the settlement of Augustus. Some great public buildings had glass windows, but cheap plate glass, and cheap glass generally, would be developed only in the sixteenth century.

There appear to have been some advances in mining techniques and in the techniques for the extraction of metal from ore. Wheels were used to raise water from the pits so that mines might be sunk deeper than had been possible earlier, and it does seem clear that the Romans made greater use

[21] Caesar *BG* iv. 21, v. 15; E. M. Jope, "Vehicles and Harness," *History of Technology*, II, 537–41, 543.
[22] D. B. Harden, "Glass and Glazes," *History of Technology*, II, 322–5.

of metals than had their predecessors. Lead was used for water pipes. Brass (*orichalcum*) came to be widely used only in the Augustan age [23] and pewter is a Roman development. Some iron was mined almost everywhere in Britain and Gaul: at many villages and villas pits about a meter in diameter were sunk and consolidated by the trunks of young oaks or chestnuts coiled and laced about to hold the earth. They were not deep but gave access to several lateral galleries. Forges, too, were found everywhere except in the towns, where ordinances probably forbade them. They were likely to be in forests where there was abundant fuel. Such forges were not efficient, for some 40 percent of the iron was left in the scories, but they were adequate for local uses.[24] In places where the ore was abundant the government exercised its right to underground wealth and let out the right to exploit. Iron mining on a greater scale took place in the Aude region of Gaul, in Noricum, and in the Sana Valley in Bosnia.[25] The some 100,000 tons of slag from Roman times discovered in Noricum correspond to some 30,000 tons of metal.

Probably more important in its general effects, certainly more vivid in our picture of the ancient world, was the advance of Roman engineering, which pressed traditional techniques to the utmost and invented some that were essentially new, like cement. The imperial period saw the wide use of cement and rubble construction, which opened up possibilities of massive building. To make a massive and almost indestructable wall, two brick faces were erected a few feet apart and the space between filled with a mixture of brick or stone rubble and cement. The faces were then extended a few more feet and the space between again filled. By various methods the separate sections were bound together to make a wall of enduring strength. (In a sunless climate the massiveness of the walls and the scarcity of windows would have been a serious drawback, but not in the Mediterranean.) In some places wooden forms rather than brick faces could be used. By such a technique the Romans were able to undertake harbor works on a greater scale than their predecessors. By combining such a construction with arches and vaults they were able to cover vastly greater open places than had any earlier architects. Cranes moved by men on a treadwheel achieved greater heights. The dome of the Pantheon was built by such methods which reached their height in such late imperial buildings as the baths of Caracalla, the baths of Diocletian, and the stupendous basilica of Constantine at Rome (early fourth century). In buildings of great luxury the brick of such construction was covered by marble, and for this purpose a technique of cutting marble into thin and economi-

[23] Michael Grant, *Roman Imperial Money* (London: Thomas Nelson, 1954), pp. 45ff.; Forbes, *Studies in Ancient Technology*, Vol. VIII (1964). Brass is an alloy of copper and zinc.

[24] André Bouton, *La Maine; Histoire économique et sociale des origines au XIVe siècle* (Le Mans: Impr. Monnoyer, 1962).

[25] E. J., Forbes "Metallurgy," *History of Technology*, II, pp. 55ff. See also O. Davies, *Roman Mines in Europe*.

cal slabs was developed. The floors might be covered by mosaics of marble tesserae. Such a technique and the facility the Romans achieved with arches also made possible the great aqueducts and bridges, some of which still stand and are in use.

Such public works did little to cheapen the prices of manufactured goods or to intensify the market economy, but they did make possible greater urbanization than would otherwise have been possible. In particular they must have contributed to the astounding progress of the western and Danubian provinces. Such work was not as great a burden to the economy as might be supposed. The basic task of building wooden frames or brick faces and filling them with cement and rubble called for much backbreaking labor, but little skill. The army or the urban poor might be employed for such work under the direction of a few professional architects or engineers. (Books by two professionals, Vitruvius and Frontinus, have survived.) At other times barbarian prisoners of war did much of the brute labor. Indeed, the great periods of imperial building seem to have followed successful wars.

The Romans' greatest technological achievements, then, were connected with the organization and direction of manpower, and they were directed to such purposes of the state as urbanization and military roads—in short, to the organization of society. Advances in the production of consumer goods were small and not of the sort to lower prices. They did not therefore radically expand the part played by the market in the economy.

BUSINESS ORGANIZATION AND THE EXTENT
OF THE MARKET

The organization of business does not show any striking advances.[26] Both production and commerce were usually conducted on a small scale. Certainly the dominant form of production and distribution in the cities was the small shop which sold goods made on the premises. Though shopkeepers might possess several slaves or might employ some hired free labor, the business certainly depended upon the work of the family which slept in or over the shop. The prosperous small town of Pompeii, buried by the eruption of Vesuvius in A.D. 79, reveals this system best. Its population must have been something like 25,000 persons. There were taverns and food shops. We are more surprised to discover a well-equipped laundry which took in wash for a price like those of modern American cities—surprised because the women of many large households were still weaving wool cloth. At Pompeii, however, there was considerable commercial production of cloth, though the city cannot have been an important wool center. There were fullers' and dyers' and wool-

[26] The standard work, now a bit old, is Persson, *Staat und Manufaktur im Roemischen Reich.* There is a summary in English.

scourers' shops [27] and a wool exchange or fullers' gildhall. A small provincial town like Le Mans in Gaul had both potteries and glass manufacturers. Both were outside the town itself (most cities appear to have had statutes prohibiting such noxious occupations within the walls).[28]

Outside Egypt the small gilds of craftsmen appear to have been voluntary and not to have had public burdens imposed upon them as yet. They were, however, strictly controlled by the imperial government, since such organizations had contributed much to the political violence of the dying Republic. They were fraternal societies without known economic functions, except perhaps to provide for the funerals of members, and they honored a patron of higher social station.[29] Shipping, too, appears usually to have been on a small scale. Most merchants possessed only a single ship, and some of these even had room to let to other merchants for the carriage of goods.

But there was certainly some enterprise on a large scale. A good deal of it involved government contracts. One eminent family fortune was built on a brickyard at Rome which supplied public buildings as well as private. The baker M. Vergilius Eurysaces left a great tomb at Rome, and Rostovtzeff conjectures that he filled contracts with the state.[30] The largest firm producing Italian terra sigillata, that of P. Cornelius, employed fifty-eight slaves. This is a great many more than the ordinary shopkeeper might own, but it is not a great number. The largest arms factory known in fourth-century Athens employed many more, but when production moved to Gaul, this level of concentration was not maintained. Mining might be carried out on a small scale, but the societates which contracted with the state for the exploitation of the great mines must have invested far more capital and employed far more persons than most industrial enterprises. They are one of the few examples of a very considerable concentration of capital in production in antiquity.[31]

Commerce and production in the West seem to have been connected with the really wealthy of the landed class in a subtler way and on a larger scale than these operations suggest. Under the Republic a law had forbidden senators to engage in trade or to own ships. They were permitted only to possess barges and small coasting vessels that could get their farm produce to the nearest market. We do not know if this law was rigorously enforced, but

---

[27] They washed freshly clipped wool to remove grease and impurities. The detergent used was root of the soapwort, for real soap had not yet been invented. The process was a delicate one if the wool was not to be injured; hence it is likely that even home producers took their raw wool to the scourers: W. O. Moeller, "The Lanifricarius and the Officinae Lanifricariae at Pompeii," *Technology and Culture*, VII (1966), 493–6.

[28] Bouton, *Le Mans*, p. 56. See the charter of the Spanish town of Urso, van Nostrand, *ESAR*, III, 196ff.

[29] The standard work is Waltzing, *Etude historique sur les corporations professionnelles*.

[30] Rostovtzeff, *Social and Economic History of the Roman Empire*, I, plate iv. Cf. plates xxiv, xxvii, xxx, xxxix, etc.

[31] The most important text on the organization of large-scale mining is the *Lex Metalli Vipascensis*. A translation may be found in van Nostrand, *ESAR*, III, 167–74.

commercial pursuits were clearly beneath the dignity of the truly wealthy and the respectable. Yet agricultural expansion naturally led the latifundista into commercial relations. He did not simply produce grapes and olives but had presses, vats, and storerooms for wine and olive oil. Some landowners appear to have produced wool cloth. Luxurious cloth was produced in the eastern cities of the Empire and sold on the market, but much good wool cloth continued to be produced at home. But even in Cato's day, the clothes of slaves had been purchased, and the production of cheap cloth for such garments had developed in northern Italy as early as Augustus' day.[32] The needs of the army guaranteed a solid market for better grades of wool cloth as well.

The father of the Emperor Pertinax in the middle of the second century A.D. had a *taberna coactiliaria* in Liguria. Pertinax himself acquired much land in the district and expanded the business. Since Pertinax at the time was a senator, he can hardly have been a simple shopkeeper and the statement that he bought up much land suggests that there was a connection between the land and the shop. The shop must have been making cloth from the wool produced on its owner's farms. Pertinax, in short, was a landowner who produced cloth the same way that others produced wine from their own grapes. He can hardly have been the only one in the district to so expand his operations.[33] The manufacturing itself, of course, was largely the work of slaves, but slaves could not tend to such matters as the purchase of raw wool and the sale of the finished product.

For such purposes as this the wealthy Roman had long made use of freedmen, just as the emperors used freedmen to manage their property (the *res privata*). Thus the freedman came to be the typical figure of the large entrepreneur in the first and second centuries. This corresponds to a rather mysterious decline in the business enterprise of the knightly class dating from Augustus' time. Augustus and his successors opened up for the knights a career in the public service on a lower level than that of the senators (though the top positions in the equestrian *cursus*, the prefectures of Egypt and of the city of Rome, were of immense importance). This cursus may have diverted some equestrian enterprise. Gradually, too, the government came to collect provincial taxes for itself and the equestrian societates in this business came to an end.[34] The equestrians' place in business life was taken by the freedmen. The prototype is the vulgar figure that Petronius created in his *Satyricon*, the tremendously wealthy Trimalchio. Trimalchio entered business as a slave. When he proved his worth and accumulated the private savings that the Romans allowed their slaves, he was liberated. After his master's death he continued in the shipping business. When his own avarice was sated, he retired from commerce, bought land, sought respectability, and, inciden-

---

[32] Strabo v. 218.

[33] *Script. hist. Aug., Pertinax* 3; Persson, *Staat und Manufaktur*, p. 51.

[34] These reasons are important but do not seem to be an adequate explanation. See Gagé, *Classes sociales*, pp. 106–22, 138–43.

tally, tried without success to acquire a literary polish. Two things about his later life are interesting. First, he kept his hand in business by financing other freedmen. His story makes the dependent status of many Roman businessmen clear. The gilds of artisans had rich patrons; freedmen were financed by the already rich. Second, the truly wealthy merchant looked to investment in land and the foundation of a respectable family, so that wealth gotten in commerce returned to agriculture. It was, after all, safest, and commercial occupations were despised. Almost the whole body of ancient literature reveals this last fact, and separate works need not be cited. Thus the commercial classes of the Roman world never developed an independent ethos or a commercial ethic.

Such men as Trimalchio were truly wealthy, but investments in commerce and in industry were limited. There seems to have been limited demand for risk capital. There were no deposit banks paying interest and no limited liability corporations, so that safe investment by small persons not active in the business in which they invested was not possible. In this relation it is interesting to note that soldiers do not seem to have received their pay periodically. Goods they needed were supplied at set prices and recorded against their pay. The surplus was paid out only on discharge.[35] There seems to have been no question of the government's paying interest on this sum, which was fair enough, when one considers that the soldiers could not have received interest on an account at a bank.

Even odder from a modern point of view is a letter by Pliny the Younger, written to the Emperor Trajan when Pliny was governor of the province of Bithynia.[36] Pliny had recovered money owed to a Bithynian city and feared that it might remain unemployed. There were no opportunities for the city to buy land, which appears to have been the common practice, and borrowers could not be found, for the state lent at the same rate of interest as private persons and demanded security as well. Pliny suggests that persons of property be forced to borrow or that the rate of interest (which may have been 12 percent) be lowered. The emperor preferred the second suggestion.

It has already been noted that ancient banking was not sufficiently developed to develop anything like deficit financing and a public debt. All this suggests that there was limited demand for investment capital, simply because trade and industry called for little investment. Even the state could do nothing to marshal the resources of the ancient economy except by increasing taxes and debasing the coinage on occasion. The crafts were thriving and produced goods for the market both by means of individual enterprise and by the undertakings of landlords themselves. Commerce was brisk, but generally on a small scale. Capital investment in neither com-

---

[35] Persson, *Staat und Manufaktur*, p. 49; cf. Jones, *Later Roman Empire*, I, 31.
[36] *Epist.* x. 54.

manded a major part of the national wealth. The basic reason was that effective demand was very limited.

The population was overwhelmingly rural. The problem of the role of the peasantry in the urban market system remains the same that we have seen in the older civilizations of the Near East: to a great degree the peasantry could not hope to buy the products of the towns and consequently the existence of the town market did not induce them to organize agriculture to produce a marketable surplus. But this appears to be less true of the Roman Empire than on any earlier large state. There is a good deal of evidence that some market gardening around the city of Rome itself was conducted by independent peasants in family-sized farms. It is generally thought that some landlords received much of their rents in money rather than in kind, but in any economy in which the price of grain can vary greatly from year to year and even from season to season, it is wise for a man of means to be able to supply his family and slaves from his own land. Otherwise he may be very hard pressed in a bad year. It was probably, too, a point of pride to drink one's own wine and eat one's own bread, as it still is in the smaller cities of France. The modest artisan or merchant would often buy a scrap of land as protection against a bad year. Only those of the urban poor who did not qualify for the annona distributed by the state were wholly dependent on the market for their daily bread. But the food market was certainly very important, and the peasantry was forced into the market system by money rents and taxes. Left to themselves many would certainly have lived on their own, confining their exchanges to bartering with their neighbors, and only selling an occasional surplus in a year of abundant crops. The impositions of the government and the landlord forced the peasants to plan their planting to sell a regular surplus every year for the urban market. If the landlord demanded rents in kind, the peasant had to plan production to supply them. Thus the cities, in spite of their lively commercial life, appear to have been largely parasitic. This was especially true in the western parts of the Empire. The central figures in the cities were the local landlords who collected rents in money and kind, who marketed much of their rents in kind, and whose tastes and pleasures were served by the artisans and merchants of the city market. Economically they resembled the aristocracy of the city of Rome, except in their modesty, for at Rome the same part was played by the senators who possessed lands scattered about the whole of the Roman world and especially the western parts of it. The public generosity of this class is recorded in thousands of inscriptions, but it was almost always directed to their cities and never returned wealth to the countryside from which it had ultimately come.

There can, then, be little doubt that a great part of the agricultural production of the Empire was planned for the market. Not only were special products like Atlantic oysters and Belgian geese sent to Rome, but the peasantry regularly supplied Rome with grain, olives, wine, beans, and fruit. The market economy was unquestionably better developed in most of the eastern parts of the Empire than in most of the western, but Palestine was not an especially important province commercially, nor, as Josephus pointed out, were the Jews much given to commerce. Yet Rabbi Hillel, an elder contemporary of Jesus, lays it down as a rule that "A woman may not lend a loaf of bread to her neighbor unless she determines its value in money, lest wheat should rise in price and they be found partakers in usury." [37] The market appears to have become the chief means by which the necessities of life, as well as the luxuries, were distributed to the greater part of the population, and the peasantry must have been in regular touch with it.

ITALIAN DECLINE

Yet the economic order and prosperity of the early imperial period were not enduring. Classical studies have revealed two essential changes: first a decline of the central position of Italy and then later a general decline in prosperity dating from the reign of Marcus Aurelius. It is not clear how the two developments were related, if, indeed, they were.

The decline of Italy's position has two aspects. The first is closely related to politics: the exploitation of the Empire became less profitable. From the time when Augustus established a more regular administration, there began a decline in the looting, bribery, and extortion which had almost systematically brought the bullion of the whole Mediterranean to Italy. Generals almost independent of the central government were no longer operating in the provinces. With a few exceptions, like Trajan's Dacian campaign, foreign wars no longer brought in great hauls. The activities of the equestrian companies of publicans were first limited by Augustus and then far more sharply curtailed by Tiberius. As the Empire advanced, more and more provincials received the privilege of Roman citizenship until under Caracalla it was extended by the *Constitutio Antoniniana* to all free men in the Empire.[38] As early as the reign of Claudius provincials began to take seats in the Senate. This is an indication that great accumulations of wealth existed outside Italy and the older senatorial circles. The new senators, drawn first from Gaul, then from Spain, and finally from most of the Empire, continued to create a luxury market at Rome, but they were less interested in investment in Italy.

The second aspect of Italy's decline is less closely connected with politics: the late Republican and early imperial system of latifundia worked by gangs

---

[37] *The Mishnah, Tractate Baba Metzia*, V, English trans. Herbert Danby (Oxford: Clarendon Press, 1933), cited by Salo W. Baron and Joseph L. Blau, *Judaism, Postbiblical and Talmudic Period* (Library of the Liberal Arts; Indianapolis: Bobbs-Merrill Co., 1954), p. 116.

[38] The possibility of some important exceptions, especially in Egypt, is much discussed.

of slave labor was declining. It appears to have been this system that raised Italy to its agricultural preeminence. (It has some resemblance to the plantation system in the American South but was not based upon one or two export crops.) With the end of the great wars of conquest, the numbers of captives must have declined and the cost of slaves have risen greatly. The old system, which was costly in the lives of men and which certainly created a most unwilling labor force, became uneconomic. Those letters of Pliny the Younger which speak of his extensive estates in northern Italy reveal instead a system of tenancies.[39] To encourage him to breed and to create some interest in production the slave, perhaps now a freedman, was allowed a hut and a piece of land for a garden. These conditions should have improved the status of the country population of Italy—other things being equal—but they did not tend to promote market production. Consequently the western provinces found that they could compete with Italy in the market for agricultural produce and soon Spain was sending great amounts of wine and olive oil to Italy. In the third century Africa would enter the market for olive oil on a great scale.

Italy lost her leadership in the production of manufactured goods for the western provinces as well. In the late Republic and early Empire she had exported terra sigillata. Already in the first century production moved to Gaul. First there developed factories in the south. They appear to have been somewhat differently organized than those of Italy. At La Graufesenque (Aveyron) or at the minor centers of Banassac (Lozère) and Montans (Tarn) there was no single producer or firm that rivalled the fifty-eight known slaves of P. Cornelius in Italy. The great pottery works at La Graufesenque had a common water supply, but each master potter worked individually, with the help of only a few or no workmen. Yet these potters captured the western market. The pottery of La Graufesenque is found in the Rhineland and at London; under Domitian it reached Scotland was exported from Narbonne to Spain. It was even sent to Italy. An unopened case of terra sigillata from Gaul was buried at Pompeii by the eruption of Vesuvius in A.D. 79. In later years production moved even farther afield. By Domitian's reign leadership had passed to Lezoux near Clermont-Ferrand. To supply the Rhineland army, men from Lezoux established a flourishing center at Heilingenberg in Alsace, and later other centers appeared along the Rhine. Pannonia, which in the first century had been supplied from Italy through Aquileia, came to be supplied from the western provinces, especially from Cologne by the Rhine-Danube route. In Gaul a great number of local centers came to supply local markets.

Clearly two forces were at work here. The high cost of transport in

---

[39] Perhaps the most convenient translation for the English reader is that published by the Loeb Classical Library in two volumes (London: William Heinemann, 1915) with the translation by William Melmoth revised by W. M. L. Hutchinson.

antiquity, especially land transport, made it economical to produce goods as close to the consumer as possible. At the same time the western provinces were learning the industrial (as well as the agricultural) techniques of the Romans. Hence there was a tendency toward provincial and even local autarchy.[40] This general decline of Italy as a market center and the general decline of Italian prosperity and leadership finally led in the fourth century to the loss of the privileged and favorable tax position Italy had had in the third century and reduced her to the same level as the other provinces.

GENERAL DECLINE

Thus Italy lost her predominant position in the West. The close economic integration of the early Empire was impaired. In the late second century a graver threat impended. Under Marcus Aurelius there are clear signs of a general economic decline. In the earlier part of the century Trajan seems to have been able to wage his extensive campaigns against the Parthians and Dacians without seriously upsetting the economy and to have drawn a very considerable booty from them. Marcus' war against the Marcomanni was not profitable and strained the Empire's economy badly. Rostovtzeff was the first to make clear the fiscal difficulties which followed.[41] To raise funds for his campaigns Marcus auctioned off the valuables of the imperial palace at Rome. This may have been largely for show; it cannot have made an important contribution to public income. It was more important that the coinage was debased. Monetary difficulties became really serious during the reign of his son and successor Commodus.[42]

In the fifty-five years from the death of Marcus in 180 to the murder of the Emperor Severus Alexander in 235 our evidence clearly shows an economic decline that starts before the civil wars and barbarian invasions of the middle of the third century. These economic troubles, then, preceded the great political crisis and cannot be explained by them. The troubles of Marcus' reign and those of his successors in the Severan dynasty are the warning signs, in the Indian summer of antique prosperity, of the winter that was to come.

[40] Frank William Walbank, "Trade and Industry Under the Later Roman Empire in the West," *CEH*, II, 33ff. (bibliography). On terra sigillata: Frank, *ESAR*, I, 375; Grenier, *ibid.*, II, 540ff.

[41] Rostovtzeff, *Economic and Social History of the Roman Empire*, I, 373ff.

[42] Very little is available in the way of price or wage series from the ancient world. Our most coherent information comes from coins, which have been discovered in great numbers. There was general stability of the currency for a century and a half after the Augustan adjustment, the single devaluation under Nero, a variety of weights in the same coin due to the difficulties of Marcus Aurelius' Marcommanic War, a gradual decline thereafter, and the complete collapse under Gallienus. At the end of the century Diocletian began and Constantine carried through a thorough reform based upon the gold, rather than the silver, standard, but by then the government took taxes and paid officials largely in kind.

Behind this crisis was probably a decline in the population. Any discussion of ancient populations must necessarily be largely hypothetical. In theory it should be possible to establish an upper limit of the population which a district could support, given the technology of ancient times. In practice even this proves very difficult.[43] We are on slightly better ground when we try to determine whether the population was increasing or decreasing. It seems likely that the population of Italy had been increasing from the Second Punic War, which ended in 202 B.C., until the time of Augustus. The raising of the land question by the Gracchi seems to prove that the Italian population recovered from the depredations of Hannibal in the course of the second century. That it continued to grow is evidenced by the number of soldiers that Italy could send abroad and by the numerous colonies of Roman citizens founded. Among the upper classes, however, postponement of marriage and family limitation seem to have become common in the late Republic. These habits were probably borrowed from Greece and went hand in hand with the Hellenization of the upper classes. Augustus found it advisable to pass legislation that would encourage the well-born to marry young and produce many sons, but this legislation seems to have been no more successful than might have been expected. On the contrary the commons imitated the aristocracy. It became necessary for landlords like Pliny to encourage their slaves to have children by granting them holdings. Under Hadrian a scheme was launched to care for the orphaned and needy children of citizens resident in Italy.[44] By the late first century colonists for such places as the agri decumates and Danubian lands were drawn from outside Italy. As the provinces were Romanized and as their population became adequate, the provincials seem gradually to have followed the Italian example and limited the number of their children. Before Marcus there is no positive evidence of population decline; rather it seems likely that a nice balance between the means of subsistence and the reproductive rate had been achieved. Under Marcus a serious epidemic, brought back by the army from a campaign against Parthia in 166 or 167, struck the Empire. It may have been bubonic plague, though there is no certain evidence of this; it does seem to have been more deadly and less local than earlier epidemics.[45] It lasted some fifteen years and is the most obvious explanation of Marcus' financial troubles. The tax base of the Empire was shrinking. The population does not seem to have recovered quickly. This plague was followed by another under Marcus' son Commodus which the historian Dio Cassius said was the greatest of which he had any knowledge. Under the Severans, the government began to complain of the paucity of men. The birth rate seems not to have risen to fill the gap.

[43] The figures given by ancient authors are usually unreliable and they are never totals.
[44] Frank C. Bourne, "The Roman Alimentary Program and Italian Agriculture," *Transactions and Proceedings of the American Philological Association*, XCI (1960), 47–75.
[45] The most careful review of the evidence is J. F. Gilliam, "The Plague Under Marcus Aurelius," *American Journal of Philology*, LXXXII (1961), 225–51.

It is not surprising, then, that at the accession of the Severan dynasty in 192 the economic outlook was somber. Expensive old habits of public munificence persisted, but the number of taxpayers and rentpayers had fallen. Both the government and the landowners were in trouble. The age of the Severans and their successors would see a formidable increase in the expenses of the state and a consequent impoverishment of the entire Roman world. The classical economy was approaching its final crisis.

13 CRISIS AND THE END OF THE ANCIENT ECONOMY

The third century A.D. is one of the most obscure epochs in ancient history. Literary sources for social and even for political history become few in number and inferior in quality, while the flood of inscriptions, so generous for the social and economic history of the first two centuries A.D., dries up. Even the papyri become less numerous. Yet we are able to see clearly the decline of population, the decline of wealth, as well as a vigorous effort by the government to save the Empire and traditional society from civil war, barbarian invasions, and internal unrest.

That the population declined from Marcus' reign has sometimes been questioned, but the evidence seems adequate.[1] The population of the Mediterranean world as a whole seems to have remained more or less stable from the Flavian period to the reign of Marcus. The only exceptions that seem well established are the continued growth of the population of the highlands of interior Syria[2] and of the high plains of Numidia.[3] Neither is typically Mediterranean in its topography and climate. Both were largely devoted to the production of olive oil and were dependent upon urban markets. Neither was profoundly Hellenized or Romanized in its culture and family life. Elsewhere birth control, exposure of infants, and late marriage seem to have stabilized the population so that in the second century the government showed a certain anxiety about maintaining numbers. Reduced under the last Antonines, the population probably continued to fall throughout the third century. The plague which Marcus' troops brought back from the East in A.D. 166 or 167 and the plague under Commodus,[4] were followed after an interval by a serious plague which broke out on the accession of Gallus in A.D. 251.[5] Thereafter our inadequate sources report a number of important epidemics down to the end of the century: a severe outbreak under Gallienus in the 260s;[6] a plague in the Balkans, Crete, and Cyprus under Claudius II, in which the

[1] See note on the population of the classical world (Appendix C).
[2] W. H. C. Frend, *The Donatist Church, a Movement of Protest in Roman North Africa* (Oxford: Clarendon Press, 1952), pp. 39ff.; "The Failure of the Persecutions in the Roman Empire," *Past and Present*, No. 16 (November 1959), 20.
[3] Georges Tchalenko, *Villages antiques de la Syrie. Le Massif de Behis à l'époque romaine*, I (Paris: P. Geuther, 1953), pp. 74–9, 140–3, 374–9, 388, 407–16, 425–9, 435.
[4] Dio lxiii. 14. 3 (epitome), Herodian i. 12. 1–2, trans. Echols.
[5] Cyprian *De mort.* 14.
[6] Zosimus i. 36; *SHA Gallus* 6. 5; Eusebius *HE* vii. 22.

emperor himself died; and a pestilence among the Germans and in Gaul in 286.[7] At the opening of the fourth century Eusebius reports a plague in the eastern provinces.[8]

Evidence that these plagues, along with the civil wars and barbarian invasions, did in fact reduce the population is first seen in the widespread settlement of defeated barbarians within the Empire. This was not wholly without precedent in earlier times, but Marcus' settlements seem to have been on a greater scale than any earlier. The status of the forced migrants was that of *inquilini*, neither slaves nor citizens, who were liable to military service. The policy would be continued by Claudius II, Aurelian, Probus, Maximian, and Constantine. At the end of the third century the Emperor Septimius Severus spoke of the "scarcity of men" and allowed his soldiers in the legions to live with their women in order to improve the sources of recruitment. Henceforth soldiers born in the camp became far commoner in the legions.[9] The Emperor Pertinax invited all and sundry to take up deserted land, whether private or imperial, in both Italy and the provinces with the promise of full ownership and ten years' immunity from taxes.[10] There is evidence that the population of some Egyptian villages fell considerably.[11] In the fourth and fifth centuries there is a good deal of evidence of land out of cultivation in Syria, Italy, and the region now called Tunisia.[12] The efforts of the government to use compulsion to get the soil tilled are even more convincing proofs, with which we shall deal below. It seems clear, then, that the population started to fall in the late second century and that there was no general and substantial recovery down into the fifth.[13]

The evidences of impoverishment will appear again and again in the course of this chapter. Here we may mention only some incidental evidences. In Egypt there is a decline in the quality of papyrus, though admittedly this trend seems to go back to an earlier date. The third century saw a decline in the literacy of Egyptian officials, including the magistrates of the cities. The quality of pottery seems to decline, and building is rarer in the cities—fortifi-

---

[7] *SHA, Claud.* ii. 3; 12. 1. 2; Zonaras xii. 26; Eutrop. ix. 8; Zosimus *Hist.* i. 28. 1–2; Victor *De Caes.* 30. 2; II Pan. 5. 2 (ed. Galletier, I, 28).

[8] *HE* ix. 8.

[9] Jean Cagé, *Les Classes sociales dans l'Empire romain* (Paris: Payot, 1964).

[10] Herodian ii. 4. 6, trans. Echols; A. H. M. Jones, *The Later Roman Empire, 284–602* (Norman: University of Oklahoma Press, 1964), II, p. 812.

[11] Arthur Boak, "The Population of Roman and Byzantine Karanis," *Historia*, IV (1955), 160–2; Hunt and Edgar, *Select Papyri*, II, pp. 300–1.

[12] Jones, *Later Roman Empire*, pp. 815–6. Why Jones concludes that this is not evidence of population decline is not clear.

[13] The basic study is Josiah Russell, *Late Ancient and Medieval Population*, Vol. LXVIII, Pt. 3, of "The Transactions of the American Philosophical Society," n.s. (Philadelphia: American Philosophical Society, 1958); Arthur E. R. Boak, *Manpower Shortage and the Fall of the Roman Empire in the West* (Ann Arbor: University of Michigan Press, 1955), should be consulted with reference to the review by Finley, *Journal of Roman Studies*, XLVIII (1958), 156–64.

cations excepted—and of lower quality. The most striking example perhaps is the one which Bernard Berenson made famous in his essay, "The Arch of Constantine." The work which the emperor himself commissioned is far inferior to earlier work, and so well did his architect recognize this that he plundered medallions from work of the second century to decorate the arch. By the time of Diocletian and Constantine the salaries of officials were far lower than they had been in the first and second centuries.[14]

USE OF COMPULSORY SERVICES

But if population and wealth were falling, the needs of the government had been increasing probably from the time of Marcus. Certainly Septimius Severus increased the pay of the army and increased its size. From his reign to that of Diocletian at the end of the century there was no possibility of relief. Expenses for war continued to increase and the extent of government activity expanded. From the reign of Septimius soldiers more and more dominated society which was in a state of siege and society itself took on a military character.[15] It is easy to blame the economic troubles which followed on the military mind. It is indeed likely that most of the emperors from Septimius, who came to the throne in A.D. 193, down to Diocletian, who abdicated in A.D. 305, had little understanding or sympathy for the problems of urban industry, commerce, and the market-oriented estates of the landed gentry. Few modern scholars today accept Michael Rostovtzeff's view that these military usurpers led peasant soldiers in a rural revolt against the domination of the cities and the gentry. But these emperors were professional soldiers. Latin and Greek possessed no real vocabulary of economic analysis, so that pleas for relief from the civil population could not argue that the long-term consequences of public policy would be disastrous. They could only oppose the selfishness of an individual or group to the pressing needs of the state. The military government put relentless pressure on the civilian producer.

Traditionally the Principate had made use of money taxes, except for those services clearly better supplied by payment in kind, like the annona of the city of Rome. Ordinarily, then, to supply its needs it bought goods and hired services on the market. Habitually, too, it left local government largely in the hands of local authorities, the magistrates of the cities. When the needs of the state, then, increased, the first move on the part of the government was to increase taxes and let out more contracts to private persons. But such a system had limits. Although the apparatus of the Roman state seems to have been able to extract money from even the most reluctant taxpayer, there

---

[14] Jones, *Later Roman Empire*, I, pp. 396ff.
[15] This is even true of art: see H. P. L'Orange, *Art Forms and Civic Life in the Late Roman Empire* (Princeton: Princeton University Press, 1965), especially pp. 85ff.

probably were limits on its ability. Probably, too, there were limits on the supply of coin (as the inflation in Marcus' reign and that in the latter part of the third century both suggest). Certainly there were limits on the ability of the ancient market system to furnish supplies. This last limitation is evident in the government's solicitude for feeding the city of Rome and in the obligations that even under the early emperors had been laid upon the subject peoples to provide carrying and carting services for the army. (When Christ told his disciples, "And whosoever shall compel thee to go a mile, go with him twain," he had in mind the service that the legionaries imposed on the Jews.[16]) The use of compulsion came naturally to the Roman army, and a military government made ever greater use of it as the crisis deepened.

Like many of the tendencies of the third and fourth centuries, this one had thrown its shadow before it. The tendency to lay greater burdens upon local officials was evident in the second century; by its beginning the liturgical principle was fully established for all state offices in Egypt except the highest, and it was already beginning to invade the sphere of urban magistracies, the "honors." [17] When Hadrian founded the city of Antinoöpolis in Egypt, drawing its citizens from the nomes, he gave them, among other special privileges, exemption from liability to both *munera* and *honores* outside the new city. By the end of the century, however, compulsion was the universal practice and in the third century the word "liturgy" was used for both munera and honores.

But the use of compulsion made it necessary for the central government to invade local government. The most famous earlier case is the commission that the Emperor Trajan gave to Pliny the Younger to reform the finances of the cities of Bithynia. In Egyptian towns there had earlier been an imperial official in residence, the strategos. Now in Egypt as elsewhere, the urban magistrates or the curia had to appoint and warrant a committee of ten men (*decemprimi* in the West, *dekaprotoi* in the East) whose duty it was to superintend the collection and storage of tax corn and through whom the central power could intervene in the affairs of the city.[18]

Something comparable happened to the craftsmen. Gilds had earlier been voluntary associations, except in Egypt where craftsmen had been licensed. Severus required artisans to form gilds for dealing with government officials, slaves being registered by their masters. By about the middle of the century gilds had been made responsible for the collection of taxes on their trades.[19]

---

[16] Matt. 5:41; cf. Mark 15:21.

[17] A liturgy was a public service, often an expensive or onerous one, laid upon a private person by the state to be carried out at his own expense. The Latin for it is *munus*, pl. *munera*.

[18] Harold I. Bell, *Egypt, from Alexander the Great to the Arab Conquest: A Study in the Diffusion and Decay of Hellenism*, Greynog Lectures for 1946 (Oxford: Clarendon Press, 1948), pp. 84–92.

[19] Persson, *Staat und Manufaktur*, p. 37.

Behind this interference in local government and extension of liturgies was the increasing exaction of taxes in kind rather than money. The pressing need was to supply the army with goods, though in the third century the civil bureaucracy was also paid in kind rather than coin. Many exactions in kind were already regular in Egypt by c. A.D. 200. The old Egyptian poll tax did not disappear, but it lost importance with the inflation. The *annona militaris* became a central tax. Properly this was a requisitioning of supplies for the army. Now the army was receiving an increasing part of its pay in kind. Requisitions could be made as and when required and to the extent called for by the momentary exigencies of the military. This was certainly a very burdensome system to the taxpayer but was convenient for the authorities. Cash could be accepted in lieu of kind, if it was expedient to the government. Receipts for the annona began to appear among the papyri in the reign of Septimius Severus.[20] Not only grain and food were taken in kind; by at least A.D. 120 the state was taking cloth and clothes as taxes from some gilds,[21] and the practice became more widespread in the third century.

STATE OWNERSHIP

Neither for agricultural goods nor manufactures did this system of taxes prove wholly adequate. The landed estates of the imperial government expanded rapidly. In the first two centuries a distinction had been made between public land and the private estates of the emperor (res privata) and the two had been administered by separate departments. On his accession in A.D. 192 Septimius Severus vastly increased the imperial lands by confiscating the estates of his political enemies. Thereafter the distinction between the res privata and the public treasury was largely lost. In the third century A.D. the emperors expropriated most of the lands belonging to the cities of the Empire. The emperor, of course, did not live from his property, but its expansion greatly increased the public sector of the economy and government income in kind.[22]

The government went another step toward autarchy by creating imperial factories for products it needed. The state's need for textiles was met in part by taxes in kind upon weavers and in part by working up materials in its own shops. The raw materials might come from imperial estates or from taxes in kind of wool, flax, dyes, and so forth. From the early fifth century

---

[20] The word "annona" has rather changed its meaning. First it meant supplies for living, means of subsistence, or rations for the army and the city of Rome. Now it comes to mean the tax that supplies these things.

[21] Persson, *Staat und Manufaktur*, pp. 27–30.

[22] That much of the production of these estates was consumed by the state is certain. Some, for example, were given such tasks as raising horses for the cavalry and the post. But we have no idea how large a part of the product may have been marketed.

A.D. there survives a list of these places for the western parts of the Empire. There were linen mills at Vienne in Gaul and at Ravenna; woolen mills at five cities in Italy, three in Illyricum, five in Gaul, one at Carthage in Africa, and even one in Britain. There were nine imperial dyeing establishments. A few other public factories were under the authority of the res privata. There is no comparable list from the East, but we do hear of woolen mills at Heraclea-in-Thrace, Cyzicus, Caesarea in Cappadocia, and at Tyre; of a linen mill at Scythopolis; and of dyeworks in Phoenicia and Cyprus. By the time of Diocletian the state manufactured all arms that the army required in its own factories (*fabricae*). There were fifteen in the eastern parts of the Empire: shops for the production of shields and arms at Damascus, Antioch, Edessa, Nicomedia, Sardis, Hadrianople, Marcianopolis, Thessalonika, Nish, and Ratiaria on the Danube. At Caesarea in Cappadocia, Antioch, and Nicomedia there were works for the armor of the heavy cavalry; at Irenopolis in Cilicia a lance factory, and at Horreum Margi a shield factory. In the western provinces there were twenty arms factories: five in Illyricum, six in Italy, nine in Gaul. There were also special factories for producing the bronze armor decorated with silver and gold which was worn by officers, three in the West and two which are known in the East. These factories were supplied with raw materials such as metal by the praetorian prefects, while the supply of charcoal was a *sordida munera* imposed upon local landowners. They must have been considerable enterprises and a large part of the population of the town where they existed was probably composed of their workers.[23]

It is perhaps with this growing interest of the government with industrial production that we should connect the surprising development of water mills. Mills driven by water had been known to the Greeks and Romans from the beginning of the Christian era, but they appear to have been little used. The circular mill driven by donkeys and slaves predominated in the first three centuries. In the light of what we have seen about the limits of investment and limits of the market this may not be surprising. In the third century the government came to be more intimately interested in the matter, since the annona of Rome came to be doled out in bread rather than grain. By the end of the fourth century—how much earlier we do not know—some mills at Rome were driven by water power. They presumably were those located on the Janiculum and were driven by water from the aqueducts.[24] At any rate when in the sixth century the Goths cut the aqueducts, one result was to stop the grinding of grain in the city until the Roman general Belisarius erected mills on boats on the Tiber. By that time other water-driven mills of considerable capacity had been erected in Gaul and northern Italy either in con-

---

[23] Jones, *Later Roman Empire*, II, 834–9, references. *Sordida munera* were such minor and degrading services as this one. The more elevated classes of the population were exempt from them.

[24] Samuel B. Platner, *Topographical Dictionary of Ancient Rome*, completed and revised by Thomas Ashby (London: Oxford University Press, 1929), p. 235.

nection with imperial estates, the annona of Rome, or of the army. Several others could be mentioned from the following centuries. The shortage of manpower, too, contributed something to this development. A late agricultural writer, Palladius, who may date from the fourth century, saw that water-driven machinery might ease the burden of men and animals, and an anonymous writer who wrote between A.D. 337 and 378 suggested a number of not very practical devices for saving money and manpower in war, some of them by the use of water power.[25]

> The state thus manufactured in its own factories all the arms and armour and a proportion of the uniforms required for the army and the civil service. It produced the marble needed for its public works from its own quarries. It obtained the gold [and probably the silver] required for the mints from its own mines, and levied in kind from the owners of the metalliferous areas the copper and iron needed for the mints and arms factories. In the late third and the fourth centuries it obtained most of its remaining requirements by levies in kind assessed on the land. It secured in this way not only foodstuffs of all kinds, wheat, barley, meat, wine and oil, to feed the troops, the civil service, the population of the capitals [by then Constantinople as well as Rome], its industrial employees and the personnel of the post, together with the horses of the army and the horses, mules and oxen of the post; but also these animals themselves, and the raw material for the state factories, such as wool and flax for the weaving mills, and charcoal for the mints and arms factories. Public works were also built and repaired by levies of material and labour assessed on the land. Among the *sordida munera* to which landowners were liable are included the provision of craftsmen and labourers, the burning of lime, and the supply of timber.[26]

One result of the crisis of the third century, then, was that the government itself retreated into a state bordering on self-sufficiency, on autarchy. It may be suspected, though, that this was not simply the result of the political crisis. Even before the age of the Antonines, the system of market exchanges stretching across the Empire had been reduced by the growing self-sufficiency of the various provinces of the West and the frontiers as these new lands acquired the agricultural techniques and the crafts of the older Graeco-Roman economy. The great extension of imperial estates dated from the reign of Septimius Severus. Such a system did not, of course, eliminate the market from the economy or even withdraw all government activity from the market. But it did produce profound effects upon the economy and social order as a whole. Its inefficiency is perhaps its most obvious feature. A system of state manufacturing may have worked fairly well in as small a society as that of an early Sumerian city, but in a great state like Rome, in which the produce

[25] E. A. Thompson, *A Roman Reformer and Inventer, Being a New Text of the Treatise De rebus bellicis* (Oxford: Clarendon Press, 1952).
[26] Jones, *Later Roman Empire*, I, 839.

of such factories was destined for a distant and unseen need, the industrious-
ness of workers must have been severely reduced. The need to move products
and to store them must have greatly increased waste. Payment of salaries
in kind cannot always have satisfied needs, and much time must have been
consumed in making adjustments. The officials could sell on the market that
part of their pay they did not consume, if and where the market was present,
but the difficulties remained considerable. It is likely that corruption increased accordingly. Certainly complaints about it became commonplace.

In another way also the system led to impoverishment and to class
change. The principle of obligatory service by local officials led to their ruin,
to attempts to escape their obligations, and then to their being tied to their
offices and functions. Membership in the local curia was required. Persons
with property enough to qualify for office could escape only by the *cessio
bonorum*, the surrender of two-thirds of their property. Liability, however,
was made collective, each curial being held liable not only for his own
shortages, but for those of his colleagues and of the body as a whole. Sons
were usually required to succeed their fathers in office. In such circumstances
the old curial class, which had been the chief beneficiary and support of the
early imperial system, was rapidly degraded. After the reign of Severus
Alexander (A.D. 222–235) the long line of inscriptions recording their benefactions to their cities and their fellow townsmen, their buildings and aqueducts, statues, forums, temples, and walls, comes to an almost complete stop.

But something of the same fate overtook other classes. The gilds of
urban workers were also required to perform necessary services. Those of
Egyptian clothworkers, we saw, were required to pay taxes in kind to clothe
the army and the imperial bureaucracy. The gilds involved in the victualling
of Rome came under similar obligations. By the beginning of the fourth century bakers were legally bound to their trade and membership in the gild was
obligatory even for persons who held property which had once belonged to a
baker. It was therefore normally hereditary, but anyone who acquired a
baker's property by legacy, gift, or purchase was enrolled, as were those who
married bakers' daughters and received doweries with them. Bakers were
forbidden in A.D. 364 to sell their property to senators and officials, who
could not very well take up the trade, and in 369 they were prohibited from
alienating any inherited property at all. Property acquired from outside
during their lifetimes might be alienated, but only to another member of the
gild. The gilds which supplied meat to the city seem to have been similarly
organized, as were the shipowners who brought in grain.[27]

The workers in the state factories would not, as a rule, be persons of
property, but they were generally citizens and freemen at law. Yet they were
tied to their occupation, and like curials, could be dragged back in chains and
branded if they escaped. The lower grades of workers, who turned the mills

---

[27] Jones, *Later Roman Empire*, I, 675–705.

and worked quarries and mines, would ordinarily be slaves. But considerable use was made of convicts, and a good many Christians were condemned under Diocletian to labor in mines and quarries in the eastern provinces.

The most pressing necessity, however, was the cultivation of the land, and for this, too, the state used compulsion. Compulsory leases of state lands became regular in Egypt, and probably elsewhere, in the third century, and the inhabitants of a village could be required to cultivate land that had fallen out of cultivation. In Egypt from the end of the second century instances of anachoresis became common. That is to say, men were fleeing their villages to escape the brutality of officials and the poverty that their obligations imposed upon them. Brigandage was the commonest alternative, while their deserted relatives and fellow peasants had to work their lands and pay the dues upon them.

THE COLONATE

To guarantee the cultivation of the land, then, the government tied the peasants to the soil.[28] By the third century rural labor in Italy, it appears, had become largely free, for the status of agricultural slaves had gradually become by law and custom much like that of serfs. Large estates were run by the owners or by their bailiffs. They consisted of a home farm directly exploited by the bailiff and smaller parcels let out to peasants called *coloni*; slaves given such plots were called by the lawyers *quasi coloni*. On the African estates of the emperor, the coloni owed rents and a few days labor a year on the home farm. (Cities, too, had let out land to coloni, but in the third century the greater part of the lands belonging to cities was confiscated by the central government.) Tenure on such lands was for payment of a rent and normally appears to have been for a period of five years but actually tended to become hereditary. While the status of the agricultural slave moved toward that of the serf, the free peasantry was also gradually degraded.

> The liberty of tenants was probably first restricted by the census of Diocletian, in which every peasant was registered in his village or under his landlord's name on the farm that he cultivated, and by legislation, which for fiscal motives, tied the peasantry to their place of registration, where they paid their head tax and annona.[29]

Landlords needing more agricultural labor welcomed the system. The whole population, free holders as well as tenants, was originally tied to the soil, but

---

[28] R. Clausing, *The Roman Colonate, the Theories of Its Origin* (New York: Columbia University Press, 1925) ; M. Rostovtzeff, "Studien zur Geschichte des roemischen Kolonates," *Archiv fuer Papyrusforschung*, Beiheft I, 1910; Jones, *Later Roman Empire*, I, 792–803.

[29] Jones, *Later Roman Empire*, II, 796.

since the landlords had no interest in tying free holders to their villages, the rule ceased to be enforced against them regularly. On the other hand the rights of landlords over their coloni were progressively increased. The law permitted landlords to chain coloni suspected of planning to flee, forbade them to alienate their own property without their lord's consent, and made the lord, not public collectors, responsible for collecting the taxes of coloni registered on their estates. Coloni were even debarred from suing their lords except for extracting more than the customary rent. Still this system does not seem to have applied in all provinces. In some, registration was by villages rather than villas. This may have been true in Judea and Gaul and was certainly true in Egypt, where the papyri reveal no trace of the colonate in the fourth century. It was probably not introduced there until the fifth. This institution created an hereditary class belonging to an estate (later called *adscripticii* in the East). They were found chiefly on large estates and were scarcely distinguishable from slaves.

Other coloni, however, were able to escape their leases. They were personally free and could enlist in the army or take holy orders. Finally there was a class of men who took only short leases and therefore remained truly free to move. They still survived in Egypt in the sixth century. The laws largely ignore them, but they were probably numerous in other provinces as well.

The increasing oppression by landlords and the state might be expected to produce both revolt and a literature of protest. Both are surprisingly rare. The Church created a new morality of alms giving, but it rarely championed the oppressed rural classes. Literature was created by the possessing class, and it was the middle of the fifth century before the priest Salvian wrote his great indictment of the injustice of the Roman order, "On the Governance of God." In both East and West this work stands almost alone.

The peasants themselves were not so temperate. Already under Marcus Aurelius enough Egyptian peasants were fleeing their villages to form robber bands called Bucoli in the delta.[30] In Gaul peasant rebels called Bagaudae were defeated by the Emperor Maximian in A.D. 285; but that movement of revolt kept reappearing until the fifth century. A recent article has even suggested that in the fifth century the Roman government and the local landlords accepted the settlement of the Visigoths in southwestern Gaul for the purpose of putting down social revolt.[31] Of all the revolts, however, the greatest appears to have been that of the peasantry of Numidia. After the peace of the Church they embraced the dissident cause of a contender for the bishopric of Carthage and came to form a religious party, the Donatists. If not from the start, they very soon showed a social hostility to the cities and the landed

[30] Dio. lxxii. 12.
[31] E. A. Thompson, "Peasant Revolt in Late Roman Gaul and Spain," *Past and Present*, No. 2 (November 1952), 11–23; "The Settlement of the Barbarians in Southern Gaul," *Journal of Roman Studies*, XLVI (1956), 65–75.

class. Saint Augustine, bishop of Hippo Regius, led the theological and practical opposition to their cause and received the full support of the imperial government.[32] There seems to be no evidence of widespread peasant revolt in any other province. The revolt in Egypt was swiftly repressed, and even in North Africa and Gaul the tendencies toward social revolt were contained by the government and the landowners.

CLASS CHANGE

The crisis of the third century and the governmental policy for coping with it reduced the prosperity of urban artisans and the cities generally, the curial magistrates and small landowners of the provincial cities, and the peasantry. All were burdened with greater obligations by the state. One class, however, prospered and grew greater: the magnates, those families which possess or acquired great estates. There even appears to have been an increasing concentration of property. The tendency certainly goes back to the second century, when it is possible to discern vaguely a profound transformation of the social order. In the early Empire the basic social distinction had been between Romans and *peregrini* (free men of the Empire who did not possess Roman citizenship but were citizens of another city or tribe). Gradually Roman citizenship was extended, first in the western provinces and then in the middle of the second century to the Greeks of the East. Finally in A.D. 212 Caracalla gave Roman citizenship to all free inhabitants of the Empire with a very few exceptions.[33] At the same time a new social and legal distinction was developing between what the Roman lawyers called the *honestiores* and the *humiliores*, the "better people" and the "humbler." [34] The honestiores of the provinces were assimilated to the privileged class of Italians and Roman citizens while the rest of the population suffered disabilities into which the poorer of the old citizenry also sank. Hadrian was the first emperor to distinguish the punishments to which curials were subject from those of the commons: persons of curial status generally were immune to corporeal punishment and torture. This change corresponds to something that was happening in local government. In the middle of the first century Saint Paul's companions were dragged before the Assembly of the Ephesians (Acts 19:28–41). A hundred years later they would have appeared before the curia of magistrates and former magis-

[32] Frend, *The Donatist Church: A Movement of Protest in Roman North Africa* (Oxford: Clarendon Press, 1952); *Martyrdom and Persecution in the Early Church. A Study of Conflict from the Maccabees to Donatus* (Oxford: B. Blackwell, 1965), index *s.v.* Donatism.
[33] His motive appears to have been to make all liable to the tax of one-twentieth on inheritances which only Roman citizens payed.
[34] G. Cardasia, "L'apparition dans le droit des classes d'*honestiores* et d'*humiliores*," *Revue d'histoire de droit français*, L (1950), 305–37, 461–85; A. N. Sherwin-White, *Roman Society and Roman Law in the New Testament. The Sarum Lectures, 1960–1961* (Oxford: Clarendon Press, 1963), pp. 68ff., 173ff.

trates. In Rome itself the assemblies had ceased to meet under Tiberius, the second emperor (A.D. 14–37). Thereafter they drop from sight elsewhere, first in the Latin West, then in the Greek East. The lively electioneering among such persons as bakers, still evident in Pompeii shortly before its destruction in A.D. 79, died down in the second century. The election of magistrates passed from the defunct assemblies to the curias, which thus became self-perpetuating bodies. Office was probably passed about among a fairly limited number of families, most of them landowners. In the second century this class, at least in the more considerable cities, enjoyed uniform privileges at Roman law throughout the Empire. The consolidation of the landed class and its interest seemed assured. The interests of such a class were, in a sense, epitomized in the great landholders who sat in the Roman Senate. It is to be noted that from the death of Domitian in A.D. 96 to the death of Marcus in A.D. 180 all of the emperors were on fairly good terms with the Senate. There was no repetition of the terror which had cost the lives of many senators under Domitian and earlier under the Julio-Claudians.

In the third century this class was sorely tried. Many of its members were tied to obligations and offices in the towns and ruined by the impositions of the central government. But there was a tendency, as public service in the cities became burdensome, for the greater men to escape. It must have been difficult for the urban magistrate to coerce a great landowner with estates in the territories of many cities, connections all over the province, and friends in the emperor's service. These fortunate families were probably the holders of offices in the imperial administration. The salaries of office under the emperors certainly fell in the third century and in the fourth they are nothing like they had been in the first. But the opportunities for illicit gain were probably greater. The opportunities for doing favors for the rich and powerful were tempting. But perhaps most important, imperial offices released the holder from the obligation to serve in local offices which might prove ruinous. It is difficult to prove directly, but we must suppose, then, that there was a close connection between the formation or the survival of great holdings and the exercise of public office, which consequently became the most tempting form of investment. It was, quite literally, an investment, for office was sold and by its purchase one could gain immunities of various sorts. We may even hazard the guess that few investments were so profitable as officeholding.

While many of the greater members of this new nobility sat in the Senate at Rome or in the new Senate at Constantinople, all did not. It was a privileged class as wide as the Empire and having members in every province. The wealth of some was very great. Typically they possessed many scattered estates and even the lands administered from a single villa were not necessarily in a single piece. Melania's estates were scattered over the Po valley, Apulia, Campania, Sicily, Africa, and Spain. One had 400 slaves and sixty-two cottages for coloni. Yet her fortune was less than that of Symmachus. Senators at Constantinople might spend as much as seventy pounds of gold to celebrate the games that high officeholders were expected to give. The Roman senator Symmachus spent two thousand pounds on the games in honor of his son's praetorship, yet Olympiodorus ranks Symmachus only among the senators of middling wealth with annual revenues of one thousand or fifteen hundred pounds of gold. Many, he says, drew from their estates incomes of four thousand pounds in gold and the equivalent of about a third as much again in corn, wine, and other produce.[35] It would be possible to give a good many other examples of great wealth and great extravagance.[36] The scale of living of these great men was princely. The fourth century was the great age of the Roman country villa, for the taste for country life was increasing. The recently excavated villa near Enna in Sicily is astounding. Others have long been known from Gaul, and the fourth century was the great age of prosperity for the possessors of land in Britain, to judge by the remains of their country houses.

THE VILLA AS AN ECONOMIC UNIT

Industrial production, too, developed on such villas. This was not a wholly new activity. There had been something of the sort to work up either the products of the farm or local raw materials. In Gaul and especially in Belgium there was a good deal of production of metal objects for sale. Potteries were common on the villas of some districts. They made rough ware for the transport of their own farm products, but in Africa some villas produced lamps for the market. There seems to be evidence of fulling and dyeing on British villas. In the fourth century this development became so intense in the western provinces as to damage urban production and the work of small independent producers in town.[37] The villa supplied the owner with income in kind, but until the fifth century it also payed rents in money. The vast incomes and luxurious habits of the Roman aristocrats prove this and show that the villa must still have been producing for the market.

There do not appear to have been many persons in the Eastern parts of the Empire who could rival the great fortunes of the Roman senators. The senators of Constantinople in the fourth century appear to have been much more modest, although landed fortunes were growing. The characteristic feature of rural Egypt during the first two centuries of Roman rule had been the rural community consisting on the one hand of comparatively small landowners, on the other of tenants of the domain lands of the imperial fisc. In the third century there began to emerge persons like Alypius, revealed in the papyri of his steward Heronius, who had large estates in the Fayyum. He was

---

[35] Jones, *Later Roman Empire*, I, 523–62.

[36] Amm. xiv. 6, xxviii. 4.

[37] Rostovtzeff, *Social and Economic History of the Roman Empire*, II, 617–8, note 40. The archaeological literature on Roman villas is large.

a kind of forerunner of those Byzantine owners of immense estates. By the sixth century the lands of the fisc hardly figure at all, "and the most salient impression we receive is of a country divided between a semifeudal nobility and a half-servile peasantry." [38]

Because of its later importance, it is worth noting that from the early fourth century A.D., when Christianity became the religion of the Emperor Constantine, the Church received a great endowment in land and revenues. Rather than say that the Church as a single corporation became rich, how-ever, we should say, the bishops of the various cities received gifts roughly corresponding to their importance. The little bishoprics of Africa and southern Italy were poor, while the greater churches, led, of course, by Rome, had im-mense properties. Constantine placed gold crosses, each weighing one hun-dred and ten pounds, over the tombs of Saint Peter and Saint Paul. The Lateran basilica received an endowment in lands that produced an annual income of 5,390 gold solidi; the baptistery had annual revenues of 10,054 solidi, and the basilica of Saint Paul some 4,070. (At the same time the pagan temples were despoiled of their hoards of accumulated treasures.) The churches were permitted to receive legacies, a privilege that Roman law allowed to few corporations, and they received vast properties from pious nobles like Melania, who gave the see of Tagaste in Africa an estate larger than the territory of the city. The Church also profited from many small be-quests; indeed they seem to have become habitual in wills. The private prop-erty of the clergy, too, swelled ecclesiastical wealth, and there is some suspicion that men were sometimes elected bishop for the wealth that they might bring the diocese. (Monasticism was beginning its long institutional career in Egypt in the fourth century, but monasteries were not wealthy in land until a later date.)

The great bishops and their dioceses, then, were endowed with the same sorts of widely scattered possessions and estates as the senatorial nobility and drew from them the same sorts of revenue in money and kind. Such wealth quite naturally sometimes introduced a worldliness into the church and pro-duced contested elections. The strife between Damasus and Ursinus for the bishopric of Rome left 137 corpses on the floor of Santa Maria Maggiore. The pagan Ammiamus remarks that those who desire the ostentation of city life are quite right to struggle with all their strength for the papal office, "for when they attain it, they will be so free from care that they are enriched from the offerings of matrons, ride seated in carriages, wear clothing that attracts every eye, and serve banquets so lavish that their entertainments outdo the tables of kings." [39]

In their contrast to the ancient polis and its economic life, these great landed fortunes, lay and clerical, resemble on a minor scale the emperor's

[38] Bell, *Egypt*, p. 97.
[39] Amm. xxvii. 3. 14–5, trans. J. C. Rolfe.

great fortune and income. Founded and maintained largely by political influence, they were largely self-contained units. The several houses and the household of the master could be supplied by the produce of the states in grain, wine, olive oil, wool, and other necessities. Chiefly only luxuries—silks, spices, glassware, and fine linens—still had to be bought. Thus there appears to have been a change in the role of the market in the economy. The effective market demand for cheap goods declined. So, too, did the demand for such middle-class goods as terra sigillata. The demand for luxuries, however, continued. It is true that the old direct trade with India, which was broken off in the third century, was not reestablished during the political restoration of the fourth, but the fourth century was an age of prosperity and luxury for the rich. The quality of *objets de luxe,* unlike that of cheap products, does not seem to have declined.

But this change was uneven. The concentration of wealth in the hands of a few families seems to have gone much further in the western provinces than in the eastern. The wealthiest members of the Senate at Rome were far wealthier than those of Constantinople, and the landed gentry earlier and more completely dominated the provincial towns of the West than of the East. Consequently, the market for cheaper local goods was far more seriously diminished in the West than in the East. The consequences were even more marked because trade and industry had never been so well developed in the Latin provinces—Britain, Gaul, Spain, and the Danubian lands—and they produced fewer of the great luxuries for which demand held up. (The splendid glass of the Rhineland is an exception.) Trade in the West became largely a matter of local barter on the one hand and of the import of luxuries for the very rich from the eastern provinces. This import trade fell increasingly into the hands of easterners whom our sources call Syrians and—for the first time particularly identified with commercial operations—Jews.[40] Both retained their contacts with the East, formed peculiar societies in the western cities, and were not assimilated by the native population. Even in the fourth century, it would seem that outside of some parts of Africa and Italy, there was hardly any native mercantile population in the West. It would appear, too, that the balance of trade must have been sharply unfavorable to the western provinces. Few western products were in demand in the East, so that payment had to be made in coin (from the reign of Diocletian chiefly in gold coin). At the same

[40] Paul Scheffer-Boichorst, "Kleinere Forschungen zur Geschichte des Mittelalters, IV: Zur Geschichte der Syrer im Abendlande," *Mitteilungen des Instituts fuer oesterreichische Geschichtsforschung,* VI (1885), 520–50; Pierre Lamprechts, "Le commerce des 'Syriens' en Gaule du Haut-Empire à l'époque mérovingienne," *L'antiquité classique,* VI (1937), 35–61; L. Bréhier, "Les colonies d'orientaux en Occident," *Byzantinische Zeitschrift,* XII (1903), 1–39. Bernhard Blumenkranz, *Juifs et chrétiens dans le monde occidental, 430–1096* (The Hague: Mouton and Co., 1960), pp. 13–30, has clearly shown that Jews in the Latin-speaking provinces in this period were never confined to commercial occupations and never had a monopoly of them.

time the government, since Diocletian's time largely settled in eastern provinces, ceased to draw great sums of money from the East to Italy and the West. The only important compensating factor may have been some rents which wealthy Italian senators drew from eastern estates. In general then, market integration, industrial production, and urbanism were far more seriously damaged in the West than in the East, and the crisis aggravated the differences between the two parts of the Empire.

14 THE ANCIENT ECONOMY IN RETROSPECT

In the course of the fifth century Germanic barbarians invaded and permanently occupied all the western provinces of the Roman Empire: Britain, Gaul, the Germanies, Spain, Africa, and even Italy. The Roman Empire in the East, to be sure, was not destroyed. With its capital at Constantinople, it survived until the fall of that city to the Turks in A.D. 1453, and during most of that period it was the most powerful of Christian states. Yet the German occupation of the West marked an epoch. From the point of view of Western development as a whole, it was the end of the ancient world and the opening of the Middle Ages. The reader should be aware that it is very difficult to assert the economic unity of the course of ancient history as a whole, or, indeed, to assert any sort of unity to the course of ancient history. Greek and Roman history, taken together, do form an obvious coherence and continuity of which the Greeks and Romans were themselves very conscious. They looked back to a cultural tradition that reached to Homer and the legendary events of the Trojan War. But beyond that the history of the Orient was unknown to them, and Egyptian and Mesopotamian culture remained something very strange and foreign, something from which they could borrow only bits and pieces.

Modern scholarship rediscovered the history of the ancient Near East only in the nineteenth century and added it as a kind of introductory chapter to "ancient" history, only because there was no place else to put it in the tripartite scheme, "ancient, medieval, and modern," that had been received from the Renaissance. We have earlier attempted to deal with the relation of the classical Mediterranean market economy to the distribution system of the ancient Near East and have stressed, perhaps too strongly, the discrepancy and discontinuity between them.

However, from the Western point of view, classical economic development does show a certain unity and and coherence of development in the form of a cyclical movement reaching from the first tentative steps toward market integration in the seventh century B.C. to a climax of the market system in the first and second centuries A.D., the creation of a state distributive system in the third and fourth centuries, and finally the collapse of the system in the western provinces in the fourth and fifth centuries A.D. The Germans who invaded the Empire—Franks, Visigoths, Vandals, Burgundians, Angles, and Saxons—were quite unable to maintain the state economy described in the last chapter. That system survived much longer in the provinces the Empire retained; in some respects it lasted until the end of the Eastern Empire in the fifteenth century, in others until the Moslem invasions of the seventh century. Hence, it is more difficult to draw a line of demarcation between ancient and medieval history in the eastern than in the western Mediterranean. This is true for general as well as for economic history.

But in the West, only the Ostrogoths who settled in Italy were a partial and temporary exception to the rule that the invasions saw the dissolution of the higher economy which had been so largely engrossed by the Roman state. Although the process is very obscure in detail, it is clear that the old system fell to pieces. The land registers could no longer be kept up so that the land tax fell into disuse. The imperial post disappeared. The armies dissolved. The imperial factories disappeared with the system of munera that supported them. The aqueducts decayed or were cut by invaders, and after their loss the cities declined sharply. From the third century they had lost much of their function as markets and manufacturers for the market. Now they lost their role as seats of the lay government. They survived as forts, as the sees of bishops, and as the sites of monasteries. What remained of the older economic system was the villa, which in the fifth century lost most of its markets and supported its owner chiefly with its own agricultural products and crude peasant manufactures. The owner in Italy (and elsewhere, if he were a bishop) might continue to live in town. In Europe beyond the Alps he more often lived on his estates. A reduced trade in Eastern luxuries survived in the hands of Jews and Syrians who catered to lay lords and to the Church.

It should be noted that this view does not offer an economic explanation of the decline of the Empire and the end of ancient civilization. Economic causes are no more ultimate than other causes and economic history explains intellectual and political history in the same degree that either of these accounts for the economy. Certainly the great political changes of the fifth century had economic causes, as any change so profound must. The demands which politics and the state put on the economy in the West proved too great in the absence of technological progress, and they seem to have played a great part in destroying it. Another social and intellectual order might have been more resilient and might have made a successful transformation of the productive system to meet these demands.

At the end of this history of the ancient economy, then, it may be worth pausing to ask why both the market economy and technology failed to advance farther than they did. Conditions after the Augustan settlement looked very favorable to further advance: there was general peace, a growing population, and immense areas of land awaiting development. Yet the only appreciable economic advances were geographical: the advanced economy of the ancient Near East, Greece, and Italy was spread to more of North Africa, Spain, Gaul, the Rhineland, and the Danubian regions. There was, however, no great intensification of market exchanges in the Mediterranean basin nor

any major advance in technology. The explanation most often given by nine-
teenth- and twentieth-century historians has been that slavery destroyed mechanical inventiveness by destroying the initiative of the mechanical classes
and that the cheapness of slave labor made labor-saving machinery unprofit-
able. This answer seems to have only limited truth. The actual cheapness of
slavery as a means of production is doubtful. Slaves, like donkeys and oxen,
cost money, and they are not willing or eager producers. It is likely that gang
labor of great estates was thought efficient in the late Republic, and this belief may have discouraged mechanical applications and investment. But the
Romans themselves came to doubt its profits, and from the first century A.D. it
was gradually replaced by tenantry. Still, it must be admitted that where and
when it was an important means of production, slavery probably did reduce
inventiveness, for the slave is unlikely to have the means to improve techniques and to reorganize production about new techniques and he is unlikely
to feel that he will profit by doing so.

There is no point in asking, as is often done, why the Romans did not
manage something comparable to the industrial revolution of eighteenth-
century England. Before anything like the cloth factories of that age could
be erected, a great number of lesser inventions were necessary, especially
techniques in metalworking which Europe took more than a thousand years
more to master. Such industry, too, demanded fuel and iron on a scale not
to be found in the Mediterranean.

It is notable, however, that the Romans hardly made full use even of
some of those inventions they knew: the Gallic harvesting machine was not
widely used and the water mill for grinding corn was very tardily exploited.
There is little evidence of mechanical ingenuity to cut costs of labor except
perhaps in the construction of public works. One reason probably lies in an
inadequate development of the market. It has already been pointed out that
the market would hardly have been a practical method for the distribution of
goods in the Bronze Age, for the far greater part of the products that a
Bronze Age technology could produce were far too dear for peasants to buy.
Hence the peasantry could not have been drawn into a wider economic system
by the market, and market exchanges could never have given a living to
artisans. In the classical period the market could perform these functions, but
only to a limited degree. It could not support heavy investment in expensive
labor-saving machinery which would lower production costs. Such machinery
produces goods in large quantity; thus before investment in it can be safely
made, a large, steady, and fairly well-assured market is necessary. In the
eighteenth century England's command of the oceans and her consequent
command of worldwide markets was a condition of investment in the machinery of mass production. The classical world could supply such a market
only for foodstuffs. Consequently the greater part of the wealth of the Empire
continued to be invested in agriculture. This was not due simply to the
prejudices of the possessing classes. Except for certain luxuries, manufactured

articles could rarely command far-flung markets. The purchasing power of the great mass of the people was very low. Their needs in a Mediterranean climate were limited and their means even more limited. It may be supposed that slavery and forced labor had a depressing effect by lowering the wage scale. (A decline in wages of artisans has been discovered between fourth-century Athens and the Hellenistic kingdoms of the third century.) Low wages and purchasing power might theoretically have been compensated for by a market spread over a wide geographical area. Had such a market been available, cheap labor might have been an advantage to the entrepreneur, as it proved to be during both the commercial and industrial revolutions of modern times. The great free trade area of the Roman Empire might be expected to have supplied such a market, but ancient transport was inadequate to the task. Like the Hellenistic kings before them, the Romans felt something of the importance of the matter as it related to shipping on the Mediterranean, and considerable investment was made by the state to improve harbors and build lighthouses. There was advance, too, in the size of ships, especially of those that brought grain to Rome. But Mediterranean shipping was not well connected with the hinterland. The excellent Roman roads were built for military purposes. They might be put to commercial purposes, but their routes were not chosen with commercial purposes in mind, nor did their builders consider the convenience of the merchant. They regularly took the straightest route and the quickest line of march with little consideration of making grades that carts could climb. The roads were not laid out to connect the hinterland to local rivers, but to connect the center of the Empire to the periphery of defense. Moreover land transport was very awkward. The horse was hardly used, for the horseshoe was unknown or little used and the Roman harness choked the team. With such a harness, it has been estimated, no team of horses could pull a load heavier than 500 kilograms. A single ass in modern harness can pull as much. The wagon lacked the whiffle tree and traces and so steered badly. It lacked the brake so that steep climbs and descents were dangerous. Tandem harnessing was unknown. Consequently pack animals were more important than carts.[1]

Under such conditions the immediate periphery of the central sea was more prosperous than the hinterland. Such specialized production as was centered in one place and found a wide market tended to be in luxuries produced in a town or district which had gained a reputation for the skill of its workmen. It did not involve great investments in machinery or buildings and was not more efficient or its goods cheaper than the same products made elsewhere. Rather they were dearer. More efficient techniques were adopted slowly and inadequately, but there was a strong tendency for production to disperse, as the histories of terra sigillata and blown glass show.

---

[1] Richard Lefebvre des Noëttes, *L'attelage. Le cheval de selle à travers les âges. Contribution à l'histoire de l'esclavage,* 2 vols. (Paris: A. Picard, 1931).

Even in these circumstances some technological advances might be expected, and there was progress in those fields with which the government and aristocracy concerned itself: the art of war, architecture, and civil engineering. But the rich and powerful little concerned themselves with other kinds of technique. Throughout the classical world, and especially among the Romans, there was a great social gap between the artisan and the aristocracy. The social position of the artisan and mechanic was low. Scientific thought seems actually to have declined well before the safety and prosperity of the Empire were endangered. The elder Pliny's credulity and the inferiority of Galen's medical knowledge to that of some of his predecessors reveal this decline.

The educational and social ideal of antiquity turned away from science and the mechanical arts to the liberal arts and language. There were two rival curricula in the schools, the rhetorical and the philosophical. Neither was much concerned with mathematics, science, or natural history, and these subjects themselves were as yet of little service to technology. There was also a strong prejudice against specialization, against anything that would pervert the whole man trained to be the ideal citizen. Hence formal education contributed little to technology and science, but rather turned men's minds away from them. This training in school for public service and oratory was, admittedly, confined to the upper classes. The literary culture was not so widely diffused as it is in modern Europe. But as far as can be seen, the same ideal was accepted wholeheartedly by those who had to work for a living. One of the most successful accomplishments of the Augustan settlement was the dignity and social position it offered to merchants and artisans in public life and in the imperial cult,[2] but fifty years after Augustus Petronius draws a picture of a parvenu, Trimalchio, who makes a desperate fool of himself trying to exhibit his literary culture. The merchant and the artisan in the ancient world seem never to have developed an ethos of their own. Rather they accepted the moral and social ideal of the aristocracy, imitated, and desired to climb into it. In this they differed profoundly from the merchant class of the later Middle Ages, whose gilds gave their members the corporate spirit necessary to create both a mercantile ethos and institutions suitable to their economic purposes.

But perhaps an even deeper reason for the antipathy of classical life and education to the practical arts lies in the difference between classical paganism and the monotheistic religions which followed it. As we started our discussion of the ancient economy with Sumerian and Egyptian religion, it is appropriate that we should finish with religion. "Man does not live by bread alone, and we cannot estimate aright even his attitude toward bread and bread-winning unless we consider also his attitude towards his god or dream or devil." [3] The attitude of Christians and Moslems toward nature results

[2] Gagé, Les classes sociales, pp. 107ff., 140, 156ff.
[3] A. D. Nock, Conversion, The Old and New in Religion from Alexander the Great to Augustine of Hippo (Oxford: Oxford University Press, 1933), p. vii.

from his belief in a transcendent god, a god not found in nature nor approached through nature. To monotheists believing in a transcendent God there is nothing intrinsically sacred and inviolable about nature.[4] In the Middle Ages men slowly learned to test nature and force her to reveal her secrets, even to abuse her. Today we dam and curb our streams with rational intention and pollute our lakes with careless abandon. Classical mythology is full of tales about the dire fates of youths and maidens who unknowingly violate springs and plants. Even so sophisticated and sceptical a pagan as Ovid expressed the innate sacredness of nature in the magnificent description of the creation which opens the *Metamorphoses* (i. 21–88). The creation of the cosmos, of the gods, of men and other animals is seen as a single organic process, not as the act of a transcendent Being. Ovid sees man as the highest animal, though lower than the demigods and the gods with whom he has, nevertheless, much in common. Man is given intelligence to master the arts of civilization, but this mastery is involved in his fall from the golden age of harmony with nature, and he is not granted lordship over all the rest of nature as Adam was.

This view is well characterized by Jane Harrison: [5]

> . . . the fundamental presupposition is, not the order and uniformity of nature, not the thing mechanical, but a belief in something like the omnipresence of life, of power, something analogous to the Stoic conception of the world as a living animal, a thing not to be coerced and restrained, but reverently wooed, a thing not immutable at all, but waxing and waning, above all not calculable and observable, but willful and mysterious, a thing a man learns to know not by experiment but by initiation, a thing not of "natural law" but mystical entirely, halting always between an essence and a personality.

Such,, indeed, is the view Pliny specifically sets forth in his encyclopedia of natural history, which attempted to collect all ancient knowledge about Nature: *nec quaerenda ratio in ulla parte naturae, sed voluntas!* [6] He closes his vast work with a prayer:

> Salve, parens rerum omnium Natura, teque nobis Quiritium solis celebratam esse numeris omnibus tuis fave.

If the ancient economy is to be regarded as having failed, the reasons lie deep within the whole context of ancient society. The ancient mind, ambitions, and social aspirations were differently directed than the modern. A purely economic explanation of ancient economic life can only be a partisan distortion.

---

[4] This view, of course, is the essential originality of Hebrew thought: H. Frankfort, *The Intellectual Adventure.*
[5] *Themis* (Cleveland: World Publishing Co., 1962), pp. 84–5.
[6] *NH* xxxvii. 15. 60.

APPENDIX A
Chronology of Inventions, Discoveries, and Political Events

	Inventions & Discoveries	*Political Events*
By c. 7000 B.C.	Cultivation of einkorn, barley, lentils, peas, or vetch in Anatolia. Their cultivation probably originated elsewhere and at an earlier date.	
Before c. 6500	Domestication of sheep and goats	
By c. 6300	Pottery	
Before c. 6000	Smelting of copper and lead at Çatal Hüyük, Anatolia	
By c. 6000–5800	Bricks at Çatal Hüyük Site of Karim Shahir (sickle)	
C. 4800	Weaving of wool or mohair Terre pisée huts at Jarmo	
By c. 4000	River valley irrigation Date palm cultivated Plow and sledge Sailboat Beginnings of monumental architecture The balance	
C. 4500–3000		al'Ubaid period

Inventions & Discoveries		Political Events	
By c. 3600	Potter's wheel		
	Cart		
		C. 3000–2850	Jemdet-Nasr period
C. 3200	Sumerian pictographs		
C. 3000	Egyptian hieroglyphics		
C. 2900	Sumerian syllabary in cuneiform		
	Cylinder seal		
C. 2800	Masonry architecture: the step-pyramid of Zoser	2750–2650	Royal burials at Ur
C. 2750	The true arch in Sumeria	2615–1991 (2686–2180?)	Old Kingdom in Egypt
C. 2650–2500	Pyramids of Cheops, Chephren, and Mycerinus	C. 2400 (2350?)	Urukagina of Lagash
C. 2500	Saddle quern	C. 2371–2316 (2360–2305?)	Sargon of Akkad
		C. 2100–1788 (1991–1765?)	Middle Kingdom in Egypt
		C. 2200–2135 (C. 2180–2082?)	Gutian domination
		C. 2135–2027 (2060–1950?)	Third Dynasty of Ur
		C. 1975/50ff.	Assyrian *karum* at Kultepe
		1850–1761 (to 1695?)	Archives of Mari

C. 1800	Spoked wheel and horse-drawn chariot
C. 1450	Egyptian shadow clock
C. 1400	Cementation process produces a cutting edge on iron in Hittite Asia Minor
C. 1250	Alphabet at Ugarit in Syria; Waterproof plaster of slaked lime and the cistern in Syria
C. 1200	Widespread use of iron in the Middle East

1792–1750 (1728–1686?)	Hammurabi of Babylon (The date of Hammurabi, though now more certain than it once was, remains a crux of Near Eastern chronology.)
C. 1678–1579 (1720–1570?)	Hyksos in Egypt
1570–1075	Egyptian Empire
1400	Destruction of Knossos
1379–1365	Tell el-Amarna correspondence
1298	Battle of Qadesh between Egyptians and Hittites
1232	Pharaoh Merneptah defeats a coalition of Libyans and the Sea Peoples
C. 1220	The Hebrews enter Canaan
C. 1200–1100	Destruction of Mycenaean civilization
C. 1188–1156	Ramses III defeats a coalition of Sea Peoples
C. 1180	The Philistines in Palestine
C. 1100	Dorians in Greece; destruction of Mycenae

	Inventions & Discoveries		Political Events
973–933			Solomon
C. 950			Phoenicians at Cadiz (Gades) and Tartessos in Spain
922			Division of kingdom of Hebrews into Israel and Judah
814			Foundation of Carthage (traditional date)
8th century	Domesticated camel in Arabia; Horseback riding introduced into the Near East		
760			Foundation of Cumae, first Greek colony in the West
733			Foundation of Syracuse
722			Fall of the kingdom of Israel to Assyria
7th century	Pulley, lathe in Greece		
C. 660			Foundation of Byzantium
C. 650–625	Coins invented in Lydia		
C. 640			Foundation of Naucratis
C. 630			Foundation of Cyrene
621			Draco at Athens
C. 620			Cypselus tyrant at Corinth; coinage introduced
612			Fall of Nineveh and end of Assyrian Empire
C. 600	Rotary quern		Foundation of Marseilles

6th century	Trireme replaces pentaconter as dominant warship	
	594	Solon at Athens
	587	Fall of Judah, destruction of the Temple
	572	Fall of Tyre to the Neo-Babylonian (Chaldaean) Empire
	560 (546)–510	Pisistratid tyranny at Athens
	550	Cyrus conquers Media
	546	Conquest of Lydia
	535	Battle of Alalia ends Greek colonization in the West
	C. 520–516	Restoration of the Temple at Jerusalem
	509	Founding of Roman Republic (traditional date)
	508	First treaty of Carthage and Rome
	490	First Persian invasion of Greece
	483/2	Discovery of new veins of silver at Laureion; Athens builds a fleet at Themistocles' urging
	480–479	Second Persian invasion of Greece
	477	Formation of Delian League
	C. 460	First coins at Tyre
C. 450	Building tackle, crude cranes	

	Inventions & Discoveries		Political Events
443	*Fl.* Hippodamus of Miletus, town planner, rebuilt Piraeus and planned the Athenian colony of Thurii		
		431–404	Peloponnesian War
Late 5th century C. 400 B.C.	*Fl.* Hippocrates of Cos, the physician. The catapult	401	Expedition of Cyrus the Younger (Xenophon)
C. 370	Xenophon, *Oeconomica*	C. 370	Theban hegemony in Greece
C. 345	Aristotle, *Politica*	338	Philip's victory at Chaeronea ends the independence of Greece
		Latter 4th century	Pytheas of Marseilles explores the Atlantic coast of Europe
C. 335–22	Aristotle, *Ethics*	334–323	Alexander's conquests
325	Quinquireme first appears at Athens		
312	Via Appia		
300 B.C.	*Fl.* Euclid, the geometer Donkey mill used in Greece		
285 B.C.	Ptolemy Philadelphus builds canal from the Nile to the Red Sea		

Date	Technology & Culture	Date	Politics & Military
C. 280	The Pharos at Alexandria	282–272	The Pyrrhic War completes Rome's conquest of Italy south of the Apennines
272	Anio Vetus, the first great aqueduct at Rome	238	Annexation of Sardinia and Corsica
Late 3rd century	Development of parchment for writing *Fl.* Erastosthenes, astronomer and geographer	227	Rhodes damaged by an earthquake.
C. 230	Hiero's great ship	225–219	Acquisition of Cisalpine Gaul
		221–201	Second Punic War and annexation of the two Spains and Provence
212 B.C.	Death of Archimedes Use of screw press to squeeze olives and grapes	200–197	Second Macedonian War makes Rome a power in the Greek world
C. 200	Apollonius of Perga, *Conic Sections* Ox-driven waterwheel	184	Death of Plautus, Roman playwright
179	Pons Aemilius (earliest dated stone bridge; arched superstructure dated 142 B.C.)	168–164	Jews under Judas Maccabeus revolt against Antiochus IV Epiphanes
176	Miller-bakers appear in Italy	168	Paullus' victory over Perseus of Macedonia brings such booty that Italy is relieved of direct taxation (*tributum*) Illyricum a Roman province

	Inventions & Discoveries		*Political Events*
		167	Rome makes Delos a free port; decline of Rhodes
160–126	*Fl.* Hipparchus the astronomer	148	Macedonia a Roman province
C. 146 B.C.	The work of Mago the Carthaginian on capitalistic agriculture translated into Latin	146	Destruction of Carthage and Corinth Africa, Macedonia, and Achaea Roman provinces
		134–132	First Servile War (Eurus in Sicily)
		133	Tiberius Gracchus, tribune; agrarian law
		129	Revolt of Aristonicus suppressed; Asia a province
		123	Gaius Gracchus, tribune
C. 120	Ptolemies appear to have made direct contact with India by sea	111	*Lex agraria*
		105	Marius' reform of the army
		103–99	Second Service War in Sicily
		91–88	Social War in Italy
		88–84	First Mithridatic War opens with the massacre of Romans in the Aegean
		87–84	Terror of Marius, Cinna, and Flaccus at Rome

83–79	Sulla's dictatorship	
73–71	Third Servile War (Spartacus in Campania)	
68–67	Metellus defeats the pirates of Crete and Cilicia	
65–62	Pompey reorganizes the East; Bithynia-Pontus, Cilicia, and Syria Roman provinces	
64–63	Client kingdoms organized Conspiracy of Catiline	
58–51	Caesar's conquest of Gaul	
C. 50		Romans learn of wagons whose front wheels are mounted on a swivel from the Gauls Cork stopper
45–44	Caesar supreme	
45 B.C.		Introduction of the Julian calendar
C. 37 B.C.		Varro, *Rerum rusticarum*
31 B.C.	Octavian (Augustus) wins at Actium; peace restored	
30	Egypt annexed	
C. 30	Production of *terra sigillata* starts at Arezzo	
27 B.C.–A.D. 14		Brass and pewter invented or introduced into the Roman world Blown glass Wooden barrel Vitruvius, *De architectura* Celsus, *De re medica* Hippalus' discovery of the monsoon route to India

	Inventions & Discoveries		Political Events
First century	*Fl.* Heron of Alexandria, author of the *Mechanica*; Claudius' harbor at Ostia		
		43	Conquest of Britain begins
C. A.D. 60	Columella, *De re rustica*		
C. 77	Pliny, *Historia naturalis*	66–70	The Jewish War and destruction of the Second Temple
		79	Eruption of Vesuvius buries Pompeii and Herculaneum
C. 97	Frontinus, *De aquis urbis Romae*		
Early 2nd century	Development of the bound codex for writing	101–107	Trajan conquers Dacia; Rome begins to exploit her mines
106	Bridge over Tagus at Alcantara in Spain		
A.D. 110–125	Dome of the Pantheon; Trajan's hexagonal harbor at Ostia; market at Rome		
		132–135	Revolt of Bar-Cocheba
C. 150	*Fl.* Ptolemy, geographer and astronomer		
150–199	*Fl.* Galen of Pergamum, medical writer		
		166–175, 178–180	Macrommanic wars and financial troubles
		166–167	Universal pestilence
		180	Death of Marcus; accession of Commodus
		C. 180ff.	Plague under Commodus
		192	Murder of Commodus; civil war brings Septimius Severus to power

3rd century First example of a carriage with shafts in the Roman world Effective use of the vertical undershot water-wheel to grind grain	212	Edict of Caracalla makes all freemen in the Empire Roman citizens.
	227	New Persian (Sassanid) Empire founded by Ardashir
	233/4	Incursions of Germans along the Rhine and Danube
	C. 251–266	A general pestilence spreads from Ethiopia.
	256	Germans invade Gaul.
	259–268	Reign of Gallienus sees height of civil disorders; Goths ravage the Black Sea, Asia Minor, and the Aegean by ship.
	270	Pestilence
	271–276	Aurelian walls the city of Rome.
	276–282	Fortification of many cities in Gaul
	284–305	Reign of Diocletian
	301	Edict on prices
4th century Earliest evidence of soap Halved bellows Jointed flail	302–311	Great persecution of the Christians
	306–337	Constantine the Great, first Christian emperor
	330	Dedication of the new capital at Constantinople
Between 366–375 Anonymous, *De rebus bellicis*	378	Gothic victory over Valens at Adrianople
	395	Death of Theodosius I; division of the Empire.

APPENDIX B
The Function of Money in Archaic Greece
by Pierre Vidal-Naquet

Was the adoption of a monetary instrument by Greece at the end of the seventh century provoked by *directly* economic causes? By the development of the international commerce of the Mediterranean and by the internal commerce of the city-states? Is it explained by the appearance of merchants as an important social class at the front rank of Hellenic society? For the immense majority of historians the reply is yes. Yet this traditional view is untenable. It was doubted already in 1931 by J. M. Keynes (*A Treatise on Money*); in 1962 at the Conference on Economic History at Aix-en-Provence by M. I. Finley; and above all by Ed. Will, who, in two articles that have or should have become classic,[1] used chiefly a text of Aristotle and the works of B. Laum to argue that the institutions of state money could not be understood apart from the general efforts at codification and measure which characterized contemporary changes in the Greek city. But could these hypotheses be demonstrated? Will did not think so: "Where are the documents which could support any hypothesis whatever about these questions? There are none." [2] Yet such documents do exist: they are the oldest coin hoards, and these are the subject of an article by the English numismatist C. M. Kraay, "Hoards, Small Change, and the Origins of Coinage," *Journal of Hellenic Studies*, LXXXIV (1964), 76–91. Although he seems not to know Ed. Will's studies, it almost seems that he is replying to the question Will poses.

Kraay has tried to verify a double hypothesis: if the first function of money was commercial, one should discover a very great dispersion of finds (for international commerce) and see small change multiply (for local retail trade). In both cases the result is negative: the coins of Italy do not pass the straits of Sicily, the coins of Sicily are scarcely found in Italy except in the region of Reggio, the coins of commercial cities like Aegina and Corinth have

Pierre Vidal-Naquet, *Annales: économies, sociétés, civilisations*, XXIII (1968), 206–9, under the title, "Fonction de la monnaie dans la Grèce antique." Reproduced by permission.

[1] "De l'aspect éthique de l'origine grecque de la monnaie," *Revue Historique*, CCXI (1954), 209–31; "Reflexions et hypothèses sur les origines du monnayage," *Revue numismatique*, XVII (1955), 5–23. See also *Korinthiaka* (Paris, 1955), pp. 495–502.

[2] *Ibid.*, p. 502.

a very limited area of diffusion (provided the hoards are examined as a whole and account is taken of numbers). On the contrary, a region like the northeast of Greece (Thrace and Macedonia), which produced silver, exported coins in great quantity and very far. Coins, then, seem to have been more an *object* than a means of commerce.

One case is wholly peculiar: Athens. Although she produced silver, she exported practically no coins before she began striking the "owls" in the last quarter of the sixth century. These coins then had an extraordinary development before the famous discovery of the "fountain of silver" in 483. The search for new veins at Laureion might even, I believe, be explained by this growth.

The development of small change was very slow throughout the Greek world as a whole. Thus at Croton, the most important mint in southern Italy, there was practically nothing smaller than the stater (tetradrachma) before 480. The picture is not so neat for central Greece, because Athens seems to have had billon money from the sixth century. In contrast billon money was very rare in the northeast and in Asia Minor (Ionia being a partial exception).

As a whole the picture is clear. There are no doubt areas of regional diffusion. Thus the coins of the great cities of southern Italy are found together in almost all the local hoards, and there were zones which exported minted silver. But the map of the circulation of coins as it can be pictured with the help of Kraay's study does not coincide with the map of the international commerce of the Mediterranean which can be drawn with the help of literary texts and archaeological finds (although the interpretation of the latter can be ambiguous). Thus if, as many facts lead us to think, there was direct and important trade between Sybaris and Miletus, these relations are not revealed by the coin finds. It must, then, be admitted that the monetary function was not at first an exchange function. The case of Athens, however, is peculiar. A sudden change took place at the end of the sixth century with the appearance of "owls" everywhere about the eastern Mediterranean. Should this event be explained by the policy of the Pisistratids with their possessions in the northeast, as Kraay thinks, or by the political revolution symbolized by the reforms of Cleisthenes, as we have suggested? [3] Whichever it was, the expansion of the Athenian coinage was certainly not independent of political decisions made by a state desirous of increasing its prestige, but it would be absurd not to put this expansion in relation also with the incontestable development of commerce.

These, however, are late data. If we turn back to the origins of coining, we must, according to C. M. Kraay, abandon the traditional explanations. Much more than with commerce and merchants, the striking of small stamped ingots by the state should be put in relation to the needs of the state itself.

---

[3] P. Lévêque and P. Vidal-Naquet, *Clisthène l'Athénien* (Paris, 1964), pp. 57–61.

In the Greek world of the seventh and sixth centuries, the functions of the state were becoming very much more complicated and occasions for hoarding and releasing precious metal were multiplying. Commerce played a part in this development to the degree that import and export tariffs were part of the resources of the state, but account must be taken of other things: the pay of mercenaries, public works, and fines, which from 570 at Chios were expressed in coins. Kraay also takes account of the fact that the state sometimes distributed the product of the mines to its citizens in the form of coin. This is exactly the point that Ed. Will had developed:

> Sociologists and ethnologists, in treating the origins of monetary practices, have laid great stress on the part played by *distribution:* distribution of gifts by the chief to his followers, distribution of booty to the members of the hunt, of the parts of the victim to the sacrificing community; the division of the crop among the members of the tribe. . . . [4]

He put forward the hypothesis that the origin of money could have been facilitated by the redistributions of land which took place in a number of Greek cities in the archaic period; the state may have distributed coin to those whose land was confiscated. Without being so bold, Kraay's study points in the same direction. No doubt it can be questioned in detail. In particular, an effort should be made to find out if, in the hoards which have not been disbursed, the proportion of coins minted in one city and overstruck in another is as limited as the published sources indicate. But such as it is, Kraay's article marks a decisive step in the study of the origins of Greek money.

[4] *Korinthiaka,* p. 499.

APPENDIX C
Note on the Population
of the Classical World

It can hardly be doubted that the population of Greece and the Aegean world was increasing from the age of colonization through the fifth century, though the only evidence is the expanding activities of the Greeks. The great outpouring of Greeks and Macedonians under Alexander and his successors is proof of continued vitality, but by the second century B.C., there is some doubt that the population of these regions continued its vigor. Polybius in the second century complains that the Greeks marry late and practice methods of controlling the number of their offspring. The exposure of infants appears to have been common, while in earlier times it had been practiced only among the very poor, in times of crisis, or for eugenic reasons. Indeed, the practice became widespread among the Greek-speaking lands of the eastern Mediterranean. Girls especially suffered. A maxim appears to have been common that even a rich man does not raise two daughters. The Roman civil wars of the first century B.C. appear to have brought a decline in population from which recovery was slow and incomplete.

Roman recovery from the devastation of the Hannibalic War was fairly prompt, as the demand for land at the time of the Gracchi shows, and this growth appears to have continued vigorously down to the Augustan age. The figures that Livy gives from the census of the citizens suggests this, although we cannot know how much of the growth was due to the enrollment of new citizens. In the late Republic, however, there are signs that the upper classes in Rome were imitating Greek methods of birth control. The literature is full of such hints. Augustus legislated in favor of early marriages and numerous offspring, with what success is not clear, but the planting of colonies of Italians continued through his reign and beyond. By the Flavian age, however, there seems to have been no surplus of Italians. The settlers of the Agri decumates were drawn from the poor of Gaul. Thereafter Gaul seems to have sent out no more settlers, and the growth of internal settlement tapered off. While the earlier settlers of the Danubian lands had been drawn from Italy, in the second century they had to be sought in the East. Hadrian's legislation in favor of Italian orphans suggests that the government was deeply concerned about the state of the Italian population in the early second century.

The population of the more Hellenized and Romanized parts of the Empire, then, appears to have stopped growing in the second century. The known exceptions to the rule of a more or less stable population in the second century A.D. are from barely Hellenized and Romanized districts on the periphery of the Mediterranean world: the uplands of Numidia and Syria. Plagues under Marcus, Commodus, Gallus, and several later emperors in the third century suggest that the population, which would necessarily have had great difficulty maintaining itself in that age of chaos, must have fallen further, and evidence from tax registers of Egypt and of deserted land in the fifth century all suggest an abrupt decline in the third century and little recovery in the fourth and fifth.

BIBLIOGRAPHY

Adams, Robert M. *The Evolution of Urban Society: Early Mesopotamia and Pre-hispanic Mexico.* Chicago: Aldine Press, 1966.

Albright, William F. *The Biblical Period from Abraham to Ezra.* New York: Harper and Row, 1963.

Albright, William F. "The Role of the Canaanites in the History of Civilization," *Studies in the History of Culture: The Disciplines of the Humanities,* pp. 11–50. American Council of Learned Societies Devoted to the Humanistic Studies. Menasha, Wis.: Banta, 1942.

Ames, Oakes. *Economic Annuals and Human Cultures.* Cambridge, Mass.: Botanical Museum of Harvard University, 1939.

Anderson, Edgar. "The Evolution of Domestication," *Evolution After Darwin.* University of Chicago Centennial; Chicago: University of Chicago Press, 1960.

Anderson, Edgar. *Plants, Man, and Life.* Boston: Little, Brown and Co., 1952.

Audin, A. "La population de Ludgunum au IIe siècle," *Cahiers d'histoire (Lyons, Grenoble, Clermont, Saint-Etienne, Chambéry),* XV (1970), 5–14.

Aymard, A. "Une ville de la Babylonie séleucide d'après les contrats cunéiformes," *Revue des études anciennes,* XL (1938), 5–52. (The city is Warka, the Biblical Erech.)

Babelon, Jean. *La numismatique antique.* Que sais-je? 3rd ed. Paris: Presses universitaires de France, 1964. (A basic introduction.)

Bailey, Cyril, ed. *The Legacy of Rome.* Oxford: Clarendon Press, 1923.

Baron, Salo W., and Joseph L. Blau. *Judaism, Postbiblical and Talmudic Period.* Library of the Liberal Arts. Indianapolis: Bobbs-Merrill, 1954.

Bates, Marston. *The Forest and the Sea. A Look at the Economy of Nature and the Economy of Man.* New York: Random House, 1960.

Belin de Ballu, E. *L'histoire des colonies grecques du littoral nord de la Mer Noire.* 2d ed. Leyden: Brill, 1965.

Bell, Harold Idris. "The Byzantine Servile State in Egypt," *Journal of Egyptian Archaeology,* IV (1917), 86–106.

Bell, Harold Idris. "The Decay of a Civilization," *ibid.,* X (1924), 207–16.

Bell, Harold Idris. *Egypt from Alexander the Great to the Arab Conquest: A Study in the Diffusion and Decay of Hellenism.* The Greynog Lectures for 1946. Oxford: Clarendon Press, 1948.

Bell, Harold Idris. "An Egyptian Village in the Time of Justinian," *Journal of Hellenic Studies,* LXIV (1944), 21–36.

Beloch, Julius. "Die Bevoelkerung Europas in Altertum," *Zeitschrift fuer Socialwissenschaft,* II (1899), 505–14, 600–21; III (1900), 405–23.

Beloch, Julius. "Die Bevoelkerung Italiens in Altertum," *Klio,* III (1903), 471–90.

Beloch, Julius. *Die Bevoelkerung der griechischen-roemischen Welt.* Leipzig: Dunker und Humbolt, 1886.

Beloch, Julius. "Die Grossindustrie im Altertum," *Zeitschrift fuer Socialwissenschaft,* II (1899), 18–26.

Bennett, E. L., Jr. *The Pylos Tablets.* Princeton: Princeton University Press, 1955.

Bennett, H. "The Exposure of Infants in Ancient Rome," *Classical Journal,* XVIII (1922–1923), 341–51.

Benoît, Fernand. *Recherches sur l'hellénisation du Midi de la Gaule.* [Gap]: Editions Orphys, 1965.

Bérard, Jean. *La colonisation grecque de l'Italie méridionale et de la Sicile dans l'antiquité: l'histoire et la légende.* 2d ed. Paris: Presses universitaires de France, 1957.

Bérard, Jean. "Problèmes démographiques dans l'histoire de la Grèce antique," *Population* (Paris), II (1947), 303–12.

Bevan, Edwyn R: *The House of Ptolemy. A History of Egypt Under the Ptolemaic Dynasty.* Chicago: Argonaut, 1968. (First published in 1927 as Vol. IV of *A History of Egypt,* ed. W. M. F. Petrie.)

Bibby, Geoffrey. *Looking for Dilmun.* New York: Alfred A. Knopf, 1969.

Blanchet, Adrien. *L'archéologie gallo-romaine.* Paris: Société française d'archéologie, 1935.

Blanchet, Adrien. *Les enceintes romaines de la Gaule: étude sur l'origine d'un grand nombre de villes françaises.* Paris: Ernest Leroux, 1907.

Blanchet, Adrien. *Les trésors de monnaies romaines et les invasions germaniques en Gaule.* Paris: Ernest Leroux, 1900.

Blegan, Carl W. "The Palace of Nestor, Excavations at Pylos, 1952," *American Journal of Archeology,* LVII (1953), 59–64.

Bloch, Marc. "Avènement et conquêtes du Moulin à eau," *Annales d'histoire économique et sociale,* VII (1935), 538–63.

Bluemner, Hugo. *Technologie und Terminologie der Gewerbe und Kuenste bei Griechen und Roemern.* 4 vols. Leipzig: Tuebner, 1879–1912. Reprinted: Hildesheim, Georg Olms, 1969.

Blumenkranz, Bernhard. *Juifs et chrétiens dans le monde occidental, 403–1096.* The Hague: Mouton and Co., 1960.

Boak, Arthur E. R. "Irrigation and Population in the Faijum," *Geographical Review* (1926), 353ff.

Boak, Arthur E. R. *Manpower Shortage and the Fall of the Roman Empire in the West.* Ann Arbor: University of Michigan Press, 1955.

Boak, Arthur E. R. "The Population of Roman and Byzantine Karanis," *Historia,* IV (1955), 157–62.

Boak, Arthur E. R., and William G. Sinnigen. *A History of Rome to* A.D. *565.* 5th ed. New York: Macmillan, 1965.

Boardman, John. *The Greeks Overseas.* Baltimore: Penguin Books, 1964.

Boeckh, August. *The Public Economy of the Athenians.* Trans. Anthony Lamb. Boston: Little, Brown, 1857.

Boëthius, Axel. "Urbanism in Italy," *Acta Congressus Madvigiani, Proceedings of the Second International Congress of Classical Studies,* IV, 87ff. Copenhagen: E. Munksgaard, 1958.

Bohannan, Paul, and George Dalton. *Markets in Africa. Eight Subsistence Economies in Transition.* Evanston, Ill.: Northwestern University Press, 1962.

Bolin, Sture. *State and Currency in the Roman Empire to 300* A.D. Trans. Edward Carney. Stockholm: Almqvist and Wiksell, 1958.

Bolkestein, H. *Economic Life in Greece's Golden Age.* 2d ed., revised and annotated by E. J. Jonkers. Leiden: E. J. Brill, 1958.

Boren, Henry C. "The Urban Side of the Gracchan Economic Crisis," *American Historical Review,* LXIII (1957–1958), 890–902.

Botsford, George Willis, and Charles Alexander Robinson, Jr. *Hellenic History.* 4th ed. New York: Macmillan, 1956.

Bourne, Frank C. "The Roman Alimentary Program and Italian Agriculture," *Transactions and Proceedings of the American Philological Association,* XCI (1960), 47–75.

Bouton, André. *Le Maine; Histoire économique et sociale des origines au XIVe siècle.* Le Mans: Impr. Monnoyer, 1962.

Braidwood, Robert J. "The Agricultural Revolution," *Scientific American,* CCIII (September 1960), 2–10.

Braidwood, Robert J. *The Near East and the Foundations for Civilization. An Essay in Appraisal of the General Evidence.* Condon Lecture Publications. Eugene, Ore.: Oregon State System of Higher Education, 1952.

Braidwood, Robert J. *Prehistoric Man.* 7th ed. Glenview, Ill.: Scott, Foresman and Co., 1967.

Braidwood, Robert J. and Linda. "The Earliest Village Communities of Southwestern Asia," *Journal of World History,* I (1953), 278–310.

Braidwood, Robert J., and Gordon R. Willey. *Courses Toward Urban Life: Archeological Considerations of Some Cultural Alternates.* Vol. XXXII of *Viking Fund Publications in Anthropology,* ed. Sol Tax. Chicago: Aldine Publishing Co., 1962.

Breasted, James Henry. *Ancient Records of Egypt. Historical Documents from the Earliest Times to the Persian Conquest.* 5 vols. Chicago: University of Chicago Press, 1906–1907.

Bréhier, Louis, "Les colonies d'orientaux en Occident," *Byzantinische Zeitschrift,* XII (1903), 1–39.

Brentjes, Burchard. "Das Kamel in Alten Orient," *Klio,* XXXIX (1960), 23–52.

Burn, A. R. "Hic breve vivitur. A Study of the Expectation of Life in the Roman Empire," *Past and Present,* No. 4 (November 1953), 1–31.

Bury, J. D. *A History of Greece to the Death of Alexander the Great.* 3d ed., revised by Russell Meiggs. London: Macmillan, 1959.

Calderini, Aristide. *I Severi. La Crisi dell-Impero nel III Secolo.* Bologna: Cappell, 1949.

Calhoun, George M. "Ancient Athenian Mining," *Journal of Economic and Business History,* III (1931), 333–61.

Calhoun, George M. *The Business Life of Ancient Athens.* Chicago: University of Chicago Press, 1926.

Calhoun, George M. "Risk in Sea Loans in Ancient Athens," *Journal of Economic and Business History,* II (1930), 561–84.

Callu, Jean Pierre. *La politique monétaire des empereurs romains de 238 à 311.* Vol. CCXL of the *Bibliothèque des Ecoles Françaises d'Athènes et de Rome.* Paris: Boccard, 1969.

Carcopino, Jérome. *Daily Life in Ancient Rome.* Trans. E. G. Lorimer. New Haven, Conn.: Yale University Press, 1945.

Cardascia, Guillaume. "L'apparition dans le droit des classes d'*honestiores* et d'*humiliores,*" *Revue d'histoire de droit français,* XXVIII (1950), 305–37, 461–85.

Cardascia, Guillaume, ed. *Les Archives des Murasû, Une famille d'hommes d'affaires babyloniens à l'époque perse, 455–403 av. J.-C.* Paris: Imprimerie nationale, 1951. (See also below, Clay, Albert Tobias.)

Cary, Max. *The Geographic Background of Greek and Roman History.* Oxford: Clarendon Press, 1949.

Cary, Max. *A History of Rome down to the Reign of Constantine.* 2d ed. London: Macmillan, 1960.

Cary, Max, and E. H. Warmington. *The Ancient Explorers.* 2d ed. Baltimore: Penguin Books, 1963. (First published, 1929.)

Cassin, Elena. "Note sur le 'commerce de carrefour' en Mésopotamie ancienne," *Journal of the Economic and Social History of the Orient,* IV (1961), 164–7.

Casson, Lionel. *The Ancient Mariners, Seafarers and Sea Fighters of the Mediterranean in Ancient Times.* New York: The Macmillan Co., 1959.

Casson, Lionel. "Harbour and River Boats of Ancient Rome," *Journal of Roman Studies,* LV (1965), 34–9.

Chadwick, John. "A Prehistoric Bureaucracy," *Diogenes,* XXVI (1959), 7–18.

Charlesworth, Martin P. "Roman Trade with India: Resurvey," *Studies in Roman Economic and Social History in Honor of Allan Chester Johnson,* ed. P. R. Coleman-Norton et al. Princeton: Princeton University Press, 1951, pp. 131–43.

Charlesworth, Martin P. *Trades Routes and Commerce of the Roman Empire.* 2d ed. Cambridge: Cambridge University Press, 1926.

Chastagnol, A. "Un scandale du vin a Rome sous le Bas-Empire. L'affaire du préfet Orfitus," *Annales: économies, sociétés, civilisations,* V (1950), 166–83.

Chevalier, Louis. "La population de Lutèce avant 275 aprés J.-C.," *Population* (Paris), 1962, 327–8.

Chevalier, Louis. "La population des villes sous le Bas-Empire et à l'époque du haut moyen âge d'après l'exemple de Paris," *ibid.,* 765–7.

Childe, V. Gordon. *The Dawn of European Civilization.* 6th ed. London: Routledge and Kegan Paul, 1957.

Childe, V. Gordon. *Man Makes Himself.* 2d ed. The Thinker's Library. London: Watts and Co., 1941.

Childe, V. Gordon. *New Light on the Most Ancient Near East.* 4th ed. London: Routledge and Kegan Paul, 1952.

Childe, V. Gordon. *The Prehistory of European Society.* Harmondsworth, Middlesex: Penguin Books, 1958.

Childe, V. Gordon. *Social Evolution.* London: Watts and Co., 1951.

Childe, V. Gordon. "The Sociology of the Mycenaean Tablets," *Past and Present,* No. 7 (April 1955), 76ff.

Childe, V. Gordon. "War in Prehistoric Society." *Sociological Review,* XXXIII (1941), 126–38.

Childe, V. Gordon. *What Happened in History.* 2d ed. Harmondsworth: Penguin Books, 1954.

Christ, Karl. "Die Griechen und das Geld," *Saeculum,* XV (1964), 214–29.

Clark, John Grahame. "Forest Clearance and Prehistoric Farming," *Economic History Review,* XVII (1947), 45–51.

Clark, John Grahame. *Prehistoric Europe: The Economic Basis.* London: Methuen, 1952.

Clausing, Roth. *The Roman Colonate, The Theories of its Origin.* New York: Columbia University Press, 1915.

Clay, Albert Tobias, *Business Documents of Murashû Sons of Nippur Dated in the Reign of Darius II, 424–404* B.C. Vol. X of *The Babylonian Expedition of the University of Pennsylvania*, Ser. A: Cuneiform Text, ed. H. V. Hilprecht. Philadelphia: Department of Archaeology and Paleontology of the University of Pennsylvania, 1904. (See also Cardascia.)

Clay, Albert Tobias. *Legal and Commercial Transactions Dated in the Assyrian, Neo-Babylonian, and Persian Periods.* Philadelphia, privately printed, 1908.

Clay, Albert Tobias. *Legal Documents from Erech Dated in the Seleucid era (312–65* B.C.) New York: privately printed, 1912.

Cohn, Norman. *The Pursuit of the Millennium.* New York: Essential Books, 1957.

Coleman-Norton, P. R., ed. *Studies in Roman Economic and Social History in Honor of Allan Chester Johnson.* Princeton: Princeton University Press, 1951.

Collingwood, R. G., and J. Myres. *Roman Britain and the English Settlement.* Vol. I of *The Oxford History of England.* 2d ed. Oxford: Clarendon Press, 1937.

Collingwood, R. G., and Ian Richmond. *The Archaeology of Roman Britain.* 2d ed. London: Methuen, 1969.

Contenau, Georges. *Everyday Life in Babylon and Assyria.* Trans. H. R. and A. R. Maxwell-Hyslop. London: F. Arnold, 1954.

Cook, Robert Manuel. *Greek Painted Pottery.* London: Methuen, 1960.

Coquery-Vidrovitch, Catherine. "La fête des coutumes au Dahomey: Historique et essai d'interprétation," *Annales: économies, sociétés, civilisations*, XIX (1964), 696–716.

Cousteau, Jacques, and James Dugan. *The Living Sea.* New York: Harper and Row, 1964.

Cumont, Franz. *Comment la Belgique fut romanisée.* 2d ed. Brussels: Maurice Samertin, 1914.

Cumont, Franz. "The Population of Syria," *Journal of Roman Studies*, XXIV (1934), 187–90.

Daumas, Maurice, ed. *Histoire générale des techniques.* Vol. I: *Les origines de la civilisation technique.* Paris: Presses universitaires de France, 1962.

Davies, Oliver. *Roman Mines in Europe.* Oxford: Clarendon Press, 1935.

Day, John. *An Economic History of Athens Under Roman Domination.* New York: Columbia University Press, 1949.

Deimel, Anton. "Die Bewirtschaftung des Tempellandes zur zeit Urukaginas," *Orientalia,* V (1922), 1–25.

Deimel, Anton. "Die Reformtexte Urukaginas," *Orientalia. Commentarii de rebus Assyro-babylonicis arabicis, aegyptiacis,* etc., II (1920), 3–31.

Deimel, Anton. "Sumerische Tempelwirtschaft zur Zeit Urukaginas und seiner Vorgaenger. Abschluss der Einzelstudien und Zusammenfassung der Hauptresultate," *Analecta Orientalia,* Vol. II. Rome: Pontificio Istituto Biblico, 1931.

Demougeot, E. "Le chameau et l'Afrique du Nord romaine," *Annales: économies, sociétés, civilisations,* XV (1960), 209–47.

Derry, Thomas Kingston, and Trevor I. Williams. *A Short History of Technology from the Earliest Times to* A.D. *1900.* New York: Oxford University Press, 1961. (A condensation and restatement of the work edited by Charles Singer et al.)

DeVaux, Roland. *Ancient Israel.* New York: McGraw-Hill, 1961.

Drachmann, Aage Gerhardt. *The Mechanical Technology of Greek and Roman*

Antiquity: A Study of the Literary Sources. Madison: University of Wisconsin Press, 1963.

Dubberstein, Waldo H. "Comparative Prices in Later Babylonia," *American Journal of Semitic Languages and Literature,* LVI (1939), 20–43.

Dunbabin, Thomas James. "Minos and Daedalos in Sicily," *Papers of the British School at Rome,* XVI (1948), 1–18. (On early trade in the western Mediterranean.)

Dunbabin, Thomas James. *The Western Greeks. The History of Sicily and South Italy from the Foundation of the Greek Colonies to 480 B.C.* Oxford: Clarendon Press, 1948.

Duncan-Jones, R. P. "City-Population in Roman Africa," *Journal of Roman Studies,* LIII (1963), 85–90.

Duval, Paul Marie, et al. *Paris, croissance d'une capitale. Colloques, Cahiers de civilisations.* Paris: Hachette, 1961.

East, Gordon. *An Historical Geography of Europe.* London: Methuen, 1935.

Ehrenberg, Victor. *The People of Aristophanes. A Sociology of Old Attic Comedy.* New York: Schocken, 1962. (Originally published in 1943.)

Einaudi, Luigi. "Greatness and Decline of Planned Economy in the Hellenistic World," *Kyklos,* II (1948), 193–210, 289–316.

Erman, Adolf, ed. *The Ancient Egyptians, A Sourcebook of Their Writings.* Trans. Aylward M. Blackman. Harper Torchbooks; New York: Harper and Row, 1966. (Originally published as *The Literature of the Ancient Egyptians,* 1927.)

Falkenstein, A. "La cité-temple sumérienne," *Journal of World History,* I (1954), 784–814.

Finegan, Jack. *Light from the Ancient Past.* 2d ed. Princeton: Princeton University Press, 1959.

Finley, John H., Jr. *Thucydides.* Cambridge, Mass.: Harvard University Press, 1942.

Finley, Moses I. "Homer and Mycenae: Property and Tenure," *Historia,* VI (1957), 133–59.

Finley, Moses I. *Land and Credit in Ancient Athens.* New Brunswick, N.J.: Rutgers University Press, 1951.

Finley, Moses I. "The Mycenaen Tablets and Economic History," *Economic History Review,* 2d s., X (1957–1958), 128–41.

Finley, Moses I. *Studies in Land and Credit in Ancient Athens, 500–200 B.C. The Horos-Inscriptions.* New Brunswick, N.J.: Rutgers University Press, n. d. [1951].

Finley, Moses I. "Technology in the Ancient World," *Economic History Review,* 2d s., XII (1959), 120ff.

Finley, Moses I., ed. *Slavery in Classical Antiquity.* Cambridge, Mass.: W. Heffer, 1960. Reprinted with a supplement to the bibliography: New York, Barnes and Noble, 1968.

Fisher, William Bayne. *The Middle East: A Physical, Social, and Regional Geography.* London: Methuen, 1950.

Forni, Giovanni. *Reclutamento dei legioni da Augusto a Diocleziano.* Milan: Bocca, 1953.

Forbes, R. J. *Man the Maker. A History of Technology and Engineering.* New York: Henry Schuman, 1950.

Forbes, R. J. *Studies in Ancient Technology.* 8 vols. Leiden: E. J. Brill, 1955–1964.

Foster, Benjamin R. "Agoranomos and Muhtasib," *Journal of the Economic and Social History of the Orient*, XIII (1970), 128–44.

Frank, Tenney, ed. *An Economic History of Rome*. 2d ed. Baltimore: Johns Hopkins University Press, 1927.

Frank, Tenney. *An Economic Survey of Ancient Rome*. 6 vols. Baltimore: Johns Hopkins University Press, 1933–1940.

Frank, Tenney. "Roman Census Statistics from 225 B.C. to 28 B.C.," *Classical Philology*, XIX (1924), 329–41.

Frankfort, Henri. *The Birth of Civilization in the Near East*. Bloomington: Indiana University Press, 1951.

Frankfort, Henri. *Kingship and the Gods: A Study of Ancient Near Eastern Religion as the Integration of Society and Nature*. Chicago: University of Chicago Press, 1948.

Frankfort, Henri, et al. *The Intellectual Adventure of Ancient Man: An Essay on Speculative Thought in the Ancient Near East*. Chicago: University of Chicago Press, 1946.

Frederiksen, M. W. "Caesar, Cicero and the Problem of Debt," *Journal of Roman Studies*, LVI (1956), 128–40.

Freeman, Kathleen. *Greek City-States*. New York: W. W. Norton and Co., 1963. (Originally published, 1950.)

French, A. *The Growth of the Athenian Economy*. New York: Barnes and Noble, 1964.

Frend, William Hugh Clifford. *The Donatist Church: A Movement of Protest in Roman North Africa*. Oxford: Clarendon Press, 1952.

Frend, William Hugh Clifford. "The Failure of the Persecutions in the Roman Empire," *Past and Present*, No. 16 (November 1959), 10–30.

Frend, William Hugh Clifford. *Martyrdom and Persecution in the Early Church. A Study of a Conflict from the Maccabees to Donatus*. Oxford: B. Blackwell, 1965.

Frere, Sheppard. *Britannia, a History of Roman Britain*. London: Routledge and Kegan Paul, 1967.

Fustel de Coulanges, Numa Denis. *The Ancient City: A Study on the Religion, Laws, and Institutions of Greece and Rome*. Garden City, N.Y.: Doubleday, 1956.

Gadd, C. J. "The Cities of Babylonia," *Cambridge Ancient History*, I, 2d ed., Chapter XIII. Cambridge: Cambridge University Press, 1962.

Gagé, Jean. *Les classes sociales dans l'Empire romain*. Paris: Payot, 1964.

Gapp, K. S. "The Universal Famine Under Claudius," *Harvard Theological Review*, XXVIII (1935), 258–65.

Gardiner, Alan H. *Egypt of the Pharaohs*. Oxford: Clarendon Press, 1961.

Garelli, Paul. *Les Assyriens en Cappadoce*. Vol. XIX of the *Bibliothèque archéologique et historique de l'Institut Français d'Archéologie d'Istambul*. Paris: Adrien Maisonneuve, 1963.

Garelli, Paul. *Le proche-Orient asiatique des origines aux invasions des peuples de la mer. La nouvelle Clio*, ed. Robert Boutruche and Paul Lemerle. Paris: Presses universitaires de France, 1969.

Garnsey, Peter. "Legal Privilege in the Roman Empire," *Past and Present*, No. 41 (December 1968), 3–24.

Gaudemet, Jean. "L'empire romain a-t-il connu les foires?" *Recueil de la Société Jean Bodin*, V, 25–42. Brussels: Editions de la librairie encyclopédique, 1953.

Gaudemet, Jean. *Institutions de l'antiquité*. Paris: Sirey, 1967.

Gelb, I. J. "The Ancient Mesopotamian Ration System," *Journal of Near Eastern Studies*, XXIV (1965), 230–43.

Gelzer, Matthias. *The Roman Nobility*. Trans. Robin Seager. Oxford: B. Blackwell, 1969.

Gilfillan, S. C. "The Inventive Lag in Classical Mediterranean Society," *Technology and Culture*, III (1962), 85ff.

Gilliam, James Frank. "The Plague Under Marcus Aurelius," *American Journal of Philology*, LXXXII (1961), 225–51.

Glotz, Gustave. *Aegean Civilization*. New York: Alfred A. Knopf, 1925.

Glotz, Gustave. *Ancient Greece at Work, An Economic History of Greece from the Homeric Period to the Roman Conquest. The History of Civilization*, ed. C. K. Ogden. London: Kegan Paul, Trench, Trubner, 1930.

Glueck, Nelson. "The Other Side of the Jordan," *The National Geographic*, LXXXV (January–June 1944), 233–56.

Gomme, Arnold Wycombe. *Population of Athens in the Fifth and Fourth Centuries* B.C. Oxford: B. Blackwell, 1933.

Gordon, Cyrus H. "Abraham and the Merchants of Ur," *Journal of Near Eastern Studies*, XVIII (1958), 28–31.

Gordon, Cyrus H. *The Ancient Near East*. 3rd ed. The Norton Library; New York: Norton, 1965.

Grant, Michael. *Roman History from Coins. Some Uses of the Imperial Coinage to the Historian*. Cambridge: Cambridge University Press, 1958.

Grant, Michael. "A Step Toward World-Coinage: 19 B.C.," *Studies in Roman Economic and Social History in Honor of Allan Chester Johnson*, ed. P. R. Coleman-Norton, 88–112. Princeton: Princeton University Press, 1951.

Granville, Stephen Ranulph Kingdon, ed. *The Legacy of Egypt*. Oxford: Oxford University Press, 1942.

Green, Peter. "The First Sicilian Slave War," *Past and Present*, No. 20 (November 1961), 10–29. (On revolutionary currents in the Graeco-Roman world in the late second and early first centuries B.C.)

Grenier, Albert. *Manuel d'archéologie gallo-romaine*. 4 pts. in 7 vols. Supplement to J. Dechelette, *Manuel d'archéologie préhistorique celtique et gallo-romaine*. Paris: A. Picard, 1931–1960.

Groningen, B. A. *Aristotle le second livre de l'Economique édité avec une introduction et un commentaire critique et explicatif*. Leiden: A. W. Sijthoff, 1933.

Gurney, O. R. *The Hittites*. London: Penguin Books, 1952.

Hackman, George Gottlob. *Temple Documents of the Third Dynasty of Ur from Umma. Babylonian Inscriptions in the Collection of James B. Nies*. New Haven, Conn.: Yale University Press, 1937.

Hagen, Victor von. *World of the Maya*. Mentor Books; New York: New American Library, 1960.

Hammond, Mason. "Economic Stagnation in the Early Roman Empire," *Journal of Economic History*, VI (1946), 63–90.

Hammond, Nicholas Geoffrey L. *A History of Greece to 322* B.C. Oxford: Clarendon Press, 1959.

Harden, Donald B. *The Phoenicians.* New York: Praeger, 1962.

Harris, Marvin. "The Economy Has No Surplus?" *American Anthropologist,* LXI (1959), 185–99. (A reply to Pearson *apud* Polanyi, *Trade and Markets.*)

Hasebroeck, Johannes. *Trade and Politics in Ancient Greece.* Trans. L. M. Fraser and D. C. MacGregor. New York: Biblo and Tannen, 1965. (Translation first published, 1933.)

Hawkes, Jacquetta, and Leonard Woolley. *Pre-history and the Beginnings of Civilization.* Vol. I of the *History of Mankind, Cultural and Scientific Development,* sponsored by the International Commission for a History of the Scientific and Cultural Development of Mankind. New York: Harper and Row, 1963.

Hehn, Victor. *Kulturpflanzen und Haustiere in ihren Uebergang aus Asien nach Griechenland und Italien sowie in das uebrige Europa.* 9th ed. Ed. Otto Schrader. Hildesheim: Georg Olms, 1963. (Originally published 1911.)

Hehn, Victor. *The Wanderings of Plants and Animals from Their First Home.* Ed. and trans. James Steven Stallybrass. London: Swan Sonnenschein, 1885.

Heichelheim, F. M. "Agriculture," *Oxford Classical Dictionary.* Ed. Max Carey et al. Oxford: Clarendon Press, 1949.

Heichelheim, F. M. *An Ancient Economic History from the Palaeolithic Age to the Migrations of the Germanic, Slavic, and Arabic Nations.* Vols. I–III. Trans. Joyce Stevens. Revised ed. Leiden: A. W. Sijthoff's Uitgeversmaatschappif, 1958–1970.

Heichelheim, F. M. "New Light on Currency and Inflation in Hellenistic-Roman Times from Inscriptions and Papyri," *Economic History Review,* III (1935), 1–11.

Heichelheim, F. M. "On Ancient Price Trends from the Early First Millennium B.C. to Heraclius I," *Finanz-Archiv,* n.s., XV (1955), 498–511.

Heichelheim, F. M. "Recent Discoveries in Ancient Economic History," *Historia,* II (1953), 129–35. (On the Wilbour Papyrus and continuity of economic institutions from pharaonic to Ptolemaic times.)

Heitland, W. E. *Agricola. A Study of Agriculture and Rustic Life in the Graeco-Roman World.* Cambridge: Cambridge University Press, 1921.

Heitland, W. E. *Iterum, or a Further Discussion of the Roman Fate.* Cambridge: Cambridge University Press, 1925.

Heitland, W. E. *Last Words on the Roman Municipalities.* Cambridge: Cambridge University Press, 1928.

Heitland, W. E. *The Roman Fate. An Essay in Interpretation.* Cambridge: Cambridge University Press, 1922.

Henry, L. "L'âge au decès d'après les inscriptions funéraires," *Population* (Paris), XIV (1959), 327–9.

Henry, L. "La mortalité d'après les inscriptions funéraires," *ibid.,* XII (1957), 149–52.

Herskovits, Melville. *Economic Anthropology. The Economic Life of Primitive Peoples.* New York: W. W. Norton, 1965. (First published, 1940.)

Heurgon, J. *Rome et la méditerranée occidental jusqu'aux guerres puniques. La nouvelle Clio,* ed. Robert Boutruche and Paul Lemerle. Paris: Presses universitaires de France, 1969.

Hill, George. "Coinage," *Cambridge Ancient History,* IV, 124–36.

Hill, Herbert. *The Roman Middle Class in the Republican Period.* Oxford: B. Blackwell, 1952.

Hodges, Henry. *Technology in the Ancient World.* New York: Alfred A. Knopf, 1970. (Probably the best simple introduction.)

Hoepffner, A. "Un aspect de la lutte de Valentinien Ier contre le Sénat, la création du 'Defensor plebis,'" *Revue historique,* CLXXXII (1938), 225–37.

Hopkins, Keith. "The Age of Roman Girls at Marriage," *Population Studies,* XVIII (1964–1965), 309–27.

Hopkins, Keith. "On the Probable Age Structure of the Roman Population," *ibid.,* XX (1966–1967), 245–64. (But see L. Henry on such use of evidence from epitaphs.)

Hornell, James. "Sea-Trade in Early Times," *Antiquity,* XV (1941), 233–56.

Hunt, A. S., and C. C. Edgar. *Select Papyri.* Vols. I and II. Loeb Classical Library; London: William Heinemann, 1932–1934.

Imbert, Jean, Gérard Sautel, and Marguerite Boulet-Sautel. *Histoire des institutions et des faits sociaux (des origines au Xe siècle). Collection Thémis,* ed. Maurice Duverger. Paris: Presses universitaires de France, 1957. (A collection of sources for use in French universities.)

Immerrahr, Sara A. "Mycenaean Trade and Colonization," *Archaeology,* XIII (1960), 4–13.

Jacobs, Jane. *The Economy of Cities.* New York: Random House, 1969.

Jacobsen, Thorkild. "Early Political Developments in Mesopotamia," *Zeitschrift fuer Assyriologie und vorderasiatische Archaeologie,* LII (n.s. XVIII), 112–22.

Jacobsen, Thorkild. "Primitive Democracy in Ancient Mesopotamia," *Journal of Near Eastern Studies,* II (1943), 159–72.

Jacobsen, Thorkild, and Robert M. Adams. "Salt and Silt in Ancient Mesopotamian Agriculture," *Science,* CXXVIII (1958), 1251–8.

Jannoray, Jean. *Ensérune: Contribution à l'étude des civilisations pré-romaines de la Gaule méridionale.* Paris: E. de Boccard, 1955.

Jardé, Auguste. *Les céréales dans l'antiquité grecque.* Paris: E. de Boccard, 1925.

Jenkins, G. K. "Greek Numismatics, 1940–1950," *Historia,* II (1953–1954), 214–26.

Jettmar, Karl. "Les plus anciennes civilisations d'éleveurs des steppes d'Asie centrale," *Journal of World History,* I (1955), 760–79.

Jevons, F. B. "Some Ancient Greek Pay-bills," *The Economic Journal,* VI (1896), 470–5.

Johnson, Allan Chester. *Egypt and the Roman Empire.* The Jerome Lectures, Second Series. Ann Arbor: University of Michigan Press, 1951.

Jones, A. H. M. *Ancient Economic History.* London: H. K. Lewis, 1948.

Jones, A. H. M. *Athenian Democracy.* Oxford: B. Blackwell, 1957.

Jones, A. H. M. "Census Records of the Later Roman Empire," *Journal of Roman Studies,* XLIII (1953), 49–64.

Jones, A. H. M. "The Cities of the Roman Empire," *Recueils de la Société Jean Bodin.* Vol. VI: *La ville,* Pt. 1, *Institutions administratives et judiciares,* 135–76. Brussels: Editions de la librairie encyclopédique, 1954.

Jones, A. H. M. "The Economic Basis of the Athenian Democracy," *Past and Present,* No. 1 (May 1952), 13–31.

Jones, A. H. M. "The Economic Life of the Towns of the Roman Empire," *Recueils de la Société Jean Bodin.* Vol. VI. *La ville,* Pt. 2, *Institutions économiques et sociales,* pp. 161–94. Brussels: Editions de la librairie encyclopédique, 1954.

Jones, A. H. M. "Inflation Under the Roman Empire," *Economic History Review,* 2d s., V (1953), 293–318.

Jones, A. H. M., ed. *A History of Rome Through the Fifth Century.* Vol. I of *A Documentary History of Western Civilization.* New York: Walker, 1968.

Jones, Tom B. and John W. Snyder. *Sumerian Economic Texts from the Third Ur Dynasty: A Catalogue and Discussion of Documents from Various Collections.* Minneapolis: University of Minnesota Press, 1961.

Julien, Charles André. *Histoire de l'Afrique du Nord: Tunisie, Algérie, Maroc. Vol. I: Des origines à la conquête arabe (647 ap. J.-C.).* 2d ed. by Christian Courtois. Bibliothèque historique. Paris: Payot, 1964.

Jullian, Camille. *Histoire de la Gaule.* 8 vols. Paris: Hackette, 1908–1926.

Kees, Hermann. *Ancient Egypt: A Cultural Topography.* Ed. T. G. H. James and trans. Ian F. D. Morrow. Chicago: University of Chicago Press, 1961.

Kitto, H. D. F. *The Greeks.* Rev. ed. Baltimore: Penguin Books, 1957.

Klemm, Friedrich. *Technik, eine Geschichte ihrer Probleme.* Munich: Karl Alber Freiburg, n. d. [1954].

Koschaker, Paul. "Zur staatlichen Wirtschaftsverwaltung in altbabylonischer Zeit, insbesondere nach Urkunden aus Larsa," *Zeitschrift fuer Assyriologie,* XLVII (1942), 135–80.

Kraay, Colin M. *Greek Coins and History, Some Current Problems.* London: Methuen, 1969.

Kraay, Colin M. "Hoards, Small Change, and the Origins of Coinage," *Journal of Hellenic Studies,* LXXXIV (1964), 76–91.

Kraeling, Carl H., and Robert M. Adams, eds. *City Invincible: A Symposium on Urbanization and Cultural Development in the Ancient Near East.* Chicago: University of Chicago Press, 1960.

Kraeling, Emil A. "New Light on the Elephantine Colony." *The Biblical Archaeologist Reader,* ed. G. Ernest Wright and David Noel Freedman. Chicago: Quadrangle Books, 1961.

Kraus, F. R. "Le rôle des temples depuis la troisième dynastie d'Ur jusqu' à la première dynastie de Babylonie," *Journal of World History,* I (1953), 518–45.

Kupper, Jean Robert. "Le rôle des nomades dans l'histoire de la Mésopotamie ancienne," *Journal of the Economic and Social History of the Orient,* II (1959), 113–27.

Laet, Siegfried J. de. *Aspects de la vie sociale et économique sous Auguste et Tibère.* Collection Lebègue. Brussels: Office de Publicité, 1944.

Laet, Siegfried J. de. *Portorium. Etude sur l'organisation douanière chez les Romains, surtout à l'époque du Haut-Empire.* Bruges: De Tempel, 1949.

Lamprechts, Pierre. "Le commerce des 'Syriens' en Gaule du Haut-Empire à l'époque mérovingienne," *L'antiquité classique,* VI (1937), 35–69.

Landry, Adolphe. "La dépopulation dans l'antiquité et dans l'époque contemporaine." *Communications présentées au VIIIe Congrès International des Sciences Historiques, Zurich, 1938,* II, 422–4. Paris: Presses universitaires de France, n. d.

Landry, Adolphe. "Quelques aperçus concernant la dépopulation dans l'antiquité greco-romaine," *Revue historique,* CLXXVIII (1936), 1–33.

Landsberger, Benno. *Assyrische Handelskolonien in Kleinasien aus dem dritten Jahrtausend.* Vol. XXIV, Pt. 4 of *Der Alte Orient.* Leipzig: J. C. Hinrichs'sche Buchhundlung, 1925.

Lattimore, Owen. *Inner Asian Frontiers of China.* 2d ed. New York: American Geographical Society, 1951.

Lavedan, Pierre. *Histoire de l'urbanisme.* Vol. I: *Antiquité, moyen âge.* Paris: Henri Laurens, 1926.

Leemans, W. F. *Foreign Trade in the Old Babylonian Period as Revealed by Texts from Southern Mesopotamia.* Vol. VI of *Studia et Documenta ad Iura Orientis Antiqui Pertinentia,* ed. M. David et al. Leiden: E. J. Brill, 1960.

Leemans, W. F. *The Old Babylonian Merchant: His Business and His Social Position.* Vol. III of *Studia et Documenta ad Iura Orientis Antiqui Pertinentia,* ed. M. David et al. Leiden: E. J. Brill, 1950.

Lefebvre des Noëttes, Richard. *La force motrice animale à travers les âges.* Paris: Berger Laurault, 1924.

Lefebvre des Noëttes, Richard. *L'attelage; le cheval de selle à travers les âges: contribution à l'histoire de l'esclavage.* 2 vols. Paris: Editions A. Picard, 1931.

Leighton, Albert C. "The Mule as a Cultural Invention," *Technology and Culture,* VIII (1967), 45–52.

Lévy, Jean-Philippe. *The Economic Life of the Ancient World.* Trans. John G. Biram. Chicago: University of Chicago Press, 1967. (Useful bibliography.)

Lewy, Hildegard. "Anatolia in the Old Assyrian Period," *Cambridge Ancient History,* I, 2d ed. Cambridge: Cambridge University Press, 1965. (See especially chapter XXIV, sections VII–X.)

Loane, H. J. *Industry and Commerce of the City of Rome.* Vol. LVI, no. 2 of the Johns Hopkins University Studies. Baltimore: Johns Hopkins University Press, 1939.

Longden, R. P. "Nerva and Trajan," *Cambridge Ancient History,* XI, 188–222. Cambridge: Cambridge University Press, 1936.

L'Orange, Hans Peter. *Art Forms and Civic Life in the Late Roman Empire.* Princeton: Princeton University Press, 1965.

Lorenz, Konrad. *Man Meets Dog.* London: Methuen, 1954.

Lot, Ferdinand. *Nouvelles recherches sur l'impôt foncier et la capitation sous le Bas-Empire.* Fasc. CCCIV of the Bibliothèque de l'Ecole des Hautes-Etudes. Paris: H. Champion, 1955.

Lot, Ferdinand. "Rome et sa population à la fin du troisième siècle de notre ère," *Annales d'histoire sociale,* II (1945), 29–38.

Luckenbill, Daniel David. *Ancient Records of Assyria and Babylonia.* 2 vols. Chicago: University of Chicago Press, 1926–1927.

MacKendrick, Paul. *The Mute Stones Speak. The Story of Archaeology in Italy.* New York: St. Martin's Press, 1960.

McNeill, William H. *The Rise of the West: A History of the Human Community.* Chicago: University of Chicago Press, 1963.

Maier, F. G. "Roemische Bevoelkerungsgeschichte und Inschriftenstatistik, *Historia,* II (1953–1954), 318–51.

Majumdar, R. C., et al. *Advanced History of India.* 2d ed. London: Macmillan, 1950.

Malinowski, Bronislav. "Culture," *Encyclopedia of the Social Sciences,* IV, 621ff. New York: Macmillan, 1932.

Martroye, F. "La répression du donatisme et la politique religieuse de Constantin et de ses successeurs en Afrique," *Mémoires de la Société Nationale des Antiquaires de France,* LXXIII (1914), 23–140.

Martroye, F. "Une tentative de révolution sociale en Afrique. Donatistes et Circoncellions," *Revue des questions historiques*, XXXII (1904), 353–416; XXXIII (1905), 5–53.

Marx, Karl. *Das Kapital*. Chicago: Charles H. Kerr and Co., 1906–1909.

Mashkin, Nicolai A., "The Workers' Revolution and the Fall of the Western Roman Empire," trans. Livio C. Stecchini, *The Journal of General Education*, V (1950), 70–4.

Mason, J. Alden. *The Ancient Civilizations of Peru*. 2d ed. Baltimore: Penguin Books, 1964.

Mattingly, Harold. *Roman Coins from the Earliest Times to the Fall of the Western Empire*. 2d ed. Chicago: Quadrangle Books, 1960.

Mazzarino, Santo. *Aspetti sociali del quarto secolo, ricerche de storia tardo-romana*. Rome: "L'Erma" di Bretschneider, 1951.

Mazzarino, Santo. *The End of the Ancient World*. Trans. George Holmes. New York: Alfred A. Knopf, 1966.

Meissner, Bruno. *Babylonien und Assyrien*. 2 vols. Heidelberg: C. Winter, 1920–1925.

Mellaart, James, *Çatal Hüyük: A Neolithic Town in Anatolia*. London: Thames and Hudson, 1967.

Mellaart, James. *The Chalcolithic and Early Bronze Ages in the Near East and Anatolia*. Beirut: Khayats, 1966.

Mellaart, James. "A Neolithic City in Turkey," *Scientific American*, CCX, No. 4, (April 1964), 94–104.

Michell, H. *The Economics of Ancient Greece*. 2d ed. New York: Barnes and Noble, 1957.

Mickwitz, Gunnar. *Geld und Wirtschaft im roemischen Reich des vierten Jahrhunderts*. Vol. IV of the Commentationes humanarum litterarum. Helsingfors, Finland: Societas scientiarum Finnica, 1932.

Mickwitz, Gunnar. *Das Kartelfunktionen der Zuenfte und ihre Bedeutung bei der Entstehung des Zunftwesens. Eine Studie in spaetantiker und mittelalterlicher Wirtschaftsgeschichte*. Vol. VIII, Pt. 3 of the Commentationes humanarum litterarum of the Societas humanarum litterarum. Helsingfors, Finland: Akademische Buchhandlung, 1936.

Mikesell, Marvin W. "Deforestation in Northern Morocco," *Science*, CXXXII (1960), 441–8.

Millar, Fergus. "The Fiscus in the First Two Centuries," *Journal of Roman Studies*, LIII (1963), 29–42.

Milne, J. G. "The Ruin of Egypt by Roman Mismanagement," *ibid.*, XVII (1927), 1–13.

Minns, Ellis Hovell. *Scythians and Greeks in South Russia*. Cambridge: Cambridge University Press, 1913.

Moeller, Walter O. "The *Lanifricarius* and the *Officinae Lanifricariae* at Pompeii," *Technology and Culture*, VII (1966), 493–6.

Mongait, Aleksandre Novich. *Archeology in the U.S.S.R.* Trans. M. W. Thompson. Pelican Books. Baltimore: Penguin Books, 1961.

Monks, George R. "The Administration of the Privy Purse, an Inquiry into Official Corruption and the Fall of the Roman Empire," *Speculum*, XXXII (1957), 748–79.

Moritz, Ludwig Alfred. *Grain Mills and Flour in Classical Antiquity.* Oxford: Clarendon Press, 1958.

Mumford, Lewis. *The City in History.* New York: Harcourt, Brace, and World, 1961.

Mumford, Lewis. *The Myth of the Machine: Technics and Human Development.* New York: Harcourt, Brace, and World, 1966.

Mumford, Lewis. *Technics and Civilization.* New York: Harcourt, Brace, 1934.

Murphey, Rhoads. "The Decline of North Africa Since the Roman Occupation: Climatic or Human?" *Annales of the Association of American Geographers,* XLI (1951), 116–32.

Myres, Sir John Linton. *Geographical History in Greek Lands.* Oxford: Clarendon Press, 1953.

Neuberger, Albert. *The Technical Arts and Sciences of the Ancients.* Trans. Henry Rose. New York: Macmillan, 1930.

Newbigin, Marion I. *Southern Europe.* London: Methuen, 1952. (A geography.)

Nicolet, Claude. "A Rome pendant la Seconde Guerre Punique: Techniques financières et manipulations monétaires," *Annales: économies, sociétés, civilisations,* XVIII (1963), 417–36.

Nicolet, Claude. *L'ordre équestre à l'époque republicaine (312–43 av. J.-C.).* Vol. I, fascicule CCVII of the Bibliothèque des Ecoles françaises d'Athènes et de Rome. Paris: E. de Boccard, 1966.

Noe, Sydney Philip. *Bibliography of Greek Coin Hoards.* 2d ed. Vol. LXXVIII of *Numismatic Notes and Monographs.* New York: The American Numismatic Society, 1937.

Oates, W. J. "The Population of Rome," *Classical Philology,* XIX (1934), 101–16.

Oertel, F. "The Economic Life of the Empire," *Cambridge Ancient History,* XXI, 232–81. Cambridge: Cambridge University Press, 1939.

Oertel, F. "The Economic Unification of the Mediterranean Region: Industry, Trade, and Commerce," *Cambridge Ancient History,* X, 382–424. Cambridge: Cambridge University Press, 1934.

Ohlin, G. "Mortality, Marriage, and Growth in Pre-Industrial Populations," *Population Studies,* XIV (1960–1961), 190–7.

Oliver, Roland, and John Donnelly Fage. *A Short History of Africa.* Penguin African Library. Baltimore, Penguin Books, 1962.

Olmstead, Albert Ten Eyck. *History of the Persian Empire.* Chicago: University of Chicago Press, 1948.

Olmstead, Albert Ten Eyck. "Materials for an Economic History of the Ancient Near East," *Journal of Economic and Business History,* II (1930), 219–40.

Oppenheim, Adolf Leo. *Ancient Mesopotamia: Portrait of a Dead Civilization.* Chicago: University of Chicago Press, 1964.

Oppenheim, Adolf Leo. "The Seafaring Merchants of Ur," *Journal of the American Oriental Society,* LXXIV (1954), 6–17.

Packer, James E. "Housing and Population in Imperial Ostia and Rome," *Journal of Roman Studies,* LVII (1967), 80–99.

Packer, James E. "Structure and Design in Ancient Ostia: A Contribution to the Study of Roman Imperial Architecture," *Technology and Culture,* IX (1968), 357–88.

Palanque, J. R. "Famines à Rome à la fin du IVe siècle," *Revue des études anciennes,* XXXIII (1931), 346–56.

Palmer, L. R. *The Latin Language*. London: Faber and Faber, 1954.

Palmer, L. R. "The Mycenaean Tablets and Economic History," *Economic History Review*, II (1958), 87–96.

Pareti, Luigi, Paolo Brezzi, and Luciano Petech. *The Ancient World, 1200* B.C. *to* A.D. *500*. Trans. Guy E. F. and Sylvia Chilver. Vol. II of *The History of Mankind, Cultural and Scientific Development*, sponsored by the International Commission for a History of the Scientific and Cultural Development of Mankind. New York: Harper and Row, 1965.

Pârvan, Vasile. *Dacia*. Cambridge: Cambridge University Press, 1928.

Pârvan, Vasile. "La pénétration hellénique et hellénistique dans la vallée du Danube," *Bulletin de la section historique de l'Académie Roumaine*, X (1923), 23ff.

Pendlebury, J. D. S. *Archaeology of Crete*. New York: Biblo and Tannen, 1963.

Persson, Axel W. *Staat und Manufaktur im Roemischen Reich. Eine wirtschaftsgeschichtliche Studie nebst einem Exkurse ueber angezogene Goetterstatuen*. Vol. III of *Skrifter urgivna av Vetenskaps-Societeten i Lund*. With a summary in English. Lund: Carl Bloms Boktryckeri, 1923.

Pharr, Clyde., ed. *The Theodosian Code and Novels and the Sirmondian Constitutions. A Translation with Commentary, Glossary, and Bibliography*. Princeton: Princeton University Press, 1952.

Piganiol, André. "Le problème démographique dans le monde antique," *Annales: économies, sociétés, civilisations*, VI (1951), 106–7.

Piggott, Stuart. *Prehistoric India to 1000* B.C. Harmondsworth: Penguin Books, 1950.

Platner, Samuel Ball. *Topographical Dictionary of Ancient Rome*. Completed and revised by Thomas Ashby. London: Oxford University Press, 1929.

Pleket, H. W. "Technology and Society in the Graeco-Roman World," *Acta Historiae Neerlandica*, II (1967), 1–25.

Poidebard, Antoine. *Un grand port disparu, Tyr; recherches aériennes et sous-marines, 1934–1936*. Paris: Paul Geuthrer, 1939.

Poidebard, Antoine, and J. Lauffray. *Sidon, aménagements antiques du part de Saïda. Etude aérienne, au sol, et sousmarine, 1946–1950*. Beirut: Ministry of Public Works, Republic of Lebanon, 1951.

Polanyi, Karl. "Our Obsolete Market Mentality: Civilization Must Find a New Thought Pattern," *Commentary*, III (1947), 109–17.

Polanyi, Karl, Conrad M. Arensberg, and Harry W. Pearson. *Trade and Markets in the Early Empires: Economies in History and Theory*. Glencoe, Ill.: The Free Press, 1957.

Postan, M. M., ed. *Cambridge Economic History of Europe*. Vol. I: *The Agrarian Life of the Middle Ages*. 2d ed. Cambridge: Cambridge University Press, 1966.

Postan, M. M., and E. E. Rich, eds. *The Cambridge Economic History*. Vol. II: *Trade and Industry in the Middle Ages*. Cambridge: Cambridge University Press, 1951.

Préaux, Claire, *L'économie royale des Lagides*. Brussels: Fondation égyptologique réine Elisabeth, 1939.

Pringsheim, Fritz. *The Greek Law of Sale*. Weimar: Hermann Boehlaus Nachfolger, 1950.

Pritchard, James B., ed. *Ancient Near-Eastern Texts Relating to the New Testament*. 2d ed. Princeton: Princeton University Press, 1955.

Purves, P. M. "Commentary on Nuzi Real Property in the Light of Recent Studies," *Journal of Near Eastern Studies*, IV (1945), 68–86

Redfield, Robert. *The Primitive World and Its Transformation*. Ithaca, N.Y.: Cornell University Press, 1953.

Reid, James S. *The Municipalities of the Roman Empire*. Cambridge: Cambridge University Press, 1913.

Remondon, R. *La crise de l'Empire romain de Marc Aurèle à Anastase. La nouvelle Clio*. Paris: Presses universitaire de France, 1964.

Richmond, I. A. "Palmyra Under the Aegis of Rome," *Journal of Roman Studies*, LIII (1963), 43–54.

Roebuck, Carl. "The Grain Trade Between Greece and Egypt," *Classical Philology*, XLV (1950), 236–47.

Roebuck, Carl. *Ionian Trade and Colonization*. Vol. IX of the *Monographs on Archaeology and Fine Arts Sponsored by the Archaeological Institute of America*. New York: Archaeological Institute of America, 1959.

Roebuck, Carl. "The Organization of Naucratis," *Classical Philology*, XLVI (1951), 212–20.

Roebuck, Carl. *The World of Ancient Times*. New York: Charles Scribner's Sons, 1966.

Roebuck, Carl, ed. *The Muses at Work. Arts, Crafts, and Professions in Ancient Greece*. Cambridge, Mass.: The MIT Press, 1969. (Published too late for use in this work.)

Rostovtzeff, M. "The Decay of the Ancient World and Its Economic Explanations," *American Historical Review*, XXXV (1929–1930), 197–214.

Rostovtzeff, M. *Iranians and Greeks in South Russia*. Oxford: Clarendon Press, 1922.

Rostovtzeff, M. "Ptolemaic Egypt," *Cambridge Ancient History*, VII (1928), 533ff.

Rostovtzeff, M. *Social and Economic History of the Hellenistic World*. 3 vols. Oxford: Clarendon Press, 1941.

Rostovtzeff, M. *Social and Economic History of the Roman Empire*. 2 vols. 2d ed., revised by P. M. Fraser. Oxford: Clarendon Press, 1957.

Rostovtzeff, M. "Studien zur Geschichte des Roemischen Kolonates," *Archiv fuer Papyrusforschung*. Beiheft I, 1910.

Rousseau, Pierre. *Histoire de techniques*. 2d ed. Paris: Hachette, 1967.

Roux, Georges. *Ancient Iraq*. London: Allen and Unwin, 1964.

Russell, Josiah. *Late Ancient and Medieval Population*. Vol. LXVIII, Pt. 3, of *The Transactions of the American Philosophical Society*, n.s. Philadelphia: American Philosophical Society, 1958.

Russell, Josiah. "That Earlier Plague," *Demography*, V (1968), 174–84.

Salvioli, Guiseppe. *Le capitalisme dans le monde antique*. Trans. Alfred Bonnet. Paris: V. Viard et Brière, 1906.

Sauer, Carl O. *Agricultural Origins and Dispersals*. Bowman Memorial Lectures. New York: The American Geographical Society, 1952.

Sauer, Carl O. *Land and Life. A Selection from the Writings of Carl Ortwin Sauer*, ed. John Leighly. Berkeley: University of California Press, 1963.

Saumagne, C. "Ouvriers agricoles ou rôdeurs de celliers? Les Circoncellions d'Afrique," *Annales d'histoire économique et sociale*, VI (1934), 351–64.

Säve-Söderbergh, Torgny. *The Navy of the Eighteenth Egyptian Dynasty*. Uppsala: Lundequistska bokhandeln, 1946.

Scheffer-Boichorst, Paul. "Kleinere Forschungen zur Geschichte des Mittelalters, IV: Zur Geschichte der Syrer im Abendlande," *Mitteilungen des Instituts fuer oesterreichische Geschichtsforschung*, VI (1885), 520–50.

Schneider, Anna. *Die Anfaenge der Kulturwirtschaft: Die sumerische Tempelstadt.* Essen: G. D. Baedeker, 1920.

Schultz, Fritz. "Roman Registers of Births and Birth Certificates," *Journal of Roman Studies*, XXXII (1942), 78–91; XXXIII (1943), 55–64.

Schwartz, J. "L'Empire romain, Egypte et le commerce oriental," *Annales: économies, sociétés, civilisations*, XV (1960), 18–44.

Seek, Otto. "Bagaudae," *Pauly-Wissowa Real-encyclopaedie*, II, 2766–7.

Seek, Otto. *Geschichte des Untergangs der antiken Welt.* 6 vols. Berlin: Siemenroth und Troschel, 1897–1921. (2d ed. in 3 vols., 1895–1909.)

Segrè, A. "Il mutuo e il tasso d'interesse nell'Egitto greco-romano," *Atene e Roma* (1924), 119–38.

Sherman-White, A. N. *Roman Society and Roman Law in the New Testament.* The Sarum Lectures, 1960–1961. Oxford: Clarendon Press, 1963.

Singer, Charles Joseph. *A Short History of Science to the Nineteenth Century.* Oxford: The Clarendon Press, 1941.

Singer, Charles, et al., eds. *History of Technology.* Vols. I and II. Oxford: Oxford University Press, 1954–1956.

Speiser, E. A., ed. *At the Dawn of Civilization: A Background of Biblical History.* Vol. I of *The World History of the Jewish People*, ed. B. Netanyahu. New Brunswick, N.J.: Rutgers University Press, 1964.

Spengler, Joseph J. "Aristotle on Economic Imputation and Related Matters," *Southern Economic Journal*, XXI (1955), 371–89.

Star, S. Frederic. "Archeology in the Soviet Union," *Yale Review*, LIV (1964), 311–20.

Steindorff, George, and Keith Seele. *When Egypt Ruled the East.* Chicago: University of Chicago Press, 1942.

Steward, Julian Haynes. *Irrigation Civilizations: A Comparative Study. A Symposium on Method and Result in Cross-Cultural Regularities.* Washington, D.C.: Department of Cultural Affairs, Pan American Union, 1955.

Syme, Ronald. "The Imperial Finances Under Domitian, Nerva, and Trajan," *Journal of Roman Studies*, XX (1930), 55–70.

Syme, Ronald. *The Roman Revolution.* New York: Oxford University Press, 1960.

Tarn, Sir William Woodthrope, and Guy Thompson Griffith. *Hellenistic Civilization.* 3rd ed. London: E. Arnold, 1952.

Taylor, Lily Ross. "Caesar's Agrarian Legislation and His Municipal Policy." *Studies in Roman Economic and Social History in Honor of Allan Chester Johnson*, ed. P. R. Coleman-Norton. Princeton: Princeton University Press, 1951, pp. 68–78.

Taylor, Lily Ross. "Freedmen and Freeborn in the Epitaphs of Imperial Rome," *American Journal of Philology*, LXXXII (1961), 113–32.

Tchalenko, Georges. *Villages antiques de la Syrie. Le Massif de Béhis à l'époque romaine.* 3 vols. Paris: P. Geuther, 1953–1958.

Teggart, Frederick John. *Rome and China, A Study of Correlations in Historical Events.* Berkeley: University of California Press, 1939.

Thomas, William L., Jr., ed. *Man's Role in Changing the Face of the Earth: An*

International Symposium Under the Co-chairmanship of Carl O. Sauer, Marston Bates, and Lewis Mumford. Chicago: University of Chicago Press, 1956.

Thompson, E. A. "Peasant Revolts in Late Roman Gaul and Spain," *Past and Present,* No. 2 (November 1952), 11–23.

Thompson, E. A. *A Roman Reformer and Inventor, Being a New Text of the Treatise* De rebus bellicis. Oxford: Clarendon Press, 1952.

Thompson, E. A. "The Settlement of the Barbarians in Southern Gaul," *Journal of Roman Studies,* XLVI (1956), 65–75.

Thomson, George. *Studies in Ancient Greek Society,* Vol. II. London: Lawrence and Wishart, 1955.

Toutain, Jules. "La densité et la répartition de la population de la Gaule romaine," *Journal des savants,* 1940, pp. 5–16.

Toutain, Jules. *The Economic Life of the Ancient World.* Trans. M. R. Dobie. New York: Alfred A. Knopf, 1930.

Turner, E. G. *Greek Papyri, An Introduction.* Princeton: Princeton University Press, 1968.

Usher, Abbott Payson. *A History of Mechanical Inventions.* 2d ed. Cambridge, Mass.: Harvard University Press, 1954.

Uslar, R. von. "Stadt, Burg, Markt, und Temenos in der Urgeschichte." *Festschrift fuer Gustav Schwanzes zum 65. Geburtstag,* ed. Karl Kerstan, pp. 33–44. Neuminster: Wachholtz, 1951.

Vallet, Georges. *Rhégion et Zancle. Histoire, commerce et civilisation des cités chalcidiennes du détroit de Messine.* Paris: E. de Boccard, 1958.

Ventris, Michael, and John Chadwick. *Documents in Mycenaean Greek.* Cambridge: Cambridge University Press, 1956.

Vidal-Naquet, Pierre. "Homère et le monde mycénien," *Annales: économies, sociétés, civilisations,* XVIII (1963), 703–19.

Villard, François. *Le céramique grecque de Marseille (VIe–IVe siècles). Essai d'histoire économique.* Paris: E. de Boccard, 1960.

Wace, J. B. "The History of Greece in the Third and Second Millenniums B.C.," *Historia,* II (1953), 74–94. (On the discoveries at Pylos and Mycenae.)

Wacher, J. S., ed. *The Civitas Capitals of Roman Britain.* Leicester: Leicester University Press, 1966. (Especially the article by Ian Richmond, "Industry in Roman Britain.")

Wallon, Henri. *Histoire de l'esclavage dans l'antiquité.* 2d. ed. Paris: Hachette, 1879.

Walser, Gerold, and Thomas Pekary. *Die Krise des roemischen Reiches; Bericht ueber die Forschungen zur Geschichte des 3. Jahrhunderts (193–284 n. Chr.) von 1939 bis 1959.* Berlin: W. de Gruyten, 1962.

Waltzing, Jean Pierre. *Etude historique sur les corporations professionnelles chez des Romains depuis les origines jusqu'à la chute de l'Empire d'Occident.* 4 vols. Louvain: V. Peeters, 1895–1900.

Warmington, Eric Herbert. *The Commerce Between the Roman Empire and India.* Cambridge: Cambridge University Press, 1928.

Washburn, Sherwood L. "Tools and Human Evolution," *Scientific American,* 3–15. September 1960.

Watson, G. R. *The Roman Soldier.* Ithaca, N.Y.: Cornell University Press, 1969.

Weber, Max. *General Economic History.* Trans. Frank H. Knight. Glencoe, Ill.: The Free Press, 1927.

Weber, Max. "The Social Causes of the Decay of Ancient Civilization," trans. Christian Mackauer, *The Journal of General Education*, V (1950), 75–88.

West, Louis C. "The Coinage of Diocletian and the Edict of Prices." *Studies in Roman Economic and Social History in Honor of Allan Chester Johnson*, ed. P. R. Coleman-Norton, pp. 290–301. Princeton: Princeton University Press, 1951.

West, Louis C. "The Economic Collapse of the Roman Empire," *Classical Journal*, XXVIII (1933), 96ff.

Westermann, William Linn. "The Economic Basis of the Decline of Ancient Culture," *American Historical Review*, XX (1915), 724ff.

Westermann, William Linn. *The Slave Systems of Greek and Roman Antiquity*. Philadelphia: American Philosophical Society, 1955.

Westermann, William Linn. "Warehousing and Trapezite Banking in Antiquity," *Journal of Economic and Business History*, III (1930–1931), 30–54.

Wheeler, Sir Mortimer. "Roman Contact with India, Pakistan, and Afghanistan." *Aspects of Archaeology in Britain and Beyond. Essays Presented to O. S. G. Crawford*, ed. W. F. Grimes. London: H. W. Edwards, 1951, pp. 345–81.

Wheeler, Sir Mortimer. *Rome Beyond the Imperial Frontiers*. 2d ed. London: Penguin Books, 1955.

White, Kenneth D. *Agricultural Implements of the Roman World*. Cambridge: Cambridge University Press, 1967.

Wilkes, J. J. *Dalmatia*. London: Routledge and Kegan Paul, 1969. (The Roman province.)

Will, Edouard. "De l'aspect éthique des origines grecques de la monnaie," *Revue historique*, CCXII (1954), 209–31.

Will, Edouard. *Histoire politique du monde hellenistique (323–30 av. J.-C.)* Vol. I. Mémoire XXX of the *Annales de l'Est*. Nancy: Faculté des Lettres et des Sciences Humaines de l'Université, 1966. (The essay on the economic aspects of Ptolemaic foreign policy, pp. 148–77.)

Will, Edouard. "De l'aspect éthique des origines grecques de la monnaie," *Revue numismatique*, XVII (1955), 5–23.

Wilson, John. *The Culture of Ancient Egypt*. Chicago: University of Chicago Press, 1956. (First published in 1951 under the title, *The Burden of Egypt*.)

Wilson, John. "Egyptian Technology, Science, and Lore," *Journal of World History*, II (1954), 209–13.

Wittfogel, Karl A. *Oriental Despotism, A Comparative Study of Total Power*. New Haven, Conn.: Yale University Press, 1957.

Woolley, Sir Leonard. *Digging up the Past*. New York: C. Scribner's Sons, 1931.

Woolley, Sir Leonard. *Excavations at Ur: A Record of Twelve Years' Work*. London: E. Benn, 1955.

Woolley, Sir Leonard. *Ur of the Chaldees: A Record of Seven Years of Excavation*. London: E. Benn, 1929.

Wycherley, R. E. *How the Greeks Built Cities*. 2d ed. London: Macmillan, 1962.

Yeo, Cedric A. "The Development of the Roman Plantation and Marketing of Farm Products," *Finanz-Archiv*, n.s., XIII (1952), 321–42.

Yeo, Cedric A. "The Economy of Roman and American Slavery," *ibid.*, 445–85.

Zimmern, Sir Alfred. *The Greek Commonwealth, Politics and Economics in Fifth-Century Athens*. 5th ed. London: Oxford University Press, 1952.

Map 1   Neolithic Settlement Sites

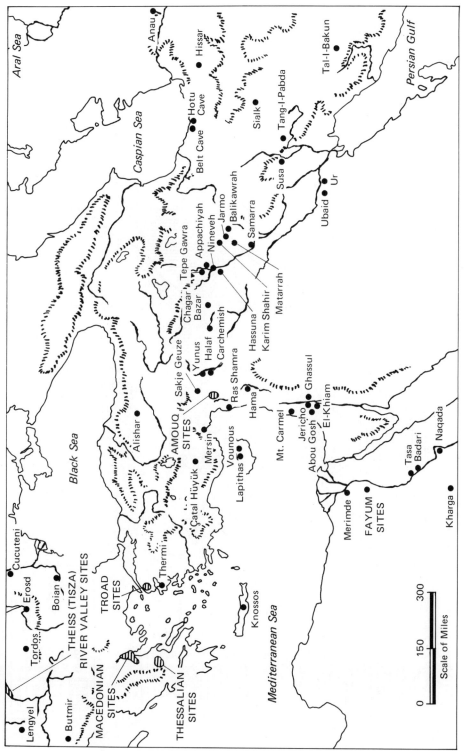

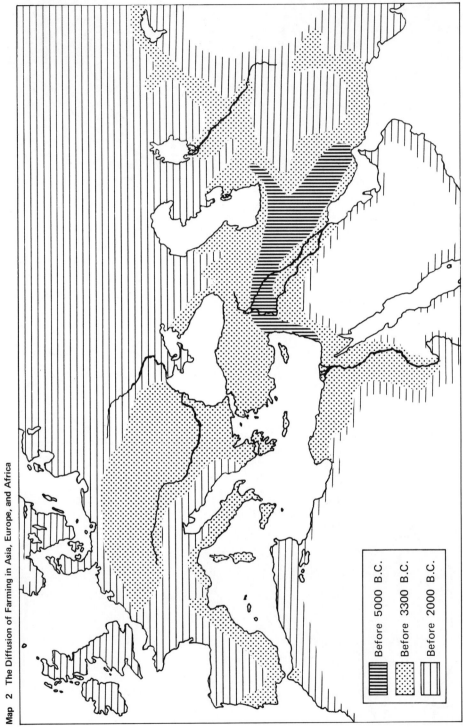

Map 2 The Diffusion of Farming in Asia, Europe, and Africa

Before 5000 B.C.

Before 3300 B.C.

Before 2000 B.C.

Map 3 The Near East

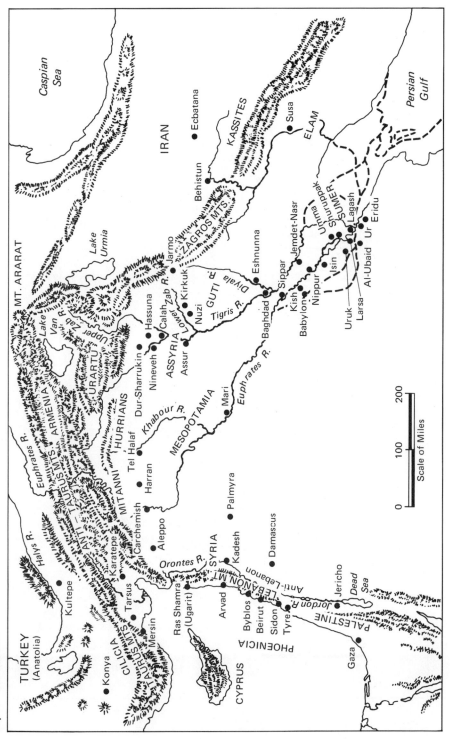

Map 4   Ancient Egypt

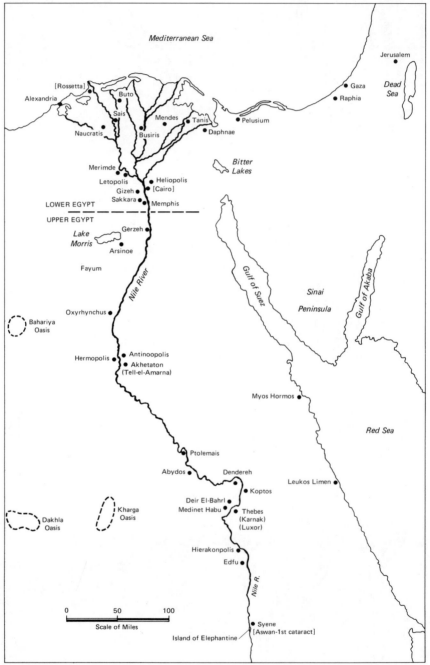

Mediterranean Sea

Jerusalem

[Rossetta]

Gaza
Dead Sea

Alexandria

Buto

Raphia

Sais

Mendes

Tanis

Pelusium

Naucratis

Busiris

Daphnae

Merimde

Bitter Lakes

Letopolis

Heliopolis

Gizeh

[Cairo]

Sakkara

Memphis

LOWER EGYPT

UPPER EGYPT

Gerzeh

Lake Morris

Arsinoe

Fayum

Gulf of Suez

Sinai Peninsula

Gulf of Akaba

Nile River

Oxyrhynchus

Bahariya Oasis

Hermopolis

Antinoopolis

Akhetaton
(Tell-el-Amarna)

Myos Hormos

Red Sea

Ptolemais

Abydos

Dendereh

Koptos

Leukos Limen

Dakhla Oasis

Kharga Oasis

Deir El-Bahri

Medinet Habu

Thebes
(Karnak)
(Luxor)

Hierakonpolis

Edfu

Nile R.

0   50   100

Scale of Miles

Syene
[Aswan-1st cataract]

Island of Elephantine

Map 5 Palestine, Southern Syria, and Phoenicia

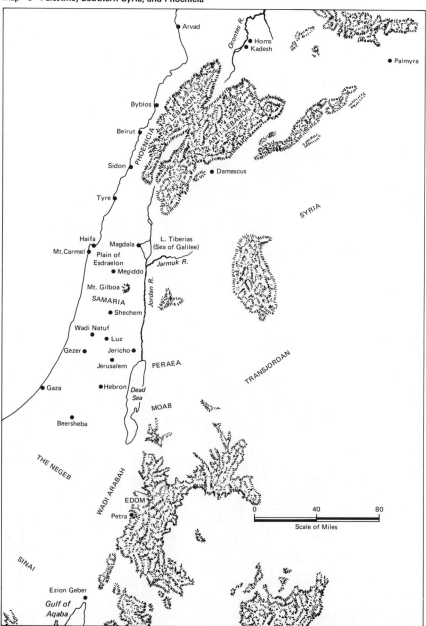

Map 6 The Aegean

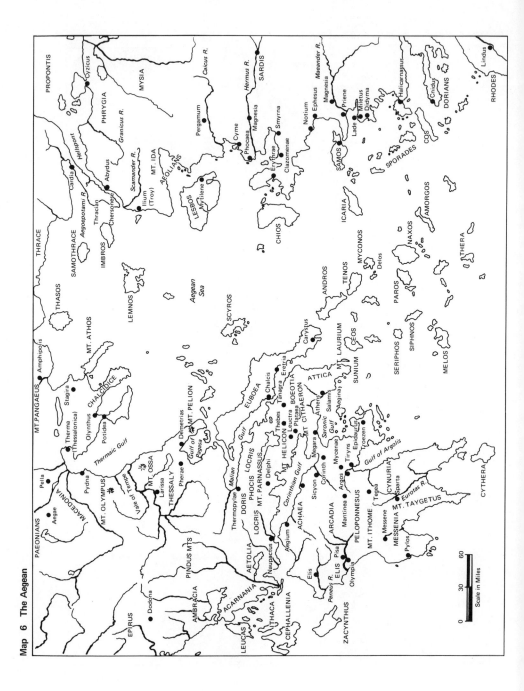

Map 7 Greek and Phoenician Colonization

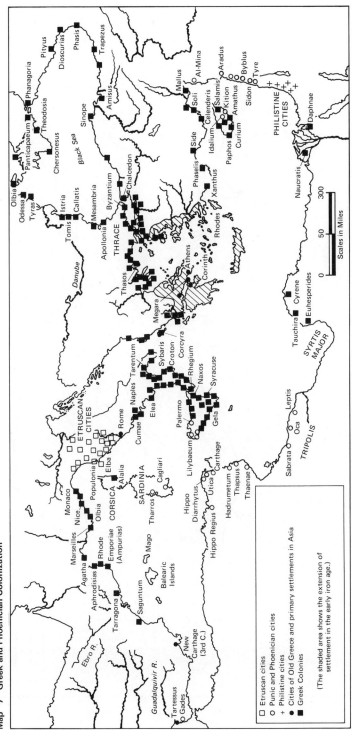

Tartessos
Gades
Guadalquivir R.
New Carthage (3rd C.)
Ebro R.
Saguntum
Tarragona
Aphrodisias
Agatha
Rhode
Emporiae (Ampurias)
Marseilles
Nice
Monaco
Balearic Islands
Mago
Olbia
Populonia
Elba
Alalia
CORSICA
Tharros
Cagliari
SARDINIA
Mago
Rome
ETRUSCAN CITIES
Cumae
Naples
Tarentum
Elea
Palermo
Lilybaeum
Carthage
Hippo Diarrhytus
Utica
Hadrumetum
Thapsus
Thaenae
Hippo Regius
Sabrata
Oca
Leptis
TRIPOLIS
SYRTIS MAJOR
Tauchira
Cyrene
Euhesperides
Gela
Syracuse
Naxos
Rhegium
Croton
Sybaris
Corcyra
Megara
Athens
Corinth
Rhodes
Thasos
THRACE
Apollonia
Tomis
Callatis
Istria
Mesambria
Byzantium
Chalcedon
Odessa
Olbia
Tyras
Panticapaeum
Chersonesus
Theodosia
Phanagoria
Pityus
Dioscurias
Phasis
Trapezus
Amisus
Sinope
Black Sea
Danube
Side
Phaselis
Xanthus
Naucratis
Daphnae
PHILISTINE CITIES
Tyre
Sidon
Byblus
Aradus
Al-Mina
Salamis
Kition
Amathus
Curium
Paphos
Idalium
Celenderis
Soli
Mallus
Tripolis

Scales in Miles
0   50   300

Etruscan cities
Punic and Phoenician cities
Philistine cities
Cities of Old Greece and primary settlements in Asia
Greek Colonies

(The shaded area shows the extension of settlement in the early iron age.)

Map 8 Mediterranean Currents and Winds

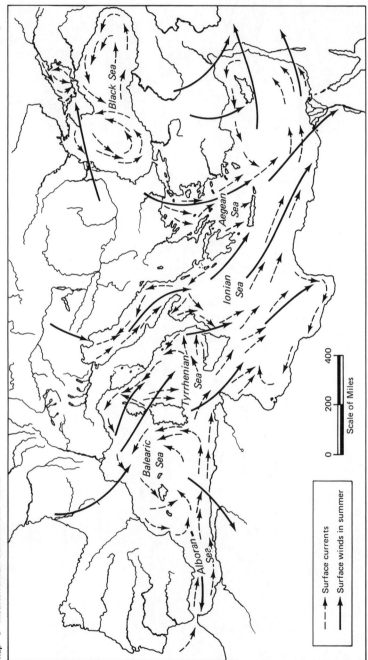

Black Sea

Aegean Sea

Ionian Sea

Tyrrhenian Sea

Balearic Sea

Alboran Sea

Scale of Miles

0   200   400

- - - → Surface currents

———→ Surface winds in summer

Map 9 Italy During the Republic

Lake Geneva

NORICUM

ALPS

ALPS

ALPS

Aquileia

VENETIA

ISTRIA

Transalpine Gaul

CISALPINE GAUL

Como

Milan

Cremona

Verona

Mantua

Pola

PANNONIA

ALPS

Placentia

Po R.

Genoa

Mutina

Bologna

Ravenna

ILLYRICUM (DALMATIA)

LIGURIA

Apennines

Luca

Rubicon R.

Rimini

GALLIC LAND

Faesulae

Pisa

Ancona

Arezzo

APENNINE MOUNTAINS

PICENES

Populonia

ETRURIA

Tiber R.

Perugia

Spoleto

Adriatic Sea

Tarquinii

Volsinii

Salt Road

Corfinium (Italica)

CORSICA

Alalia

Tarentum

Veii

SABINES

Rome

Praeneste

Ostia

Arpinum

APULIA

Tusculum

Cassino

Antium

CAMPANIA

Beneventum

Terracina

Cumae

Brindisi

Puteoli

MT. VESUVIUS

Naples

Salernum

Tarento

Herculaneum

Pompeii

Paestum

Metapontum

CALABRIA

SARDINIA

LUCANIA

Gulf of Tarentum

Tyrrhenian Sea

Thurii

Croton

Ionian Sea

Hippo Diarrhytus

Eryx

Palermo

Messina

Locri

Drepano

Segesta

MT. ETNA

Rhegium

Utica

Lilybaeum

Himera R.

Carthage

Selinus

SICILY

Catana

Hippo Regius

Girgenti

Enna

Leontini

Gela

Syracuse

Zama

Camarina

Thapsus

MALTA

NUMIDIA

0   50   100

Scale in Miles

LEGEND:
— — — Northern Boundary of Italy in the Late Republic

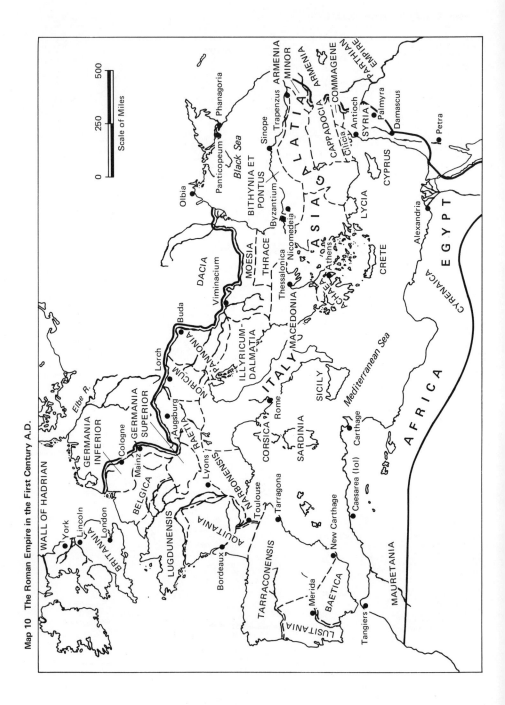

Map 10　The Roman Empire in the First Century A.D.

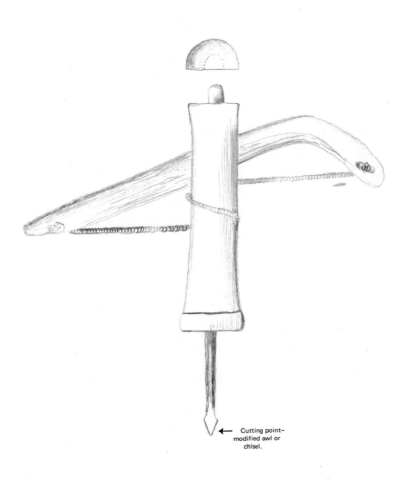

Cutting point–
modified awl or
chisel.

Figure 1
Bow Drill

Figure 2

Iron Bits

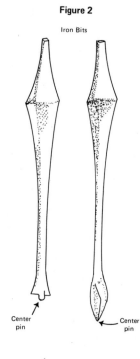

Center
pin

Center
pin

Cutting
edge

Cutting
edge

Carpenter Drill

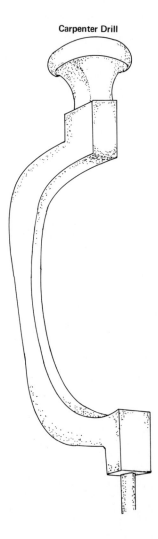

Figure 3

Saws

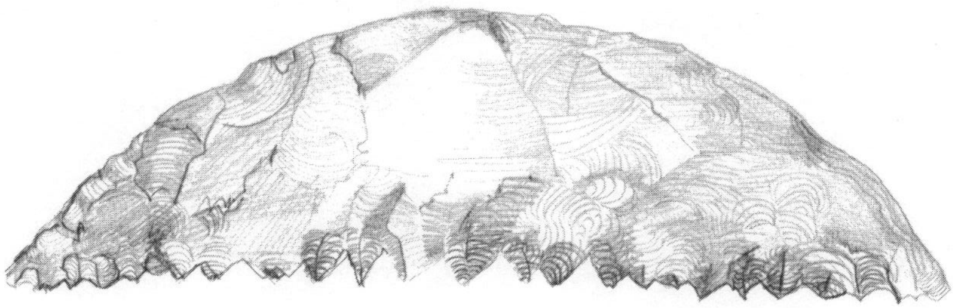

Stone saw

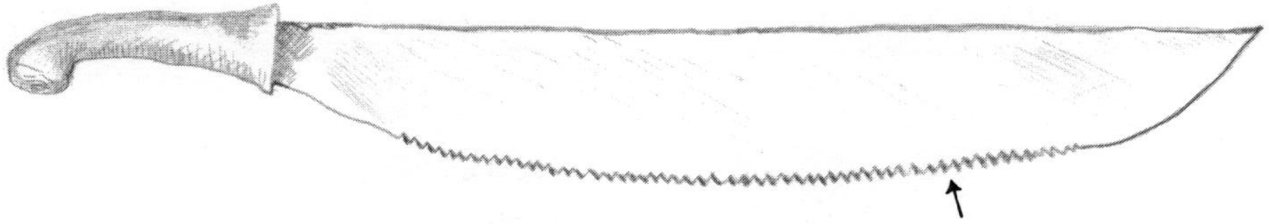

Parallel teeth extending completely across the saw blade.

Bronze saw

Figure 4

Iron Saws

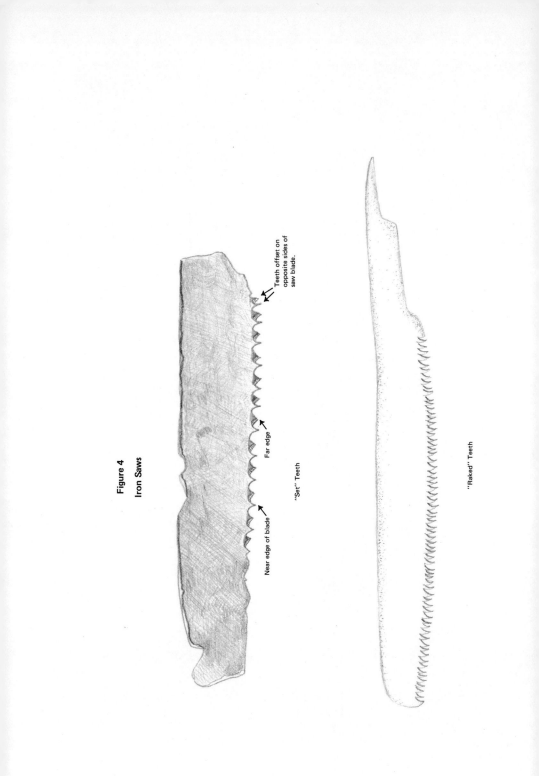

Teeth offset on opposite sides of saw blade.

Far edge

Near edge of blade

"Set" Teeth

"Raked" Teeth

INDEX

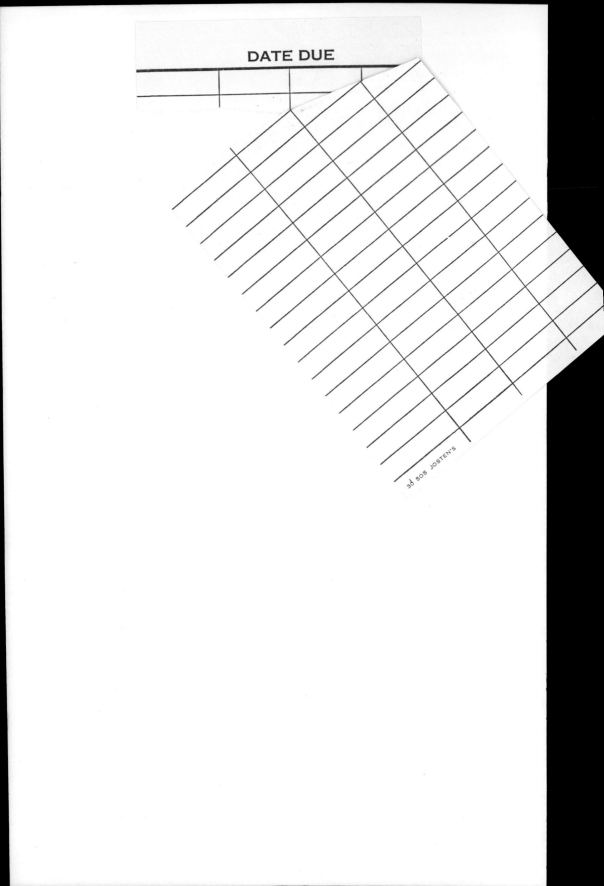

DATE DUE

30 505 JOSTEN'S